The Whole Story:
A Journey into the
20th Century

Irving Abrahamson

"Irving Abrahamson and I have been close friends for some forty years. A superb teacher and literary critic, his striking personality comes through in this autobiography, which I warmly recommend. Written with talent and passion, and tears as well, it covers large segments of the twentieth century historiography. Its many readers will emerge from these pages with a sense of enrichment."

Elie Wiesel

ISBN 10: 0615575099
ISBN-13: 978-0615575094

DEDICATION

For Perle--who has traveled
these pages, and more, with me
.

ACKNOWLEDGMENTS

Rick Onyshko brought these pages into the light of day. For some unfathomable reason he undertook the task of seeing the manuscript of *The Whole Story* into publication and beyond. His creative mind saw the project as a challenge to be overcome. And armed with his technological skills, his wisdom, his experience--and with a determination beyond belief--he has single-handedly lifted the manuscript pages of *The Whole Story* from the twentieth century into vibrant life in the twenty-first, and perhaps beyond. Whether he knew it or not he was on a rescue mission.

In the Jewish tradition to save a life it is as though one saved an entire world. Surely the same is true of a book. I shall be forever grateful to him.

It was neither possible nor necessary to educate people who never questioned anything.

Joseph Heller, *Catch-22*

There is no sun without shadow, and it is essential to know the night.

Albert Camus, *The Myth of Sisyphus*

When the imagination sleeps, words are emptied of their meaning.

Albert Camus, *"Reflections on the Guillotine"*

Imagination makes the world.

Tulu

Who doesn't go to the end, can know only a truth that is partial and mutilated.

Elie Wiesel, *The Gates of the Forest*

The Path

In Highland Park, where I live, the Green Bay Trail for much of its route parallels the old Chicago and Northwestern railroad line. Though the line has changed its name, the route hasn't. The train still runs north from Chicago to Kenosha, Wisconsin. In Highland Park the main stop on the line is a quaint station just off the center of town. Except for its clock tower it is not much more of an affair than the station at the south end of town.

I have walked the trail north to town and south into the village of Glencoe hundreds of times, in all seasons, every hour of the day. In the late spring, during summer, and in early fall the trees on either side of the path arch over it for long stretches and form a natural tunnel, blocking out the city streets on one side and the railroad and its embankment on the other. They hide the telephone wires and power lines that follow the tracks. Except for the gray gravel path underfoot, most of the year I could for all the world be hiking through a forest rather than be where I am--in the middle of a suburban Illinois town.

Bicyclers, joggers, walkers use the path. Some pass me with a nod or a smile or a "Hello" or a "Good morning" or a friendly wave of the hand. Some just look straight ahead, earphones glued to their ears, grimly determined to ignore my existence. Disguised behind dark glasses, oblivious to trees, bushes, wild flowers, the red flash of a cardinal, they could just as well be cycling on Mars or jogging on the moon.

Sometimes I meet a neighbor or a friend, and we stop to chat awhile. But I like the path best when I can feel the pure, clean pleasure of walking it alone, without a soul in sight, when the hard ground under my every step assures me I am still alive and haven't fallen through yet.

Sometimes, without thinking, I strike a perfect, effortless rhythm-- and it's as though I can go on to forever. Then, maybe after a mile, from nowhere some fragment of the past will come streaking across my mind. And in that same split second I will know I have just been at one with myself, that I have just experienced happiness--and already left it behind. And I become conscious that I am no longer happy in the mindless way I was happy when I did not know I was being happy.

It's then--while I'm just walking the path and hearing the measured crunch of the gravel underfoot, or seeing the sudden arc of the squirrel I have startled, or listening to the flutter of invisible wings in the underbrush--that I find old entries in the diary I carry in my mind or jot down new ones. These remains of the past, these remnants, these memories that lie strewn through my mind are all I have left of life lived. In my more optimistic moments I look forward to some Unified Field Theory to gather them up and make some grand sense out of them. Otherwise I think to myself that there's no point in trying to make sense out of them. Or maybe that there's no other point than the effort of trying to make some sense out of them.

I am sure of one thing, though. If meaning lies anywhere at all, it must be in what I remember, not in what I've forgotten. You don't remember an experience unless it had--and still holds--some sort of significance for you. Trouble is, there are so many of these memories and they come in such odd sizes and shapes that it's hard to sort them out and slow them down and give them their due. They don't live in isolation either. You have to make the connections that give them their meaning. Sometimes the connections point one way, sometimes they point another. But one thing I know: everything lies in the connections. Everything.

When the horn blasts of the sleek northbound for Kenosha split the air, I know it will be only seconds before its onrush will leave me far behind, still listening in my memory for the chug-chugging steam engine of my youth and its long, lingering "youwhoooowoooo" that will not let me go.

At such moments--as I reach my turning point and begin to retrace my steps--I sometimes tell myself that my familiar path could well have been another, that it could as easily have led to the Ninth Fort as to my home.

4

Mameloshen

My mother called them "October's golden days." She held them dear, and now I too treasure them. A balmy day in October is like a balmy day in spring that uplifts the heart because it carries the promise of new beginnings. But a soft day in a Midwest fall breaks the heart. Disguised by a warm sun that sets the trees along the path ablaze in gold, its faint, cool breeze from the north warns me against October's alchemy.

To walk the path in October is to walk into a pointillist dream of leaves fallen and falling. This is when I can't help hearing the sound of "Time's winged chariot hurrying near." I heard it in my student days. I heard it in my teaching days. The sound is much clearer now.

It's a marvelous line, three hundred years old. No shaking it out of my mind, on the path or off. In my own time and place, a very different sort of poet, an American, put it a bit differently when he said, "Don't look back now--something might be gaining on you." At once Biblical, mysterious, nightmarish, his words strike home too. And they're all the more threatening because I know I can't help looking back. And I have to admit I feel the same "slow, persistent breeze" blowing toward me that Meursault feels as it comes at him from "the dark horizon" of his future.

I see the curtain rising. I hear the very first speech of the play. In all innocence Lopahin asks, "What time is it?" By now I know the entire play is in those words, that they already signal the inevitable sound of the axe against the cherry trees as the final curtain falls.

I hear these lines on my walks. They target me from very different worlds. They are the very essence of poetry, and they do what poetry does: they unsettle me. They have mined the fool's gold littering the path beneath my feet.

I love the English language in which I know these words. It is the language I know best, the language that has given me entrance to worlds I might never have known, the language that has given me my

living, my history, my life. But it was not my first language. Yiddish--
mameloshen--was my mother tongue. It was my mother's tongue. I
knew it before I knew any other. I knew it even before I knew who I
was.

In my time I have seen Yiddish ignored and scorned, mocked and
murdered. As a grammar school boy learning to be an American, I
was ashamed to hear it spoken on the street or in the department store
or on a streetcar. Back then, to me Yiddish belonged elsewhere, to a
different time, a different world, a world somewhere beyond oceans,
not here in America where I lived. I did not know it then, but Yiddish
was already an indelible part of my being, more profoundly a part of
me than I could measure, a world within the worlds in which I would
live, a language more vital, more life nourishing, more ingrained than
any other I would know, connecting me forever to my mother and my
father, to the world they had left behind, connecting me to my brother
and my teachers, to Europe, to Jewish history. *"Tzu heren ah Yiddishn
vort"*--to hear a Yiddish word--means to yearn for it, to long for it from
the deepest reaches of the heart. Today when I hear *ah Yiddishn vort* the
heart leaps up, for it signals the sweetest of tongues, a language that
speaks of the deepest love, of a homesickness beyond home. Today I
am ashamed that I was ever ashamed of it.

The Englishman, the American, the Frenchman, the Russian--I
hear what they have to say. Who has ever said it better? But it is my
mother's Yiddish that cuts through the years. I can still hear my
mother saying it: *"Ay kinderlakh, s'iz shane nehenter vie vayter."* "Oh, my
children," she was saying at an anniversary meeting, addressing her
contemporaries with the diminutive reserved for good friends in
moments of affection, and containing both sadness and love for them,
"Oh, my children," she was saying, "it is nearer rather than farther."
There was no mistaking the knife-edge of her truth. She knew they
would understand what was closer rather than farther for them all. I
do too.

The Boat

Bryant Grammar School--on the West Side of Chicago, where I grew up--was named for William Cullen Bryant, a white beard looking sternly down on us from inside a wooden oval frame hanging above the front wall blackboard of Mrs. Carmody's classroom, where she taught General Science, among other subjects. We knew he had written a poem called "Thanatopsis" when he was seventeen. He didn't look as though he could ever have been seventeen. It was no poem for a nine year old either.

In Mrs. Carmody's room we sang a round that was poem enough for me. We sang:

> Row, row, row your boat
> Gently down the stream.
> Merrily, merrily, merrily,
> Life is but a dream.

I loved that round. Mrs. Carmody would start a group of us singing. When we finished the first line, she'd get another group going with the first line while the first group was starting the second line, and the third group would get started after the second one had completed its first line, and so on through the song, all the lines gloriously merging, then each group dropping off after completing all its lines, until the final line drifted off all alone down the stream.

It was one of the few songs I would dare to sing. Though it was hopeless for me to try to carry a tune, that round was one of the few songs I liked to sing, maybe because I knew my voice would be safely lost inside the chorus of voices all around me. I loved the sounds of it. But the sense of it always lingered behind. Life a dream? Would I row my own boat? Could I? What boat? To where? What stream? And merrily? Its promises contradicted what I already knew of life. But I loved it anyhow.

The Miracle

Suddenly, out of nowhere--in 1970 or 1971--my brother Philip began to sculpt in wood. He rented a studio and left it only to teach at the college. Nights, weekends, holidays he spent every spare hour in his studio. Sometimes he would take a rest and phone me from his studio, and we'd talk. Or I would phone him. Either way I could hear classical music coming from the radio he listened to while he was at his work. Whenever I could I would go to his studio and sit there on a high stool and watch him for hours at a time. Sometimes we'd talk family talk. "Do you remember when Ma said...?" And there'd be laughter. Always there was laughter. "Do you remember what Pa did when...?" Sometimes we'd joke about the Yiddish in the Tante's letters to us from Russia. Sometimes he'd explain the piece he was working on while he was working on it in front of me--the problem he was facing and trying to solve. For him every piece of wood contained a problem he had to solve--solve with his mind, his imagination, and his hands.

Mostly I loved watching him with his chisels and mallets. I never saw him happier. In a way, I don't think he was ever happier. Chisel and mallet came to life in his hands. Stroke. Tap. Tap. Tap. Stroke, tap, tap, tap. The rhythm. The chips would fly, and the mark he wanted would appear on the block of wood before him. In time the miracle would emerge--an eye, a beard, a hand, a mouth. A few days later a figure would appear with a hand that held a beard and a mouth that smiled enigmatically and eyes that followed you wherever you went around the room. It didn't matter--a block of wood or a log--in a few days the piece of wood took on life where there had been no life before. It existed where there had been no existence before, except in my brother's mind. It had come into being. It had entered the world out of nowhere into the present. It was something new in the world. It had presence. It spoke and told a story. From a non-existent past it had a future because it had a living present.

My brother was fifty-seven years old when he died. He never touched chisel or mallet until the last three years of his life. In those three years or so it seemed he hardly ever put them down--until he could no longer hold them in his hands. He knew something in those years. He put what he knew into what he created with his bare hands. Like all poets he was a maker. He did not tell me what he knew. It would have been too painful for him to tell me. And it was too painful for me to ask.

In those three years he created a whole world. If only I knew where his statues were and could retrieve them, I would have to build a *shtetl*--a small town--to hold them all. Those of his figures that I have managed to gather into my home are only a small part of his creation, a fraction of the world he created. Each carries its private message for me, something of what he knew. Each has its story to tell, the Jewish story, the Jewish poem, the Jewish *niggun*--its melody.

Many of them are based on a Biblical theme. But they are not religious statues, not in any ordinary sense. They are, heart and soul, Jewish statues, Yiddish statues, whimsical, humorous. He gave Yiddish names to most of the statues. *Der Klezmer* (The Musician). *Eliyahu Hanavi* (Elijah). The Hasidic Dancer. *Der Schneider* (The Tailor). Rosh Hashanah (The New Year). Job. *Ah Malakh Veynt* (An Angel Weeps). *Fahrtrakht* (Lost in Thought). *Gevalt* (Hue and Cry). Somewhere out in the world someone owns his *Minyan* (The Quorum), ten pieces, each two feet tall. Someone else owns his *Akedah* (The Binding). One way or another they are connected to each other, even to God, in a way. After all, they are all *landslayt*, all from the same *shtetl*. But at their center they are my brother, and they tell me what he knew.

I also have his two mallets. They sit on my desk like watchful sentinels. Worn down from long and honorable service--how many sculptors had owned them before him?--they have their private message for me too. It's something, after all, to carve out a piece of time so that you can walk around it and look at it from all sides and every angle, and watch the figure of it and see the way its eyes follow you wherever you walk in the room.

Remnants

Before I was old enough to go to school, my mother would often take me Downtown with her. Downtown was when you crossed the River. When you crossed the bridge over the River, you were in another world. It was where the office buildings were. Skyscrapers. Crowds. Yellow cabs. Checker cabs. Police whistles. Museums. And department stores. We would sometimes go to Marshall Field's or Carson's, department stores that didn't cater to the West Side, but mostly we went to the Fair or L. Klein or Mandel Brothers or the Boston Store. On the way Downtown she would always be sure to point out the "House of Correction" as we were approaching it, a jail for people who had broken the law and for little boys who had done something wrong. My heart always pounded until our streetcar had safely passed it by.

Always she warned me to keep close, not to get lost. There was always so much to see that it wasn't easy to keep up with her. She loved to stop at the tables that carried something called "yard goods," where she was always on the lookout for what she called "remnants." It did not take me long to understand that these were leftovers, odd-length pieces of cloth that were bargains because they were remainders. She had a quick eye for those that could be useful to her.

She would make things from these remnants. The clickety hum of her Singer sewing machine and the steady rhythm of her foot on the treadle at the bottom of its cast iron frame are as much among the sounds of my childhood as the cling-clang-clong of the red streetcar that took my father to work every morning and brought him back at night--when there was work. From remnants of remnants, old and new, she designed and sewed quilt covers as colorful and beautiful as any done by the Amish or in the Carolina hills. From stockings that no longer had any hope left in them she wove rag rugs like new. It was a sin to discard those remnants and old stockings as long as there was still use in them.

My mother was an artist. She cut the remnants to size and shape, she matched colors, she made the pieces fit the design she had in mind, patterned them into a whole. She could envision the total effect of her work. She knew the secret of how to fashion new life from fragments.

Notes

Sometimes a Jew on a transport to Auschwitz would manage to fling a letter out of the cattle car in the hope someone in the outside world would find it, perhaps even hand it on. In the face of death, the historian Emanuel Ringelblum and his comrades in the Warsaw ghetto collected their notes of life in the ghetto, sealed them in milk cans, and hid them for a future they would never see. Elsewhere in that same ghetto the Hebrew teacher Chaim Kaplan wrote, "If my life ends--what will become of my diary?" It was the last sentence he ever wrote. I can imagine myself into the absolute terror in it.

Litvak

I am a child of immigrants to America. I am something called a "first generation" American. I can never be anything but a child of immigrants. Now I know that such a child is forever unalterably different from those born into any other generation, over and beyond the universal truth that it is in the nature of things for every generation to be different from every other generation.

Perhaps because I am first generation, I have always been fascinated by stories of where people come from. On the road, "Where ya from?" is the first question a perfect stranger will ask you on a first encounter. Everyone has to come from somewhere, and "somewhere," until you know better, is a ready-made mystery story. Even as a child I knew my own story was somehow bound up with where my mother and father had come from. I learned early on that they had come from some far-off place people called "the Old Country," a place that, to hear them talk, was somehow very different from the country I had been born in. Both were born in Lithuania--he in a distant city called Kovno, she in a town called Krakonovo.

11

Actually, Kovno then was a big city, the capitol of Lithuania. We could never find Krakonovo on any map.

Lithuania was called "Liteh" in Yiddish, and a Lithuanian Jew was a "Litvak." Since both my parents were Litvaks, I can claim to be a Litvak too, and, in a way, a "Kovner" as well, a Litvak from Kovno. There is both more and less to my claims than meets the eye.

Had I been born in Kovno and remained there, my life would inevitably have taken some very different turns. As it turned out, I was born a Litvak on the West Side of Chicago, an area so densely inhabited by Jews of the poorer classes that my schoolmates called it "the ghetto." My destiny was bound to my father's. In Kovno it would have been quite another. At the Ninth Fort my destiny would have been quite another.

The Album

The time: summer, 1982. The place: Skokie, Illinois, a suburb north of Chicago. Evening. Some members of the Lithuanian Club have gathered at the home of William Mishell. They are all Litvaks, some of the pitifully few Lithuanian Jews to survive the Holocaust. Most stem from Vilna or Kovno or Siauvli. Some sit on the sofa or on easy chairs in the living room. They are gossiping, for all the world just like normal people. Others gather around the dining room table to look at a picture album. The pages turn. They stop at a group picture--three or four rows of a "gymnasium" graduating class. At first glance I might well be looking at a class picture in my own high school yearbook.

They speak to each other in Yiddish. For a moment I have entered a scene in a Chekhov play. One finger points and asks, "What happened to...?" and gives a name, while another finger points elsewhere, hesitates, and says, "What was his name? I've forgotten," and a third asks, "Where is...?" and a fourth, "What became of...?" This one was a partisan killed in the forest, that one disappeared altogether, another had escaped and is living in Israel. When they

12

speak of *Der Nayenter Fort* and this one or that one who had gone there, it is clear that they all know something that no one else does. I listen to them as they pour over that school photograph and reminisce about their classmates, for all the world just like normal people. I am only a member of the audience.

Almost ninety-five percent of Lithuania's Jews were murdered, probably the highest percentage of Jews lost of any country. These Litvaks lived the war against the Jews. Each of them is a story to tell.

"Go with God"

Dani Birger was a member of the Jewish police in the Kovno Ghetto.

I met him only once, in 1982, at the home of the Mishells in Skokie, when I was a guest at an informal gathering of the Lithuanian Club. If I were to see him on the street I would not recognize him, though I do remember him as a short, stocky, rugged man. After that meeting, after hearing several of his stories, I tried twice by phone to gain his consent to an interview. He rejected my request both times, no matter how much I appealed to his sense of history.

He did not want to remember. "It is better to forget," he said. "I haven't told the children. Why should they know?" It was better for them, he said, to know only good things. I reminded him of the stories he had told about himself or that others had told about him, and of how I wished to hear them again, only with more detail. No, he wanted to forget it all. It was as though he wanted nothing more to do with them. I am sure he had his reasons.

I remember only fragments of those stories. Before the Holocaust Birger was that absolute rarity in Lithuania: a Jewish boxer--and not only a Jewish boxer but a champion Jewish boxer, known throughout the country. One night while he was walking in the street, he saw three hoodlums starting to attack a man who looked Jewish. The man cried out, "I am not a Jew!" But his screams made no difference to them.

Birger crossed the street, went up to the Lithuanians, and said, "But I am--" And he proceeded to show them what he meant.

Another time, during the days of the Kovno Ghetto, Birger was evidently one of the Jewish police involved in underground activities. Someone betrayed him to the Gestapo. Too late, Birger saw several members of the Gestapo climbing the stairs toward him. He was on the landing at the top of the stairs. He had no way out. In an instant he knew what he had to do. With all the force he could muster, he hurled himself down the stairs at them, knocked them over, and fled before they could shoot.

Birger knew he had to get out of the ghetto. He knew he had to get out of the country. Aware of escape routes, he managed to leave the ghetto and somehow acquired a train ticket. He boarded the train, casually took his seat, perhaps in a compartment. In due time the conductor came by, had a long look at him, took his ticket, eyed him again, and moved on without saying a word. The train rattled on, coming closer and closer to the border. The train finally came to a halt at the border. As Birger was about to get off, the conductor approached him once more, paused, raised his hand in a salute, and said, "Go with God, Dani Birger."

The Gestapo shot forty members of the Jewish police at the Ninth Fort for giving aid to Kovno's Jewish underground. Birger remains a mysterious figure for me because I do not know his story. What I do know is that he played a greater role in my life than I ever could have in his. What he does not know, and could not have known--is that without him there would have been no story.

Golus

My parents were born into the last years of the nineteenth century. Like so many of their generation they left home and Russia for the New World and its hopes. They were, in part, playing classical roles in the drama of Jewish history--so heavily marked by its central themes of exodus, exile, expulsion, wandering, migration. In an era of emigration my parents were immigrants. When they were still children in Russia, Konstantin Pobedonostsev, advisor to the Tsar, was supposed to have proposed a solution to Russia's "Jewish problem": one-third would die...one-third would be converted...one-third would be forced to emigrate. They belonged to the one-third that emigrated.

My parents were Lithuanian Jews. I knew that much. But at first, as a child, I could never quite understand how sometimes Lithuania was part of Russia, sometimes it was part of Poland, and sometimes Poland was part of Russia. They were Russian Jews--but they were still Lithuanian Jews. They were Lithuanian Jews--but not Polish Jews. Even more difficult for me to understand, somehow a Lithuanian Jew was never simply a Lithuanian, or a Russian Jew a Russian, or a Polish Jew a Pole.

My mother had relatives in Chicago and Baltimore. My father had them in Kovno, London, Glasgow, Charleston, S.C., even, he thought, somewhere in Capetown or Johannesburg, where many Lithuanian Jews had gone. Another thing I couldn't understand was how all those children could leave everything and everyone they knew in Lithuania and put countries, continents, and oceans between each other, between themselves and their parents, most of them never to see each other again, settling down onto foreign soils to sprout new life, windborne and scattering like the white dandelion parachutes I could send off into the world with a single puff of air. I had no idea that this is what the word "Diaspora" meant. Dispersion. My mother used the word *Golus.* I had no idea where *Golus* was or that Jews had been living there--"in *Golus*"--for almost two thousand years. And I with them.

As a child I could not understand how children could leave their parents behind--forever--never to know what became of them. Not to know what happened to one's mother? Not to know what happened to one's father? To cut oneself off from them forever? How could my own mother and father have done this? What power had driven them to go? It was unnatural for a child to leave his parents alone and unprotected. What was natural was my own fear that something would happen to my father or mother to leave me alone and unprotected.

Kovno, Charleston, London, Glasgow, Capetown--the very sound of those names struck an exotic note. Lithuania, the South, England, Scotland, South Africa--they called up images very different from "the West Side of Chicago." That I had relatives--real family-- somewhere in those places was simply incredible. Who were they, and how did they get there? Why did they go there? What had become of them? What were they to me? Or I to them? Would we ever meet? Would any of them ever come to look for me--or I ever go to look for them? How would I do such a thing? I had no concept of the distances I would have to cover to get to them or of the distance--more than miles--that I would have to overcome if I ever found any of them.

In the Thirties and early Forties, when Chicago was the only home I knew, distance was still distance, physical and out of the question. Oceans and continents were still obstacles measured in miles and days, not hours and minutes. When Hitler swallowed Czechoslovakia in 1938, I was twelve years old. I was thirteen when he attacked Poland, and not quite fifteen when America declared war against Germany and Japan. When I was in grammar school, the War was an unseen presence on the West Side of Chicago. It was remote, somewhere far off "overseas." The War would surely be over before I would be called up. But with the graduation of each senior high school class, its menace drew ever closer. Distance took on hard reality for me only when the Class of '43 entered the War, and I with it. I was eighteen when I entered the Navy and left the West Side. It was a month after D-Day. We had long since lost touch with my father's family in Kovno. It was 1944. The War was still on.

The Mind's Eye

A cold, grey afternoon on the trail. The snow underfoot is packed hard. The trees are brown and bare, etched against the sky. Not a soul. Only the sound of snow crunching under my boots.

I walk past the plots where local farmers from across the street dug the earth last spring to grow their annual crop of tomatoes, carrots, beans, corn, and such. Old railroad ties mark off each parcel of land, neighbor from neighbor. They do not own these rectangles measured out alongside my path. But come spring, they take possession of them, sprouting secretly out of nowhere like the crops they plant. Something there is that impels these city dwellers to dig and plant and grow. Now their little plots are empty, blanketed with January snow, but in the summer I will see these squatters carefully tending the soil again, absorbed in their weeding or watering. Sometimes around harvest time one of these farmers will present me with a tomato or two, the fruit of his labors.

I am something of a farmer too. I do not have the green thumb my father had, but I know what the squatters have to do, even though I grow only some foolproof annuals in the garden I cultivate. The most important thing, I have learned, is to clear the land. You have to clear the land. First of all, you have to dig up the stones and haul them away. Then you have to dig up the weeds. Stones don't grow back once you've taken them away. But you always have to keep after weeds. If you don't, you'll have a jungle in no time at all, and you will lose the clearing you need for your flowers to grow freely. Of course, you have to fertilize and water the soil. Everything is important. But first you have to have a clearing.

Sometimes on the trail I will spy a fallen log, a tree stump, or a broken branch, and I will see in the twist or turn or the angle of it a figure to be carved out of it, if only I were a sculptor like my brother. What I do with my mind's eye is to try to see the figure he would have seen, to see with his eyes. I think of how good it would have been to go hunting for wood with him, how he would have examined each piece, appraised it with a knowing eye, decided whether or not it was worth carting off in his car and setting it aside to dry for a year. I cannot prevent my eye from surveying the landscape for wood for his mallet, even though I know it is useless to do so. All I have left of him are some sketches, a few of his statues, and the mallets he used to make them.

I do some of my best thinking--and remembering--on my walks, especially on a winter's day when the trail is white and empty, except for the sound of the wind. A stranger would say the path looks like a place where "nothing happens." I know better.

The Magic Lantern

Prague. July 24, 1985. At the *Lanterna Magika*. I am overwhelmed by the performance. I have never seen anything like it in my life. Generally skeptical of multi-media theater, I am completely overcome this time by the ingenuity and poetry on the stage. What I am seeing is a portrayal of what happened "One day in Prague."

What happens begins innocently enough. Ever so gradually the eye picks out a worker on screen wending his way through a crowd in Wenceslas Square. He carries a full-length mirror on his back. He is bringing it to the theater. Suddenly, there he is on the screen. Suddenly, he walks out of the screen onto the stage. Suddenly, he is in the theater. It is a magical mirror. Sometimes it reflects. Sometimes you see through it. Sometimes it turns up on the movie screen. You go inside it and out of it for half a dozen scenes, in fantasy, in reality, with the same live actors on the stage as are on the screen, behind the screen, emerging from it, circling around it, all with music, song, and fun and sadness and joy. I am amazed, stunned by *trompe l'oeil* come to life.

Each time the scene shifts to a new episode, the magic lantern takes my imagination to the edge. The mind is a magic lantern.

Click.

Lifting the Lid

My mother saved postcards, photographs, letters. Not in albums but in two boxes. One, made of grey tin and hinged on its long side, had originally seen service as a candy box. The other was coated with orange lacquer on the outside, black lacquer on the inside. They held some of the few tangible reminders she had of the home, the parents, the friends she would never see again.

After my father died, my brother asked for the tin box. And after he died, the tin box disappeared and with it a photograph of my father that I treasured. If it still exists somewhere and someone should happen upon it, he is sure to be struck by it, not so much by the slenderness of the man in the dark grey suit or by the propriety of the grey felt hat he is wearing as by the eyes that do not smile for the camera. They look far beyond the camera. He appears distant, severe, almost haughty. The photographer has caught my father's austerity, perhaps even a faint touch of scorn for a world on the verge of the first World War, or for a world already launched into the Twenties.

Time has chipped away at the orange lacquer lid of the second box, though not at the black lacquer inside. Measuring six inches by eight, its lid is two inches deep and slips over the slightly smaller bottom. During my childhood it became a treasure chest. I needed both hands to lift the lid. Most of the photos inside had no meaning for me. The picture postcards were just as unknowable, what with their funny handwriting, strange stamps, and unreadable messages.

During the Depression years of the Thirties and the war years of the Forties, during the years of study, into the years of teaching and the concerns of living, I returned to the orange lacquer box in idle moments to speculate over its contents, but mostly they remained little more than curiosities, inert, dormant, latent, stubbornly withholding their meaning. Many of the photos have no meaning at all for me. I cannot even guess at the faces or the stories behind them. Most of the portrait postcards are the sort of anonymous curiosities that turn up in dusty bins in antique shops, their vitality all but gone. The reverse sides are either blank or covered in an illegible hand, Yiddish or Russian. To be sure, some pictures were clear enough. There was one of Jacob Gordin, the Yiddish playwright, another portrayed "Mozart's Death." Others were of scenes from Russian plays.

But for years I made little effort to solve their mystery. After my parents died, what had been mementoes to them became relics to me,

19

growing more ancient with each passing year. They were the remains of broken connections between sender and receiver. Both sender and receiver were no longer in existence. These postcards were already old before I was born, before "my" time. What had they to do with me? Still I could not bring myself to throw them away. If they no longer connected sender and receiver, I felt they were still somehow connected to me.

For the last quarter of a century since the beginning of the Seventies--living my own history, my own deaths--my curiosity has grown, not out of any sentimental, fashionable search for "roots," but because stories interest me, family stories that answer questions and raise new questions that will lead to still other answers that are worth knowing. It is too late now to put the questions to my mother or my father or my brother. But I am convinced they knew what I want to know. When I might have asked the right questions, I could not bring myself to do so, because death was already in the room listening to our conversation. But for the most part I was too young, too stupid, too foolish. Mostly, too ignorant. But that is an old story.

Long ago, in the Thirties, when bad times had not yet turned into war times and our family had not yet come apart, humor made life bearable for us, and my brother and I, though we were almost ten years apart, could always find something to joke about in family matters. Oh, yes, Pa had come from Kovno. Everyone had heard of Kovno. But Ma's home town? Krakonovo? Who had ever heard of Krakonovo? It wasn't on any map we had ever seen. And Slobotkeh? What kind of a name was Slobotkeh? The very sound of the word was made for laughter. We teased her. Minsk rhymed with Pinsk. Were there really such cities? And Kishinev? Another joke. Who could possibly come from a place called Kishinev? Or Yehupetz. Or Chelm. Wasn't Chelm a fictional Jewish town located somewhere in Russia, a town you made jokes about, a town of logical fools, lovable fools--but fools. There were so many stories about them, the *Chelmer naronim*, that it couldn't be real. To my American ears, still being Americanized, these names somehow sounded Yiddish, unreal, easy targets. Did they really belong to the world Ma and Pa had come from? The names rolled off the tongue with a smile or a laugh. My brother joined in the joking, even though he knew far more than I, better than I, had studied Yiddish far longer than I. I would learn later of the Kishinev pogroms, but he already knew Hayyim Nahman Bialik's poem about the 1903 pogrom.

But since the beginning of the Seventies I have been drawn to these innocent postcards as never before. Their secrets had grown deeper, more troublesome, more disconcerting because I had done so little to uncover them. What dreams, what hopes, what events did they speak of? Or were they only postcards after all, quick remarks... having wonderful time... see you soon. There were letters, too, stored in other boxes. Beginning with the Seventies and with each passing year, as I have studied them, cards and letters and photos, and learned more about them, they have gradually turned into manuscripts. They are relics of a time before the Destruction, before the *Churbn*, before the Holocaust, before the Shoah.

In November, 1997, in a somewhat nostalgic mood over my own years at the University, I visited my friend Norman in his office at the Oriental Institute. He has a high-ceilinged, old-fashioned office, a double desk--that is, two desks meeting and directly facing each other-- appropriately cluttered with books and pamphlets and papers, a perfect setting for his work on manuscripts, old volumes, and the other texts of his trade. Norman is an authority on the Dead Sea Scrolls. From the evidence he drew from his examination of old texts, manuscripts, ledgers, letters, maps, he predicted the exact location of an ancient yeshiva in the heart of Rouen. Excavations proved the accuracy of his claim--to the astonishment not only of Rouen and France itself, but of archeologists, Jewish historians, and others. A stunning achievement.

But that day we were not talking about the Dead Sea Scrolls or the yeshiva at Rouen. He was in high spirits. "You know," he said, "I spent the whole day here today deciphering an old manuscript. It was tiring work. Time consuming. I am very tired right now. But do you know what? It's exhilarating! It makes me happy. I can't tell you how happy it makes me." His eyes gleamed, his cheeks glowed. No mistake about it. He *enjoyed* his work. He had enjoyed the day. His pleasure held a meaning for him beyond the pleasure he took in his classroom down the hall or in the Auditorium below. He had spent hours "elsewhere," exploring, extracting meaning, solving puzzles, finally making a small discovery for the day. He had come across a solution to a mystery of lives lived elsewhere long ago, he had made a connection between now and then, achieved a little revelation that would take its place in some future pattern. His was a special, private happiness. It could not be shared.

But I knew exactly why he was happy.

I had my own sacred texts, manuscripts lying around not for centuries but for decades, waiting to be discovered, deciphered, translated. Waiting to be recovered. And I handled them as I had been taught to handle them in my own work during my University days. Most of the cards are addressed to my mother, either in America or when she still lived in Krakonovo. They bear the stamps of the Tsar. The cancellation marks date them. Many were mailed in the first decade of the twentieth century, before that "other" war. They go back to the time of that "Nikolai" who occasionally cropped up in my mother's comments about the old country. Now to hold one of these cards in my hand it is as though I am touching a whole world gone.

My mother received New Year's greetings, idealistic political remarks, romantic, sentimental messages--from Ponevesz, Slobotkeh, Minsk, Brisk, even from Kishinev. One card showed a street scene-- Ulica Wilkomierska--in Poniewicz, another a market scene from the same city. A third pictured Kuczkuriszki, a nature scene from Wilno. And as for Chelm, there really is a Chelm! There has to be. One of the cards portrays a market day scene from there.

The orange lacquer box also contains two sepia colored postcards, still sturdy after their Atlantic crossing just before that other war. They are addressed to my father. When I first saw them I did not know they were also addressed to me.

RELICS, 1914

27.4.1914--Kovno

Much loved brothers and sister-in-law. I can share with you that I am in perfectly good health, and I am happy to hear the same from you. Dear sister-in-law, am I as big a fool as I look on the postcard that I should make myself foolish with the boy who invites me to America? I am not excited by a handsome boy. I love only ugly ones. Dear brother Henoch, what you wrote about your sending tickets, we have not yet received them. I believe that now is the best time to travel. About the border we will see further. To make a governor's pass it must cost 18 rubles. Further write us all details and what class tickets you are sending--only not third class. My dear sister-in-law, we expect to bring with a present that will please you--a pair of candlesticks or a nickel samovar. Choose which will please you or some other such things that you need. My dear ones, I can hardly believe that I shall yet see you. Dobe Abramson. Please answer immediately.

11.5.1914--Kovno

My dear brothers Henoch and Mayshel and sister-in-law, may you live and be well, like me. My dear ones, we are very uneasy about your health. It has been long since we received a letter, and we are uneasy about the ship's tickets. We have become very upset. I have left my position, and we have sold certain things because according to the letter you wrote we should have received the tickets the same week. Only it is already 5 weeks and still no tickets. Now it is a much better time to travel. It is warm. My dear brother Henoch, as I read your letter I cried from joy that we shall be able to see each other and at the same time be rid of loneliness. How lonely we are--more lonely than a stone. A stone has other stones near it, but we have no one. There is nothing to do now in Carmelita. Once at least there were foreigners, but there is no spirit. Yankel is not on speaking terms with Di Mameh. He has entirely changed. He has a beautiful daughter. Di Mameh has no joy from him. His behavior with her--it is too much to write about here--better we shall talk about this. I give friendly greetings to my dear sister-in-law and Motele. Write us all about where we stand at present in the world. We are very uneasy. From me your sister who wishes to see you already, Dobe Abramson. Please write immediately. We are very uneasy.

Postcards

Sepia tinted picture postcards. The first bears two faded green stamps, two kopeks each, canceled by the April 27, 1914, postmark. They are from the time of the Tsar and carry the unmistakable exotic aura of the long ago and far away. At first glance they are the sort of postcards curators put on display in museum exhibits called "Immigrant Years" or "The Jewish Experience in America: 1880-1920." Retrieved from albums and attics and placed on display, they attest to the reality of "history." But at the same time they are reduced to lifeless artifacts, their real messages--often illegible or undecipherable--are lost even to those who have preserved them. If the museum visitor stops and looks at all, he hardly ever listens.

Dora, my father's sister, wrote both of them to my father a decade before I was born. She sent them to him at 1921 West Taylor Street in Chicago. My father's Yiddish name was Henoch--Henry in English. The cards were meant not only for him and my mother but for his brother Motl. Motl is Yiddish for Max. My father had brought Max over to America and was looking after him. Yankel--or Jacob--the third brother, did not reach America until the Twenties.

The first card pictures the Adam Misckevich Valley. A tree, bushes, and a fence occupy the foreground, along with two boys, about seven or eight years old, one of them carrying what looks like a milk can. A vague forest disappears in the misty background. The second card offers a Kovno street scene, a view of Prospect Mikolajewski, with its shops, cobblestones, streetcar rail lines. The cards became relics, never explained, never discussed. After my mother and father died there was no one left to explain them.

From time to time during the Seventies I would attempt to read them. Time after time the minuscule Yiddish handwriting defeated even the magnifying glass. I could make out parts but never the whole.

Year after year the cards lay there, becoming ever more of a reproach, ever more of a challenge. By the Nineties I had stopped and looked long enough. It was time to listen to their voice, to their message from another world, from another time. I was convinced they held clues to my father's life--and therefore to my own. But even after

I deciphered them I could feel that a mystery remained buried inside them.   I had no idea that they also held a key to the mystery.

Dora and her mother, who were to have left for America from Antwerp, turned back to Kovno. World War I broke out in August, 1914.

1936

An Invitation

The orange lacquer box held many treasures. As a child I did not know--could not have known--their value. They were playthings piled two inches high--picture postcards, snapshots, a pamphlet. Somewhere haphazardly in the middle of the pile lay a card. Elsewhere in the pile: a photo. Playthings.

The card is an invitation to my parents from "Ch. Dembovitz and Wife" to the Bar Mitzvah of their son Aharon on "7/XI-36"--November 7, 1936. In small print their home address: "Kaunas, Laisves Aleya 11, Residence 1."

My parents had also saved a photograph of Aharon. The photo shows him wearing a dark, high-collared tunic, perhaps a student uniform. He is serious, fresh-faced, looks straight out of the photo as though in anticipation of what the world is about to bring. On the back of the photo he writes in a clear Yiddish hand: "For my Uncle Henoch that I have never met, and family, from your nephew, Aron Dembovitz. Kaunas. 1936.X.22." The date is two weeks before his Bar Mitzvah.

In 1936 I was only ten years old, and I did not know the name Dembovitz, nor could I have known that "Ch." stood for Chaim. But this much I did know: that my father had a sister in Kovno, that she was married and had two children, a boy and a girl, and that the boy was around my age. I don't think I knew that Kaunas was actually Kovno under another name, or why it had the other name. All I think I knew was that "Liteh," as my parents pronounced it, was very far away, across an ocean, and that I had a Tante there that I had never seen. I knew my father sometimes wrote to her. But she and her family lived in another world called Europe. Europe was a mystery. My mother and father had come from that world. There was something exotic, even romantic, to me in the idea that I had unknown faraway relatives who still lived in it. But the fact of the matter was that that world was so far away that I didn't even know their names.

Forty years after my father received them I held them in my hand--my aunt's announcement of Aharon's Bar Mitzvah and Aharon's photo and message to my father. They came suddenly to life--came suddenly into my life.

EARLY LETTERS, 1958 - 1968

Vilnius, 20. V [1958]

To my dear and only little brother Henochl,

You should live and be well. Dear Henochl, I beg you, do not travel anywhere because of me. Do not strain yourself. Remain in your beautiful home and garden. Guard your health. It will do no good to travel because, after all, my girlfriend Chana has been in America forty years. I beg you, do not go.

Further, my dear Henochl, I sorrow for you in your great loss--that you lost your wife, your friend in life. I imagine how you feel, and I feel for you. It is in one's older age that one must, above all, have just this friend, but life does not work out as one wishes. Dear Henochl, be comforted and look after yourself.

The package you sent us is a very good one, all bought in good taste-- wool for a coat for my daughter and a suit for my son-in-law, and two fine dresses for her. Everything she sent is very good. Many thanks for everything.

I will write you again and more who the Biskovs are. Now I am tired. Be well, my little brother. Regards from my daughter, son-in-law, and grandchild. Regards to your good, handsome children. I lie in bed and every day I read the letter I awaited so long from you.

From me, your sister, who wants only to hear you are well.

Dora Dembovtiz

Vilnius, October 28 [1958]

My dear brother Henochl,

You should live and be well. Thank God that I can now write you myself. I can tell you that I have had a bitter summer. I became ill May 1 and lay in bed at home. They exerted much effort to help me. But, unfortunately, I had to be taken to the hospital where I was immediately placed on the operating table. The operation was not successful. It was for gall stones. It was too late. There was nothing else to do: either life or death. Everything would have been all right if the gall had gone into the food, but it went to the side, and they had to perform a second operation. You can imagine the suffering and pain I endured. I had three transfusions, and I barely got through it all.

My daughter suffered terribly. She turned the hospital upside down. She never left my bedside, and the present you sent turned out to be very useful. It was ordained that I not have pleasure from the beautiful present. I was in the hospital four and a half months. Now I am at home. I am still weak. The wound hasn't healed, but it is better.

Yes, my dear brother, *Mann trakht uhn Gott lakht.* I have always thought that we might still see each other at least once more in life. Only you and I are left. If you had wanted it to be, it would surely have been. But there is nothing more to say about this anymore.

Dear brother Henochl, you once asked me who are the Biskovs. If you remember, Bayle, who used to bring us milk, lived near the tunnel. It is her daughter who was my friend. Her brother lives near me. He once wrote her about me. She got very much excited and wrote back an excited letter saying she would help me: I should send her my measurements, and she would send everything. I ask nothing of her. She is very rich but very stingy. Let her be well. If not for her brother from Newark, she would not help her brother in Vilna. The Yankl Yankiski who wrote you is an extraordinary fellow.

My dear good brother, I have asked you to send the photos of you, your children, and grandchildren. I would like to see everyone, if only from a distance. But my dear brother, you are very cold to me. And our children are also cold to each other and do not even want to know about one another. I am after all not a stranger. I am after all an aunt. You can't deny it.

Dear Henochl, our brother Yakov had a son Feivel by his first wife. What has happened to him? Why don't you write about him? I have nephews in America, and I don't want to be so alone. It is not an evil thing that I ask. Dear Henochl, forgive me--but am I not right?

Well, my dear good brother, only be well. My daughter, son-in-law, and grandson send you regards. If we cannot see each other, let us hear from each other. From your sister, Dora Dembovitz

Chicago, Illinois December 30, 1958

My dear sister,

It is a long time since I wrote you. I am very sorry about this, but what could I have done? I have been very sick. This year I have been in the hospital four times. And even now I am not well. Your letters are also not very cheerful. But we cannot help ourselves. Nevertheless, it is good to be alive to hear from each other. At least we are among the living.

My dear sister, today I sent one hundred dollars to your friend Anna Biskov so that she should send you a package. I hope it will be of use to you. I cannot send it to you from here because I cannot get around easily. My heart does not permit it. Perhaps you could write what is best for you. A letter from you takes eight days, as from me to you, my dear sister. I hope you are feeling better.

I wrote to Anna Biskov some time ago that I would travel to see her, but I could not keep my word. Perhaps I will go this spring if I feel better. It is more than a thousand miles.

I have read that Shayndel Chaya's is looking for her brother Abraham, who now calls himself Stein. If you should see her, greet her for me. I once heard that he lives in Brooklyn.

I send regards to your daughter and her husband and all those you see.

Your brother, Henry Abrahamson

Vilna, January 20, 1959

Dear brother Henochl,

Only live and be well, you and your good children. I received your short letter. You cannot imagine my joy. Dear Henochl, because of me God will grant you years. I am so alone, after all. I pray to God you should only live. As you say, we should at least be able to write each other from a distance and hear from one another.

Dear Henochl, I beg you over and over--with your poor health and weak heart, do not journey to my friend Biskov. I will tell you who Anna Biskov is. If you remember from long ago, her mother was called Bayle the Tunnelerke. She lived near the tunnel. She used to bring us milk. Anna is her daughter, already forty years in America. And Yakov Yankiski is her brother. And one brother, Abraham, lives near us in Vilna. When the brother who lives nearby sent Anna regards from me, Anna answered immediately with much joy that I am alive and that I am her dearest friend and that I should send her my address and my measurements so that she can send me whatever clothing I need. And she asked if I had anyone in America so that together they might bring me over. How naive...Anna is.... As soon as she learned I had a brother she became cooler. Now she says she has lived through much trouble: her husband was very sick--he had a serious operation but now he is better. She is rich and stingy. So now you know the entire matter. Therefore guard your weak health. Do not travel to see her.

This Yakov Yankiski is not long in America. After Hitler's concentration camp he got in touch with Anna, and she immediately brought him over--that is, after the liberation from the trouble and torture. This Yakov is a marvelous human being.

Now, dear Henochl, I will write you about Shaynke Chaya's. She has two brothers in America, if they are alive. One is called Abraham Stein. The second is Chone Stein. And she is unable to find them. She is much to be pitied. No one is left from her family. All killed. She is as alone as a stone--no child, nothing. Hitler murdered them all. All her years--she is near eighty--she is still working for others. Dear Henochl, perhaps it is possible to find them. Do not overexert yourself. Ask your good son. Perhaps he can write somewhere to a search bureau or a newspaper. You will earn a mitzvah.

Now, dear Henochl, a few words about myself. I have, thank, God come back to myself and feel not bad. I am in the home and run it. My daughter and son-in-law work. They send you their regards and wish you much health. My son-in-law had a beautiful suit made from your former present, and my daughter a beautiful silk taffeta dress. They thank you very much. I also thank you for what you sent. From this present I will be able to go to take the cure where I shall have to drink the waters that heal the liver and the kidneys. I will immediately write Anna a letter about what she should send. Dora

January 23, 1959

Dear friend Abramson,

I am sorry that I must bother you so much. Your sister writes me that she was very sick and is in much need. Therefore I would like to send her the package as soon as possible. If you cannot send any more money, I can return a piece of the cloth goods. Then I will have enough money to send it. But I need the receipt that I sent you. Be well.

From me, Chana Biskov.

Vilnius, March 22, 1959

Dear Henoch and your dear son,

Be well and of good fortune. Dear Henoch, I received the package you sent. It came exactly on my birthday. A great thank-you. God grant you health and long years. Dear Henoch, you are very far away from me. But in my heart I am happy that I have, thank God, a brother and am not so alone in the world.

Dear Henochl, what is happening with your children? How many times have I already asked you for a photo of yourself and your children and grandchildren? And perhaps you have a little photograph of me from long ago, please send it. Dear Henochl, you write so little. There is so much blank, unfilled paper that I fear you must be ill. Write a few sentences each day until they accumulate into a whole letter.

Dear Henochl, why has your son not married? It would be good to have a *baleboste* in the house. I wonder how you live. Who takes care? Two men! Dear Henochl, how is your second son? What is happening with his two children? And is there already perhaps a third? Write everything. Does he know he has a Tante here? Only one.... I send him my best regards.

Dear Henochl, I ask you not to travel to my friend Biskov--it is so far. Now that it is almost summer you must not strain yourself in your garden. My friend Chana Biskov put up her own dollars for the package, so she must now be in financial trouble....Why did she do this? All she had to do is buy as much as she had money for--and figure this out beforehand. Anyhow, dear Henochl, send her back the few dollars. She wrote you about this and you did not answer, so I suppose she will not be able to make ends meet. She is very stingy but very rich....

Best regards from my daughter and son-in-law and a big thank-you for writing, the package, and all you do for me. God grant you years and health. I send you an addressed envelope so you will not have to ask anyone. I am surprised that you have forgotten the Russian language. Have a happy, healthy Pesach and give my regards to your children. From me, your sister, who wants only to hear good things from you. Dora Dembovitz

[Vilnius, undated]

Dear Henochl,

Do you remember the address of my husband's tante Malka Laypman? You once went to visit her. I have lost their address.

About your telling me to give your regards to the Kovner that live in Vilna, to my sorrow, I must answer you that not a single one is left. All were killed. No one is left.

I want you to write. You can write even less than your last letter, but I should know how you feel and what you are doing. Forgive me for giving you a headache. Please answer quickly. Perhaps you have the photos of my youth. Send them to me. I will be very grateful. I hope this letter finds you in the best of health. From me, your ever-longing sister.

Vilna, 1959

To my dear brother Henochl,

You should live and be well. I want and wish only that we shall hear from one another. But give me the pleasure: write a few words. After all, more than you I do not possess. You are everything to me

Dear Henochl, it is also a long time since I have had a letter from my friend Biskov. When she sent the package, she wrote that she added some of her own money. Dear Henochl, write me if you have sent it back to her. No doubt she is in need.

My daughter and son-in-law send regards and wish you all the best. I send regards to your good children. Send photos of all of you, at least one of you. It will give me great joy. I hope you will give me this pleasure. From me, your sister, who impatiently awaits your answer.

Vilnius, [after June] 1959

To my dear nephews Itzik and Feivel and his family,

May you all be well and have good fortune. Dear Feivel, I wish with all my heart that you have joy from your family and that they be healthy. To be healthy is to be rich.

Now my dear Itzale, what is going on with you? No doubt you have long since married--and you did not invite me to the wedding. But don't be upset. I know: it is because you did not have my address. It has been so long since I have heard from you that I think all of you have forgotten me. But I have not forgotten all of you. I long to hear good news from you. My dear ones, you have not earned anymore complaints...I am your one and only, so I hold myself very proudly....

I have all the letters you wrote in the past. Even your Papa's letters, which I hold most dear. I possess your friendly letters, Itzikl, and the letters from Feivel, so full of laughter. Also the sorrowful letter that my brother is no longer here. My dear Itzale, I hope that you and Feivel will not forget me, and that you will answer me.

Now dear Itzale and dear Feivel, I will tell you why I have not written for so long. I have been very sick. I have had two operations on the liver. The first was not successful, so they performed a second one. I barely managed to escape the *Malakh Hamoves*, the Angel of Death. Now I am pure sweetness-- without a gall. Also, three years ago I took a bad fall in our flat and broke my arm. It did not heal properly. I suffer very much from it. The doctors have suggested an operation, but I will not be able to withstand such a thing.

Another disappointment. I had a girlfriend in New York. Your Papa wanted to go there and see her about me. Since he was so sick and the trip was a thousand miles, I quickly wrote him not to go because my girlfriend is already fifty years in America, so what could she have known to tell him about me? When he was unable to travel to see her, your Papa wrote her and sent her money for a package for me. This was a human being without gall—I mean your Pa.

I suffered through Hitler's war and just barely managed to escape. In the year '14 we had two tickets for ship's passage--Mama and I--that my good brother sent to bring us to him in America. But it was not to be. The tickets were for passage from Antwerp. Just then the war broke out. Before he sent the tickets I had a young man who wanted to marry me, who went off to America and who also wanted to send two tickets. I did not want it to cost your Papa, but your Papa answered immediately that I should not dare to accept them. That was the kind of man your father was. Then came the war. And that, my dear ones, is how my life worked out.

Dear Itzale, write me about everything. What is going on with your automobile? Are you happy with it? When you receive my letter, drive over to Feivel and write me an answer immediately. May my letter find all of you in the best of health.

Your Tante Dora

Vilna [1961]

Dear Itzik,

May you live and be well. Dear Itzik, send me the addresses of my nephews, Yankel's sons. I believe they have no idea that they possess a Tante, alone and sick. In this respect, I believe perhaps they have good hearts and warm souls and will surely not reject me.

I am even more angry with you than with your brother Feivel. He is busy with a large family, thank God. You are quite alone. Or perhaps you are already married and did not invite me to the wedding--so I give you a Mazel Tov that you should have good fortune.

I understand you have already bought an automobile and that your brother Feivel has finally covered the naked walls of his house. Use everything in good health. Also, you have the photos of my mother and me from my youth. Because they are not especially dear to you and you don't need them, please send them to me. Be well. From me, your Tante, Dora Dembovitz.

Chicago, Illinois [September 3, 1961]

Dear Tante Dora,

Do not be angry with Feivel. With me, perhaps--but not with him. As you say, he is occupied with his family, while I am alone. He has worked the whole summer long, and I have not. But there was much for me to do in my home also. And--do not laugh--it is also hard work to read the books I have to read, to think about them, and to talk about them in my classes and elsewhere. I run from one end of the city to the other. I am lucky to have an automobile. Do not be angry with us. We both work hard.

Dear Tante Dora, I also have a complaint against you. I once asked you to write whatever you can remember of my father, and you have not yet done so. I want you to tell me everything you can remember.

I have not married yet, Tante Dora. I am not in a hurry. But when the time comes, you will know. I will tell you and invite you--with my whole heart. Dear Tante Dora, to you and yours a good New Year. Be well.

Yitzhak.

Vilnius, June 1, 1962

Dear Itzik and Feivel, also his family,

You should all be well. I have not answered your last letter because I have been very sick. I had problems with my nerves, and now that I have made an analysis I have a new illness--diabetes. I have become very sweet--nor do I lack salt either. Well, my dearest ones, what I possess--it is you.... Yet you did not find it necessary to write to ask the reason for my not writing. However, my dear ones, one cannot be held dear by force....

Dear Itzale and also Feivel, I am not angry with you. I am also not mean. But, after all, you do not know me.... But I have imagined it [would be] quite otherwise.

Once long ago your Papa loved me very much. It is a very great loss to me that he is no longer here. I have the last letter that your Papa wrote me. And I cry and cry the way he writes me that he wants to travel to my friend in New York except that his health does not permit it, and that he has written her, and that he has sent her money to make a package to send me a present. How loving it was of him. He told me to look for an uncle who would help us with everything. I cannot forget his dear good words. But I no longer have my Henochl. Dear Itzale, you ask and you do not forget to ask me to write about your Pa. Can one write out everything in a letter? There are certain things one cannot write.

Dear Itzik and Feivel, many Americans come as tourists to Russia. Perhaps one of you will make a pleasure trip to come take a look. Soviet Russia is very beautiful. After all, Yankel's Feivel was born here in *Liteh*. He can certainly come and have a look at his homeland. He can stay with his Tante, just as though he were at home. This is the only Tante that remained alive from the bitter-dark Hitler war--and who went through so much: the concentration camps.... He certainly does not know that somewhere there still is a Tante. He left here when he was six years old. Together with my daughter he turned the apartment upside down. I invite you all--anyone who wishes to come and has the opportunity. You are all dear to me.

43

Dear Itzikl, I am proud that you write that you will marry--that is, when the time comes. And that you will invite me and perhaps come to get me with your automobile.... You understand, I would not refuse. Believe me, I would also take a beautiful speech with me.

My dear ones, I greet very heartily Feivel and his family. His writing makes me laugh very much. As I understand it, Feivel must be a merry one. He should only be well and have joy from his children. If possible, send photographs of everyone. Itzik, send photos of yourself--also of your automobile. I hope that now I will receive the addresses of my two nephews. Afterward, I will ask about two more nephews--Yankel's twins. You will no doubt be wondering what it is I want from you! With regards and love, your Tante Dora.

Vilna, June 12, 1967

Dear Feivel,

A big thank-you for your present--I mean the photo of my unforgettable brother Henoch. Also the pictures of your dear, beautiful children. I wish you much joy from the children and your grandchildren. A young grandfather.

Dear Feivel, I have a big request. You must surely have old photos of me and my parents. You must surely have pictures of my youth. You don't know them. After all, you don't know me. Another request. I had another brother. His name was Max. Also very handsome. You were still little children. Perhaps you weren't even here yet. Your Pa brought him over and a short while later he became ill and died. I beg you, if you or Itzik has a picture, send it to me. I once had an album full of pictures. I still remember how you looked when you were maybe twelve years old. My dear brother wrote on it "My son, Philip."

Dear Feivel, quite a number of years have flown by, and I went through quite a bit of trouble. I went through two wars--in '14, when my mother and I were to have traveled to your Pa, they sent us away [from Kovno], and we had to leave everything scattered behind. When we returned we found nothing remained of what belonged to your Pa.

Now, dear Feivel, count up how many years went by until we again went through another dark war, Hitler's war--the ghetto, the concentration lager--but this time already with my family. Through great wonders and miracles my daughter and I remained alive. My handsome good husband and my handsome good son--who had just, at eighteen, finished gymnasium--were murdered.

44

When we turned back home--what home? when home?--you can imagine how tragic it was. We didn't even have anything to eat or anything to begin life with.

We were freed in that beautiful lager Bergen-Belsen. It was a death lager. You must have read of it in the newspapers. The English freed us. Dear Feivel, can any books describe these matters? Impossible.

Now, dear Feivel, you ask what my children are doing. I can tell you that my son-in-law works in a construction ministry. My daughter runs a business dealing with textiles--but the business is not hers. It belongs to the government.... Do not make the mistake that the business is her own. My grandson studies physics and mathematics. He has finished the third course. And I run the house--that is, I am the *baleboste.*

Be well, all. I send many kisses.

Tante Dora

Vilnius, [end of 1968]

Dear Itzale,

I wonder much at your not writing. Are you, God forbid, ill? It is already more than 8 months that we have not written each other. I long very much to hear from you--so I wrote you a letter and you gave it to Feivel, but you did not write a word about yourself and what is happening with you. Feivel answered me that you will write me yourself but, alas, you haven't. Dear Itzale, I asked Feivel to send me my photos of long ago--of my youth. Also of my mother. Also of my brother Max, who died. Your Pa most certainly told you about him.

You should all be well. The new year 1969 should bring you much joy, good things, and much success in your work.

Now my dear Feivel and Itzik, I want to invite you to the marriage of my grandson. It will take place February 1. Yes, my dear ones, time flies. On January 28 he will be 22. He is a fourth year student, in physics and mathematics. He will finish next year.

Dear ones, if I were a little younger, I would come as a guest and we would still be able to see each other. But my dear ones, it is too late. But for you it is not too late. You are still young. After all, you consider yourselves Litvaks, so you can certainly take a pleasure trip. Many Lithuanians who live in America come as guests--understandably, when they can afford it. After all, Yankel's Feivel was born in Lithuania. But he does not long to see his birthplace and his Tante. It seems to me he is a very cold nephew. But that's how it is--love cannot be forced. Dear ones, may you all be well. Regards from my family.

Your Tante, Dora Dembovitz.

DI TANTE'S VOICE

Stones

In the spring of 1914 Doba Abramson was eighteen and in the springtime of her life. She and her mother lived in the Carmelita section of Kovno, a district that took its name from the church at its center. Her brother Henoch had already brought their brother Max to America, to Chicago. And now he was sending for her and their mother, and she was waiting impatiently for the arrival of the *schifskarte*, the tickets he was sending for ship's passage across the Atlantic to the New World. She was eagerly looking forward to the great adventure of her life.

Doba had written my parents that a young man had already invited her to America and was ready and eager to send her *schifskarte*. My parents had immediately warned her that she would be making a dreadful mistake to accept his offer. To do so, they tried to explain, would mean a quick marriage upon her arrival--and they let her know she was simply far too young for that.

On April 27 she sends them a postcard to allay their fears. Do they really think, she wants to know, that she is so big a fool as to fall in love with a handsome boy? "I love only ugly ones," she fires back at them.

Two weeks later she sends off another card. The *schifskarte* have still not arrived and she is growing anxious. Her joy at the thought of being reunited with Henoch is undiminished. To see him again will mean she will "be rid of loneliness." For life in Kovno has turned empty and dull. America and other countries have claimed her peers. "There is nothing to do now in Carmeliteh," she complains. "How lonely we are--more lonely than a stone. A stone has other stones near it, but we have no one."

In the years that followed there must have been some correspondence from time to time between Doba and my father. But the earliest of her letters in my possession date back only to 1958. By that time she is my Tante, but I know of her only vaguely. In 1958 I do not know she is a woman of sixty-two. Nor do I know that forty-four years have passed since she sent her postcards because I do not know that it is she who sent them. Nor do I have any idea yet of what the postcards say or mean; they are still untranslated curiosities to me, and I have no idea of the story they tell. In 1958 I am too busy living my own life to be curious about some old postcards. And I have no comprehension at all of what *meshpokhe* means to her. It is an idea as far away from me as Kovno.

Nevertheless, in 1958 I knew my father's sister had lived through two World Wars and a revolution. I knew she and her daughter had survived the concentration camps. I knew her husband and her son had not. I did not know she had endured the ghetto. I did not know she herself had escaped death at least three times. I did not know how she and her daughter Fanny had survived. In 1958 I knew she was living in Vilna with her daughter, her son-in-law, and her grandson. And I knew that whenever he could my father had sent packages to them. I knew they were living in the Soviet Union, and I knew the Soviet Union was a dark place on the earth.

In one of her earliest letters--October 28, 1958--she describes the physical wounds of a four and a half month stay in the hospital. But it is clear that she finds her spiritual wound more difficult to bear. "I have always thought we might still see each other at least once more in life," she writes my father. "Only you and I are left." Without knowing of his circumstances, she reproaches him, "If you had wanted it to be, it would surely have been. But there is nothing more to say about this anymore." What is most on her mind is the ache in her heart: her need for family, for *familye*, for *meshpokhe*--and our failure to fulfill her need. She complains that he has not sent photographs of himself, his sons, his grandchildren: "I would like to see everyone, if only from a distance. But my dear brother, you are cold to me. And our children are also cold to each other and do not even want to know about one another. I am after all not a stranger. I am after all an aunt. You can't deny it." Nor has he written her about their brother Yankel or his sons. "I have nephews in America," she says, "and I don't want to be so alone." How can a *meshpokhe* exist somewhere and forget her, an aunt who is so alone?

"It is not an evil thing that I ask. Dear Henochl, forgive me--but am I not right?"

In self-defense, my father attempts to explain. "This year I have been in the hospital four times. And even now I am not well." And, he continues, "Your letters are also not very cheerful. But we cannot help ourselves. Nevertheless, it is good to be alive to hear from each other. At least we are among the living."

Three weeks later, she tells him of her tears of joy upon receiving his "short letter." Then, more gently, resorting to the diminutive, she says, "Dear Henochl, because of me God will grant you years. I am so alone after all. I pray to God you should only live. As you say, we should at least be able to write to each other from a distance and hear from one another."

She also takes the time to answer my father's inquiry about Shaynke Chaya. Shaynke Chaya, she informs him, has been unable to find the addresses of her two brothers in America. "She is much to be pitied. No one is left from her family. All killed. She is as alone as a stone--no child, nothing. Hitler murdered them all. All her years--she is near eighty--she is still working for others. Dear Henochl," she pleads, "perhaps it is possible to find them...."

Two months later she has received a package from my father which "you sent exactly on my birthday. A great thank-you. God grant you health and long years. Dear Henoch, you are very far away from me. But in my heart I am happy that I have, thank God, a brother and am not so alone in the world."

In March, 1959, she asks my father does his son Feivel "know he has a Tante here? Only one...." Then, wickedly, she adds, "I send him my best regards." In her letters during the Sixties our cousins do not escape her tongue either. Yankel's sons, she believes, must "have no idea that they possess a Tante, alone and sick. In this respect, I believe they have good hearts and warm souls and will surely not reject me." She cannot believe our cousin Feivel does not "long to see his birthplace and his Tante. It seems to me he is a very cold nephew. But that's how it is--love cannot be forced."

In January, 1971, she recounts a double catastrophe, Fanny's hospitalization and her own suffering from a fall that prevented her from going to see her. "You can imagine. Fanya was in the hospital. And I lay at home--alone the whole day, lonely as a stone."

In 1971 I begged Di Tante to write me something of her life. In 1972 she wrote me ten pages of it. On one of them she recalls the expulsion of the Jews from Kovno during the first World War--it must have been in May, 1915--and how she and her mother, fleeing eastward toward Vilna, "came to the little *shtetaleh*" where they experienced hardships so ugly and dark that they left her feeling "as alone as a stone."

My Biography

I was eight years old in 1905. My parents had four children: three boys and I the only girl. One was called Henoch. The second was called Jacob (Yankl), the third Max, and they called me Doba. As I remember, the Revolution was annulled--that is, it was choked off. But the time was unsettled. So my Pa immediately sent Henoch off to America. We lived in Kovno on a street not far from where soldiers were quartered.

One day during the Revolution a soldier we knew was passing by where my Pa sat on the stairs of the house where we lived. He pulled my father's feet from under him--an example of goyish humor. Der Pa began to feel ill from the day this happened. With each passing day he felt worse. His lungs were affected. The soldier--not meaning to--had struck his lungs. He was sick for a while. Then he died. Our situation became frightening. In a short time my brother Henoch began to send 15 dollars every month. Anything was better than nothing.

The First World War began in 1914. This was also terrifying. When the war began all the Jews of Kovno were sent away. The reason given was that Kovno had a fortress and the Jews were considered the worst enemies and spies. So I, a little girl, and my sick mother were considered enemies. You can imagine the suffering and troubles I endured. This can in no way be written out. I was still a little girl but faithful....Would you say otherwise?

In addition to all this trouble we had a little bit of luck. An inspector of railroad cars lived in the courtyard where we lived. He counseled us not to go far, that we should stop at one station before Vilna. He said the war would not last long and we would be able to return. We followed his advice. When my mother and I arrived at the little town, the station before Vilna, the train failed to stop. As the train was moving slowly, we threw out our poor packages, and I jumped out. My mother did not have time to jump, and she went on toward Vilna. But later she turned back to me. You can understand my situation.

We came to the little *shtetaleh*. A few Yiddish families lived there, but they were bad people. They put us up in an empty barn for horses. We had to clean out the manure from the horses. A little later Di Mameh became ill. She caught a very bad cold. I did not lack for trouble. I was as alone as a stone. But it was an exciting time.

In a short time the situation worsened. The war approached. We saw the fire, heard the cannon. One of the leaders of the *shtetl* had horses and wagons. He was already preparing to run from the *shtetl*. He took pity on us and took us with him toward Vilna. We ran away to Vilna. Luckily, I met a schoolmate who had come to Vilna before us. We found a place to live, and it turned out that what the train inspector had said was true.

We returned home quickly. We came to the watchman. He received us warmly, gave us something to eat, and we lived with him. The city was destroyed. The stores were destroyed, broken. No windows either--all broken. We restored everything and set up a grocery. The military ran from the front. Both of us worked day and night, and we did well. Many hungry soldiers came and we earned much. But we did not understand that the Tsarist money was no longer good. So we were in trouble again. We had worked for nothing.

My brother Motl [Max] left for America. He was the youngest. He had fallen in love with a girl who had gone to America. When he came to see her she already had another. He took this much to heart, became very ill, and died. As I remember, your Pa had plenty of trouble with him.

My brother Yankl also went into the army. He came home after his service. A few years later he married. A little later a son was born. He was called Feivel. This is the Feivel who was by your brother Feivel. Feivel once wrote this to me, and your brother did not even tell him about me. Well, anyhow....

The October Revolution took place in 1917, and after the Revolution Lithuania became independent. At this time I met my husband. He was good, handsome, had all the virtues. He respected my mother very much and used to call her "Mama."

By trade he was a cap maker. He made caps for army officers. He worked in a shop that worked for the army. We met by chance, by a miracle, and we were married. We lived together with Di Mameh, and it was all very good. We all lived in the old place. When my husband would come home from his eight hour job, he would work even more in the house, and I would help him. We did not spare our strength and worked hard because we wanted to reach a goal. That is, we saved money and ignored fancy clothes and such things. Finally we saved a little money--we were able to take in enough to rent a shop on the main street. It was called Freedom Avenue. But we had credit. We got everything we needed and it worked out well. My husband and I worked side by side.

After we made a little money, we wanted to have a good place to live. I was very bold and obtained a beautiful apartment of five rooms, with central heating, and a beautiful kitchen. However, in order to save money I rented out two rooms to a lawyer. But this cost me much more.

My son Araleh became thirteen, and we had to make a Bar Mitzvah. This is a very beautiful holiday. There were many guests. We ate and drank. And when all had left, the lawyer entered, congratulated us on the festivities, and said to my husband, "Come, Dembovitz," and he went with him to the restaurant. They drank a little and came home. This was on a Friday. Saturday, when we had to bring our boy to *shul*, there was already a misfortune. My husband was taken with a paralysis. A vein had burst in his head. We immediately called doctors who did everything they could, but unfortunately with little success. The doctors advised us to send him to Estonia, where there was a professor who cured such sick ones. So he went there. The professor sent him to Latvia. There they made good procedures.

When he came home from Riga, we did not recognize him. He had become even more handsome, but the two fingers with which one must handle the needle no longer worked. Well, we found a way out. We hired a worker. The enterprise did not stop. We ran it as before. At this time Fanya was already a big girl, and she helped out very much.

In 1941 the Second World War began. No matter how much one writes one cannot write out all that happened. Everything was taken away from us, and we were sent into the ghetto. We were able to take something from the house to sleep on, bedclothes, pots, and other little things. But what was the use of pots when we had nothing to cook? We received portions of bread. In a word, it was a sorrowful time.

We were fenced in with barbed wire and guarded by many soldiers. They used to force us to work. Lithuanians also worked there, and they would trade bread for our things. But there were also good Lithuanians who threw bread and other things over the fence when the guards were not looking. In a word, you can imagine for yourself how they tormented us.

Suddenly they sent us to Estonia. There, too, we found a sweet camp. We were not allowed to take anything with us--only a handbag. They used to force us to do "black work"--that is, to dig the earth and pile it up, whether is was necessary or not, as long as the Jews were tormented.

After being in Estonia for a time, I asked permission to work in the kitchen. Many Jews worked there. The block leaders of the camp were also Jews. I barely succeeded in my request. They allowed me to work in the kitchen. They needed to have a supply of potatoes peeled. I asked the leader of the lager to decide who should peel the potatoes. Little children, 11-12 year old little girls, would come to the kitchen. The little girls had mothers and fathers. And other hungry children. The little children would steal little pieces of potato and hide them in their clothes. Every once in a while they would say they were going to the toilet. Instead they would carry the pieces of potato to the barrack where they lived. I was not stingy with them. But if a German were to see this, I would receive 25 blows on my rear.

My husband did black labor and suffered frozen feet and became ill. My little son Araleh also lived nearby. I was well off, after all. Suddenly, they sent him to another lager--a young boy without a mother. In a short time he became sick. There was no help from the Germans--they wanted only to annihilate the Jews more quickly--and my Araleh died.

I did not know of his death for a long time. Then, one time I, some other women, and some little children were sitting in a bunker picking over potatoes. One of the women workers, an acquaintance, wanted to tell me something. She began, "Frau Dembovitz--" But one of the young boys shouted out, "I know! Young Dembovitz has died!" He said that Araleh was sick, all worn out--that a German SS had entered his barrack, saw him, took out his revolver, and wanted to shoot him, but the leader of the room begged him not to shoot and said that he would soon die on his own. This is what the young boy told me.

You can imagine the effect of all this on me. I write in brief: one can't put everything down on paper. My dear little boy, my little son. Araleh completed Hebrew Gymnasium. I cannot forget. Just now, as I write my biography, my heart aches. And I have had a good cry, remembering everything of the concentration lager. How I was able to survive I do not know.

They sent us by ship from Estonia to Stutthof, where we remained for three weeks. When they brought us to Stutthof, we were hungry, frozen, glad at least to have arrived. They immediately led us to the baths. They took away our clothes. I had a poor little packet--a few little photos, an old dress. They examined us while we were naked--in places where one should not and in the mouth. Some who did have something of gold swallowed it, but this was seldom. I had a little photo of my little son, as large as on a pass. I placed it where they looked for gold. An SS girl discovered it. I wanted it very much, at least to be able to look at sometimes. But it's all the same. He is in my deepest heart, and I cannot forget him.

Now I will describe our life in Stutthof. We slept on small wooden "beds"--two women to a bed--one head on one side, the second on the other. We had to get up at four o'clock, before dawn, without a coat, with not even a cloth for one's head--all just to torture us. Not everyone had a bed. Many lay on the ground. If you did not get outside quickly enough, they would douse you with cold water to force you out. The women would move close together in groups, each warming the other. One cannot describe this either. This is more degrading than one can imagine.

Now about eating. In the morning they used to give a soldier's loaf of bread for three persons for a whole day. At midday they would give as if to a pig. A good *baleboss* would give a pig better than we got. The food was poured into wooden tubs in the yard, and everyone would have to go in twos with one bowl. There was no spoon--eat as best you can--as if one could eat with his hands. By great good luck, Fanny and I had a toothbrush, so she ate first, and sometimes I. And what kind of food was it? If you know what is called *kropiveh* [poison ivy nettles]...well....

I remember an acquaintance of mine, a respectable woman, who after eating her portion went to clean out the tub in order to get a little more. An SS girl saw this. She ordered the woman to stand on a bench and doused her with cold water. And she had to stand like that for an hour.

In Stutthof I saw my husband again. We women were fenced off from the men by barbed wire about 100 meters long. I saw him and we spoke silently and waved our hands. A German guard saw this and struck him over the head with something. I saw this with my eyes. I never saw him again. This was my farewell to him.

After three weeks in Stutthof we were sent deep into Germany, to a concentration camp near Hamburg. It was hard and terrible for us there. We had to work in an arms factory. We worked at night also. I worked, but they got no joy from my work. Wherever I could I would make damages.

When the front drew near, they sent us to a death lager, Bergen-Belsen. There it was altogether horrible. They gave no food or water for ten horrifying days. On the eleventh the English surrounded the lager and freed us. After freeing us, the English gave us food. Those without brains threw themselves on the food, ate, and died in a short time. Thousands of people.

On the day we were freed an SS girl gave me a shove. I fell and broke my foot. They placed me in a hospital. A French woman lay near me. She was a doctor. She placed a plaster of Paris cast on my foot. The cast that the doctor made was not good. I had an x-ray and they made a new cast. The English were gentle and good. There was also a professor who proposed that I go to Sweden to rest my foot. To this day I still remember what he looked like--very handsome, good, and gentle. The English would give us chocolate cigarettes.

I lay in the hospital for a time. In this lager there were people from all nations. While I was lying in my room in a good bed, a tall, handsome Russian came by and made me a gift of the cane he had used for his broken foot. Time passed, and after a while I began to use the cane.

There was little joy. Fanya and I journeyed home with a great eagerness. I had lost such a good husband and a son. Fanya had lost a good Pa and a brother. The English asked if I had anyone in America. I answered that I had a brother but not his address. So we came home--to the bloody home, in Kovno.

In Kovno we found a girlfriend of Fanya's and her brother. We lived with them a month. After a month we learned that Osya had also come and was living with his sister, whom you met. He was living in Vilna. So we also went to Vilna and lived with his sister a short time. Osya and Fanya began to work, and a little while later we were lucky to get an apartment. At that time, in 1946, the Poles left for Poland....

"Ah Brievele"

Di Tante has one long-standing complaint: that I do not write her often enough. When weeks, even months, go by without a letter from me or my brother, she does not directly berate us for failing in our duty. No. That approach would be too obvious. She has a more powerful, unfailing weapon at her command: Jewish guilt. Which, if not more powerful, is arguably unlike any other kind. "I want you to let me have pleasure from my life," she says. Clearly, we are depriving her of that pleasure. Then, with unerring accuracy, she strikes home with "Who knows how long I shall be able to answer you?"

My brother and I hear her classic, unassailable argument. Unable to restrain ourselves, we burst into laughter. "It's *Ah Brievele der Mamen!*" We both instantly recognize the debt she owes to "A Little Letter to your Mother," the most famous Yiddish folk song of

59

her time, the sentimental lament of a mother in the Old World writing to her son in the New:

> A little letter to your mother,
> Do not delay it,
> Write speedily, dear child,
> Grant her this comfort.
> Your mother will read your letter
> And she will recover.
> You will heal her pain, her bitter heart.
> You will revive her soul.

After suffering from yet another of my long silences, she writes, "I and all of us are wondering why for so long there is no letter from you, Itzale. What has happened? Are you all well?" Then she zeroes in with "Don't you want to know about my health?" Guilt again. Next, as if she has read our minds and heard our laughter all the way across the ocean, she writes, "Once they sang a song 'Ah brievele der mamen,'" then draws a line through the word "*mamen*" and places the word "Tante" directly above it. And like the song, she adds, "Do not be late. When we receive a letter, the whole mood changes."

Di Tante knows how to strike exactly the right note. I can hear it. Unmistakably.

"Dear Itzale ..."

...is how all my aunt's letters to me begin. Those she writes to my brother begin "Dear Feivel" rather than "Dear Feivele." Itzale (pronounced *Itz-ah-leh*) is the diminutive of Yitzhak, a form full of special loving connotation. Older female members of a family--a mother, an aunt--will use this form toward a younger member of the family and have the right to do so. That my aunt does not use the diminutive form of my brother's name does not, however, mean that she has any the less love for him. More probably, it is simply that he was older than I and that she "knew" me better than she knew him.

"Dear Yitzhak," the form of address my cousin Fanny uses, indicates a certain equality, appropriate between cousins, for example.

My brother and I would share our aunt's letters, and we would have a high time of it working our way through them, not at all because of her handwriting--she wrote a clear Yiddish--but because of her way with punctuation, or, more accurately, her way without punctuation, for she used neither commas nor periods. No dashes or question marks or exclamation points. No paragraphs either. But her Yiddish was our Yiddish, after all. It was *mameloshen*. It was the Yiddish of our parents. It was a Lithuanian Yiddish. Because its vocabulary, phrasing, rhythm, and intonation were natural to us, we had little trouble translating her Yiddish into our English.

Neither of us had ever met her, seen her, or spoken to her. Yet we could hear her voice in her letters as though we had known her all our life. We laughed over her wit, her humor, her way with Yiddish proverbs, her sayings--her *vertlakh*.

We also had to laugh at the Old World repetitions that characterized her letter-writing style, and when we finally ventured to tease her about them, she was quick to respond: "Do you know, Itzale, I feel drawn to write 'dear Itzale,' 'dear Feivel.' But I remember how you and Feivel made fun of me when you told how when I write you a letter it is full of 'dear Itzale' this and 'dear Feivel' that. Remembering, I try not to write "dear Itzale," "dear Feivel." But I cannot write otherwise--because you are very dear to me. Who else other than dear Itzale and dear Feivel do I have? As you wish. You can laugh at me, but I shall write the way that is dear to me...." And, no doubt laughing to herself all the way, she follows this last "dear" with one more thrust, a sentence that begins "So again, dear Itzale...." The Tante could give as good as she got--if not better.

Nor did she fear to take my father to task for having "forgotten the Russian language" and for sending letters filled with more white space than words. All he has to do, she instructs him, is write a few sentences a day, and in a few days he can have a full, respectable letter. Then, without transition, she faults him for failing to attend to a matter of classic Jewish concern. "Why," she wants to know, "has your son not married?"

Tante Dora was a woman to reckon with.

The Stamp Collection

It was an event in our home whenever my parents received a letter from my father's sister Dora. It was an event because the letter came from Stalin's Russia. One of the events I remember arrived sometime in the late Forties, a year or two after my return from the War. I remember how my parents put their heads together over it. They always spoke in subdued tones when any word came to them from her. But this time they spoke more earnestly than usual.

Aunt Dora wished us the usual, that we should live and be well, gave us the news that all was well with her and her family--and she remarked, among other matters, that they had everything they needed. She insisted that no one lacked for anything in the Soviet Union. To my parents, who had long known the murderous truth of the Soviet Union, her remark sounded a wrong note. Dora was no true believer. It was not like her to protest so much.

In a postscript, a casual afterthought directed to my mother, she further remarked that she had placed some especially beautiful postage stamps on the envelope and that my mother might want to save them for her stamp collection. Odd again. My mother was no stamp collector and she had no stamp collection. What could Dora have been thinking about? The remark made no sense. My mother guessed that because it made no sense, it must make sense--there had to be sense to it. She inspected the stamps. They were indeed colorful enough, just as her sister-in-law had said. Otherwise there was nothing unusual about them.

Finally, she decided they had to be removed from the envelope. She boiled water in the tea kettle and held the envelope above the white steam that puffed from the spout. The stamps gradually loosened. Carefully she lifted them from the envelope. The envelope revealed nothing. But the underside of each stamp did. On each Aunt Dora had written an obviously urgent message in Yiddish. "*Shikt gornit.* Send nothing." "*Ah groys rizik.* A great risk."

Little as they had, my parents understood that Dora and her family had less. Clothing, shoes--they knew anything they could send her would be a help. But Dora's words brought them up short. Few as they were, they spoke volumes. What they meant was that the Russians were suffering shortages of food and clothing and shoes. What they meant was that the Soviet workers' paradise was something less than perfect. What they meant was that any package she received from abroad would arouse suspicions and bring on accusations that she and her family possessed more than their neighbors and were therefore living contrary to the fundamental and holy Communist principle of equality. Moreover, to have connections to the outside world meant you were a "cosmopolitan"-- that is, a Jew--and therefore not genuinely loyal to the State. Dora and her family would have paid dearly if her stamps had been discovered. She and her family would have paid dearly if my parents had sent the package. If anyone had taken a great risk, she had.

Another time. Another letter from Dora. Instant anticipation. News from Dora! My father opened the envelope. Instant pleasure: several photographs slipped out. Followed by instant puzzlement: the photos were of no one we knew! Instant disappointment: nothing in the letter explained who these people were or that photos were enclosed. The only possible explanation: the Censor. With so many open envelopes on his desk, he had forgotten which one had contained the photographs and had mistakenly enclosed them in Dora's letter to us!

The Censor. Whether in Stalin's Russia or Brezhnev's, he--or the fear of him--is in every letter. His eyes are always looking over the writer's shoulder. Because he is a presence in the letters we receive from the USSR he is also a presence in those we send to the USSR. And behind his unseen eye is the unseen fist. An iron one.

DIARY, 1970

The First Letter
Highland Park
Spring, 1970

Dear Tante Dora and the whole family,

My little Perle and I have been overcome with a desire to come to see you all. We hope to come to Vilnius this summer--if all goes well and we get our papers in time. Maybe we will yet be able to be together for a few days.

As things stand now, we will come to Moscow on the evening of the 21st of July (the seventh month), a Tuesday. On Wednesday evening (July 22) we hope to fly to Vilnius. If all goes well, we will be able to stay in the city until the 27th of July, a Monday. Then we fly back to Moscow and then on to five other cities in the land, and then to Copenhagen, and finally back home. But everything waits for what your country will tell us. From our side, till now, all goes well. But everything must still be approved by Intourist, the Soviet Bureau for foreign tourists.

We want to bring with us what is most appropriate for the weather and the time of year. Perhaps you can tell us a little about these matters. We also want to bring presents for everyone, things you would perhaps like to have. Therefore you must write us quickly, a little faster than I have been in answering your last letter. Perle says she wants to know your height, your weight, the colors you like, and anything else you can tell her so she can have an idea what to bring for presents for all of you. Perhaps you want something special. We do not want to come with empty hands--as *pusteh fressers* [free loaders, more mouths to feed]. It is not proper. My mother and my father would not be happy if we did. Nor do I want my brother Feivel to take me to task.

If we cannot come on the 22nd, we will let you know. Then we will come on other days.

Yitzhak

Wild Geese
July 20, 1970

We are finally at O'Hare airport. We still have a couple of hours to wait before we board. I don't know what I am doing here. Mr. Gordon, our travel agent, a man wise in the ways of Russia, said "Go," even though the two letters we sent announcing our arrival have gone unanswered. In answer to our misgivings, he said, "Go. You will find out."

I have a few old photographs in my handbag and an old ink-stained envelope in my wallet to go on. That's all. I think we are off on a wild goose chase. What business do we have chasing wild geese in the Soviet Union? In the Soviet Union! Who goes to the Soviet Union?

And why am I writing a journal? Mr. Gordon said, "Go." Something tells me, "Write." It's time.

I've seen him more than once. In silent rare old "home" movies or maybe in early Yiddish "talkies," faded and grainy and flickering. The set is a dusty yard in front of a ramshackle wooden cottage. A well. A tethered goat. A wandering cow. Chickens scurrying about or scratching a living out of the dirt. The Jewish "Yankee" has returned from his America to visit the mother he has left behind in *der alter heym*, in the old home, in the shtetl. His flat-topped straw hat, his bow tie, his white suit tell us everything. He is all smiles, all success. He is an animated performer, moves faster than life. He embraces his mother, plants a kiss on her cheek. She wears a babushka. A shawl covers her shoulders. A white-maned, white-bearded grandfather sits stoically on a bench, a hand resting on each knee. Wide-eyed, curious children surround the stranger from the New World. He dispenses candy, a pat on the head. He removes his hat, fans himself with it. Instead of writing ah brievele der mamen he has come to visit her. He's a stock figure who once lived on the Yiddish stage and screen.

But he's a character out of an innocent pre-war world I never knew. We're going into a very different history. We're going into a police state, the land of the KGB, the country Stalin built. Ehrlich and Alter are names I know--murdered. Like Solomon Mikhoels--murdered. I know about the farce of Birobidzan. I know the monstrous May Day parades in Red Square--the marching soldiers, the rolling tanks, the rocket missiles. I know of the gulag, the executions, the trials. I know of the crackdowns on the dissidents and refuseniks. I know of the relentless anti-Semitism in the books, the cartoons, the newspapers. Most of all, I know the bitter hatred my mother and father had for the communists, their ideology, their corruption, their vision of "the radiant future."

I can already feel the Iron Curtain. Intourist has told us that Kovno is a "closed" city. Off limits. Vilnius is open though. The USSR is a closed country, a Dark Continent. Our friends think we're mad to go there. At first I thought so too. Not anymore. My father would have said, "Go." To explain our going I'd have to explain my love for him. It's impossible to explain such matters to them. I'd have to write a novel. They'd never understand.

Tseylem kop
July 20, 1970, 1900 hours

We have been aloft for three hours. It's dark and we must be over the Atlantic by now. Perle has managed to spill some dry instant coffee all over my flight bag. Surely an omen of a successful trip.

We met Mr. Greenbaum as we were climbing up the ramp to the plane. Since then he has come by to talk music with Perle. He was her cello teacher many years ago. We see him at Orchestra Hall in the cello section of the Chicago Symphony. He is a Scotsman from Glasgow and speaks Yiddish and English with a wee bit o' a burr.

The night lights are going on. Pillows and blankets are appearing. And we are heading steadily eastward into the night toward the Old World. From my window seat the night glows faint and blue.

We drone steadily into the night, and it is as though with purpose. There is a mystery in our going--quest and mission both. *Tzu gefinen di Tante*--to find the Tante.

When he heard we were going to Vilnius, our friend Mr. Daiches told us that there is no one of his family left in Vilnius--no uncles, aunts, cousins, nothing. Only he remained alive, one out of eight. But perhaps, he asked wistfully, perhaps we might find someone there who still remembers one Yitzhak Daiches. And he wrote out his old address. "Maybe you will find it," he said. He wrote it out for me: "Glezer Gass, 8/15." On the street of the glaziers. He called Vilna "*di vigaleh fun Yiddishn kultur in Liteh*"--the cradle of Yiddish culture in Lithuania, and that means in Europe. He said that Vilna once had 90,000 Jews--"*ah historischeh shtot*," he called it, an historic city.

Mr. Daiches told me, too, why a Litvak is called a *tseylem kop*. The literal translation is "cross head." But that doesn't make much sense. Being a Litvak myself, I have always wondered what it really means and why and how the term came to be applied to the Litvak. If anyone would know, he would. Here is what he told me. It seems that a Polish Jew once complained most bitterly that he could never win an argument with a Litvak. To express his exasperation and frustration he said, "You can place a Litvak in the length, and you can place a Litvak in the breadth, and still you cannot defeat him in logic!" (Mr. Daiches pronounced the word "*log-ik*.") And this is why the Litvak has received the name *tseylem kop*--you can place him lengthwise and crosswise--you can place him on the cross--and he will still not surrender his logic, nor can one defeat it

.

It is a pleasure, though always a sad one, to talk with Mr. Daiches. I like speaking Yiddish with him, and he said to me, in Yiddish, "You speak a good Yiddish." A compliment. Mr. Daiches has the deep, hollow-eyed look of the tortured man. "It's the same look," says Perle, "that we've seen on Elie Wiesel." And she's right--it's the same look. "Most of the Jews of Vilna," he said, "were murdered. Maybe a few survived. And maybe you will still find someone there who has heard of one Yitzhak Daiches...."

Why do I love so much to hear *ah Yiddishn vort*--a Yiddish word? Today I thought of the *hard*ness of English. In English we say "Goodbye," and the word has the hard ring of finality to it, with no thought of a return, to meet again. Not so the French of *au revoir*--to see you again, or even the German *auf Wiedersehen*. In Yiddish it is *geyh gezunter heyt* or *geyht gezunter heyt*--go in good health, or *hoht ah guteh rayze*, have a good journey. "Goodbye" doesn't even come close to the generosity of the others. And so I long to hear *ah Yiddishn vort*. Perhaps I have a share in Mr. Daiches' sadness, for who will come after us to know or remember the sweetness and sorrow of our Yiddish? Did this too die in the Holocaust?

And so we are going to Vilnius. How far from the Kovno or Krakonovo, where Pa and Ma once walked the streets and had mother and father, sisters and brothers, friends and companions? Perle tells me that two nights ago I talked in my sleep and kept repeating "find...find..." It is not like me to talk in my sleep. Of course it has to be that the Tante is on my mind. I wonder if she is alive. Oh, how I hope she is alive! She is Der Pa's *ah shvester*--my father's sister. It would be a miracle to meet her, who is indeed from another world. We go armed with an address and two photos of her daughter. Maybe someone will know and tell us. Pa would find her, and I will too.

But what if she is not alive? What if we have come too late? Why didn't she answer the last two letters we sent? Is it really too late for even our jet to overtake her? It would really be something to find her, make her laugh, tease her, joke with her. She'd be like that--full of wit and with a quick tongue. Her letters showed her so. And there would be something of Der Pa in her, too, maybe the crooked, warning index finger. I hope she is still alive. It's important to stay alive. There isn't anything more important than that.

KGB

Tuesday, July 21, 1970, 1300 hours

We are sitting in our seats on a two jet Aeroflot--this is no KLM airliner. A half hour ago we were in a corridor at the Amsterdam airport looking at it from a distance, as it stood isolated in a remote area of the field, not another plane anywhere in sight. It has the red flag on its white tail. While we looked through the corridor window, KLM crews passing us took a long look at it and lowered their voices to whispers. When it came to boarding, we couldn't help but notice the redhead in the trench coat, his hands buried in his pockets, standing too casually in front of the ramp leading up to the cabin door. He didn't seem to have any reason to be there except to eye the passengers boarding. KGB.

Perle is quiet and I joke, but we both have mixed feelings. When we climbed aboard we discovered that under Communism no one has reserved seats. It's grab-as-grab-can. In three hours we will be in Moscow. Moscow!

We're off! Holland is already green, rectangular, and red-tiled below us. We have gone into a steep turn and we are already flying through murky white clouds, breaking through and climbing above them. I thought that turn would never end. CCCP on the left wing.

No instructions on emergency measures. No soundproofing. No dramamine--just when it would have been a good idea. A bearded American professor-type just across the aisle is already writing away furiously in his notebook while I look out my window.

1430. Finished first rate lunch. Heavy but good. Turkey, salad, eggs, wine, mineral water, tea, cake--and a green apple. Also a linen napkin. But the stewardesses do not smile.

The first eeriness of traveling to an unknown world, and a forbidden one, is beginning to shift to curiosity and suspense. How will it go? Many of the Russians on board seem to be athletes, maybe tennis players. No one speaks to us, however. No one smiles.

Ploshet Krasnaya

July 21-22, 0115 a.m. Moscow.

Arrived at 6 p. m. We have just returned from our first adventure in the CCCP--a walking tour and a bus tour all on our own and without a kopek in our pockets!

The bastard who flew our plane must have thought he was still in the Russian Air Force. He didn't give a damn about his passengers. No smooth flying for him. That first terrible turn should have been the tip-off. Perle gave up her lunch just as we landed at Sheremetyevo International Airport, but she recovered quickly. There were delays at the airport, not by customs but by the young blond bureaucratic Intourist man, who seemed almost to be following a policy of delay.

We were taken to the Hotel Ukraina. Once we arrived here Perle was already saying, "Let's go. We're in Moscow! We can't just stay here in the hotel. Let's go. We'll exchange some money downstairs. Then we'll go." Down we went. The Intourist office: closed. The cashier: closed. No money. "We're going anyhow." "But we don't know where we are...we don't have any money...we don't know the language," I protested. "It doesn't matter. We're only going to be here overnight. How can we be in Moscow for the first time in our lives and not go to the Kremlin? C'mon!" The question could have only one answer.

We learned the name for Red Square--*Ploshet Krasnaya*--and went out into the street looking for a streetcar, asking, "*Ploshet Krasnaya?*" "But we don't have money for the fare," I said. It was no use. "C'mon. They can see who we are. They won't kill us. We'll play dumb."

"*Ploshet Krasnaya?*" The driver nodded. We boarded, took our seats. The conductor came checking for tickets. We looked helpless, trying to explain we had no money. An international incident was in the making. But quickly averted. A little old *babushka* smiled at us, got up, and deposited 4 kopeks for each of us in the coin box. She accepted my hug of gratitude.

73

A few minutes later while we were gobbling up the scene through the window, hoping to spot our destination, suddenly, there it was. Red Square! We hopped off and simply started to walk, two crazy Americans alone in Moscow, barely two hours in the country, gaping at the onion towers of St. Basil's at the far, far end of the wide open expanse of the Square--and, yes, a picture postcard large as life. The dark red brick of the Kremlin. The measured march and swinging arms of the goose-stepping soldiers at Lenin's tomb. The strollers.

"Perle, look at that flag up there. What do you notice?" Atop the highest tower of the Kremlin there was the red flag, waving in the dark, hot summer night, caught in the white light of spotlights for all to see.

"It's their flag."

"OK. OK. But what else do you notice?"

"What are you talking about?"

"Can't you see? Look--the flag is fluttering like mad--but there's no breeze!"

There was no mistaking it. We were in the USSR all right.

We wandered around *Ploshet Krasnaya* for almost three hours. It was after eleven when we started to walk back to the hotel. The streets were quiet and empty, only a drunk or two. Incredibly, Perle remembered the way back!

I have to get some sleep. Today we fly to Vilnius.

Address Unknown
Wednesday, July 22, 1970

The Intourist taxi took us to Sheremetyevo around three. We are aboard the local to Vilnius, an hour and a half flight. Amsterdam, Moscow, Vilnius--the distances shrink. The suspense and doubts increase
.

A whole soccer team is flying with us, also a heavyset old woman dressed in black. She is from New Jersey, flying to see her family for the first time in how many years? She tells us she is eighty-three. She expects them to greet her at the airport.

What should we expect? Maybe the Tante will be at the airport waiting for us too. But maybe not. We've written two letters--no response. What if she's dead? Or maybe she has moved and isn't even in Vilnius anymore? What if the letters never reached her? How will we ever find her?

The Russian government is giving us only five days in Vilnius. Only five days.

Only five days to find the Tante.

Vilnius
Wednesday afternoon, July 22. Vilnius.

We are at the Hotel Neringa. Intourist is putting us up in a room reserved for foreigners. We have inspected the place for hidden "bugs"--in the chandelier, in the phone, who knows where? We are suspicious and recall all the tales we have heard of visitors being observed, spied upon, recorded. We laugh at these stories, but we're cautious nonetheless. Instinctively.

Our plane landed on what looked to be a farmer's field, not an airport for a major city. The auburn-haired Intourist guide simply walked out onto the field and right up to the plane looking for us. As we disembarked we saw a crowd, about twenty-five or thirty people, all dressed in their best, come to greet their relative from New Jersey. And all of them bearing flowers! They lined up row on row right on the field for a classic family picture.

We looked around for someone to greet us. No Tante. No flowers. Nobody. Nothing.

Only the Intourist guide, who walked us back across the field to the waiting room in the terminal building, then took us here in a taxi. Only a hollow, sinking feeling.

Michyurina Street 64/76
July 22/23, 2:15 a.m.

It is already Thursday morning, but I am still living Wednesday night. How am I to tell it all? How does one tell the "all" of anything?

How do I describe the disappointment, the envy, the jealousy I felt at seeing the New Jersey great-grandmother being greeted by her own family at the airport? Or the loneliness, doubt, and fear in my disappointment? We had come thousands of miles only to be greeted by silence and emptiness. Nor was there anyone to greet us at the hotel.

I was impatient. I wanted to believe there was still hope. I wanted to set out on the final leg of our journey--to the address on the ink-stained envelope. I wanted to find the Tante. Something about the way Mr. Gordon had said "Go" promised an adventure, one way or another.

But no: I discover Perle is famished. She simply has to get something to eat. I am in no mood for eating. I don't care about eating. I want to go to Michyurina Street. I have not come all this way to go to a restaurant. At first I am blind to her suffering. But Perle is genuinely starved. She hasn't eaten since yesterday's lunch ended in the disaster of last night's arrival at Sheremetyevo

So in the end I take pity on her, I relent, and we go looking for someplace to eat. There is nothing in the Neringa, our hotel. We get vague directions from the desk clerk and begin to walk the streets. No restaurants anywhere. Nothing. We walk not knowing where to look or where we are going. Suddenly Perle hears the clatter of silverware. The smell of food is in the air. But there is no restaurant in sight. We know we are near food. But where? At last we take a chance, descend a short flight of stairs, and open the door.

A restaurant! A pure Lithuanian restaurant that has probably not seen an American in years. We enter cautiously. Everyone looks up at us. They can see we are Americans. Our clothes give us away. Though we don't exactly know what to do, we aren't afraid. We seat ourselves at a rough wooden table, our backs to the wall. A waiter comes, presents us with the menu. But it's no use. We can't read a word of it. Nor does he understand a word we say.

It's not necessity that's the mother of invention--it's an empty stomach. Bravely we go up to the food counter. It is as mysterious as the menu: not a single recognizable item. Abandoning all caution, we resort to the international sign language. We point to one of this and two of those and some of that. We eat and pay our bill. Finally, we show our ink-stained envelope.

Michyurina Street? We are sent back in the general direction we have come from. We see no taxis. The ink-stained envelope in hand, we stop a passerby who hands us on to another who hands us on to a third, a young German woman who looks at it and quickly grasps our plight. I understand some of her German. She understands some of our English. Incredibly, she offers to take us there! She seems to know where we have to go. We walk back again to Lenin Square. It is Vilnius's Red Square, dominated by a statue of Lenin, his arm flung out in the pose of an orator. She takes us to the far corner of the Square where we wait for the bus.

The bus driver looks at the address on our envelope, nods, motions us aboard. The location, he says, is in a new *rayon*, a new district. On our way I manage to ask our guide why she is going through all this trouble for us, two total strangers. "Out of *humanisme*," she says. The bus takes us to the end of the line. We are the last of his passengers. He drops us off on a dusty street, points up ahead, and drives off.

***

We were alone. The sun was still high and hot. Nothing seemed right. Could the bus driver have been mistaken? Where on earth were we? What were we doing here anyhow? Chickens scrambled on the road ahead of us! A new *rayon*--and chickens scampering on a dirt road? Chickens? My heart sank further and further. The discrepancy grew with each step we took. Not a new building in sight anywhere, only shaky old wooden houses that angled surreally off center.

We walked gamely up the road for a while, five minutes, ten. Sure enough. A whole block of Soviet-style grey concrete, four levels high, materialized out of nowhere.

Our German guide left us to reconnoiter the area, then returned a few minutes later. She had found Michyurina Street 64, apartment 76.

***

My heart began to beat faster. "You go up," Perle said. Maybe she wanted the moment to be mine alone. I walked up one flight of stairs--alone. There were two doors, one on each side of the first landing. I rang the bell of the right-hand door. Could it really be? I rang again. This was the right address. No answer. I rang again and knocked--and again no answer. Again. And again nothing.

The neighboring door opened. A woman's head appeared, spied the stranger, then furtively disappeared behind a door quickly shut.

I went down the stairs and outside again.

***

78

While the three of us stand around outside to consider our next step, a blond-haired boy, about eleven or twelve, wheels his bike out the entranceway. We stop him. I show him the picture of my cousin, and I point to the first floor.

He nods. The answer is "Yes!"

Our guide questions him in Lithuanian. Yes, an old woman lives there with her daughter and her husband. And he rides off on his bike.

A stone falls from the heart.

***

But where are they? What are we to do now? All we can do is stand around waiting, waiting. Ever resourceful, our German guide disappears, then reappears: she has found a neighbor to help us. She takes us around the corner to an apartment on the second floor and introduces us to a beautiful, tall Lithuanian woman, a teacher of English as it turns out. As our guide prepares to take her leave, her mission accomplished, I take her address. She wants nothing. I promise her she will hear from us, and we thank her as best we can.

The Lithuanian teacher takes us in, shows us her apartment, her art books, speaks openly and freely about her work and about the books she cannot get. She is not afraid to be talking to foreigners, and we are surprised at her openness. She puts her two lively children to bed. And we wait, interested in all we hear and see around us. Though our guide has left us in good hands, we grow more nervous with each passing minute. We are imposing upon strangers. And who knows when the Tante will come home?

"Maybe they have gone on vacation," she offers. But in the next breath she reminds herself, "No. They were here only yesterday. I saw them on the balcony." She goes to her telephone directory, then to the phone. She rings them. Once. Then again a few minutes later. No one home. A half hour passes. We talk and wait. I promise to send her *The Old Man and the Sea*, which she cannot buy here. We hear steps on the stairway. A knock on the door. The Lithuanian teacher opens it.

It is the Tante.

The Second Letter
July 22/23, cont'd.

She is wearing a belted brown raincoat. She takes a few hesitant steps into the apartment, exchanges a few words with her Lithuanian neighbor, eyes us warily. This is the Soviet Union, after all. Speaking in Yiddish, I explain that we have come from America to look for her. "Who are you?" she asks. "*Ich bin Henoch's ah zun,*" I tell her. Giving my father's Yiddish name, I tell her I am Henoch's son.

"*Du bist Feivel?*" she asks. She uses my brother's Yiddish name: "You are Feivel?" No, I tell her. "*Ich bin Yitzhak, Feivel's bruder.*" She still does not believe me. She can't believe me. Why should she believe me? Perhaps we are spies of some sort. KGB. But who would want to spy on her? Why would anyone want to entrap her? Then I show her the picture of her daughter.

What worlds raced through her mind in that instant as she held in her hand that precious photograph decades old, her own copy long since lost, as she must have lost everything else?

But she remains cool, reveals no sign of emotion. Then, crooking the index finger of her right hand, in a gesture that belonged to my father, she beckons us. "*Nu, kumt arayn in shtub,*" she says. "Come with me to our apartment."

After a thank-you to the Lithuanian neighbor, we go down the stairs, out, back around the corner, and back up to apartment number 76.

Our German guide had told the neighbor at the left-hand door where we were waiting and she had told the Tante that strangers had come looking for her.

***

Now the evening really begins! She is 75 years old. And where has she been? Out visiting a sick friend! At the other end of the city! "What do you think?" she says with feigned indignation. "That I cannot go wherever I want to? I am not sick, after all."

I take out the photographs we have brought with us. I know what will happen with the first one I decide to show, but I have to risk it anyhow. Tears. It is the one of her daughter and her son. He is sitting on his bicycle and his sister stands behind him. "He was such a fine, good young boy--*ah guter yingaleh*--he died in the *concentratzionz* lager...." I try to fight back my own tears. Perle, too.

I try to make a quick joke or two while she looks at a photo of my father. "That...that was my Henochl--such a good one. There was only one like him in the whole world. I remember how he took me to the theater, how he loved me."

She pauses, remembers. "When I wrote him in America that there was a young man who wanted me to come to America and marry him, Henoch immediately wrote back to me that I must not do this, that as soon as one got off the ship I would have to marry him--while I, I had not yet had time enough to live a little and find out about the world. And in the same letter he sent me and my mother *schifskarte*-- tickets for our passage to America from Antwerp. Just then the war broke out--and we did not go."

I show her a photo of my Uncle Jacob. She says, "My sweet, good Henoch was better than Yankel. If I did not do what Yankel told me to do," she remembers with a smile, "he would call me over to him and rub his beard against my cheek. He was wounded in the war."

81

And when I show her a picture of Max, her third brother, she recognizes him immediately. "That is Motl. He brought a lot of trouble to Henoch. He went to America, fell in love with a girl, and wanted to marry her. But she threw him over for another. He fell ill-- and died"

The stories pour out, one after another. I had heard the one about Max, who, I had been told, had died of spinal meningitis and a broken heart, all before I was born.

***

She begins to speak about the concentration camp of Stutthof-- "the worst of them all," she says--when the door opens. Osya enters, the Tante's son-in-law. Moments later, my cousin Fanya enters, carrying the mail. She sets it down on a sideboard together with her keys. Shock. Disbelief. Explanations. Osya speaks some English. But our Yiddish is good. Amid tears, laughter, and bewilderment both of them understand everything.

During a momentary pause, Fanya goes to get her keys. She glances at the mail for the first time. She holds in her hand the second letter we had sent from America! The first had never arrived....

The First Night
July 22, 1970, Wednesday night cont'd.

Everything is new. Everything is strange. We have met for the first time in our lives. And yet everything is familiar. Our Yiddish is the same. The sounds are the same. The rhythms are the same. The twists and turns of phrase and idiom are the same. The proverbs are the same--I have heard them all my life. It is as though we have known each other forever. We begin to attempt the impossible--to put all our lifetimes into words. In five days.

What do I learn of their lives? Osya is a construction engineer, a minor official in charge of ten other engineers. He earns 180 rubles a month, a good salary. Fanny travels the country as a buyer for a textile firm. She makes her quota every time. She should win a Lenin medal for her work one day. Their son Fima, already married, is a student of physics at the university and earns extra money as a private tutor. He will never reach his father's station in life because he is probably not as necessary to the state. Not yet, anyhow. All five live in four rooms.

Questions and answers fly every which-way across the table. It will take time to fit the pieces together. The eye tries to take everything in, even the bowl of pears on the table. I tell myself I have to remember everything. Who could ever have imagined this scene? Fanny makes instant coffee. The apartment has a tiny kitchen which boasts a new refrigerator of which they are very proud. In America it was already obsolete 25 years ago. A bottle of brandy appears, and I drink a "L'chaim" to the Tante.

The Lithuanians? They were the worst of all. When the Tante and Fanny returned after the war, no one offered them even a pair of shoes. Nor did their neighbors return what the family had given them for safe keeping. Nothing. All was lost. As for the English at Bergen-Belsen, they were good people. "You could talk with them," says Fanya.

Why, the Tante wants to know over and over again, why did I stop writing after Feivel had written her saying I would soon be answering her letter. *She* had given *me* up for dead! Killed either while driving my car or as a result of foul play--for the Soviet papers write only about the terrible things that happen in America. Is it true what they say, that people kill each other in the streets? I try to explain that there is some truth in what the papers write, but that the Soviet papers, as she well knows, do not tell the whole truth about anything. Ever.

I ask if we can go to Kaunas--to Kovno--where my father was born, to see the home where he and Uncle Jacob and the Tante once lived. And I want to see where the Tante and her family lived too. Is there anything to see there? Will they let us go? The great-grandmother on our plane to Vilnius was going to her family in Kaunas, but Intourist had informed us back in America that Kaunas was a "closed city," off-limits to visitors. It is too risky to go there. We do not want to jeopardize our stay.

The Tante has raised Fanny's son Fima for twenty years, running the house while Fanny and Osya were working. He and his wife Bella are on vacation at a dacha just now. We will see him soon. I learn from the Tante how he has "made her sick." He has married a girl she disapproves of and already a child is coming. She is dissatisfied with his marriage, and so he is angry with her. It is the old, old story--but still full of pain, for everyone. Though Fima calls her his "Granny," she has really been a mother to him.

The night grows older and older. It is 1:15 in the morning, and we have to return to the Hotel Neringa. They call a taxi and insist on taking us there. I realize that if they come with us they will have to make a trip back from the hotel. "Perele," the Tante says with a twinkle, "is a good wife that she does not let go of you a whole night." Twisting her words, I answer that Perele will not let go of me at all if they do not let me pay the taxi fare! The hotel is locked when we arrive, but at last someone comes to the door to let us in.

It is 3:45 Thursday morning of our first night in Vilnius. Pa crossed the ocean one way. I have crossed it in the opposite direction, backward in time, to a different world, a foreign world, yet mine, too, in a way. Tonight I have crossed more than an ocean. I must get some sleep. But I am wide awake.

I have found the Tante.

Behind the Curtain
July 23/24. 12:30 a.m.

Today, Thursday afternoon, we took Fanya and the Tante for lunch to the Hotel Vilnius. The Tante had never been there. We went to the Cathedral; the Tante had never been there. Then we went to the landmark Gediminus Castle. We climbed all the way to the top, the Tante only part way. We had a view of all Vilnius.

The Tante wanted only for us to eat at home tonight. However, Osya and Fanny insisted on taking us out to dinner, but we refused to hear of it. We returned to the Neringa area for dinner. Smoked sable, my first beef stroganoff, vodka--and a toast from Fanny that brought me close to tears.

Earlier today we met Fanny's friend, Sarah Fischerina, a sweet and gentle woman. She has two boys and one girl. She is either divorced or separated--and has been for a long time. "If you don't work," she said, "you become cut off from the world." Osya says the same.

Beyond its universal truth, it is as though work is the lifeline to sanity here, the only one left. As we all talk together, little by little, I am beginning to understand something of life here. It is one thing to come here with what one has learned about communism and the USSR from a lifetime of reading and hearing and thinking about this country. It is quite another to see and hear firsthand something of the actuality facing Jews who have been living here behind the Iron Curtain ever since it came down. For Fanny, the Tante, and Osya it is 25 years. One gets a sense that Fanny and the Jews she knows feel life slipping away from them even as they try their best to hold onto it. "All three of us need iron nerves to live," says Fanny. *This* is the USSR.

What is ever present is the fear--even if, like Fanny, one is unafraid. We ourselves are not afraid: we are Americans, sure of ourselves, protected by our passports. Is our room bugged? Are we being watched? Followed? We are aware of these possibilities. We have read enough about them. Is it an accident that only certain rooms are reserved for foreigners at our hotel? In our American innocence we do not take these possibilities seriously. It is enough for us to think we have nothing to hide. But Fanny and Osya, if they talk at all, will barely talk above a whisper while they are in our room.... Their caution takes hold of us too. This is a country where letters fail to arrive or somehow arrive too late....

These are the realities of ordinary daily life. What's clear is that a state that has the power to do these things does not actually have to do

85

them to exercise control. Whether they are being watched or not, people behave as though there is a watcher. Once the state creates the atmosphere of fear the very idea of fear is all that's necessary to control life. It is in the very air people breathe. You can't see it. You can only feel it--and feel others feeling it. It weighs one down.

For the first time, after only two days, I have already gained an idea of what it means to live under a different system than our own, a communist system. Though I have read and thought enough about these matters, there is nothing like the direct encounter with a foreign political system to open one's eyes to the very meaning of "system," that it exists in reality. One way or another, Jews feel the weight of the Soviet system. They felt it in Stalin's time. They feel it now in Brezhnev's time.

There are eight to sixteen thousand Jews in Lithuania, most of them in Vilnius. They are afraid of being accused of Zionism. Once or twice a year Jews manage to come together to attend a performance of the Jewish theater or to enjoy a Jewish choir--most of all they come "*tzu heren ah Yiddishn vort*," to hear a Yiddish word. There is a deep longing for the language, a sad and bitter sense of its absence. Their love for the language is bound to all those murdered in the Holocaust who spoke it. But gatherings are rare.

Mainly, Jews keep a low profile. The adults seldom go out at night. "Night is only for the young, the romantics," says Fanny. They are resigned to living out each day as best they can. Except for a Saturday or a Sunday, the weeks steadily grind life away.

Fanya and Osya have good jobs. They belong to the "middle" class, the professionals: engineers, teachers, scientists, doctors, managers, and so on. They hold the same place in Russian society that many Jews hold in America. They are "in-between." In-between the upper, ruling class and the vast working class. All this in a "classless" society. Those who are in-between perform the function that Jews have so often performed in history--they have the necessary, invaluable skills to enable the system to operate within its own terms. Their skills provide them with a certain safety net. At the same time, their position in-between makes them vulnerable to pressures from those in power above them and from the large masses below them. It is not easy to be Jewish in Vilna. It is not easy to be Jewish.

Meshpokhe
July 24. Friday.

We meet Fima and his wife Bella at the dacha given him for a few days' vacation. It is near the Neris River, only forty minutes away from Michyurina Street. It is a barren wooden cottage: a table, three chairs, a bunk, a couch, a sink, and a *balcon*. Pears and an orange on the table. Fima smokes. We spend the day on a picnic. For Russians a picnic means "being with nature." It is also safer to talk out in the open fields.

He tells us of how Fanny returned to Lithuania after the war because the Tante insisted on going back--and how the Iron Curtain came down to trap them there. I learn of how Osya belonged to the Kovno underground and of how he too returned to Liteh after the war.

When we return to Michyurina Street, it is late afternoon. Fanny calls her friends on the telephone. We hear her excitement as she says, "What guests have come to us!" We have literally come down from the heavens.

In mock exasperation Fanny scolds the Tante, where had the devil taken her that she was not at home when we came? The Tante had gone to visit a sick friend at the other end of the city. But Fanny herself? Where had the devil taken her that afternoon? She had gone to visit her old teacher Kanterovitch, whom she had not seen for many years. The Jewish way.

The Tante has been cooking all afternoon while we have been gone. She treats me to the cherry compote I love, and in jest she taunts me, "Well, you are a professor. Why don't you ask where *di beyndlakh* are?" I well know the time she has taken to extract the cherry stones. It is a matter of love.

When the topic of childhood education arises and I suggest that an occasional "potch" might sometimes hasten the learning process, she answers--a better psychologist than I am--"If a word does not help, then slaps certainly won't either."

During the afternoon the Tante shows me a letter from my father. It is dated 1958. Fima translates some old Russian postcards for me. Is it the mystery of Pa's brother Max that one of them solves? And Fima not knowing. He shows us his photographs. He is very handsome, very talented. Privately the Tante tells me he has lost weight since his marriage because he no longer eats her cooking....

In command of the kitchen, she has made a magnificent meal: mushroom soup, cold borscht, pickles and tomatoes, caviar and bread and butter, Morocco sardines, 60 kopek Russian champagne. "One glass," says Fima, "is enough to keep a man alive for a day." Also meat, chicken, ice cream bars. Tea. Linen tablecloth, but no napkins. No paper goods in the USSR. Perle supplies Kleenex as a substitute for napkins. I eat everything in order to make the Tante happy.

As we sit around the table speaking Yiddish and English, I think to myself we could all just as well be sitting around the table on Touhy Avenue on the North Side of Chicago in my mother-in-law's home. There is so much joking and laughter that Fanny cautions us not to disturb the neighbors. Fanny cannot believe that we are sitting here in Vilnius at her table. It is impossible for us to believe it too. Or that they are unable to get out of their country.

We are *meshpokhe*. Family.

In Lenin Square Lenin stands day and night with his arm out flung in a heroic pose. There are benches to sit on.

Past and Present
Saturday, July 25

Osya takes us sightseeing: parts of the old city, parts of the new. The ghetto, the University, the amusement park, the Cathedral of Anna. Osya has trouble pronouncing "th." Each time he snaps a picture of us he says, "Sank you very moch."

Intourist has warned us not to leave Vilnius city limits. I want to go to Kovno, but Kovno is off-limits, a "closed" city to us. Ponar, only ten kilometers away, is off-limits too. I want to go to Ponar. I know of Ponar, but I don't know anyone at home who has heard of it. The forests of Ponar used to be a spot for an outing on a summer's day. Osya is willing to risk it. We go by taxi. Osya, Fanny, Perle, and I. On the way I see banners stretched high across the city streets. "What do they say?" I ask. Fanny translates their shameless propaganda for me. One says: "Long life and happiness to Soviet Lithuania." Another: "With words and song we honor you, Soviet Lithuania."

The taxi takes us past factories, through forests of birch. Ponar is the grave of tens of thousands of Jews, the burned and the buried. Tiny flowers are in bloom--white, yellow, red. Signs mark the burial pits--5000, 3000, 2500--but the numbers tell only a part of the story. What the signs don't say is that the dead are Jews, only that they were "victims of the Fascists." We wander from one mass grave site to another. One sign says "Between 1941-45 the Fascists killed 100,000 people of various nationalities and professions, of whom 70,000 were inhabitants of Vilnius." No one would ever know that the 70,000 were Jews. Another reads: "Graves of the fallen of the Fascists: ATTENTION." Another says: "For the Fallen to Fascist Terror, 1941-1944."

The woods are quiet and still. The grave pits are inescapable. Osya stands beside us, Osya, the partisan. Fanny breaks into the silence. "*Kumt, kinderlakh,*" she says. "Come, children," she says, as we linger among the wild flowers. "*Genug.*" "Enough," she says uneasily, "these troubles we have seen." Somewhere, close by, a train whistle lingers in the air. We carry the dust of Ponar on our shoes.

We visit the museum, see the iron shoe of a victim. Keys belonging to victims who were deceived into thinking they would be returning home to unlock their doors. Eyeglasses. False teeth. Wire bindings. I sign the comment book. We spend three hours at Ponar.

Later--every minute counts--we go to the Intourist Beriozka shop with the whole family. The shop is open only to foreigners. Visitors to the city can take their relatives into the shop and buy all sorts of things for dollars or pounds or marks or francs, things denied to the general population. The USSR needs foreign currency. We are foreign currency. Fima chooses a radio, only to discover its shortwave band to the U.S. has been blocked out.

We go home to the Tante and cherry compote. I learn that Fima wears exactly the same size shoe that I do, and I give him the shoes I bought just before we came, the most expensive pair I have ever owned. I steal some cherries and pieces of sour apples from the Tante. I copy my father's 1958 letter. We sign old photographs and take new snapshots. We have meat blintzes, chicken soup (de-fatted by the Tante), chicken *cutletten*, *kartofflen* (potatoes, small), fresh mushrooms that Fima and Bella have picked, chopped cod liver and egg, more cherry compote.

Then we visit close friends of the family, the Pomerantzes and their two children. Dr. Pomerantz, a psychiatrist, finally joined the Party, not out of any conviction but to get a better position, an apartment, the usual thing. His joining the Party is a sign that he has given up hope of getting out of the USSR. Fanny and the family have little hope, but he has even less. He lives in a new *rayon*, a district that will eventually hold 50,000; 25,000 have already moved in. I go with Dr. P. to the *magasin*, the supermarket, and pay 4.83 rubles for two boxes of Russian candy, one for the Pomerantzes, one for Sara Fischerina. The district has built a kindergarten in the forest. Dr. P. is proud of his flat, his lovely wife, his twin girls. We drink a *mkabel ponim*, a toast, to the Tante, the *babushka* so much beloved by all. She dabs her eyes, saying only "*s'iz mir gevoren ahzoy hase*," allowing only that she has become very hot.

ZORG
July 26, 1970

A Sunday afternoon. The Tante is making our lunch. Fima is showing me photographs. The Tante pokes her head out of the kitchen to say, half seriously, "Do not tell Feivel that I am not a *berieh*. It is almost midday--and the lunch isn't ready yet!" I promise her that I will not tell my brother what a terrible homemaker and cook she is.

Osya and I begin to talk about the Kovno Ghetto. He goes back to those days and the part he played in the resistance. It was a small part, but he is very proud of it. He belonged to a group called *ZORG*, which in Yiddish means "care."

"In the beginning," he said, "we thought to defend the ghetto and we cooperated in underground work with the communists. The partisans said we couldn't save the whole ghetto--but that we could save some in the woods. They were right."

He went to a bookshelf, took down a volume, and opened it. It is written in Yiddish. He read a paragraph to me. In English the book would be called *Partisans of the Kovno Ghetto*. Its authors are Meyer Yelin and Dima Gelpern, and the book was published in Moscow in 1948. I copied the Yiddish for future translation. On page 62 they write, "Good human material flowed toward the organization in the form of the group 'ZORG,' led by Moses Milner, Solomon Brewer, Osya Taraseisky. The group saw as its main task the defense of the ghetto in the event of a German attack or liquidation and was not originally oriented toward the partisan view of the struggle. The name ZORG is an acronym for 'self defense organization' [*zelbschutz orgonozatzieh*], which indicates its main purpose."

"We were youngsters," Osya said. "We wanted to defend the ghetto. But the communists said no--that we should take to the woods and continue the fight from there." Osya was proud of his part in the Kovno underground. And he was proud that the book had placed his name in history.

The Fence
Monday, July 27

We leave today. I feel terrible inside. Fanya will be here in an hour, at ten.

Having met her *chaveyrim*, I know how important *chaveyrim* are to survival here. *Chaveyrim*--in both Hebrew and Yiddish--signifies more than "friends." They are comrades too. *Chaveyrim* are those who have gone to school together or shared the closeness of a cause with you or suffered in the war together, in the camps--or all of these. In Vilnius it means Jews who, year in, year out, share life within the communist state to make living a little more bearable than it might otherwise be. This is all that Fanya and the others have in this society, while life goes on as the system goes on as Stalin went on as Brezhnev goes on.

Soon I will see Fanya and the Tante for the last time, and Aeroflot will take us back to Moscow. Our five days will be over, gone, turned into history. The sights, sounds, tastes, smells, jokes, and tears--in an instant all will turn into memories. To have walked the streets of Vilnius, the city that once was Vilna, and the paths of Ponar--it is more than strange. The beautiful Fanya, lively, lovely, loving. And *Di Tante*...the Tante...her half-lidded eyes...her blue eyes...her *brilln*, those eyeglasses of hers, fallen low on her nose...

At first I thought it would be better to leave without saying goodbye to her, that it would be easier for her. Besides, I cannot stand partings. But Osya said, "You cannot do this to her. You cannot take this parting away from her. For her it is as if you have come down from heaven. She thought she was all alone. She thought she had lost everything. Now she has a *meshpokhe*--a family."

92

On my last walk in the street with the Tante, she says, "*Fanya lozt mir nit shtarbn*--Fanya does not let me die." And it is true. Fanya has guarded her, fought for her, saved her time after time--in the camps, in the hospital. She will not let her mother die. The Tante tells me a secret--that she has managed to save enough money for a grave and a stone for herself so that Fanny will not have to worry about these matters.

While we stroll and talk, we pass a department store. On the sidewalk in front of it we see a dark-featured, white-bearded old man, a peasant from the farm. He is as gaunt as an El Greco. He is selling lottery tickets. She wants to take a chance. I buy two tickets for her. 80 *kopkes*. Later I give Fanny "*Tascheh gelt fahr di Tante*--pocket money for the Tante," to give her once we have gone.

What else will I always remember? The language, always the language, the Yiddish. The Tante said "Itzahleh" the way I haven't heard it said to me since my mother died. And the way it will never be said to me again. "Arahleh"--her son. "Itzahleh." How do you explain all the connotations of the Yiddish diminutive? How do you translate the sweetness, the tenderness, the meaning of the Yiddish diminutive into English, a language that does not contain the diminutive and cannot convey its sweetness, tenderness, and meaning?

At the airport we make small talk trying to keep up our spirits. "Be cautious and careful in Moscow," the Tante warns me. "Give Feivel our heartfelt greetings. Maybe he will come too?"

"There are many bees in Russland," says the Tante. "Did you know that? Do you know why?" Puzzled, I shake my head. "No, Tante." "They are what makes us all so sweet," she laughs and wants to make *me* laugh.

"If we live we shall see what the future will bring," says Fanny.

"Make him come back," the Tante says to Perle.

I remember her saying, "*Ahz m'fahrlirt dem hoffenung fahrlirt men ahless*--if one loses hope, one loses everything."

We board the plane, settle into our seats. I take the window seat. From behind the visitor's fence the Tante waves her poor hand in farewell, but she does not cry. In return I wave the flowers they have brought us at parting. Perhaps they will see me.

The Volga
August 2, 1970. Volgograd.

Always, always I see the figure of my father doing what I am doing--standing at the railing of our hydrofoil as it speeds between the banks of the Volga, sitting in my seat at the theater as the curtain rises and the lights dim, strolling from painting to painting of pictures at an exhibition, or just taking a walk, a *shpahtzier*, to take in the sights. How he would have enjoyed returning, a stranger, but not quite a stranger, recalling his young time, recalling the language--a thin, slight figure searching out his little sister Dora. I always see him--without seeing him. Slender, silent, reserved, carrying the mystery of his own hidden history from Kovno to Chicago.

Di Tante told me how his employer once came to their father to shake his hand and say, "One day you will have much joy from him. He is a good worker and faithful and bright."

It is a wet, damp, cool night on the Volga. A rainy, damp night inside too.

The Soccer Game
August 7, 1970. Sochi.

From high up at our hotel window I can look down on the soccer field and watch the goalie and a kicker at practice in the early morning sun. The far distance turns their movements into slow motion, then into ballet. A while later two teams march onto the field in parallel file, one in red uniform, one in green. The referee blows his whistle. The match begins.

To watch soccer is to think of Pa and his European love for the game, of how he took me to Sunday afternoon matches played by Jewish teams with names like Maccabee or Hakoah against Bohemian or Czech teams with names like Sparta and Sokol. Pa would wear his straw hat. The dust would fly and the sun would burn. We'd sit in the bleachers and marvel at the skill and speed of the players, the way they could strike the ball with head or toe and send it flying exactly where they wanted it to go. We'd walk home after the game. Sometimes I'd give him my hand to hold. At home he'd take off his straw hat and there'd be a perfect black line where the sweatband had touched his forehead. Above it his forehead would be white, below it would be dark and dusty from the sun and the field.

I look at the game swirling first one way, then the other across the green field. With the flight of the ball, my thoughts turn to Pa and his "return" here through me. I see him looking, seeing, striking up a conversation, recalling his Russian. I see the quiet smile every time he passes "Apotek," for in his youth he was apprenticed to a pharmacist in Kovno. I think of how much he must have loved his little sister. What a reunion they would have had! Pa, Pa--always Der Pa, his austere look, his gold watch, its chain looped across his vest, his cigarette. Pa would have gloried--quietly--in taking our flights, our boat rides, our train rides. I think I have come here as his surrogate in search of the Tante.

The soccer ball is still in play. I hear the distant whistle of the referee, the far off cries of the players.

The Locked Door
August 14, 1970. Leningrad.

It is 6:50 a.m., departure day. But it is yesterday that I write about. We went by hydrofoil up the Neva to Petrodvoretz. Returned toward evening to our hotel, the Hotel Astoria, the very same hotel where

Hitler planned to celebrate his victory over the Russians. Left the heat of the day and entered the cool damp of the lobby.

A voice. A familiar voice was calling out, "Meestair Ahbromson!" Fanya! Dear Fanya, come from Vilnius to surprise us on our last night in the Soviet Union! And timing her appearance so as not to interfere with our enjoyment of Leningrad. We embrace, kiss--in joy and pain, with laughter and hidden tears.

10:35 a.m. Have just boarded our Aeroflot jet that will take us to Copenhagen. Fanya is already on her way to see her doctor friend at the polyclinic.

She remained with us till the last moment. A figure costumed in white and gold, she stood on one side of the locked door, we on the other. I tried to send her off, because partings hurt. But she would not go. I called her *baze*, mean. Nothing helped. I tried to lighten our parting by making fun with the guitar and the samovar I am carrying home. I give her a message. "Tell Di Tante to send me a jar of compote," and she bursts into a laugh.

"*Pajalesteh*," says the stewardess, bringing us hard candy one more time as the motors begin to whirr. Soon we shall be leaving Fanya behind, and the Tante, and the *gantzeh meshpokhe*, the whole family. Leningrad, Vilnius, and the whole CCCP, too.

Airborne. Our shadow on the earth below is already chasing after us. We are not quite free of this country yet. But now I know something more of what it means to be free.

It is sad to leave a newly found family behind. Fanya said, "*Es gefelt mir zich tzu bahgegnen, ober nisht zich tzu gezegnen.*" "It pleases me," she said, "to meet but not to part." In Yiddish it rhymes. Both of us fought back tears.

"You will remind yourself of everything," said Osya. Now is the time to begin remembering. Fanya is far less afraid of their situation than he is. She has to believe all things are possible. Now for sure. She is a woman who goes as my mother said one must go, *shtoltzer hate,* head high, proud, unafraid.

In our last hour together she told how she and Di Tante came home naked from the concentration camp. They had absolutely nothing. Given a train ticket and promises of jobs and more, they returned home to Liteh--and nothing. Their neighbors ignored them, gave nothing back. Last night she told us her son Fima had no future in the USSR because he is Jewish. He can tutor. He earned 150 rubles last month tutoring mathematics. All four of his students passed. This is extra money for him. "He has golden hands," she says. "You can see it. He can do everything." But what he needs is a *direh,* an apartment, because Bella is due to have a baby in the next few days. It is next to impossible to get a *direh.*

As a little boy, she said, Fima would often be beaten by the neighbor children and come crying home for help. Osya would say, "I will not help you. Hit back!" And he did--and became feared in the neighborhood, even though he was small and slender.

She told us about her old *lehrer,* Kanterovitch, the teacher she had gone to visit the day we arrived. She recalled how he had given her a 2 in Hebrew (or was it Latin?), how she had become angry and cut school for two months, how her father had punished her when he discovered her truancy, and how she had returned to school. During her absence her girlfriends had kept her informed of her assignments to enable her to keep up with her studies. When she returned to class, Kanterovitch asked her a question. "Can you answer?" he said. "Yes," she said, and gave the correct answer. He gave her a 5, and thereafter they became fast friends.

You will remind yourself of everything, said Osya. Little by little, pieces of a picture begin to fall into place. But there are many blank spots. Twenty-five years behind the Iron Curtain?

Homeward Bound
August 18, 1970

This morning I thought of the suspense Philly must be feeling, waiting for us to bring him the whole story. All I did was write a postcard. I wanted to write on it in Yiddish *"Di Tante--gefuhnen."* Instead I wrote in English "The Tante--Found!" I did not want to take the chance of writing in Yiddish. Who knows what the censor would have done? Maybe Philly will take the day off today and meet us at the airport.

In a couple of hours I shall be crossing the Atlantic for the fourth time, this time as the Tante's "Itzahleh." Yesterday, as I passed the walls of Tivoli on my walk home from the waterfront, for a second I thought I saw Fanya, and I almost heard her "Meestair Ahbromson."

***

In another hour or so we will come back down to earth, 29 days after Mr. Greenbaum and a thousand *pajalestehs*, after ballets, operas, folk dances, and circuses, after Moscow, Rostov, Sochi, Kiev, and Leningrad, after the Archipova Street Synagogue, after eternal flames and obelisks. What does it all mean? It's one thing to be a tourist, to be on the outside looking in. It's another to be on the inside looking out.

In the USSR a tourist gets to see only what Intourist wants him to see. Even so, one gets impressions, deeper ones if you manage to lose the guide and get off on your own. Sometimes even the simplest impressions can be the most telling. In the street, in the metro, almost everywhere you see people carrying something, usually in a net-like stretch sack. Mostly they carry food--bread, tomatoes, pickles, potatoes, apples. Restaurants shut down at eleven o'clock. Afterward, though the streets are safe, it is not unusual to see drunkards in them. Every floor in your hotel has a concierge who holds your key for you when you go out and gives it back when you return.... Block after block of apartment houses, built and being built. Drab architecture, drab clothing, drab streets. To go from the USSR to Copenhagen is to gain a special, unexpected appreciation for the invention of the colored neon sign and for the lights of Tivoli. Whatever ordinary daily life is for the Russian, it is the same for the Jew, but with the inevitable addition of the "burden" that only Jewishness brings in the Soviet Union.

I have let stand the last line of my July 25th entry. In a way it makes no sense. I have let it stand to remind myself that even keeping a diary in the Soviet Union can be a risky business for a Jew, even for an American Jew. You say to yourself, "Why take a chance? Why say anything that might jeopardize the family?" So, to outwit the possible inquisitor you jot down things that are harmless but which, once you have crossed the border, you can translate into the truth.

Beneath the strength and beauty of this country, under its arts and sciences, its banners and slogans, below the surface of what the tourist sees lies something else, something dark.

"You will remind yourself of everything," said Osya. Yes. I remember the pride he took in telling me of *ZORG*, the underground organization to which he belonged in the Kovno Ghetto, how the word means "care" or "concern." I remember the paragraph about *ZORG* in the book he showed me. I remember copying its Yiddish to carry back home with me.

I remember Ponar and Babi Yar.

I remember taking a walk in the street with the Marcuses after they had come to see us one evening at the apartment. We passed Lenin Square, and he pointed his finger, "Do you see that building across the street? The Gestapo tortured prisoners in there. Now the Communist police do the same thing. Do you see any benches in the Square?" I did not see any. "Do you know why? They took away the benches so that people could not sit and watch to see who was going in and who was coming out." His voice began to rise in the street and I could feel his hatred for the police and all that they stand for. His wife tried to quiet him.

Marcus is a dying man. Fanny says he has the *roc,* cancer. He has been operated on, but there is no help for him, and he will have to suffer much. But this night he was keen and funny and clever. And I shall always remember our parting in front of the Neringa after a night of laughter.

The Marcuses, the Pomerantzes, Fanny and Osya--they are *chaveyrim* in an enclosed, futureless world. They know the rot and corruption, the bribery and lies just below the surface of what the tourist sees. They try to find ways to make life interesting, *"interesahnt,"* as Osya says. But maybe there is a future. The silence has been broken. Jews are demonstrating to get out of the country. In spite of fear.

Soon we shall be landing. Perle will carry the guitar. I'll carry the samovar. We found it in a dark, dusty antique store in Kiev. Paid 21 rubles for it. As we passed through Russian customs the officer eyed it curiously. What could these Americans want with a dull grey beaten-up samovar? "Silver?" he asked. No, nickel. He held a short discussion with another officer. Both smiled, surely at our stupidity, then sent us through.

I remember the toast to Di Tante at the Pomerantzes, how she was caught in the act of wiping away a tear and protested *s'iz mir hase.*

We are still young. *L'chaim* to us all.

The Lamp

I remember that my head was in a whirl. The first twenty-four hours in Vilna had been incredibly full of questions and answers, memories, stories, and, most of all, of emotions. Needing a few moments to myself, I wandered off into the living room. To say that I "wandered" is an exaggeration. There was precious little space to wander into in the little *shtub,* the little apartment, on Michyurina Street. My eyes took in a television set, a record player, a couch with pillows done in needlepoint flowers, like the ones my mother would make.

I found a chair and sat down to rest my brain. The sun had just gone down. I wondered about the new world that had opened up--that we had opened up in the old one. There was no telling where it would lead. A real Tante. A real cousin. There was much to think about.

The room grew darker. It was time to turn on the lamp. I went over to the little end table beside the couch and turned it on. Instantly the light flooded the photograph below it. And instantly I knew I would never be able to forget that moment.

The face of a teenage boy looked up at me from beneath the glass that covered the table. I knew who it had to be. I stared at the photograph. I looked at those eyes: they were my eyes. I looked at the nose: it was my nose.

It was Aharon--Fanny's brother, Di Tante's son--murdered in one of the concentration camps. I was looking at the fate that might well have been my own.

Afterwords

The words remain with me. Three words in Yiddish. I cannot get them out of my mind.

Our trip is over. We are home. The house is quiet tonight. But my head is full of our five days in Vilnius. Only five days in a lifetime. Only three words. And something has happened.

We were at the Vilnius airport waiting to board our plane for Moscow. Fima and Osya had brought us flowers. Departures. What are they? A shake of the hand, a kiss, a tear, a hug--and farewell. But this departure was different. Something remarkable, something extraordinary had happened. Lifetimes were involved. Histories were involved. First of all, my father's sister: my brother and I had acquired a real Tante. And a real cousin. And Osya, Fima, and Bella. Even a child. Two once separate, and separated, families were now members of one *meshpokhe*.

We stood around doing what is universally done at partings. In the shadows--you could not see them, but they were there all right--the Tsar, Lenin, Stalin, Brezhnev. And Hitler. The Germans. The camps. A revolution. Two wars. Two murders. And fears and hopes and suffering. The five days were concentrated into the few minutes before our departure. The future was a question mark. The heart was full. The breathing had an unwelcome catch to it. To do something, to do anything, I straightened the belt of Di Tante's brown raincoat. She was wearing the blue babushka Perle had brought her.

Then it was time to walk onto the airfield and toward our plane. Osya snapped his last shot with his camera. I turned for one last look back, and at that very moment he called out to us, "*Fargest unz nit!* Do not forget us!"

I hear those words tonight and every night. Three words called out in Yiddish--in desperation and hope, both plea and command. Jewish history. They chill the heart.

LETTERS, 1970-1971

Vilnius, immediately after our first visit, 1970

Dear Itzale and Perele,

I trust my letter will find you in good health. I thank you again and again that you write and let us hear from you. I take much joy that you are pleased by all that you see in our country and even more that you discovered Di Tante...and the family.

Dear Itzale, in the first letter you wrote that I am not one given to tears at parting. You are indeed highly educated, a professor, but a professor can sometimes make a mistake. I did not cry as we said our goodbyes because I did not want to cause you pain. Dear Itzale, everyone sees when you laugh. No one sees when you cry. When I came home and Fanya went shopping, I lay down and cried till early morning and did not sleep. Wherever I go I see you. I look through the window and I think you will soon be here with Perele. Alas, you were here only five days.

Dear Itzale, I remember my brother and your Ma, may they rest in peace. They gave you a good upbringing. I am really proud because of you. When I go to see my friends I speak only about you. But I am grieved. The five days were like one. After you left, Fanny learned that you could have extended your stay here another five days. I am so very sorry. Again too late.

Dear Itzale, I have also sent off a letter to Feivel to share with him the unexpected joy of your coming. He has probably received it by now. A letter takes eight days from us to you--that is how your Pa once wrote us.

I thank you many times for the gift of the pocket money that you gave through Fanny. But why? You gave us so much. I was very angry with her that she accepted it. My dear ones, your love and friendship is far, far higher.

Did I ever think that you, Itzik, would one day come to us--and I take such poor care of you? To this day I cannot forget how everything took place. You will laugh much with Feivel. I was crazy, all mixed up. What can happen in a lifetime! This I truly cannot forget.

Dear Feivel, I am jealous that Fanny will see you. A miracle can still come to pass for Fanny. That you and she will see each other--but not so any longer for me. Forgive me, Itzale, for expressing myself. And, Itzale, if possible, send the photo where I stand with my mother. She is really your grandmother—and my mother—and that is really me.

Well, my dear ones, have a good, successful journey.

With love, your Tante, Dora Dembovitz

Vilna, July 29, 1970

Dear Feivel and family,

May you all be well. I want to share with you my great, great joy with our unexpected, beautiful guests, Itzik and Perele. How quickly one can get used to good fortune--meeting for the first time a person one has known only through writing. You cannot imagine how we have fallen in love with each other now. Itzik has shown me so much love--he held me, took me around, kissed me, and took many photos. He says he is an orphan. So I told him I would make him into a son. He laughed much and was happy and said, "Yes, yes, Tante."

Itzik told my daughter I should not accompany him to the airport because perhaps I would cry. His heart is like gold. I controlled myself and did not cry. But when I came home, I cried hard. I did not sleep for a whole day and night. I took sleeping pills, but I could not sleep.

This was all a great, beautiful dream, but it went away very quickly. Only five days. It was very little. Good Itzik asks me to come to him as a guest, at least for a year. But I cannot do this. You know about my good daughter. If I go out and come home a bit late, she runs to look for me. So how can I leave her? She is good, like Itzik, and probably like you.

Now, dear Feivel, I must write you that Itzik and his wife took us all to a store where things are bought for dollars, and they bought us many beautiful gifts. They also brought many gifts with them. This was so very beautiful and very loving that I cannot describe it. But the gift of the love that Itzik and Perele have given us exceeds everything.

Dear Feivel, you can come to us in peace. You do not have to bring anything. For us the love is very dear, the best of all. Wherever I go or stand, Itzale is near me. But he is already in Moscow. Your Tante, Dora Dembovitz

Vilna, July 29, 1970

To Dear Cousin Feivel and family!

I hope my letter finds you all in the best of health. I add a few words to Di Mameh's letter. She has already written you everything. The coming of Itzik and Perele was an overwhelming experience for us. They wrote us a letter which we received on the very day they came to us. They found us by themselves. They will tell you about this themselves.

We are lucky to have such good, fine, dear, warm-hearted friends. I hold Itzik for a brother and Perele for a sister--such a dear, good woman. The five days flew away like a dream. They added twenty years to Di Mameh's life, but if you were to come she would live forever.

Di Mameh will soon become a great-grandmother. Regards from all of us. Your Fanny

Vilnius, August 2, 1970

Itzik, your coming to us was very beautiful and very good. But your going away gave me no pleasure. You made me a gift of so much love and goodness--Perele, too--that this is only to be read in stories. But, after all, this is true.

I jump up in the middle of the night and begin immediately to think of you, the goodness, so I do not sleep anymore--I imagine you are coming and that we will go together, that I will give you a glass of cherry compote without *beyndlakh*, and that you are with me wherever I go and wherever I stay. That I possess such a good nephew and niece--there are no words to express my feeling of love.

My dear ones, I have also written a letter to Feivel to share with him the unexpected joy you brought me--so he should be happy and laugh. I am proud because of you. I long for you and hope that when you come home you will write us everything.

My dear ones, excuse my crooked handwriting, but better crooked than nothing, with such a hand as mine. May this letter reach you in the best of health.

From your Tante, Dora Dembovitz, many, many kisses.

Highland Park, August 22, 1970

Dear, dear Tante and the whole family,

It is a gray, rainy day, but not in the heart--because I have found a Tante. We are home four days, and the telephone rings with calls from our friends. Everyone wants to know what happened with us. Feivel and his family have been here and bombarded us with questions. But how can one tell of such a Tante and Fanya? and Osya and Fima and Bella? We talk and talk but one cannot really tell everything, especially not about a love for such a Tante.

We have not yet really come down to earth. But under Perele's hands everything is already in order, scrubbed and clean. The children are in good health. I have already given four lectures in three days. So all is as before. But nothing can ever again be as before. At my first lecture my students already knew that I had just returned from Russia. They did not let me speak about my subject. They wanted only to know what I had seen and done. Soon the whole city will know that I have a new Tante and a new sister!

***

I have read the beautiful letters you and Fanya wrote Feivel. I see your Yiddish words--and at once I begin to long for you, for a glass of compote....But, Tante, I am homesick not only for what your golden hands can make but for your wise words and sayings and your newly acquired sweetness (not that you were sour, only that you have become *more* sweet). I only hope that in my older years I shall be as quick of hand and foot and brain as you are. When I saw you climb the hills around the house as well as Gediminus Hill, I lost all my fear for you.

***

I am not one to dream much in my sleep, but since we have been home I keep dreaming in my sleep about Vilna, the Tante, other places in Russia, and even about the Pomerantzes! Every night the same!

It's true, Tante, we had only five days. But it was enough time to take you into my heart--from which no one will ever be able to take you. You remind me much of my father. I loved him as much as Fanya loves you. Your wisdom and goodness--everything in you reminds me of Der Pa.

***

Perele hoped to see Fanya in Copenhagen and looked for her there. And once I thought I saw her--near the Tivoli Gardens. And there, there I thought I saw her walking toward me. I ran toward her, but it was not Fanya. The beauty of a Fanya is not to be found in Copenhagen--only in Vilnius.

I have left a piece of my heart in Vilnius. Feivel envies me that I know you and the whole family. We continue to talk of you. I tell him only a little at a time. He is impatient with me. But I am stingy. I keep the Tante for myself. But I will tell him everything eventually. He is a brother, after all, and you are his Tante also. Be well, Tante. And all. Yitzhak

Vilnius, September 27, 1970

Dear Itzale and Dear Perele, together with your good, beautiful children,

Dear, good Itzale, I see that you can already make a book out of my cherry compote! What would have happened if you were to eat what I can bake? You would not have left here. I bake what is called a napoleon, and other beautiful things. If we had only received your letters earlier, all would have been ready for you. Well, next time you come it will be different.

Now, dear ones, I have become a great-grandmother, and Fanya a grandmother, Osya a grandfather. Bella gave birth to a daughter who has every virtue except one--she cries at night and does not let us sleep.

You tell me I am wise. You know women. When you give a woman a compliment, she becomes proud. No doubt I tell the truth.

My dear ones, regards from the family Pomerantz. If you had been here five more days, more would be sending you regards but, after all, there were only five days.

Do you know, Itzale, I feel drawn to write "dear Itzale," "dear Feivel." But I remember how you and Feivel made fun of me when you told how when I write you a letter it is full of "dear Itzale" this and "dear Feivel" that. Remembering, I try not to write dear Itzale, dear Feivel. But I cannot write otherwise--because you are very dear to me. Who else other than dear Itzale and dear Feivel do I have? As you wish. You can laugh at me, but I shall write the way that is dear to me....

So again, dear Itzale, you write that I was angry with Fanya that she went to Leningrad, but you made something of an error. I was glad she had the opportunity to be with you. Who knows when there will be another such opportunity....

109

Now some bad news. There is a great misfortune in the house. Fanny is ill almost a month. Unfortunately, she had to go to the hospital and was there several days. All the analyses were good and we took her home. Again she became ill and again we took her to the hospital. Now they have found that she does not digest her food. Even thin soup causes an attack and great pain. Many doctors have consulted on her case, and she will need an operation--on September 28. I sit and end this letter--tears are falling on it. Better it would be if this happened to me rather than her. She protected me so much. She does not deserve this.

Your Tante

Vilnius, October 25, 1970

My dear Yitzhak and Perele,

I hope my letter finds you in the best of health. We received one letter from you, Yitzhak, that you are already home. We already await a second.

Unfortunately, I could not answer your letter. A misfortune occurred. I fell ill. I have never been sick. I have never had to turn to a doctor. It happened suddenly. We did not know what it was. I could not eat anything for three weeks. I lost ten kilograms. I had an operation and the doctors found gall stones. How do you say it, Yitzhak? Another miracle occurred--and I continue to live again. I am still very weak. I cannot eat everything. But I am better than before. I can already go outside for fifteen minutes at a time.

But this isn't all. Di Mameh, very much upset, became dizzy and fell in the house and suffered bleeding on her foot. A hard swelling formed in the place where one sits. She lies in bed for three weeks already and cannot sit. It is called a hematoma. It will take a long time to dissolve. I am weak and with my last energy I am caring for her. I hope she will be well by the time you receive this letter. I am very sorry that my letter is not a happy one. I hope my next one will be better. My dear ones, if only you knew how I long for you! But unfortunately you are so far from us.

I have become a grandmother but have seen only the beautiful photos of the little one. My dear ones, give Feivel and his family greetings from us all. I wish you all a good year, a year of health, a happy year, and good fortune.

Your Fanya

Highland Park, October 31, 1970

Dear Tante Dora,

Dear Tante, I know you remember all my questions. Make me a gift of your answers. Write me a book. I saw paper in a corner of your room. Write me a hundred books. Tell me everything--about my father and your other brothers, Max and Yankel. And your mother and father. Only now have I learned that I also had a grandmother and a grandfather! Tell me about the olden times. I beg of you. You will earn a mitzvah. And give joy to a nephew who loves you very much.

Dear Tante Dora, here the leaves are already flying from the trees. Many already stand naked. Others are so full of color they take one's breath away. But each day moves us closer to winter. But we shall live through the snows, and spring will come for all of us, believe me. The cherry trees will bloom again. And the Tante will again make my compote.

Fima writes that Fanya is getting better and that you will soon be up and around. I hope there is an end to the misfortunes. Write us good news already. On the photo the new little Irina looks very lively and like our side of the family. Tante, does she cry in Yiddish or Russian?

With much love, Yitzhak

Vilnius, November 24, 1970

Beautiful, dear Yitzhak and Perele!

About us some good news. I am already steady on my feet, am able to go to work, but I have leave coming to me, and I will use it. Di Mameh is already much better, moves about, and is allowed to go out. The heart is already happier.

Irina grows into a beautiful child. She resembles both sides of the family, but she has Di Mameh's index finger, that is, the Tante's, that is, the grandmother's. Fima works at his job at the university. Bella studies. They visit us once a week. Osya works as usual. He tired himself out with our illnesses. But now everything is good again and life is normal again.

111

Dear ones, we are not the only ones concerned about you--the Pomerantzes are also. They always ask whether we've had a letter from you. When does Feivel expect to come to us? We await him with great impatience. I hope he will write us about this, so that we can meet him, not as it was with you. He should not have to go looking for us....

Fanya

Highland Park,   January 2, 1971

Dear, dear Tante Dora,

I cannot begin the new year without writing to my one and only Tante. When we came to Vilnius and awaited your entrance, I wondered who knows what I would find--perhaps she would be ugly, perhaps blind or deaf, mean, sour. I trembled hand and foot. And what did I find? A beauty...sharp eyes that saw everything...sharp ears that heard everything...and a happy person with every virtue, who could climb Gediminus Hill better than I could! All who see you in our films cannot but wonder at my Tante!

Perele and I quarrel over you. She already says you are *her* Tante. I say you are *my* Tante.   I say she has enough tantes--that what is mine is mine. She will not hear of this! So we fight. You will be a cause for divorce here yet.

We received Fanny's cablegram on my birthday, the first cablegram in my life. How she learned about my birthday I do not know. It made a great *simcha*, a great joy, in my heart.

Dear Tante,   in a few weeks you should receive a package with a few things Perele has chosen for you.   Everything in the package is washable--except the jacket. Enjoy it all.

Other news. Feivel has been sculpting in wood for a year and a half now. His statues are extraordinarily wonderful. He has a great talent in his hands. A few weeks ago a half hour program on television showed eighteen of his works. Feivel spoke easily and with humor. His statues spoke for themselves. You would have been pleased. One statue was about five feet tall. Others were two feet high. He will be a master yet. You will have to see them.

We wish you all the best for the New Year. Give our regards to the Pomerantzes and their children--a good year to them also.   And to the Marcuses. And to Fanya's tall blond friend Jana and her husband Max. And for you, Tante, and my little sister--many kisses. Yitzhak

112

Vilna, January 5, 1971

Dear Itzale, Perele, and your daughters,

When Fanya was in the hospital and I fell, I lay at home--alone the whole day, lonely as a stone. A whole day the door was not locked. You can imagine my situation, my grief--such pain, such suffering, not being able to go to Fanya. I did not eat for a month. I became weak from all this and had a heart attack. Luckily, the next-door neighbor came in, saw I was in trouble, and called the emergency squad. And they revived me.

So when Fanya came home from the clinic, barely alive, she had to look after me--and a few days later she became ill. The house doctor, a doctor of internal medicine, came and immediately called a surgeon. He examined me and said I needed an operation. Seeing the situation in our house, he did not let me go to the hospital. He performed the operation in his laboratory and gave me an excellent nurse. She came to change the dressing every day. I lay another three weeks. All this cost much money. Now all is in order with both of us. But to try to match you going up Gediminus Hill...well, I do not have the strength. Not even to your hotel. Fanya looks as thin as Perele. She has lost ten kilo, and I a little less. For now all's well that ends well.

How good it is to be able to sit again and write this letter. But to write all that you ask is impossible. This can only be done verbally. 1 hope what you want I will be able to give you. If I were to write you everything about the war when I lost such a husband and such a son who had just ended his classes...what will all this be for you except grief? I do not want to tell you what Fanya and I suffered. I cannot forget this. But why do you too need this grief?

Dear Itzale, I thank you and Perele and Feivel for the pocket money you gave Fanya for me. You did this quietly. I gave it to Fanny and she bought material from which I am having a fall coat made. The coat is very beautiful, and when it is finished I want to dress up with a pretty pocketbook from Leningrad and have my photograph taken and send you the pictures. So I became ill. I'll do it in the spring.

Dear Itzale, all your letters on your journey over Soviet Russia are very sweet and loving, and not only one has read them. When I have time I read them again--how you write from Sochi that Perele swims like a fish and you like a stone.

Be well. Give my regards to Feivel. A good, healthful 1971. Your Tante.

113

Vilnius, January 23, 1971

Dear Itzale, Perele, and your beautiful daughters,

We are all well, and I want to hear the same about you. If one is healthy, he is rich. But we do not understand this. Well, anyhow, some yes, some no.

Dear Itzale and Perele, thank you for the beautiful package. My dear ones, I well understand your good taste. It is enough for me to understand that you both found each other and have bound your lives together.

I understand, also, why you sent the package by air mail and spent so much more--so that I should be able to use the coat. Dear ones, the coat is very beautiful and the fit is just right, except it must be shortened. The beautiful things you sent for the little Irina are extraordinary, as well as the other things, all in much good taste. Our thank-you is as large as our city Vilnius.

Dear Itzale, one cannot write out everything in a letter. When you come for the second time, I will tell you everything and we will see everything. We will go to Kovno, and I will even show you where your Pa lived, and all of us. I can boast about showing it all to you. In my mind everything is as it was before, but it is already more than fifty years ago. I will soon forget, I am afraid. Everything has already changed. Never mind, I'll find it all.

Dear Itzale, when I go to bed I reread at least one of your beautiful letters. Then I cannot fall asleep. Two sleeping tablets do not help. I start to remember your good Pa, who raised two such good, concerned children, you and Feivel. Do you see, Itzale, what can happen in life in just five short days?

Dear Itzale, Perele, Feivel...we would certainly have invited you to greet the New Year because we had a double holiday. It was also Fanny and Osya's thirtieth wedding anniversary. We had planned to have a ball, but Fanny and I were too weak. But we had our friends, all my dearest and best. When we raised our glasses of champagne, we also drank to the health of all of you, and this is how we enjoyed ourselves until five in the morning.

It is almost Purim, my birthday. And I am baking tasty *hamentashen*. I ask you, Itzale, how can I send some over to you so you can at least have a taste? I am afraid that by the time you send me your advice it will be too late. My dear ones, be well. Your Tante Dembovitz.

Vilnius, January 23, 1971

My dear Yitzhak and Perele!

      I hope my letter finds you in good health. Di Mameh and I are already, thank God, well. I have returned to work. I did not work for four months. Di Mameh also works, in the house. I was very thin. I lost ten kilo in three weeks. But now I have begun to recover and started to eat more. In general I feel not bad. I have become *ah guter mensch*--a person without a gall.

      I thank you very much for your beautiful presents. Why do you do this? I know my talking won't help, you will do what you please. We were overcome by the beautiful things.

      My dear ones! If only you knew what a beautiful child is growing up here. The children and the little one were with us for the New Year. The 31st of December was our anniversary. It would have been different if I had been healthy. It is thirty years that we live together. We thought of how to celebrate, but unfortunately we did not have the strength. The children and two other couples came. We had a quiet celebration.

      From your sister Fanya

Vilnius, March 9, 1971

Dear Yitzhak, Perele, and children!

      I hope my letter finds you all in good health. A long time has passed and we do not have a letter from you. We are very uneasy. Di Mameh becomes sour when she does not get a letter for a long time. She is also afraid to scold you about this. She knows you work very much and are tired, but she still wants a few words from you. Since you were here she does not let your pictures out of her hands. She knows all your letters by heart.

      With us everything is the same. We are all well. A few days ago we celebrated Di Mameh's 75th birthday. A whole group gathered and we celebrated a whole evening long. The Marcuses and Pomerantzes thank you for your regards and send you their own. Also regards from Jana and her husband. Your Fanya

115

Vilnius, March 18, 1971

Dear Itzale and Perele, also Feivel and his family,

May you all be well. I go twice a day to the mail box, but unfortunately I have found no letter. Dear Itzale, your last letter is from January 2, long ago. My longing is very great.

Dear Itzale, you should write more often--at least one letter in two weeks. If you knew how much joy your letters give me, you would surely do this. I understand that you work much and are tired and do not have the time. But I want you to let me have pleasure from my life. Who knows how long I shall be able to answer you. Do not write long letters--only often. I am already pushing time until you come again, with Feivel. Three months after you write your letter, it will already be the time for you to come to us.

Dear Itzale, if only I could write you everything. Great changes are taking place in our land. Many Jewish families are leaving. I am sure you read the newspapers. Your little sister has a great desire to go.

I am happy to learn that Feivel has such a talent. He promised to send me a photograph of his work. I would be pleased to see it. But unfortunately I do not even have an answer to the last two letters I have long since written him. I understand well enough: he has no time. Secondly, we are not acquainted. Perhaps he thinks, as you did before you saw me, that I am perhaps deaf, blind, or with other faults. Dear Itzale, tell him of all my virtues. Maybe this will persuade him to write.

Well, dear Itzale, I send heartfelt greetings to all. Tell Perele that I am her Tante also, that I have the same love for her that I have for you. Since you are my nephew, she is also my niece. I am proud of you both. But you are so far from me--one letter in three months....Be well. Regards from the children.

Your Tante Dembovitz

Highland Park, April 7, 1971

Dear Tante Dora,

I have almost forgotten to wish you a happy Pesach. I think Pesach is one of our most beautiful holidays. I still remember how Di Mameh would put out a white tablecloth and how I would get a drop of red wine. Perele also sets a beautiful table. You would enjoy seeing it. Tante, do you over there open the door for Eliyahu to come in for a while? Ours is the only house in

116

the world that he comes to stay. You see, Feivel has made a sculpture of him-- an Elijah who is already a little drunk from the wine he has sipped at all the houses he has visited on Pesach night.

So we wish you a good Pesach. Henoch also sends you greetings. Also Feivel and his family. I'm afraid Henoch and Feivel are both lazy, lazier than I am. I will see to it that Feivel writes you a letter. Possibly you will hear from Henoch too. Do not faint if you hear from him. He is *ah guter mensch*, and he hopes only the best for you and the whole family. Just imagine that such a lazy person as Henoch will write to you!

Here it is still winter. But the days grow longer, and the bird we call a "robin"--it has a red breast--has arrived so we know spring is coming also. It sings a sweet song.

Dear Tante, I want to write more often. I do write you more often but the words are in my head. They are my best letters. I hope a day will come when I can put them on paper. Yitzhak

Highland Park, April 24, 1971

Dear Fanya,

Your Russian chocolates arrived exactly on Pesach! Imagine! Why did you do this? Better to spend money for chocolate for the Tante to make everything sweet for her.

The sun warms and we are already in our spring. Years ago my father was a real gardener. Everything grew for him. Wonderful flowers, also tomatoes, strawberries, cucumbers, raspberries, rhubarb, carrots--and weeds, too. Many weeds. The wind blew, the sun shined, his hair flew--and he was king in his garden. A good, sweet, dear human being, *ah guter mensch*.

How is Osya? And the Pomerantzes and their beautiful children? And the Marcuses and Jana? And Irina--is she reading yet? Is she holding discussions with the Tante yet?

Both of us work as always--we are forever running. Feivel works hard with his mallets and chisels. He will be a great sculptor one day. Most recently he has sculpted a *minyan*, ten *menschen*, each two feet high. You can imagine. We have not heard anything from Henoch, but we are not worried about him. If we get news of him, we shall write. As long as he is well. Tell the Tante I

117

love her even more than chocolate. A kiss to you--and for her. Greetings to Osya, Bella, and Fima.

Your little brother, Yitzhak

Vilna, April 27, 1971

Dear Itzale, Perele, and children,

Dear Itzale, we received your letter and read with great joy that you are all well. Also I learned with great joy that my dear brother Henoch lives in Israel. We will be happy to receive a letter from him from Israel. I will try not to faint from surprise. That he is very good, I already know from my younger years. He is the best of all my brothers....I shall wait impatiently for his letter, but better late than never....

The Pomerantzes, Fima, Bella, and Irina were at our first Seder. We had Pesach mead and all that is necessary for Pesach. We remembered you and drank to your good health. Dear Itzale, how is it that you skipped Purim? I wrote you some time before Purim and invited you to taste my good *hamentaschen*--it was also my birthday and Osya's too. I gave you a good idea-- to take an airplane and come with Perele and the children and Feivel and his family. That would be a great holiday. But I can see this only in a dream, and perhaps not even there.

Your Tante

Vilnius, May 11, 1971

My dear Yitzhak, Perele, and children,

I hope my letter finds you all well. I received your letter with great joy. A letter from you is a holiday for us. We read and read again. Di Mameh, she knows all your letters by heart, Yitzhak. We are all well. Little Irina is growing. She is a clever little girl. A very lively child. When we take a look at her, we forget all our worries.

And there is plenty to worry about. Many are leaving us. They are going to Israel. The Marcuses have left already. And we are also considering this. I understand that Henoch is in Israel, but according to the second letter I am not sure. But I believe he is there and that we will soon meet. Imagine what a joy

118

this will be. We would very much like to be at my cousin's daughter's wedding at the end of the year.

Dear Yitzhak, do not worry. The Tante has chocolate too, but she must not eat too much sweets. She is sweet all by herself. Believe me, I do not begrudge her.

The Pomerantzes send you hearty greetings. We were at their home not long ago, sat at their table, but you were not there. They thank you for your regards and wish you all the best. Jana and her husband Max also send their regards. Give Feivel and his family our regards. With many greetings and kisses--

Your little sister Fanya

Chicago, June 7, 1971

Dear Tante Dora,

I am in my classroom. My students are struggling over their final examination, and I sit here with them. This means I have a found hour in which to write to you.

Dear Tante, we hope to see you again. If it is possible--that is, if the Soviet government permits it--we will once again come down out of the heavens...to Vilnius. One does not let go of such a Tante. We hope to come in time for the cherries. But we have had no news from the Soviet government yet. If all goes well, we shall have another five days with the family.

Perele and I long for you. You cannot imagine how much. Our family-- from Tante to Irina--is really extraordinary. Perele says our whole life here has changed because we found you. I understand now why Yankel and Henoch loved you so much. Speaking of them, before we come to you we will go to see them in Israel. We hope to bring you some news of them. Feivel says that Henoch is a *foyler* and a *ligner*. I say he is neither lazy nor a liar. He is *ah guter mensch*. We hope to bring you greetings from him.

Yitzhak

June 11, 1971

Dear Tante,

We expect to arrive in Kiev on July 30. As things stand now, we can come in from Moscow. We do not have all the information yet. We don't even know if we can stay the whole five days. We are a little afraid that the Soviet time plan works against us. But we shall see. Not everything is set yet. But we must come to see the Tante. It is our bad luck that Aeroflot does not fly in exactly when we wish. But if it is at all possible, Tante, we shall come to see you. I will write more before we go. Until I can bring it to you, I send you our love via air mail.

Yitzhak

Vilnius, June 21, 1971

My dear Yitzhak and Perele!

By us there is news. We have received the required papers from my father, who has been found after so many years. He lived in Africa and did not know of us. Now he lives in Israel and has found us and wants to be reunited with us. We are doing everything to be reunited with him and at the same time be close to you. This is our latest news. Dear Yitzhak, if only you knew how we long for all of you, how we want to be together with you. I cannot even write you about this....We are all well and live with only one thought.

Little Irina will already be ten months old. She already has two lower teeth and a third coming in from above. She does not sit still but crawls on all fours. She understands much. In a word, she is a pleasure. Next week they will go to the forest with her--to the same place where we went with you [to talk in safety].

Di Mameh is at home. She is very sour. Only you can make her sweet again with a few words. Please make us all a little happier. Take the great stone off our hearts. We await an answer.

Your sister Fanya

120

DIARY, 1971

A Jewish Life
July 28, 1971. Tel Aviv.

Mrs. Feigenbaum just called and spoke with me for half an hour. We met on a tour earlier this week, and I told her and her husband that we are going on to Vilna--and why. It turned out that she has two brothers there! "You must tell my brother--the one who has cancer-- that he must come to Israel," she said tonight. It seems she has changed her mind. She knows how dangerous it is to choose for another. But now she's willing to state her choice for him.

"Israel is the only place for him and his family. Since maybe there is a God," she said, "if he came here he might get a new outlook on life and regain life. Tell him to send all his furniture. And if they are rejected, tell him they have to apply again and again. There is no question even for their daughter, who is studying to be a doctor. She must come too. They will adjust. People make things. Things don't make people. Israel is the only place to live a Jewish life. There is no way to live a Jewish life in Vilna." I said I would try.

Her brother, she said, had accumulated rubles. "But what," she asked, "does being rich mean there?"

Mr. Feigenbaum, I learned earlier, is a survivor, a Polish Jew. Of the three hundred Jews from his home town he is the only survivor. "Wouldn't you want to go back to see your home again?" I asked him.

"No. Never."

"Why not?"

"If they knew I was a Jew from there--and the only survivor--I am sure they would kill me too.

A Speck in the Sky
0745, Saturday, July 31, 1971. Kiev.

Have had a good night's rest. From our room in the Dniepro Hotel I can see a department store, wide streets, buses, fountains, massive buildings that dwarf people. Green trees. The red flag.

I still feel a little weak, but I am better and wonder again how it will be this afternoon. Will the Tante be there? With flowers in her hand? Or will we have to take a taxi to Michyurina Street? I felt terrible yesterday, but it was no time for going to a hospital. And now Sabena has lost our baggage too! Two bags. It is Sabena's fault, and, oh yes, Sabena will say it's sorry, but that isn't going to alter *our* situation. We had to make out papers, and Intourist gave us promises, but what will turn out I don't know.

Back from waiting for our vouchers, passports, etc. From behind his counter the "Administrahtor"--fat and blond--saw me coming for the passports and knew exactly what I wanted. We both laughed. He knows we must leave for Vilnius shortly. "These are your tickets to Vilnius. Everything is all right. I vish you all the best. Goodbye."

We are at a minor Kiev airport, alone in a room, isolated, intentionally cut off from all Russian passengers. We are in an Intourist room reserved for foreigners. The place is full of propaganda pamphlets in French and German. Below the big, bold letters reading "Under the Banner of Leninism" are the familiar pictures of the Revolution. "You may take these books as souveniers."

1115, Saturday morning.

We are aloft aboard an old twin-prop rumbling smoothly. Rich, green lands below look planned and worked. There was some commotion about our seats, but in the end we got them.

Passengers read books, newspapers. We are the only tourists aboard. It is a bright day, and we are on our way to Vilnius and a genuine Tante. We have been heading for this day for a whole month.

124

How sad to think it will be over almost before we are started. But it is worth it--to bring life to the Tante and her poor hands. The Aeroflot stewardess passes hard candies. All the passengers have the stocky, burly, Slavic look. They are a good looking people--in a strong way.

Yesterday, one of the women on our plane from Vienna was greeted in the classic style--by a large family and with flowers: cousins, uncles, aunts, in-laws, brothers, sisters. Many jokes, many smiles, much laughter. Peasant faces, weather-worn and time-creased. They took the classic group picture that they will call "at the Kiev airport."

It is getting very cold on the plane now. First you sweat, then you freeze: Aeroflot.

Each time I leave the States I have to learn all over again that the whole world is not America, that there's more to the world than America. I should know better by this time, but each time I am shocked at my provincialism, intellectual and physical. There's nothing like going to see another country to start making comparisons and contrasts and learning that the world doesn't revolve around us, that we're only in it, on it, with many others, of different ways, carrying their own baggage. Perspective. It makes for a certain humility.

What a *simcha* it will be for the Tante! I hope she is well. How she must be waiting for us at the Vilnius airport! They will see our plane from far off, just a speck in the sky, but they will know it is our plane, the plane from Kiev. And the Tante's heart will pound with excitement. And it will all be very good for her. And tonight we will drink *L'chaim* to her--and to all--and she will wipe away a tear and say something like what my father once said under very different circumstances, "It is nothing--something has fallen into my eye." Poor, dear Tante--who has lived through revolutions, wars, concentration camps, deaths, and so much else. And now I shall see her a second time.

But there will be no large family to greet us. There aren't any large Jewish families anymore.

The Return

0130, Sunday morning, August 1, 1971. Vilnius.

We are "home" at the Neringa Hotel again, in Room 11, reserved for Americans. We have been gone all day and have only just discovered our plight: the plumbing doesn't work and the lights don't work. It is insult added to the injury of our lost baggage. Perle has a terrible case of allergy and has sneezed bitterly all night. She thinks she picked it up in Jerusalem. She suffers much with it but has now fallen asleep.

Pure luck brought us to the family again. We were leaving the airport to take our taxi to the Neringa—just as Di Tante, Fanya, and Fima, flowers and all, were coming in at the very next door. An excited reunion, cut short by our Intourist guide, who took us and Di Tante to the Neringa, Fanya and Fima following after. All look well, though Fanya and Di Tante suffered bitter illness and operations in the last year. Di Tante looks a little heavier, Fanya a little lighter. Fima is as calm, cool, and handsome as ever.

We weren't able to get a taxi to Di Tante's home, so we took the autobus. We passed the ice cream stand at the same end of the line. The same apartment #76, the same mail box, where so frequently they look and do not find. Osya is home. He did not feel well the other day, but he looks well now, and we sat and talked of many things for the rest of the day.

We ate much, especially *karshen* compote. Three glasses full. "*Di ershte*," Di Tante said. She meant the first cherries of the season. Special for me. Cold borscht, which I do not like. Chopped herring, which I do not like. Duck, which I do. Torte, which I had to skip. Di Tante made it herself.

It was terribly hot in the apartment. Little Irina was the inevitable center of attention, a tireless and beautiful child. Bella is still quiet and heavier than I remembered. Only Fima is mainly unchanged, though now a father. Food, champagne, talk of our recent past and their future. We remained until twelve, then caught a late bus "home."

Tisha b'Av

Sunday, August 1, 1971. Vilnius.

Jora and his wife Bebba burst into the apartment in the late afternoon, full of the excitement they witnessed at the *demonstratzie* at Ponar. Their description of the event crackled with electricity. Today, Tisha b'Av, 500 demonstrators went to Ponar to mark the day with flowers at the grave sites. The Germans and Lithuanians killed 70,000 Jews here. There is not one Jewish family in Vilna that does not have its dead in the graves of Ponar. But what they really came to do was to protest the government's policy toward the Jews. The KGB and the police had learned of the demonstration. They came and gave warning: no one would be permitted to enter the grave sites. The response was a Jewish sit-in. For four hours the demonstrators sat quietly outside in the heat of the sun. Then they placed their flowers on the road and stood fast. The police broke up the demonstration, threw many of the demonstrators into the waiting police wagons, and drove off, deliberately running over the flowers. Bebba and Jora were there. They saw it all. You could feel their excitement. There will be phone calls and within hours the outside world will know. Exactly what the 500 want.

Fanny was not surprised. She knew about the planned demonstration all along but kept the information from us for fear we would have wanted to join it. She did not want to risk our being arrested and putting an end to our visit. So she had kept us with her all afternoon.

The Pomerantzes were at our table too. They were the quietest of all. But they listened intently. When I think of them, I cannot help but think about the terrible plight of all who are caught "in-between." The Jews. This is the eternal position of sensitive and educated people like the Pomerantzes. It's the source of much of their suffering. It's what makes Jews different from everyone else and thus makes others recognize their own difference from the Jews.

Fanny says that Der Litviner--the Lithuanian--can once again chase the Jew in the streets of Vilna. Because the Jew is "the different one." Four years ago, she said, a little three year old girl was reported missing from a Lithuanian kindergarten. "It was just before Pesach. The child simply disappeared. Rumors began...the Jews.... Incitements began. Jewish boys were attacked in the streets. Then they discovered her body in a cellar. A young Lithuanian boy had strangled her. A neighbor saw him. What would have happened if a crazy Jew had done it? For this reason alone it is time to get out."

It is the old story. She has heard, and seen, the slogan "Kill the Jews! Save Russia!" "Di Litviner," she says, "in their hearts they hate the Jew--the Russians first, then us."

Jora and Bebba have nothing more to lose. They have burned their bridges. They declared their desire to emigrate, were refused, and have suffered the usual, expected crackdown: loss of job, and so on. The Pomerantzes, on the other hand, are uncertain, ambivalent. They are gentle people. Though they sense that, once again, the game is up, they know that to oppose the government is to put homes and friendships and careers and families at risk. It's the old story. As they listened to the events at Ponar--of the 500 at Ponar--I could imagine only too well the thoughts of the Pomerantzes caught "in-between."

The Butcher
August 2, 1971. Vilnius.

No entry.

The entry for August 2 is missing because I never entered it.

No matter. A quarter of a century later I can still remember myself back to that date, to that afternoon, to the events I chose not to record, the half hour when six lives, perhaps more, were at stake. In the hands of the KGB such an entry could have had consequences. Therefore no entry.

The late Sixties and early Seventies were heady days for Jews in the Soviet Union.   Jewish activists were demanding the right to leave the country, openly challenging the government that would not let them go.   No one knew it then, but their protests signaled the beginning of the end of the Soviet Union.   In time demonstrations outside the Soviet Union and *demonstratzies* inside it began to take effect. Perhaps out of a sense of guilt or remorse for the silence of American Jews during the Holocaust, American Jews a generation later, young and old, began to visit the USSR, smuggling in Torahs, phylacteries, prayer shawls, Jewish calendars, Hebrew grammars and other texts.   They came for political reasons.   They came for religious reasons.   They came for humanitarian reasons.   What they were really smuggling in was hope.

We, however, did not come in the name of any organization or with a political, religious, or humanitarian agenda, though in some way all these elements played a role, provided a backdrop for our coming. We went because of an address on an ink-stained envelope, because of some old letters that still exerted a magnetic pull through time and space. Ultimately, I trace my journey back to memories, back to my father, a silent presence behind all these pages, a man for whom I had limitless love.

What would my father have done?   I know what he would have done. He would have gone to find his sister.

My father despised the communists for the murderers that they were, and his anti-communist beliefs might well have lent force to his search for his sister. He would have denied any religious belief in the commandment of *pidyon shevuyim*, the obligation to ransom a fellow Jew held captive.   But without knowing it, he would have followed the commandment.   Nor did he ever cease to work for social justice.   But as influential as these ideals were in his life, ultimately, if he had lived and been physically able, he would have set out for Vilna because his *sister* was there, because of her suffering, and because of his own memories of her and of his youth.

What it had come down to was that our promise of help meant rubles. Ransom money. Ransom money to buy out six people: Di Tante, Fanya, Osya, Fima, Bella, and Irina. There could be no escape without money. Rubles for exit papers. Rubles for crating household goods and furniture. Rubles for carrying the crates and cartons down the stairs. Rubles to move everything to the shipping warehouse. Rubles to load everything. Rubles to ship everything to Israel. Rubles every step of the way. More rubles than the family had.

Rubles were the problem. Outside the Soviet Union they were worthless. Inside the Soviet Union the government had set an artificial exchange rate of, roughly, one ruble for a dollar. And one could get these rubles only from the Intourist office. On the black market, if I wanted to take the risk, I could get considerably more than one ruble for the dollar. If I wanted to take the risk.

There was one more way to get rubles. Some Jews in Vilna had managed to accumulate rubles, but had nowhere to spend them, for there was little enough to buy. Most of them wanted dollars--in anticipation of the time they would be able to leave the country. One of these was Milner, the butcher, who knew Di Tante and trusted the family. Fanya went to talk to Milner. She knew his trade had made him well-to-do, that he had rubles that would be worthless to him in Israel, where he planned to go. The result: he would give Fanya the rubles the family would eventually need in order to get out of Lithuania if we promised to send dollars to him in Israel. Fanya would tell him how many rubles the family wanted, and she would tell me how many dollars to send him in Israel. If we all agreed, it would be a three-way arrangement--a verbal contract.

I had Milner's offer in mind on August 2 when the doorbell rang. It was mid-afternoon, Tuesday, a sunny day out. Fanya opened the door and Mrs. Feigenbaum's two brothers entered. We introduced ourselves, shook hands. While I gave them regards from their sister, Fanya hurried away to smother the phone with pillows and blankets, in case it had ears. Then she drew the curtains and blocked off the windows, in case they had eyes. Perle, Fanya, and Di Tante disappeared in another room. I was alone in the semi-darkness with the brothers.

I am no bargainer. I refuse to bargain. I am embarrassed to bargain, even though the Arab or Turkish or Indian shopkeeper who faces me is not. Mrs. Feigenbaum's brothers had come precisely to get the most dollars they could for the rubles they possessed, nor could I blame them. They knew as well as I that outside the Soviet Union their rubles were worthless. "But what," Mrs. Feigenbaum had asked, "does being rich mean in Vilna?" What she meant was that there was little one could buy with them.

The bargaining did not last long. Mrs. Feigenbaum's brothers could not match, let alone exceed, Milner's offer. After their final offer, I had to tell them that my cousin had managed better terms.

As the brothers got up to take their leave, I could see that the one who carried the *roc* within him had tears in his eyes. They were not tears of anger or frustration that we had come to no agreement. Not at all. It was rather, I think, that Israel was now only a dream for him, while in time it would become reality for Fanya and her family. He gripped my hand in his and gave it a powerful shake. "Have a good trip," he said. And for him? What trip?

The Napoleon
Tuesday, August 3, 1971. Vilnius.

We parted with the Pomerantzes tonight. How sad, how terribly, terribly sad. As we said our final goodbyes with them, Dr. Pomerantz said, wistfully, "Perhaps you will write us a letter too...."

They came with one of their daughters, who has just today landed a job as a model. At seventeen she is in the throes of her first love. Her young man has gone to Israel, and she says she wants to learn English and Hebrew--not Yiddish--in anticipation of some future reunion with him. Dr. Pomerantz recently joined the Party. He did so not out of any idealism. His joining the Party means he has resigned himself to his lot and that he has decided he might as well at least improve his material situation here, just as many others have done. Now that he is a member of the Party it will be more difficult than ever for him to get out of the Soviet Union--just when his daughter may have stirred thoughts of Israel in him.

Once again, but for the last time, the table was full: pickles (sour and sweet), tomatoes, herring, tongue, brisket, salad. And dessert. I complained about dessert. I bemoaned the end of Di Tante's napoleon. Suddenly she disappeared from the table. Seconds later she was back. With a twinkle in her eye she said, "*Oyb azoy....*" "If so,"-- and she gave a triumphant little laugh, as though she had scored again-- "I have something for you." And sure enough, she had saved the last piece of her famous napoleon torte for me! When I first saw the entire torte it was at least eight inches high and at least twelve inches in diameter. A dozen eggs had gone into it, though I don't know where. It was a masterpiece. And she had hidden and saved the one last piece for me!

During the evening she sat at the corner of the table, listening to all the jokes, some even a little off color. But she is a good sport. Rather than laugh outright at these jokes she smiles and raises her hand to cover her eyes in a show of modesty.

As we sit around the table, Perle has a drink of what she calls "*heyseh vasser*" or "hot water," the name she has given to vodka. The others say it should be drunk with pepper. I can't believe them.

Earlier in the evening we had Di Tante's noodle soup and her wonderful *kuckletten*, a sort of chicken hamburger. Victor, Fima's best friend, liked them too. He is darkly handsome, sports a mustache. He came around 4:30--told us of the results of the demonstration at Ponar on Sunday. Ten or twelve demonstrators got fifteen days each in jail for failure to obey the militia. One, a doctor, received a twenty-five percent loss of pay for a whole year. Fima called the sentences "simply communist fascism." The demonstrators got what they wanted though--worldwide publicity. The BBC and Israel had the news the next day. The government can't stop the news from getting out.

Behind the Fence

1245, Wednesday, August 4, 1971. Moscow.

We are rolling toward the flight line. Aeroflot is on time. We are aboard CCCP Flight 331, from Moscow to London. Our plane is a large one, six seats across, the largest Russian plane we've been on, a far cry from the local from Vilnius this morning.

Intourist told us to be ready at 6:30 this morning to get the 7:27 to Moscow. We were ready and waiting for the Intourist taxi. No taxi at 6:30...6:40...6:50...7:00. The situation grew more serious by the minute. We urge the clerk of the Neringa Hotel to do something, anything, to call Hotel Vilnius...Hotel Gerintas.... From sign language we learn that the Intourist office at Hotel Vilnius does not open till eight! And anyhow--the phones don't start operating till later...! No taxi.... In the CCCP one learns nothing if not patience. If not God, then Intourist will see one through...in time, or there will be hell for someone to pay. And the poor porter knows it. Frantically, he tries to flag one taxi, then another. No luck. At last the Intourist car pulls up for us--and we take off, breaking all speed limits, flying through two red lights as though we were already on Aeroflot! We make it to the Vilnius airport in time. In time to be greeted quickly by last year's auburn-haired Intourist guide.

But there--standing and waiting patiently, always waiting so patiently--are Di Tante, Fanya, and Fima. Hurried kisses. A few words. "*L'chaim,*" I say to Fanya. "It means to life," I say. And considering yesterday, she understands exactly what I mean. A hug.

"We must go quickly," says the redhead. No tears. There is no time for them. Osya comes late. We see him in his white shirt, waving to us from behind the fence, where he stands with the others watching us walk toward the plane. We wave back, then enter the plane.

We see them through our porthole. They are far off...behind the fence...waiting to see us off. Perle waves back one last time. They are tiny figures far off, left alone once more. But perhaps, for once in their lives, not quite alone.

133

WORDS AND LETTERS, 1971

Vilnius, August 4, 1971

Dear Yitzhak and Perele!

A few hours after you flew off customs called and informed me that your luggage arrived and wanted to know what to do. I went to Aeroflot, spoke with an official, and told him to send them back home to you. I gave him your address, and they sent it all to Moscow and from there to you. I believe you will have it by the time you receive my letter.

It is very gloomy in the house. We go from corner to corner and we imagine you are in the other room and that in a moment you will come out and we will see your beautiful, bright faces. If there are dear things in the world, you are to us the dearest.

My dear ones, Osya went with a taxi to take you to Aeroflot. He saw you leaving, so he went back, but he was late. You were already near the airplane. But what can one do when things are not always what one wishes? Osya has just gone to send you a telegram, and I am writing this letter....

Fanya

My dear ones, both,

Fanny has already written you everything. But I am also writing a few words from deep in my heart. I never imagined such a thing could occur in life--such love and concern for us. I thank you many times and wish you much health and a good, beautiful New Year. Dear Perele, I wish the same for your parents and the children. And you, Itzale, greet Feivel and his whole family. I do not lose my hope still to see him. All the best from your Tante--who was barely able to say goodbye. But better a little while than nothing at all.

Highland Park, August 6, 1971

Dear Tante--

We came home last night--two o'clock in the morning--without our third *tchemodon*! Aeroflot has lost it for us. But we think it has already been found. We also received the telegram from Fanya--that they are sending us the other suitcases. Don't worry. As Osya says, everything will be "all right." What a business with *tchemodones!*

We came home tired and dirty. Perele sneezed and I coughed. Together we sounded like an orchestra. It's a lively world here--*ah lebedikeh velt.* Everything would be much better if only I had cherry compote--the best medicine. But my "doctor" is elsewhere, far away. I am afraid we tired you and Fanya with our visit. You did so much for us. You probably need a vacation. I know that now *we* need one. But we have to go back to work.

Tante, you look very good, even better than last year. You were even sweeter than last year. Truly. You and the whole family, I feel, will have a good future. Give our regards to the Pomerantzes. It was a pleasure to be with them. Also to the Chesnows. It is good to know such strong, happy people--all.

With great love, Yitzhak

Highland Park, August 7, 1971

To Chaim Dembovitz:

My name is Yitzhak Abrahamson, and I am a nephew of Dora Dembovitz. My dear Tante is a sister to my father.... Last year I went to see her, and this year once more. We are home only two days from our journey. And this is why I am writing you.

The situation of the Jews in Vilna and in the Soviet Union is worsening. Soon the situation of my own family in Vilna will also worsen. They have made their request to go to Israel--and you know already what can happen when such a request is made. Six people are involved: my Tante Dora, my cousin Fanya, her husband Osya, their son Fima, Fima's wife Bella, and their little girl Irina, 11 months old. They have given the authorities your name as my Tante's husband and Fanya's father. Therefore, I ask you, for myself and for all of them, and from the bottom of my heart, to write them a letter from Israel. This is very important. You must write to your "wife" and your "daughter." It is very important they should be able to show that they have an immediate relative in Israel. It is a question of helping rescue six lives. I beg you--*write them many letters.* I believe you well understand their situation. And I believe you understand what to write.

My cousin's husband is a construction engineer. Their son Fima is a physicist. Israel needs them both. There the young ones will surely have a future. For my Tante, Fanya, and Osya to live in freedom--you can imagine what this can mean to them. Write them as often as you can. You will earn a great *mitzva*.

With deepest hope,

Yitzhak Abrahamson

Vilnius, August 10, 1971

Dear Itzale,

Fanya has flown off--to a spa--four hours flying time and then even more traveling. Now it is very lonely--you left so quickly--if only we had had the fifth day. That day was a real loss.

Three hours after you flew off customs phoned us. At customs Fanya met a friend who had come to receive a fine package full of beautiful things, but she could not take it because she had to pay too much duty. She did pick out certain items and paid 300 rubles. The other beautiful things remained: for the officials, of course. Dear Itzale, your Perele is very wise. She was right to have us send the *tchemodanes* back. She understood Haman's mind.

So now again I write "Dear Itzale" and you will laugh at me. Give me an alternative. What shall I do? Shall I write "inexpensive Itzale?" I cannot write this. Laugh at me if you will, but you are very dear to me, and I am proud because of you. I tell all my acquaintances everything about you. I cannot stop talking about you.

I write with many thanks and love for what you are doing for us. You have perhaps opened the doors. I don't know how things would look without you. Now we have more hope than before.

Fanny was able to buy two beautiful imported blankets--the kind you do not see here--one for you, one for us. When I journey to my husband I will take it with me....

My mother would say that a *mensch* must live with hope. If you lose hope, all is lost. So I do not lose hope that I will yet come to you and no longer cook noodles three days straight. I do not lose hope. I follow my mother's words.

Dear Perele, I hope to meet your mother and father. Regards to your beautiful children.

Your Tante

Vilnius, August 21, 1971

Dear Itzale and Perele,

I hope you have recuperated from your long and difficult journey. It was good to see each other again and take pleasure in each other. If you didn't live so far from us we could see each other more often. But this can't be done....

Do you know, Itzale, the guest who met you at dinner with us telephoned me and said he had the best impression of you and Perele and that I could be proud of you. And I can write you that I am so proud that no one can compare himself to me....

Dear Perele, thank you for the beautiful wardrobe for little Irina. May you become a grandmother and buy nothing worse for your grandchild. May your daughter get a husband no worse than my dear Itzale. Am I not right?

About the main news so far there is nothing. As it happens, we are very puzzled. Many families are unhappy. Who knows? We have to try to hope. As soon as there is something we will write.

With best wishes and love, your Tante Dembovitz

Highland Park, August 27, 1971

Dear Tante,

Our suitcases have been returned to us. You don't have to worry about them. And, yes, Tante, in many respects Perele is much wiser than I. She is a rare one, wise and good. I have long known this. That is why I took her with. She is a *berieh:* she can do anything around the house. And she is a *tummlerkeh,* too--wherever she goes, she is the life of the party. As soon as she enters there begins a *tararam*, a great *tummel*. She cannot be stopped. Already she speaks only of *her* Tante! *Her* cousin! I have to remind her that this is *my* Tante, *my* cousin!

Fanya wrote that it became a little gloomy in your house. Tante, it is not like that in my heart. Can you understand how happy it is to have such a Tante? You will come to us on a journey--and we will not let you cook. *I* will cook for *you*! I know how to make a good, hot, red beet borsch, like wine. You will only have to make cherry compote and your great napoleon torte. I tell everyone about the torte. Have you saved another "last piece" for me? Be well, Tante. Regards to Osya and the children.

With great love, Yitzhak

Highland Park, Illinois September 1, 1971

Dear Miss Pomerantz:

....While we were in Vilna last year we met your nephew, Dr. Pomeranc--a highly respected neurologist-psychiatrist, a close friend to our family in Vilna. He and his beautiful wife have two lovely daughters, twins, of university age. Last year we were guests in his home. This year we were invited there again but were unable to go. However, he and his wife and one of the twins came to see us in my aunt's home.

Last year, and this year again, he expressed a strong desire for us to get in touch with you so that you might write to him and his family. I cannot possibly tell you how important it is that you correspond with them. From my own experience with my own family in Vilna, I know what it can mean to soften a little the loneliness of people in their situation. All they wish is to hear from whatever family they still have left to them. It would bring Dr. Pomeranc and his family the greatest joy to hear from you....It would be a great *mitzva* if you would write to them....With kind regards from Dr. Pomeranc and his family,

Irving Abrahamson

Vilnius, September 7, 1971

September 7, letter

Dear Itzale, Perele, and children,

I am very glad that you have already received the *tchemodones.* I had a good rest on my vacation. I drank *heyseh vasser*--tasteful water--not like the "hot water" vodka I gave you to drink here. The whole time I thought only of you... much upset by the lost *tchemodones.* What can one do? Most important was that we were all together and saw each other again.

While I was on vacation, they fired Osya from his work. You understand why, of course. Now he is looking for work. He will find something, do not fear. We expected this. I am working. They are not touching me. Meanwhile all is quiet--we hear nothing. What you write--that Perele is both wise and good--is true. She is also beautiful. We love her dearly. Both of you are burned deep in our hearts, and we can't imagine where the years have gone without you. What is gone is gone. But now that we have you we will not let you go....

Fanya

Highland Park, September 11, 1971

Dear Tante mine--and Fanya, Osya, Fima, Bella, and Irina,

We wish all of you all the best in the New Year: health and hope for the year 5732 and for all years. I myself cannot imagine how we have managed to survive 3,500 years. But we have done it. One does what one must do. I myself take an example from you, from what you have had to go through in life. People like you will live another 3,500 years, I am sure. When I look at my sweet, dear, young Tante, I believe in everything. She reminds me always of my father.

I have received a letter from the Tante and yesterday a letter from Fanya and a beautiful card with a red flower. Feivel also received a card. I no longer break my teeth over Fanya's handwriting. It is so clear that I thought it was the Tante who was writing! Fanya, your handwriting is now a pleasure to read-- very clear, like mine. We send you--with great warmth and greater love-- greetings on the New Year.

With love to all, Yitzhak and Perele

Highland Park, September 25, 1971

Dear Tante mine and Fanya, Osya, and family,

I am sorry Osya must look for a new job. We expected this. But everything will turn out all right yet. He will find work, you will see. As you say, Tante, one must not give up hope.

We received the six photos. Unfortunately, we will have only the photos that Osya and Fima made of our journey. The photos we made with our new apparatus did not turn out. Our films, however, did. You are laughing and walking with me and you are waving your hands, and Fanya chases the chickens in the street. Everything turned out beautifully. You will see.

Rosh Hashanah night we and our guests drank a glass of wine to all of you and your guests, and wished for you what you wish for yourselves, and more. Regards to the Pomerantzes, and all, for the New Year. Dear Tante, be well. And do not worry. I have sent letters to Fanya's friends and to my uncle and told him all about our journey. He must be happy that we saw you. We also sent a letter to Dr. Pomerantz's tante.

With much love from Perele and me, Yitzhak.

Vilnius, October 1, 1971

Dear Yitzhak, dear Perele, and dear children,

We received your wishes for the New Year and thank you much for them.

Today they denied our request to reunite ourselves with our dear father, husband, and grandfather. I do not know why. We are very disappointed and will write further. We often receive letters from my father. He awaits us impatiently, and we yearn for him, but unfortunately not yet.

....When our longing is very great, we look at you on the white wall--in the film--and we are together again. Di Mameh becomes happy when she sees you and how you kiss her. The four days you were here were like a dream. What can one do? Perhaps a time will come when we will be able to see each other more often and be closer.

Dear Yitzhak, we await your letters with great impatience. I am much pleased that you are able to read my handwriting. I believe you will be able to read it even better in the future.

Fanya

Vilnius, October 12, 1971

Dear friends Yitzhak and Perele,

We received your letter. Many thanks for your good wishes for the New Year. Permit us as well to send you greetings and good wishes, good luck, health, and success in the New Year.

We speak of you often. Fanya and the Tante tell us of the clever letters they receive. We often laugh heartily at your *khokhmas*. We often speak of Perele, her beauty and especially we cannot forget how she said the popular words *"pa blahtu"* [*protektzie*, clout]. I believe that you have not forgotten either.

It was a great loss that you were here this last time for so short a period and did not have the opportunity to be our guests. We hope that we shall yet meet again by us, by you, or in some other place, it is not important. Many thanks that you did not forget our request and wrote my tante. So far she has not written us.

Forgive me if I write with mistakes. It is many years that I have not written in Yiddish. I hope your letter is not the last one. You will write us more, and I shall have to learn how to write Yiddish better.

Warm regards from my wife and children. Special regards to Perele and your whole family.

Zelik Pomerantz

Vilnius, November 1, 1971

My dear ones, Yitzhak, Perele, and children!

I trust my letter will find you in the best of health. You have no doubt received my letter. Every day we wait for an answer from you, but so far the

143

mailbox is empty. I have already written you that our request has been refused. We have written again to be considered again and to be allowed to leave. So far we have no answer.

We receive frequent letters from my father, and good letters. He awaits us with great impatience and much longing. He hears the same from us. He asks me if he should also write and demand that we be let out. I have written him that he should write. Whether he will be able to argue the case...he is an old man already.

By us several families have already received permission to go. Among the lucky ones is also Milner. He came to us and told us the news. He asked about you and asked us to give you his regards. The Pomerantzes also send you regards. They received your letter and answered you immediately. We always talk with them about you. We long so much for you. Each time we send so many kisses--in our thoughts, that is--that when I add them up, they would surely come to two thousand. Today imagine if we were to kiss you so much at one time. Now do you understand how much we love you?

Dear Yitzhak, am I writing clearly enough? Or must you break your teeth? Write a few words. Di Mameh runs again to the mail box. Give her work. Let her read your letters.

Answer my letter immediately. Remain well. We wish you all the best.

With many greetings and kisses, your Fanya.

Chattanooga, Tenn. [1971, after our return from our second trip]

Very worthy Mr. & Mrs. Abramson, Shalom--

First of all, we thank you for your warmheartedness--that you took the time to speak with my brothers. And at the same time for telephoning and sending off the presents that my brother sent through you. I hope that one day we shall be able to do the same for you. I have received a letter from my sick brother. He writes that so far they have not been able to decide to leave Vilna. You cannot at all imagine how thankful we are for your regards from my brothers. Please write: did you see my brothers' children? What impression did they make upon you? What do you hear of your family?

A heartfelt greeting from Abraham. Be well. Please write.

With love.

Abraham and Esther Feigenbaum

Highland Park, November 5, 1971

Dear Tante,

We are greatly disturbed that Osya has no work. I hope he will soon find something.

I am also sorry that you cannot be reunited with your husband. I do not understand why they are holding back such a reunification. However, I hope, Tante, you will all still see each other. If one lives long enough one discovers that life holds many wonders. And you, dear Tante, are still very young, and not only in my eyes. I can very well understand why my uncle is so impatient.

Feivel showed me the letter you and Fanya sent him not long ago. It is a *simcha* to know you are all well and that you do not even think of losing hope. Just look at what you have found in the last two years! Perele and me, your husband, a whole family! I am also beginning to believe in miracles.

Tante, give our regards to Mrs. Feigenbaum's two brothers, the ones who came to see us. Also to Dr. Pomerantz. Tell him we received his wishes for the New Year, that he writes a good Yiddish, and that he is part of the family. Is little Irina talking yet or only babbling? A child of ours should already be talking philosophy, otherwise she is not ours. A kiss for her. And for Fanny, from her little brother and her little sister Perele, the same.

Yitzhak

November 20, 1971

Geherte Family Abrahamson!

Your Cousin Fanya and Tante who live in Vilna wrote you a letter five weeks ago in which she thanked you for the 2,000 kisses, that is, the 2,000 dollars which you must send me.

I am Milner, Zelik. I imagine you remember me. We spoke of this together. I arrived yesterday in Eretz Yisrael but I did not find the money in Jerusalem at the address I gave you.

I imagine you know that your cousin received the money and I am in much need of it now. I thank you very much and send you greetings from your cousin and Tante, Frau Dembovitz. I wish you all the best.

From me, Zelik Milner

Vilnius, November 24, 1971

Dear Yitzhak, Perele, and your children!

We do not have good news. Unfortunately, our request to be reunited with my father has been refused again. This is the greatest disappointment for us. You must understand that we live only with the thought of being reunited with him. He is already old and God knows what can happen. We have written again and asked that our request be reconsidered and that we be allowed to be reunited with our family.

Dear Yitzhak and Perele! I am trying to write clearly and more. Di Mameh says I am already writing better. But in your last letter you do not answer my questions, so I do not understand whether or not you received it-- the letter at the beginning of October, where I wrote of Osya's work, how we live, sent regards from the Pomerantzes, Milner, and from us for you two thousand kisses. Di Mameh also wrote you that our friend Milner has left. He asked that we send you his heartfelt regards. He is already there, but he has heard nothing yet from my cousin. He said that he will write him and send a greeting from us.

It has turned quite cold here--the true winter, with frost and snow. Today our mood is the same as outside. But what can one do? It does not depend on us. We await better news.

I still hope the day will come that we shall be reunited and meet again. My heart aches with longing. Our children also cannot wait. I hope that you, Yitzhak, will understand my letter. I believe I am writing clearly. I wish to receive an acknowledgement that you have understood me. Answer immediately, just a few words, even in English. We wait impatiently. Di Mameh wrote you earlier. With many greetings and kisses, your longing Fanya.

Highland Park, December 1, 1971

My dear Tante, my little sister Fanya, Osya, and children,

Tante, tell Fanya I understand her handwriting, and I do not suffer with it as I did a year ago.

I am very sorry, Tante, that the government does not permit you and the family to be united with your husband. I do not understand this. They allowed Milner to get out but not you! Well, he is lucky; I wish him all the best. Would that all of you could be united again. It will yet be so. I have the address of friend Milner's brother. We must really send him a Mazel Tov. He has earned it. If I were to see him, I would kiss him on both cheeks. (As I remember him, he was a little too round and thick to take around.) Since I cannot see him in person, I will send him my kisses through the mail. I will even write him my first letter tonight!

Dear Fanya, do not be uneasy. Believe me, you will see your father yet, and us for sure. I understand your longing. Perele and I are homesick for you too--and for the Tante and everyone. Take an example, as I do, from my dear, strong, wise, proud, wonderful Tante. She is extraordinary--and not only for her French torte and Lithuanian cherries.

I am glad Osya has found a job. Regards to the Pomerantzes. Now I must write Milner not to be angry with me. The story of the *tchemodones* has come to an end and we are sending out your package by air mail next week. With much love--

Yitzhak.

Highland Park, December 1, 1971

To our dear good friend Milner who has just recently arrived from Vilnius and whom we met in Vilnius the first week of this August:

We have just learned the good news of your arrival in Israel and that you have already found your place there. May you have much luck and good health in your new home. My cousin Fanny Taraseiskaya has already written me the good news. As I understand her, I must send you the money that you were good enough to lend her in Vilnius. Please be good enough to write me all the details. Please send me your address, your full name, and everything else that I must do from my side here. Please forgive my hasty letter, but I want you to know as quickly as possible that you must not worry about our side of the bargain. Please write us soon about my family, about what I must do from here, and all about your journey. Please write us everything. My wife and I send you our kindliest good wishes.

Irving Abrahamson

Highland Park, December 11, 1971

Dear friend Milner:

The 2,000 dollars that we had to send you have been sent. The money is at the Bank Leumi Le-Israel in Jerusalem. We thank you from the bottom of our heart for all you have done for us. And we hope all the best for you in your new life.

If you know anything else we can do to rescue my family, be so good as to write us as soon as possible. We have great love for my Tante and my cousin and their family, and we must help them. You, above all, understand. Be well, and once again a thank-you.

Yitzhak Abrahamson

Highland Park, December 11, 1971

My dear Tante,

Last night I saw you (and Fanya, Osya, and the children) in the films we showed our friends. They saw how you laugh and run. And Fanny ran after the chickens once again. Wonderful.

Wonder of wonders, our weather is still warm. A bigger and better wonder is what we hear in our newspapers--that your government is allowing out more families to be reunited with their families in Israel. It troubles us that they are still blocking your reunion with your husband. We hope your situation will improve, Tante.

We have had a letter from friend Milner. He has been reunited with his brother. We have already sent him a Mazel Tov--and a kiss on each cheek, but, of course, from a distance.

Well, Tante, now I wait for a letter from you! Why are you so lazy! I am a nephew after all, and you must not forget me. Greet everyone for me.

Yitzhak

Israel, December 20, 1971

Dear friend Abramson!

I Milner's brother-in-law am writing this letter [for Milner], the same who met you in Vilna:

Your letter arrived. We thank you very much! We have already received the money. *Alles in ordenung*--everything is in order. It is only three days that I am with my family in the land. I send you heartfelt greetings from your cousin and her family. I hope that they will be able to come soon. I did all I could to help them. That is why I am sure they will come.

The brothers Milner send you heartfelt regards.

Arkady Gurevitz

Western Union Telegram

Sent from Vilnius
To Irving Abrahamson
December 22, 1971. 8:30 AM

THEY PERMIT US GO TO ISRAEL BEST WISHES TO YOUR BIRTHDAY. FANNY

149

Vilna, December 26, 1971

Dear children, Itzik and Perele,

We received your last letter of 11 December. Also your beautiful package. The sizes fit, and everything shows Perele's good taste. I have never yet had such a beautiful wool suit. Again many thanks.

I believe you have received a telegram that we have been given permission to go to Israel. We will send another telegram when we leave. You no longer have to write at this address. We will send the telegram when we already have our tickets. It is very difficult to get tickets, but we will get them, don't worry. We have already packed everything. I am writing this letter standing on a packed carton. The tickets have been ordered for the 10th or 12th of January. Everything is with your help....

Dear Itzale, you wrote that I am lazy to write. For you that can never be. But that I am lazy--certainly not. I am from your father's family, after all, you should know.

We love you all very much. Also Perele, with her two beautiful daughters. I hope to be at your eldest daughter's wedding. Time moves on. It can still be. Warmest regards, Perele, for your parents, and Fima thanks you extra for the beautiful clothes for Irina. Itzale, give our regards to Feivel and his family, they should be well. I beg his pardon for not answering his letter. My head has been in such a whirl. I believe you will certainly understand that moving is quite a heavy piece of work. Once again, from me, your French Tante who bakes napoleon tortes.

Dear Yitzhak, Perele, and children!

I thank you many times for the beautiful package you sent. I hope we shall soon see each other. We are all very fortunate that we shall soon be reunited with all our own. We hope to be in Vienna January 14. The Pomerantzes send you their regards. They are deeply moved by our leaving, while they meanwhile remain behind. Well, my dear ones, I will soon write a long letter from there. I thank you again for all you have done for us. Our best regards to Feivel and his family. I kiss you thousands of times and wish you the best.

Your Fanya

Vilnius, December 30, 1971
[Card, in English]

Dear Friends!

We congratulate you with the New Year!

We wish a Happy New Year, a lot of health and happiness.

Thank you for the presents sent for the girls.

Pomerantz

[PS, in Yiddish] I hope you understood all that I wrote in English. At the moment I cannot do better. We will be thankful for your letters.

Yikhes

In the Old Country social standing among Jews was ultimately a matter of *yikhes*. If you had *yikhes*, it meant you had status in the community. In fact, *yikhes was* status, the highest rung of it. In those days *yikhes* was a matter of family descent, of belonging to a line of learned men. If your father was a rabbi, a teacher, or a scholar, and his father before him, and generations further back, then you had *yikhes*. You didn't necessarily merit it. You inherited it. It simply adhered to you because your ancestors had acquired it. Wealth did not confer it. There was only one way a wealthy man could acquire it: he could not buy it, but if he wanted it badly enough, as he often did, he could buy into it. He would seek out a young man who had *yikhes* as a match for his daughter. It didn't matter how poor he might be. What mattered was that he came from a line of rabbis, teachers, and scholars--and was on the same track himself.

In the New World--in America--the meaning of *yikhes* has gradually given way before new times, new ways, new values. Wealth itself has taken over completely and replaced learning and knowledge as the basis for *yikhes*.

151

In Vilnius, however, Di Tante acquired a special *yikhes* all her own. "What can happen in only five days!" she said. Its source was neither learning nor wealth. Suddenly she had something that hardly anyone in her circle had. For so long a have-not among have-nots, at one stroke she found herself transformed into a "have." Where she had been an equal among equals she found herself lifted above her equals. For decades she had desired *meshpokhe* above all. She who had irretrievably lost *meshpokhe*, she who had been cut off from *meshpokhe*, suddenly had *meshpokhe*. The impossible had occurred. The improbable had happened to her. A miracle.

Di Tante and her daughter had survived the war and the Holocaust. Like all those in her circle who had endured those years, she had suffered bitter losses. She had salvaged something from life, but like her contemporaries in Vilnius, every day she lived a life without the *familye* that might have been. Could a day ever have passed without a thought about what had happened to what might have been? Now, without warning, she had become different from the others. She who had lost everything now possessed something the others could not match, had no possibility any longer of matching unless they still had an old uncle or a distant aunt or a cousin somewhere in the world outside the USSR. She had acquired something no one else she knew could any longer imagine.

We had materialized out of nowhere, and our appearance had given her distinction, a special status--*yikhes*. It did not matter that she had acquired it through none of her own doing--all that mattered was that she had it. And she held her head a little higher and walked all the taller for it. "Do you know, Itzale," she wrote, "the guests who met you at dinner with us telephoned me and said they had the best impression of you and Perele and that I could be proud of you. And I can write you that I am so proud that no one can compare himself to me."

If she boasted of what had befallen her, she did so only in the privacy of her letters, nor did she identify her feeling as *yikhes*. It was not in her gentle heart to exploit it in public. Nor would she have begrudged anyone else her same distinction. If she knew its joy, what she knew even more was the bittersweet taste of that joy. taste that only the twentieth century could have afforded her.

Gerus

Though many of these letters were written in Highland Park or Vilna during the early Seventies, I already have to call them "pre-modern." They do not belong to the age of television, computers, e-mail, and voice mail. As the twentieth century fades into the twenty-first, their subject matter and the language that shapes it, their context and its implications have been overtaken by the modern world. Outshouted, too. To translate them from their pre-modern world into the modern one is more than a problem of turning their Yiddish into English.

Take the word *gerus*, for example. Some Jews say *grus*. Kovner Litvaks say *gerus*. Either way it is the Yiddish word for "regards" or "a greeting." *Optzugeben ah gerus* means to give regards or to transmit a greeting to a third person; it is a mission, a responsibility. The *gerus*, or the request to hand one on, is a fixture in all the letters. Though at first glance it appears to be an innocent convention, a formality easily taken for granted, in these letters it is a lifeline.

Undreamed of, unheralded, our appearance in Vilnius was a shock to Di Tante, Fanny, and the family. Our arrival, literally out of thin air, also caused an immediate sensation among their friends. Such an event simply did not happen in the real world, let alone in the Soviet Union. Di Tante, Fanny, and the family suddenly became the center of attention in their circle, and when Fanny invited some of her friends--her *chaveyrim*--to meet us, we instantly became a source of curiosity, wonder, and speculation.

Even more, we represented a link to the outside world for them too. When, soon after our return from our first trip, Di Tante writes, "My dear ones, regards from the family Pomerantz. If you had been here five more days, more would be sending you regards but, after all, there were only five days," she herself becomes a link in the lifeline.

And when, in return, I commission her to give a *gerus* "to the Pomerantzes and their children....And the Marcuses. And to Fanya's tall blond friend Jana and her husband Max," she is unfailing in her role, for more letters follow and more regards--to and from the Marcuses, the Pomerantzes, Jana and Max.

In 1971, after returning from our second trip, I know how every *gerus* we send will have an impact and blossom into a topic for conversation, discussion, analysis. I know how a *gerus* can turn into a shared connection, offer a touch of hope, perhaps warm a heart. Esther Feigenbaum writes us, "You cannot at all imagine how thankful we are for your regards from my brothers." In the fall Dr. Pomerantz sends us greetings for the Jewish New Year. Wistfully, he writes, "We hope that we shall yet meet again by us, by you, or in some other place, it is not important."

But it is important. All important. For Dembovitz, Taraseisky, Pomerantz, Marcus, Jana, Max, and their friends. Unforgotten in the shadows behind every *gerus* to us is the history of twenty-five years of life lived behind the Iron Curtain. Twenty-five years of history under the iron fist. Twenty-five years marked by outright murder of the leaders of the Jewish community and by relentless, virulent anti-Zionist--anti-Jewish--propaganda spread by radio, newspapers, books, and television. Marked, too, by the steady undercurrent of ordinary anti-Semitism at school, on the job, in the street. Twenty-five years of discrimination, alienation, isolation. Twenty-five years under the eyes of the secret police, the censor, the informer. Behind every *gerus* we exchanged lay the sense that maybe there was hope, after all, of breaking through the Curtain.

It is important because Fanny and her circle were well aware of the growing movement for emigration to Israel. They knew of the protests by Jewish activists, of their demonstrations, petitions, and open letters to government officials in Moscow. They knew of protests and demonstrations in America and other countries. They also knew of KGB threats, court trials, and jail sentences. In 1970, during our first visit, we met those who were certain they wanted to leave for Israel despite the doubts and rumors and fears that swirled around them. We knew some who were ambivalent. We knew some who remained silent. We felt the strains and tension in the air. But we felt the excitement too in those who saw a chance of getting through the Curtain.

In 1970 only 999 Jews left the Soviet Union for Israel.[1]   When we came to the family that year to offer our help we saw that though Fanny and Osya were not emigration activists, they were committed to Israel. They had Di Tante and her age to consider. They had Fima and his family to consider. They had the problem of a new language to consider. They had a new life to consider. And they knew the reprisals they faced when they would present their request to leave. They would lose their jobs. They would be denounced as "traitors" to their coworkers and to the country. And they could be refused.

In 1971 the family joined the ranks of the refuseniks. Twice they applied for permission to emigrate, and twice they were denied. Their third request was granted at the end of the year.   Di Tante, Fanny, Osya, Fima, Bella, and Irina left the Soviet Union for Israel in the first few days of January, 1972. They were among the very first of the 31,652 Russian Jews who left for Israel that year. They became part of the first wave of Jewish emigration to Israel from the Soviet Union in a decade that would see 160,561 Jews arrive there.

In her last letter before her departure from Vilnius Fanny writes, "The Pomerantzes send you their regards," but adds, "They are deeply moved by our leaving, while they remain behind." Four days later, on December 30, at the very end of 1971, Dr. Pomerantz writes us his New Year's greeting. The Yiddish postscript to his *gerus* reads: "We will be thankful for your letters."

One day during our first trip to Vilnius I squeezed into Di Tante's tiny kitchen while she was performing her magic for our Sunday dinner. I said, "Tante, do you have anything left from my father? Did you save any letters? Anything?" She eyed me curiously. She must have heard the wishful note in my voice. She wiped her hands on a dish towel and, without a word, disappeared into her room. A minute

155

later, she returned with a letter my father had written her. She handed it to me. "*Na*, here--," she said, and turned me out of her kitchen.

Osya was playing old-time recordings of Jewish folk songs. I held the letter in my hand, saw the familiar handwriting, noted the date: December 30, 1958. I read and re-read it. I could hear my father's words. I knew Di Tante would not part with her letter, so I sat down to copy it. The translation could wait. As I was writing, Fima entered with a basket of mushrooms he had just picked for our dinner.

As my father comes to the end of his letter he tells his sister to convey more than one *gerus* for him. One, to Shayndel Chaya's: "If you should see her, greet her for me." A second: "to your daughter and her husband." And a third: to "all those you see." Back then in Vilnius I had no idea who Shayndel Chaya was. I understood his second *gerus* referred to Fanny and Osya, but not what he meant by "all those you see." But Di Tante understood.

Years later, when I began translating these letters, I learned about Shayndel Chaya. Only then did I realize that a letter Di Tante sent shortly afterward carried a response to his third *gerus*, so well meant, so ultimately completely hopeless. "About your telling me to give your regards to the Kovner that live in Vilna, to my sorrow, I must answer you that not a single one is left. All were killed. No one is left."

Di Tante's words strike a hammer blow. They are stark, crushing, unalterable. When I hear them, I can think only of my father. I cannot imagine what he thought. But Di Tante's words could only have been a bitter, mind-numbing pain added to all his own silent suffering.

In 1970 and 1971 every *gerus* we sent carried a message of hope to its destination. In 1958, long out of touch with his sister, my father sent his *gerus* to his *landslayt*--to his countrymen, friends of his youth--in gentle hope. Only to learn of its immeasurable futility.

As much as anything else in these letters, the *gerus* is their truth.

156

The Game

Di Tante, Fanya, and I decided to bring my father back to life.

In 1970 the Soviet Union permitted emigration only on the basis of "the reunification of families." An applicant for emigration to Israel had to have an "invitation" from an immediate family member living there. Without such a relative he was simply out of luck. Di Tante, Fanny, and the family no longer had any immediate family members living anywhere. We had only one choice: to circumvent Soviet law. Eleven years after his death we brought my father back to life. He first appears in our letters in January, 1971.

Di Tante begins to play the game--by complaining to me that her brother Henoch has not answered the latest letter she has sent him. Mindful of officials who might examine our letters, Di Tante keeps her remarks about him natural and innocent. Her comment is no more important than her news about the celebration of Fanya's thirtieth wedding anniversary or her desire to send me *hamentaschen* for Purim.

By mid-March Fanya writes me openly about their goal. "Great changes," she says, "are taking place in our land. Many Jewish families are leaving. I am sure you read the newspapers. Your little sister has a great desire to go."

Early in April I send Di Tante a Pesach *gerus* from my father, and I caution her not to faint if she hears from him firsthand. Yes, I tell her, her brother Henoch might be lazy, but I add, "*Er iz ah guter mensh*-- he is a good human being, and he hopes only the best for you and the whole family." Late in April, continuing the game, I write Fanny, "We have not heard from Henoch, but we are not worried about him. If we get news of him, we shall write. As long as he is well." By the end of April Di Tante is playing the game with as much relish and skill as Fanny or I. "I learned with great joy that my dear brother lives in Israel. We will be happy to receive a letter from him from Israel. I will try not to faint from surprise. That he is very good, I already know from my younger years. He is the best of all my brothers....I shall wait impatiently for his letters, but better late than never...."

By May the pace of events in the USSR begins to quicken. Fanny writes, "There is plenty to worry about. Many are leaving us. They are going to Israel. The Marcuses have also left already. And we are also considering this. I understand that Henoch is in Israel....I believe he is there and that we will soon meet. Imagine what a joy this will be." Early in June I promise her that I will see Henoch and the Marcuses in Israel before we come on our second trip to Vilna.

Then, suddenly, late in June, everything changes. It is Di Tante's husband who has returned from the dead! "There is news," Fanny writes. "We have received the required papers from my father, who has been found after so many years. He lived in Africa and did not know of us. Now he lives in Israel and has found us and wants to be reunited with us. We are doing everything to be reunited with him and at the same time be close to you. This is our latest news. Dear Yitzhak, if only you knew how we long for all of you!....We are all well and live with only one thought." Fanya has discovered a distant cousin or uncle in Israel! He is a legitimate Dembovitz, a "Chaim Dembovitz" namesake who has sent letters and the required invitation to Di Tante and her family.

The game was over. Back and forth we had played it. We had speculated about my father's whereabouts, his health, his laziness, and his other character flaws, all the while knowing the stakes were high, all the while feeling the pure irony, the gentle bittersweet humor of our every word about him as father, as brother, as uncle. As long as the game continued, I took special private pleasure at the thought that at last--in his own quiet way--my father would have the opportunity to outmaneuver the communists he hated so much. I enjoyed imagining the whole scenario: how he would rescue from the Commissar the sister he had tried to rescue from the Tsar. It would have been a real triumph--and a delicious joke--if we had pulled it off.

But the game we played was not wasted. We put the skill we developed in playing it to good use when the time came to employ our code.

Khokhma

In the autumn of 1971 Dr. Pomerantz writes from Vilnius, "Fanya and the Tante tell us of the clever letters they receive. We often laugh heartily at your *khokhmas.*"

In literature as in life the Litvak has come in for a good bit of criticism--half humorous, half serious. In his famous short story "If Not Higher" Isaac Leib Peretz asks, "And who, I ask you, is going to argue with a Litvak?" In *The Great Fair* Sholom Aleichem remarks of one of his characters that his "genius lay in contradiction. Whatever you said to him, he contradicted--a true Litvak." When Prime Minister Yitzhak Shamir was called upon to explain the resignation of Moshe Arens from his cabinet post, he said, "He is stubborn. He is a Litvak. They are all stubborn." The Litvak's skepticism, his distrust of emotion, his literalism--the list of his character flaws is not short. Understandably, I see these qualities as virtues rather than flaws. But no matter.

What does matter, what cannot be denied, however, is the Litvak's instinct, his capacity, his affinity for *khokhma*, that happy combination of wit and wisdom that unerringly strikes the target. Wisdom without wit is not *khokhma*. Wit without wisdom is not likely. Genuine *khokhma*--and there is no *khokhma* that is not genuine--requires wit and wisdom, intelligence and a way with words. It is quick, clever, and fun. It delights the mind that creates it, and it delights the mind that recognizes it. It takes *khokhma* to create *khokhma*. It takes a certain measure of *khokhma* to perceive it.

If Dr. Pomerantz enjoys our *khokhmas*, it has to be, first of all, because he is aware of the game we are playing against the USSR. If he laughs, it is because he is aware of the enormous difference in the power of the opponents. When we saw him during the summer he could explain the situation of the Jews in Vilnius and the USSR in terms of its "meenooses" and "plooses," but he knows, as well as we do, that the situation is serious and growing increasingly urgent, even for him and his family. If his laughter is full and deep over the *khokhma* of the game we are playing, it has an edge to it, for he knows there is no *khokhma* in the game he is playing with the Soviet Union.

Di Tante says openly that we are dealing with "Haman's mind." Before they can emigrate, Di Tante, Fanny, and the family know they must overcome the two major obstacles Haman has placed in their way--they need his permission to go and they need the financial means to cross his border. Other uncertainties abound--political and domestic. Newspapers, radio, television relentlessly spread ominous anti-Zionist and anti-Jewish propaganda. Rumors. Fears. Every bit of news of demonstrations, protests, and petitions releases new doubts, new uncertainties: to remain...to wait...to go...to risk being left behind...to be cut off once again.... The only certainty, overriding everything else, is that freedom and the future are actually at stake. Each letter from Vilnius is a little episode of domestic life caught in the unfolding drama of yet another huge upheaval within Jewish history.

Early August. We are home only a few days. A letter from Di Tante. "I don't know how things would look without you. Now we have more hope than before." Then, without missing a beat, she remarks, "When I journey to my husband...." and resumes the game. Two weeks later, tucked away in a letter's end: "About the main news so far there is nothing. As it happens, we are very puzzled. Many families are unhappy. Who knows? We have to try to hope. As soon as there is something we will write."

Every letter I send her is a project somehow to keep up her morale or to lift her spirits. I am proud, I say to her, "that you do not even think of losing hope." Osya is fired from his job? I assure her "everything will turn out all right yet." I sing her praises: I admire her wisdom, I extol her courage, I tease her, cajole her, praise her beauty. Anything to elicit a smile, a laugh. She is too clever, by far, not to see through me. She refuses to succumb to my flattery. Always underlying the *khokhma* in our letters is the situation of the Jews and the mounting pressure on the family. They are one and the same.

November 1. Fanny writes, "By us several families have already received permission to go. Among the lucky ones is also Milner. He came and told us the news. He asked about you and asked us to give you his regards." Then she brings our simple code into play. It is the signal we have been waiting for. "We long so much for you. We are always together, and each time we send so many kisses--in our thoughts, that is--that when I add them up, they would surely come to two thousand. Today imagine if we were to kiss you so much at one time. Now do you understand how much we love you?"

December 1. I promise a Mazel Tov to Milner. "He has earned it. If I were to see him personally, I would kiss him on both cheeks." Then: "Since I cannot see him in person, I will send him my kisses through the mail."

December 11. I deposit two thousand dollars to his account in Bank Leumi Le-Israel in Jerusalem.

December 22. I receive a Western Union Telegram from Vilnius. "THEY PERMIT US GO TO ISRAEL BEST WISHES TO YOUR BIRTHDAY. FANNY"

December 26. Di Tante writes her last letter from Vilnius while she is "standing on a packed carton." And with a final touch of *khokhma* Fanny ends her own last note with "I kiss you thousands of times."

December 30. A Happy New Year card from Dr. Pomerantz. The last words we receive from Vilnius are his. "We will be thankful for your letters."

BEYOND THE IMAGINATION

First Witnesses

Bergen-Belsen was in a category all its own.

Bergen-Belsen began operation in April, 1943, as an internment camp, a holding camp for prisoners who were supposed to be exchanged for German nationals in Allied hands. In spring, 1944, it became a holding camp for the sick and otherwise unfit workers from labor camps in northern Germany. Hauptsturmfuhrer Josef Kramer, who came to be known as "the Beast of Belsen," took command of Bergen-Belsen in December, 1944. He immediately turned it into a concentration camp. It became a very different kind of holding camp. Never an "extermination camp" like Auschwitz-Birkenau or Treblinka or Sobibor--camps that produced death on a factory mass production basis--Bergen-Belsen nevertheless became a death lager. Deportation to Bergen-Belsen was tantamount to a death sentence.

In December, 1944, Bergen-Belsen held 15,000 prisoners. On April 15, 1945, when the British entered the camp, it held 60,000 inmates, survivors of death marches and evacuations from other camps threatened by the approach of the Russians. So many prisoners were dumped into the camp that the camp administration broke down completely. For all practical purposes chaos reigned. What the British found was a camp full of the dead, the walking dead, the dying, a camp in the death grip of starvation, tuberculosis, dysentery, and a typhus epidemic.

From January to mid-April, 1945, 35,000 died. In March alone 18,168 prisoners died, Anne Frank and her sister Margot among them. Freedom did not stop the dying. Fourteen thousand died in the first five days after the British took over. In the next few weeks 14,000 more died.

The soldiers of the 11th Armored Division of the British 2nd Army entered the camp at 3 p.m. on Sunday, April 15. The first war correspondents and photographers arrived the next day. All were stunned by what they found--piles of corpses everywhere, horror upon horror, 10,000 unburied dead. The battle-hardened reporters, men who thought they had seen it all, were shocked beyond measure. A half century later their impassioned words have lost none of their devastating power. Their initial visceral responses to what their eyes have seen are honest and pure. Incredibly, their reflections upon what they have witnessed announce the essential issues that ever since have haunted all serious consideration of the Holocaust.

The correspondents who came to Bergen-Belsen were the first to record what lay behind the barbed wire. They feared exactly what survivors were to fear later: that no one would believe their stories. Theirs were the first full, direct eyewitness reports of the concentration camp universe to reach the outside world. The words they were the first to burn into history lie on the page far beyond the reach of historians and theologians.

"S.S. Women Tied Dead To Living: Belsen Horror"
Special Correspondent R. W. Thompson in the *Sunday Times*, April 22, 1945

It is my duty to describe something beyond the imagination of mankind. I do not know how to begin except to say that I have been told that the women S.S. guards for their pleasure tied a live body to a dead body and burned them as a faggot while dancing and singing around the blaze.

It did not shock me because life and death had ceased to have meaning, because it is a fact that the living were dead.

In this terrible camp of Belsen, where thousands have been reduced to bestiality each month by a cold, systematic process and then reduced by the same process to the ultimate release of death, all normal standards change.

When for hours you gaze on the human body distorted beyond recognition, and come to the point when there is literally no difference between the living and the dead, you are beyond shocking because you are beyond human standards.

This Nazi concentration camp of Belsen is one of many. It is the expression of Adolf Hitler and Nazi Germany. It is a thing you read about and refused to believe in from 1933 onwards.

Now if the words of Christ are to mean anything, if all the aims of humanity are to be more than just idealistic clap-trap, you must read and you must believe.

We few who have had the opportunity to view this atrocity against mankind have the right to demand your attention.

There are, perhaps, three or four hundred of us, war correspondents perhaps 20, the rest soldiers, and our words, our honour must suffice that this terrible deed against the human spirit may be known to all the world.

The terrible work of clearing up the dead, of cleaning the fearful, stinking huts in which as many as 700 lost souls had their whole existence, is going ahead fast, but it has not been possible yet to keep pace with the dying.

The Nazi S.S. guards, both men and women, utterly without shame, are doing the work of collection of the corpses, riding with them on the trucks and piling them into the great burial pits.

The shock and horror of it all grows with each day. The extent of the Nazi crime slowly dawns on the mind, with all its fearful frighten[ing] implications. Sadism, brutality, rape and murder--all the usual crimes of humanity against humanity pale to insignificance beside this conception of the German mind.

You recognize this deliberate reduction of people to the level of the beasts and slowly to death as the destruction of the soul. The living and the dead lie often side by side and the only difference is the purely physical one of the still beating heart. Clothing is without meaning, for these bodies are no longer people. In a sense they are less offensive naked than in the grey-striped filthy rags that hang on them, serving only to accentuate the awful shame.

Soon now this fearful evidence will be destroyed. Now and then one pauses to wonder at the mentality of those who, coolly and without the remotest sense of shame, handed this colossal evidence of the complete corruption of their race to the world.

One would have thought that this, above all, would have been fought for until every last shred of evidence had been obliterated.

Kramer, the commandant, and his guards are actually proud of this camp. They do not see anything wrong about it. In fact, these Germans are without hope. They are not as other men. The thing is satanic.

Now, as the terrible filth of the living and the dead is cleared, and food and water and milk begin to nourish the starving bodies of the survivors, and the burying keeps pace with the rate of death, it is of the first importance that as many people as possible should visit Belsen before this horror is wiped from the face of the earth.

The threat of typhus must be eliminated at the earliest possible moment, and the fires burn ceaselessly, destroying the obscene litter of the shameful enclosures.

Tonight, at six, the 300 Wehrmacht guards were passed across the Elbe, in accordance with the terms of the military agreement. They went without seeing the horrors of the atrocity which they had guarded, and for which they and the whole German race share the guilt.

Under the headline "Burgomasters At Belsen Say 'We Didn't Know,'" Christopher Buckley, Special Correspondent for the *Daily Telegraph*, writes, "Ever since our armies began to penetrate into Germany, nearly three months ago, I have been trying to find some clue to the problem of the German people." He is upset by his inability to reconcile "the fiendish cruelties and inhuman callousness" in Bergen-Belsen and Buchenwald with "the manifest docility and what would appear to be the kindliness of the ordinary civilians in the Rhineland and Westphalia." Even if one grants that "the German people, collectively, are guilty of nothing more than ignorance and negligence," he acknowledges "...you are still faced by the fact that the German people, collectively, produced the men and the women in requisite numbers to maintain this system."

"Belsen," Buckley concludes, "is the nearest thing I know to a spectacle of absolute evil. I have visited many battlefields in this war and Belsen is incomparably, immeasurably more terrible a sight."

"Prison Camp Horrors Will Be Shown To Germans"
Harry J. Ditton, War Correspondent on Western Front, in the
Daily Telegraph and Morning Post, April 20, 1945

...In the interests of truth and justice, however, and in case there are still some at home who want to forgive the Germans, the stark story must be told, even though a lump comes into my throat and my heart seems to bleed as I picture, again and again, in my mind's eye, the diabolically revolting and shameful crimes the Germans have systematically practiced for five years.

Let me say at once that these are crimes which, in the name of all that is righteous, call for swift and merciless vengeance--vengeance that would be demanded by anyone seeing the acres of graves of men, women, and babies-- victims of German torture and murder--whose only crime was that they were not Germans or Nazis.

I do not want to make your flesh creep, but I confess that I still squirm and shudder as I seem to see again the piles upon piles of naked men and women not yet buried, but whom a merciful Providence had released from their agony and misery.

As I see again, too, the thousands upon thousands of half-crazed, diseased, and emaciated humans herded worse than cattle, whom the kindly hand of death will strike at any moment.

There are 50,000 bodies in the graves to which I have referred, buried in groups of 10, 30, 40, 50, and a hundred at a time, without any religious ceremony and without any cross to identify them.

Joseph Gar, Research Associate for the YIVO Institute for Jewish Research, writes, "...the German forestry administration in the

169

neighborhood of Bergen-Belsen prohibited the taking of timber from the woods for bonfires. Besides, the German military personnel in the vicinity objected to the strong odor of burned human flesh which reached their barracks. Then the bonfires were discontinued and the corpses were allowed to remain where they were piled up in large mounds near the barracks or even inside."[2]

Brigadier General H.L. Glyn Hughes, Senior Medical Officer of the British 2nd Army, and Captain Derrick Syngton were the first to enter Bergen-Belsen. In a dispatch headlined "The most terrible story of the war," Edwin Tetlow, Special Correspondent of the *Daily Mail*, quotes Hughes: "I am afraid you may think I am exaggerating, but I assure you I am not. It is the most horrible, frightful place I have ever seen."

Robert Daniell, a British tank commander, was among the first to enter Bergen-Belsen. He was a Lieutenant Colonel commanding the 13th Honorable Artillery Company of the 11th Armored Division. "What I saw in those two hours changed me for the rest of my life," he told the Associated Press in a 1992 interview. "Since then, I have not had any normal feelings about any German man or woman who was alive at that time. I hate them all."

Di Tante and Fanya entered Bergen-Belsen April 4th or 5th, 1945.

DISCOVERIES

A World Between

Kaunas...Vilnius...Lithuania...

A chance remark overheard. A dateline in my daily newspaper. The words are stop signs. They bring me up short--memories stir. The words turn my mind straight to my father. They take me back to where he "came from," to the course of his life and its meaning for me. Today I know Kaunas was once the Kovno my father came from, that Vilnius was once the Vilna that Jews everywhere knew as the *Yerushelaim d'Lita*--the Jerusalem of Lithuania. In my young time my parents and their friends spoke of Kovno, not Kaunas; of Vilna, never Vilnius. Back then I did not know my father's "Kovneh" was Kaunas, or that "Vilneh" was the same as Vilnius.

But of course Kovno is not the same as Kaunas, nor is Vilna the same as Vilnius. A whole world came between Kovno and Kaunas, between Vilna and Vilnius. History came between. A history in Lithuania of unimaginable destruction. The Lithuanian Jews, to their sorrow, could not imagine the unimaginable. Only the Germans could. And not only did the Germans imagine it: they created it. In Lithuania, together with their Lithuanian accomplices, they began the destruction of European Jewry. The twentieth century *Churbn*--the Third Destruction--is what came between.

The Kovno my father knew no longer exists. The Kovno Di Tante and Fanny knew no longer exists. When I ask my cousin Fanny if she would ever go back to Kovno just to see it again, she replies, "No. Never. I know every stone of Kovneh. I cannot go back. The heart hurts too much. I will never go back."

In search of Kovno--not only of my father's Kovno but his sister's--I have turned to diaries, memoirs, histories of the Holocaust, encyclopedias, to maps and indices, looking for word from another time, another country. No archeologist excavating some ancient dig and unearthing a gold coin or a clay tablet, a mosaic hunting scene or an exquisite bronze could be more thrilled than I when I hold a letter in my hand or turn a page in a book and discover a name, a date, a story that will help me pull together pieces of my own story and perhaps lead me to decipher whatever truth it might hold.

I am desperate for any scrap of information that will connect me to my father or his sister or his niece, for anything that will fill the blank spaces in their story. Many of those spaces remain blank. Still, I never know when I will come upon a clue and fill in a blank space. My expectations run high with Avraham Tory's *Surviving the Holocaust: The Kovno Ghetto Diary,* a gold mine about life in the ghetto, written by the secretary of the Kovno Ghetto Jewish Council. In it I discover Order No. 15, the decree of July 10, 1941, ordering the Jews of Kovno into the ghetto by August 15. Something makes me return to Order No. 15 and to stop at the eighth clause, which commands the Jews of Kovno to turn their radios "over to the housing department (at 9 Laisves Boulevard, third floor)" and warns them that they "will be severely punished" if they do not.

Laisves Aleya...Laisves Aleya.... And then I remember. I make the connection: Di Tante's invitation to Aharon's Bar Mitzvah! I retrieve her card. In the lower right-hand corner, in Yiddish, is the Dembovitz address: "Kaunas, Laisves Al. 11, Apartment 1." Laisves Aleya was where Di Tante and her family lived and worked! Only a few doors from number 9.

In *Light One Candle,* his memoir of the Kovno Ghetto, Solly Ganor brings Laisves Aleya alive for me again. Laisves Aleya is one of Ganor's first memories of Kovno. Fondly he recalls it as Kovno's "main street, a wide boulevard...divided by a broad pedestrian promenade, where tall chestnut trees grew in rows as far as...eyes could see. Modern buildings with elegant shops stood on both sides of the street." And when I wander among the photographs in Ehpraim Oshry's *Churbn Lite,* suddenly, there it is, a photo of Laisves Aleya, Kovno's main street, in which I can make out the chestnut trees down the center, a double row with a promenade aisle between them. And shops with awnings. And traffic and passersby.

In the darker ghetto days workers in the city brigades, those who were put to work inside Kovno itself, would be marched from the ghetto through the streets to their workplaces. Often they would use Laisves Aleya. An individual ghetto Jew entering Kovno on "official" business for the ghetto would also use Laisves Aleya. But on November 14, 1942, Tory records a "warning from the city governor," that "Jews are forbidden to walk along Laisves Boulevard in Kovno, either in groups or singly." "Freedom Boulevard" suddenly became off-limits to Jews.

My father never mentioned Laisves Aleya. When he spoke of Kovno, what he remembered was "Carmelita," the name of the neighborhood in Kovno where he grew up. "And there was a railroad station there," he said. I always liked the sound, just the sound, of the word Carmelita. In Martin Gilbert's edition of Tory's *Diary*, sure enough, I come upon a map of Kovno proper. There, clearly marked in the southeast, is my father's "Carmelita." And Kovno's main railway station is right there too, just as my father said. The railroad tracks from the station lead west to Konigsberg and east to Vilna. In my father's day, and even in his sister's time, before the war, the station was innocent enough.

Kovno's main railway station was also waiting for me in Rabbi Ephraim Oshry's *Churbn Lite*. I have no idea how that book found its way into my library, but it lay there dormant and unread for years--until the Nineties. Published in 1951, it is Oshry's harrowing account of "the destruction of the sacred Jewish communities of Lithuania, 1941-1945," forty-four of them. A chronicle of horrors and a martyrology, his book is difficult reading, made all the more painful by the Yiddish in which it is written. Oshry was himself one of the few who emerged alive from the total destruction of the Kovno Ghetto.

As Oshry tells it, the Kovno railroad station marked the beginning of the end of innocence for about 40,000 non-Lithuanian Jews, who were disembarked there. The first transports arrived there in early December, 1941, bringing Jews from Frankfurt, Vienna,

175

Berlin, Hamburg, Breslau, Prague, and other small towns in Austria and Germany. "When they arrived at the railroad station in Kovno," he writes, "the Jews saw that they had been deceived."[3] Instead of taking them into the Kovno Ghetto as they had promised, the SS marched them three or four kilometers up a hill directly to the Ninth Fort and their death. The Germans called the road *Der Weg zum Himmel-Fahrt*, "the Way to Heaven."

Thousands of Kovno Jews and thousands of "foreign" Jews took that road. Tante Dora and her husband Chaim, Fanny and her brother Aharon and her husband Osya did not. They survived in the ghetto until October, 1943, when they were transported to Estonia.

Postscript

Avraham Tory's *Surviving the Holocaust: The Kovno Ghetto Diary* was not published in English until 1990. Once I discovered the *Diary* and read its first pages I could see that the next five hundred would bring me closer to the Kovno Ghetto than anything I had previously read.

Nor did it disappoint. The *Diary*, which includes numerous official documents, is an eyewitness account of the ghetto between June 22, 1941, and January 9, 1944. Whether an entry is a single sentence or three pages long, a report of a personal experience or the text of a German decree, the *Diary* provides a dramatic record of life-- and death--in the ghetto, by a man profoundly committed to the Jewish people. Tory emerges from these pages as a man prepared to risk his life to testify to the fate of the ghetto.

If any figure aside from Tory dominates the *Diary*, it is that of Dr. Elkhanan Elkes, who was chairman of the *Aeltestenrat*--the Jewish Council--from the beginning of the ghetto until SS Capt. Wilhelm Goecke, following Heinrich Himmler's orders, turned it into a concentration camp. Dr. Elkes appears in about a hundred entries in the *Diary*. Tory vividly portrays the blood, terror, and agony of the ghetto, but perhaps the single most moving entry of all is Dr. Elkes's Last Testament,[4] a last letter, which Tory managed to bring out of the ghetto. The letter is dated October 19, 1943. Elkes addresses it to London for his son Joel and his daughter Sarah, both sent to England in 1938 to study medicine.

"We have now heard," he informs them, "that in a few days our fate is to be sealed. The Ghetto is to be crushed and torn asunder. Whether we are all to perish, or whether a few of us are to survive is in God's hands. We fear that only those capable of slave labor will live; the rest, probably, are sentenced to death." Thereafter for three pages, with the unflinching lucidity of a man who knows only the truth will, finally, do, Elkes recounts the deaths suffered by their immediate family, the great massacres that have cut Kovno's Jewish population by half, to 17,000, the slaughter of thousands of foreign Jews at the Ninth Fort, and the murder overall of 220,000 of Lithuania's quarter million Jews.

In the face of his own stark summation of German murderousness and the Lithuanian betrayal of the Jews, Elkes remains the Jewish father, concerned with the destiny of the Jews, with the meaning of being a Jew. "Joel, my beloved!" he writes. "Be a faithful son to your people. Take care of your nation, and do not worry about the Gentiles. During our long exile, they have not given us an eighth of an eighth of what we have given them." And he urges him, "Immerse yourself in this question, and return to it again and again."

Sent from the brink of death, Dr. Elkes's words bring him intensely to life. But as powerful and as memorable as they are, it is not Dr. Elkes's last letter that stuns me: it is his postscript to it. It is dated November 11, ten days or so after the ghetto has become a concentration camp. "Our share of misery is not over yet," he writes. "On the twenty-sixth of last month they took 2,709 people out of our Ghetto. According to information we have received, they separated the children and the elderly--they are probably dead by now. Those who were able to work were sent to Estonia to hard labor."

The words are like an electric shock. It is as though they have been lying in wait for me for five hundred pages. More than a half century after the fact, Dr. Elkes was giving me news of Di Tante, Fanny, and the family! News that they never gave me long ago in Vilnius--because they did not remember it or no longer remembered it clearly or simply because the tumult of our arrival gave them no time to look back into the past when the future itself had come calling upon them. Back then in Vilnius it was "old" news, more than a quarter of a century old, and in a way it no longer mattered to them--living it had been enough. But it did matter to me. Until I read the postscript, I knew only that the family had been sent from the ghetto to Estonia, to Vaivara. Now, from Dr. Elkes himself, I had discovered not only that they had been caught in the Estonian *Aktzie* but the exact date they had been deported, only a few days before the Germans transformed the ghetto into a concentration camp.

William Mishell, who knew the family, reports that Jewish police "accompanied by Germans" entered the ghetto on the twenty-sixth and rounded up as many as they could of those whose names appeared on the lists the Jewish Council had been forced to provide. Catching wind of the *Aktzie*, many Jews managed to go into hiding, and the Jewish police came up short of the 3,000 demanded by Goecke, the commandant of the ghetto--with the result that the Germans sent in Ukrainian and Lithuanian police to complete the Aktion. "Men, women, and children," writes Mishell, "were bloodied by the dozens. In the process furniture was destroyed, windows broken, and doors smashed. The picture was of a real pogrom, with people bleeding and falling to the ground and being kicked all over. At the ghetto gate they were loaded into trucks and taken away," taken, as it turned out, to Aleksotas "near the railroad station." [5]

There SS Hauptscharfuhrer Helmut Rauca held a *selektzieh*. The Germans sent the children, the weak, the elderly, the sick directly to their death in Auschwitz. They sent the others to Estonia. The Estonian *Aktzie* occurred two years almost to the day after Rauca had

178

directed the selection for the Great *Aktzie* at Democratu Square on October 28, 1941.

When I asked my cousin Fanny if she remembered the date of the Estonian *Aktzie*, she said she did not. When I told her the exact date, and how I had "looked it up," she was astonished--that I who had not been there knew it, while she who had been there did not.

"But I remember what happened," she said. "Der Papa had a job in one of the ghetto shops. The night before it happened, we were told that the next day there would be an *Aktzie*--but that his shop would not be touched. So, early the next morning we all went to the shop to hide there--Di Mameh, Der Papa, my brother, Osya, and I. And we waited. We thought we were safe there. And what happened? All of a sudden the police entered the ghetto and surrounded Der Papa's shop. They fired shots from the outside into the shop, and a bullet went through the wall right by Der Papa's head--it just missed his eyes he said. They broke into the shop and rounded us up. Then they took us outside and forced us into the lorries that were waiting for us. They drove us straight to the main railroad station, in Carmelita, and loaded us straight into cattle cars. The train started and went and went...I don't know how long or how far. But finally we came to Estonia, to Vaivara. There they separated the men from the women. Di Tante remained with me.

"They put us to work digging the ground. The earth was so hard you could not dig into it. But they made us do it anyhow. And for what? For nothing. There was no purpose to it except to torture us.

"I became a nurse in Vaivara. And when Di Mameh caught the typhus, I did whatever I could to take care of her. She lay on a wooden board--that was her bed--and I washed her and kept her clean. One day while she was sick I said to her, 'Mama, you will never guess who has come here to the camp. Would you like to know?' She guessed at once. 'Araleh,' she said. And I brought him to her--her dearest.

179

"She got over the disease. And they sent her away to another camp. They sent me to Kivioli."

Alex Faitelson, a member of AKO, the underground Anti-Fascist Fighting Unit in the Kovno Ghetto, is both memoirist and historian of the Kovno Ghetto, recording names, dates, places, events that might otherwise be lost to history. Listing his own losses in the Estonian Aktion, Faitelson states "my wife's family was also evacuated to Estonia, my sister and her family, Eliezer Zilber's mother and young brother..." and, suddenly, in the same breath, he adds, "and Ovsei Taraseiski, one of the leaders of 'Zorg' (Self Defense). Taraseiski was a Revisionist who had studied for a time at a naval academy in Civitavecchia, Italy, to which he had been sent by the Betar youth movement." And by way of further explanation, Faitelslon quotes from Meishe Milner's *Beyond the Life Line--Memoirs* (Tel Aviv, 1981): "Zorg was an illegal group, which came into existence in the ghetto in November, 1941, under the leadership of Meishe Milner, Shleime Brauer, and Ovsei Taraseiski. They joined AKO in January, 1943."[6]

Home in Highland Park on a golden October day fifty-six years later I stare out the window, then back at the names--Eliezer, Shleime, Meishe, and I can't help but think back to the Old West Side of Chicago where, as a high schooler, I heard names like "Sam" and "Davy" and "Morrie" in the study hall, on the streets, in the gym. Only, while my classmates were playing basketball or baseball, Shleime and Meishe and Chaim were playing for their lives in the ghetto. And Ovsei.

He was Fanny's husband. When I first met him in 1970 in Vilnius, I came to know him as Osya or Ossie. I remember his telling me how he had once dreamed of becoming a naval officer. And how he had belonged to a small underground cell that had had to choose between fighting to defend the ghetto from within or fighting the Germans by supporting the partisans outside the ghetto. How proud he was to show me the recognition he had won in the book he owned on the history of the partisans in the Kovno Ghetto!

180

My discovery of Ossie's name: it was another postscript to the Estonian *Aktzie*, which had ensnared them all.

Slobothkeh

*"Nem zich ahrop ah Mu*sar" is what my mother would say, only she said *"Musser,"* not *"Musar."* I was only six or seven when I must first have heard her utter these words. I never stopped hearing them. She always seemed to have them ready for me. I still hear them. Back then I had no idea what *"Musser"* actually was. All I knew, in a general way, was that she was telling me to take notice of someone's right action, of a good deed performed, from which, it was clear, I was to take an example. Back then I did not know that *"musar"* was the Hebrew word for "morality." All I knew was that *"Musser"* was just another Yiddish word whose meaning I sensed and took for granted, a word I understood without being able to define it.

A half century and more would go by until I learned something about *"Musar."*

When my mother spoke these words I knew she intended them to be part warning, part advice, part instruction. I knew that they were an injunction already meant to guide me in the right direction in the life toward which I was growing. I had no idea that Musar was a Jewish religious movement or that its mission was to teach ethics and morality to yeshiva students. Nor did I know that the Slobotkeh Yeshiva was one of the major centers of the movement or that in its time Musar--in terms of Jewish thought and belief--had made Slobotkeh one of the most pious places on earth.

During my childhood Slobotkeh didn't exist. It couldn't exist, not with a name like that. "What kind of a name is Slobotkeh? There's no such place," we teased our parents. Slobotkeh was just one more mythical name of a mythical city in a mythical Europe that existed only in my imagination, only as a word. My brother and I pronounced the word "Slobotkeh," just the way our parents and their friends did. Only decades later did I learn that the maps and the encyclopedia spelled it "Slobodka."

But now, more than half a century after the war, I have learned about Slobotkeh.

I have learned what I never knew, not even after having twice visited Lithuania. Slobotkeh--the Lithuanians called it Vilijampole--was a suburb of Kovno. It lay on the other side of the river Neris (the Vilija River), just across from Kovno proper, and was connected to Kovno by the Vilijampole Bridge.

Hitler's armies attacked the USSR on June 22, 1941. The Germans took Kovno on the 24th. The Soviets, who had occupied Lithuania since the previous June, abandoned Kovno a day later. On the 25th and 26th Lithuanian "partisans," who were already killing Jews throughout Lithuania, entered Slobotkeh--the home of Musar. According to German statistics, the Lithuanians killed 1,500 Jews during the first night's rampage and 2,300 more in the next two days. Ironically, it was the Germans who "restored order," disbanding the Lithuanian irregular forces two days later. But the Lithuanian partisans and their local accomplices in Kovno nonetheless retain the distinction of being the first to put the Final Solution in motion. Even as Lithuania itself has the distinction of becoming the first great killing ground of the Holocaust.

Mostly the victims were the very pious--the yeshiva students and their teachers--and the very poor. "Very few remained. How much they went through there...," my cousin Fanya said, her words thirty years after the event still touched by the horrifying savagery of the Slobotkeh pogrom, still full of its pity, sorrow, and pain.

Di Tante, her husband Chaim, Aharon, Fanny, and Osya were behind the barbed wire of the Kovno Ghetto from the very beginning. But not until I began to read about the Kovno Ghetto did I learn that

182

what I and everyone I knew had all along called the Kovno Ghetto was not in Kovno at all but in Slobotkeh.

The Handwriting on the Wall

Kadushin was his name--Zvi Hirsh Kadushin. After the war he took the name George Kadish. I never met him. But because of what he did and how he did it I know something of him. What he did was to take about a thousand photos in the Kovno Ghetto. He took the photos secretly, risking his life with every snap of the shutter. They are the best photographic record of life in the Kovno Ghetto--and probably the best photographic record of any ghetto. He hid his prints and negatives in milk cans that he buried under his house, and he managed to retrieve them after the war. All the photos that appear in Avraham Tory's *Diary* are his, as are many of those in *Hidden History of the Kovno Ghetto*.

Though I never met him, I did see him--as George Kadish--in a documentary film about the Kovno Ghetto.[7] Though he died in August, 1997, you can see him there in his studio, surrounded by walls covered with his photos, his life's work. He is white-haired, wears an open-collared white shirt. He is a Lithuanian Jew, whose English is still colored by his Yiddish syntax and accent. "I took over a thousand photos, but not all of them were exactly to my subject and not every take was perfect. Film I used to bring in from the city, from outside the ghetto. A lot of film I used to steal from the x-ray nurses--they used to have Leica film. And I went on taking those pictures," he says, "for later--for eternity."

At an exhibit of his Kovno Ghetto photographs at the United States Holocaust Memorial Museum he recalled the Slobodka pogrom: "I remember on the very first day of the killings I heard shooting and yelling in my neighbor's house. After this noise stopped, I decided to go see what had happened. When I opened the front door, I found my neighbor's two children and my neighbor's wife on the floor shot to death. I ran to the kitchen to escape through a rear door and I found my neighbor lying in a puddle of blood. His right arm and pointing finger were outstretched toward the white wall. On the wall, before he died, he had written in his blood two words... '*Yidn Nekomah!*' I ran back to my apartment, I grabbed my camera and went back to my neighbor's house to record this terrible scene." Kadushin took those words written in blood as a "sacred order" placed upon him "by the millions of my people who were killed and exterminated for their beliefs." From that moment on, he said, "I continued to secretly take photos inside and outside the Ghetto." Thereafter he saw his photos "as a kind of revenge directed at the Nazis, the murderers of my people." [8]

That first photo of his still screams loudest for later, for eternity. It pictures nothing more than an empty wall and two words. The words are in Yiddish. "*Yidn Nekomah!*--Jews, Revenge!" The words are not a statement. They are an exclamation, a demand, an imperative, a command. Their message is unmistakable to anyone within earshot. The words leap from the wall and will not be denied.

Kadushin photographed the deportations to Estonia in October, 1943. Afterward, he escaped the ghetto and its liquidation, but returned to it immediately after the Russians liberated Kovno, on August 1, 1944. "I had to go to the ghetto to see, to visit or revisit it with my camera....When I came over, I saw a terrible, terrible non-liberation scene--hundreds of dead people, charcoaled people, burned-to-death people."

"*Yidn Nekomah!*" Once you hear the words, you cannot silence them or put them out of your mind. Nor can you erase them from the wall.

The Garage

The frightened eyes below his cap, the bare knees below his overcoat, his knee socks, the   little boy with his hands upraised while a German soldier, rifle in hand, stands behind his captive.... The German rifleman caught at the very moment he fires at the woman fleeing before him, as she clutches her baby to herself.... Once you have seen these photos you can't forget them. They harrow the mind. You don't have to see them again because they remain imprinted there on your mind. They are more than evidence of the Holocaust. Like thousands of other photographs, they survive to tell stories that suggest the essence of the Holocaust.

For me the sheer brutality of the Holocaust lies in the photo that is stark witness to the massacre at the Lietukis garage. The photo is not especially well-known, though it appears occasionally in a textbook or in an encyclopedia. But each time I encounter it directly, the image on the page reimposes its horror on the image already in my mind. Each time the heart chills down again to absolute zero, down not only to the ineradicable existence of pure evil but to its triumph.

The picture is not hard-edged. But the facts are visible despite the darkness that shrouds the scene. Two of the killers stand out in their white shirtsleeves in the center foreground. They are in the midst of their work. One is in motion. He stands over his victim and has just swung his iron bar or is about to deliver yet another blow with it, a final one. The second, also in civilian clothes, his shirtsleeves rolled-up the more comfortably to go about his work, also stands above his fallen victim. The bodies of Jews lie crumpled everywhere on the floor. A third killer stands further back at the left edge of the photo, club in hand, his cap still perfectly in place. He looks stonily at his handiwork on the floor. Only one Jew lifts his head from the floor--but it is no use: he is a dead man. In the background spectators in uniform stand around viewing the scene with professional interest. Among them there appears to be another civilian killer, also in a white shirt. Most horrifying of all is what has gone on, or is still going on, beyond its edges: more killers, more bodies, more uniformed witnesses. How does one fathom the mind of the Lithuanian slaughterer--or the mind of the German onlooker? Or that of the photographer?

Reprinting the photo, but not identifying it, the *Encyclopedia of the Holocaust* explains, "When the Germans occupied Kovno on June 24, 1941, they saw bands of Lithuanians seizing Jews in the streets and beating them to death. Here, Lithuanians beat Jews while German soldiers watch." Avraham Tory, diarist of the Kovno ghetto, writes that 52 Jews were mercilessly tortured and murdered at the Lietukis garage on June 27. That day came to be known as "Bloody Friday." The killers on the photo are Lithuanians, either ordinary civilians or members of "partisan" bands, who took matters into their own hands all over Lithuania almost immediately after Germany attacked the USSR on June 22. The Germans had no difficulty finding accomplices in Lithuania. They had no difficulty recruiting accomplices almost everywhere they went.

The cold, glaring contrast between the vicious fury of the killers as they go about their work and the steady interest of the spectators captures the relentless, implacable, profound hatred toward the Jews that lies at the heart of the Holocaust. The Holocaust was a frenzy of killing: the killing of Jews. It was a single-minded manhunt designed to run down and execute every last Jew, first in Europe, then in the world.

Hitler's design and its incredible success raise many questions. We know where the Holocaust happened. We know when it happened. We know to whom it happened. We know how it happened. Scholars have explored and documented these matters at great length. The bibliography on the Holocaust is immense. But *why* it happened is a question that gets short shrift.

The question of the *why* of the war against the Jews forces us to raise related questions. Why was this war so successful in almost every country in Europe? How are we to account for the near universality of it? Why the brutality, the fury of it? Why the overriding singleness of the target? Why the near totality of it? If Hitler and his totalitarian accomplices were responsible for sins of commission, how are we to account for the sins of omission of the democratic West, its near abandonment of the Jews during the war? How do we account for the silence of the USSR toward the Jewish victims on its soil--during and after the war?

What, after all, was the underlying "Jewish problem" for the Germans? What, after all, was the "Jewish question" for the Germans? What did it ask? Why was there a Jewish problem at all? Who created it? The Jews? How did they create it? When? Where? For whom? Only for the Germans? What about the Austrians, the Rumanians, the Hungarians, the Poles, the Russians? And the English, the Americans, the French? Why did it necessitate a Final Solution? What were the previous solutions? Why did they not suffice? Why were they inadequate?

The question remains: *why* the Holocaust?

Why do museums and monuments, scholars and the lay public generally ignore this most fundamental of all questions?

Why did my first encounter with the photo of the massacre at the Lietukis garage on Vytautus Boulevard strike home? Why has my every encounter with it since then done the same? Di Tante and her family were living in Kovno on that day.

Aktionen

The Germans sealed the ghetto on August 15, 1941.

Three days later they held what came to be known as the "Intellectuals Aktion." The German aim was to cut down the potential leaders of any resistance. SA Captain Fritz Jordan ordered the *Aeltestenrat* to recruit 500 men from "the educated classes" to report at the ghetto gate for white collar work in the Kovno city archives. The prospect of a good job in the city drew over 300 teachers, lawyers, accountants, and other professionals to the ghetto gate. Gestapo Master Sergeant Helmut Rauca ordered Lithuanian partisans to round up enough men from the streets to fill the quota. Eventually 534 men marched through the gate--never to return. According to Joseph Gar, William Mishell, and other historians of the ghetto, they were executed at the Fourth Fort.

On September 15, Captain Jordan brought 5,000 special certificates to the *Aeltestenrat* and ordered the Council to distribute them to essential skilled workers. These work passes were supposed to be life passes, a promise to exempt the bearer from any roundup, any selection, any Aktion he might be caught in. Two days later the Germans held a selection and exempted those with the passes. Then, after they had assembled the others to begin the march of death to the Ninth Fort, they suddenly, without explanation, aborted the Aktion. On September 26, however, the Germans turned a false accusation into a genuine Aktion. This time, claiming some Jews had attempted to assassinate a German officer, they sent a thousand Jews--those without Jordan Passes--directly to their death at the Ninth Fort.

A week later, on October 4, they struck again. They locked doctors, nurses, and patients inside the infectious diseases hospital in the Small Ghetto, then burned it down. Exempting almost all who held the passes, they selected over 1,800 others from among the Jews held in the Small Ghetto and executed them at the Ninth Fort. They transferred the remaining Jews to the Large Ghetto and closed down the Small Ghetto.

Two years elapsed between the Great Aktion that took place October 28/29, 1941, and the next major Aktion, the Estonian Aktion of October 26, 1943, when Di Tante and her family were deported. Some historians of the ghetto claim these two years were a "quiet" period.

The Germans clearly won the war against the Jews of Kovno in the major Aktions on the execution grounds at the forts outside the ghetto. Just as clearly they also won the psychological war they waged against the Jews inside the ghetto.

The Germans were masters of relentless ongoing psychological warfare. The agony for the 534 victims of the Intelligentsia Aktion ended at the Fourth Fort. The Germans did not reveal their fate. The agony of those waiting for the return of the 534 continued day after hopeless day--a torment that would end only when they themselves met their own fate.

Nor could the Germans have designed a more fiendishly ingenious instrument of bloodless mental torture than the Jordan Pass. It offered hope to those who acquired one but immediately sowed fear and panic among those who did not. The cancelled Aktion--it bore all the signs of a mock Aktion--could only have aroused feelings of relief and hope in those who were "saved," feelings the Germans must have known they would crush little more than a week later at the Ninth Fort. The burning of the hospital in the Small Ghetto and the executions immediately afterward at the Ninth Fort--almost 2,000 men, women, and children died in this double Aktion--could only have been an added torment to those left alive in the Large Ghetto.

A quiet period after the Great Aktion in October? After 10,000 executions? Hardly a family remained untouched: wives without husbands, husbands without wives, children without parents, parents without children, almost everyone without someone, whole families destroyed. The "quiet" immediately afterward could only have been the stunned, tormented silence of those who remained alive.

A quiet period from mid-November to mid-December? The Germans halted the mass killings of the Jews of the ghetto. But they transported thousands of foreign Jews to Kovno and executed them at the Ninth Fort. The first German Jews to be deported from Germany were executed at the Ninth Fort. From behind the barbed wire of the ghetto fence Kovno Jews, Fanny among them, saw the long lines of the doomed walking toward the Ninth Fort. The Kovno Jews knew what awaited the foreign Jews there. And they had to live with what they knew.

A quiet period? In January, 1942, the Germans ordered the Jews to collect stray cats and dogs from the ghetto and bring them and their own pets to the Veliuonus Street synagogue. Then they shot the animals. Tory records, "It was a cruel and sadistic spectacle: wounded cats and dogs running around in the synagogue, wailing and shrieking." For several months the Germans refused to allow the Jews to remove the bodies. In his *Responsa from the Holocaust* Rabbi Oshry writes that they forced the Jews to cover the bodies with sheets of the Torah scroll.

Oshry remembers how the Germans chose Purim, 1942, to break into the ghetto to round up Jews for forced labor in order to take the joy out of the holiday and "demonstrate once again that there was no hope for the Jew." They did the same on Tisha b'Av in order to add still more sorrow to the day.

A quiet period? By May, 1942, the Germans had flooded the *Aeltestenrat* with 2,500 orders that kept the Jews in a constant state of anxiety. "Waves of decrees and decisions," Dr. Elkes writes in his Last Testament, "threaten to drown...[the ghetto] every day." From one day to the next the ghetto Jews did not know whether they were obeying or breaking a law. A Jew who acquired a newspaper, tried to smuggle food into the ghetto, removed his yellow star, left his workplace, or walked on the sidewalk on Laisves Boulevard risked a beating, an arrest, or worse.

On February 4, 1943, during the quiet period, the Germans executed 45 Jews--to deflate any hopes raised by the German defeat at Stalingrad. In the shadow of the "Stalingrad Aktion," Tory saw "work and bread"--the ghetto workshops--as the only hope for the Jews. Extra food on Purim sparks hope in him that the Germans need "the working and producing Jewish hands." But Tory's "hope for better days," cannot still his fears of "Calamities [that] wear different disguises, and never fail to catch us off guard." Speeches by Hitler and Goebbels promising the annihilation of the Jews touch off "a new wave of fear in the ghetto. People see themselves teetering on the brink of an abyss of destruction." But when the Germans assure Dr. Elkes that no Jews fit for work will be killed, hope rises once again.

Only to be shattered when the Germans break their word with an Aktion at Ponar, just outside Vilna, where they massacred an entire trainload of Jews from the Vilna area who, like a number of Kovner among them, had accepted a German promise of resettlement for work in the Kovno Ghetto. The news that German and Lithuanian units had shot down 5,000 Jews devastated the Kovno Ghetto. "No words can express the feelings of each one of us," writes Tory.

"Ponar," he says, "has taught us once more that neither work for the Germans, nor slavery, nor submission, will be of any avail when our time comes. Our irrevocable sentence, signed and sealed has already been passed somewhere in Kovno." No one, he adds "will come to our aid when we finally face extermination." He fears new tricks, new lies. But the human need to hope is irrepressible and surfaces again with the slightest suggestion from the Gestapo "that for the time being nothing is going to happen." Any hope will do. But only two weeks later, May 7, Tory is again saying, "We no longer believe that work will save us. The ground under our feet does not feel secure anymore."

What sort of quiet could there have been in the ghetto in the fall of 1943 when day after day the Germans, attempting to destroy all evidence of their crimes at the Ninth Fort, burned the corpses of Jews that had been exhumed from the mass graves? "The corpses of the Lithuanian Jews were naked," writes Tory, "and lying on one another lengthways and crossways." Day after day the Jews back in the ghetto knew what was happening. They saw the smoke that hovered over the Ninth Fort.

The Estonian Aktion ended the quiet period. Until they were caught and deported in it Di Tante and the family could only have felt the same daily pressures that all their neighbors did. Life, after all, went on after the *Aktionen*. The Germans relentlessly crowded the Jews into ever narrower quarters. They demanded more and more work out of the workshops and at the airfield. They gave ever shorter food rations. They robbed the Jews of everything--of their food, clothing, shoes, books, valuables. They handed down ever more decrees, imposed ever greater restrictions, presented the ghetto leadership with ever more impossible choices. The German aims, Rabbi Oshry writes, "were to make our lives ever more miserable."

Work was the only hope for remaining alive. But the German priority for the Jews of the Kovno Ghetto was not work but death. The Germans never intended work to be anything other than a reprieve from death. Though they kept some Kovno Jews alive longer than almost all of Lithuanian Jewry, they never intended anything other than death for all Lithuanian Jews, the Kovno Jews included, the Dembovitzes included.

Hope was the ultimate weapon employed by the Germans in their psychological warfare against the Jews of the Kovno Ghetto. And they wielded it with exquisite skill before and after their *Aktionen* against the Jews. They exploited the Jews with it and they tormented the Jews with it. They were able to exploit the Jews with it because they could torment the Jews with it. Hardly a page of Tory's *Diary* is free of the tension the Germans created as they played hope off against fear, fear against hope--over and over again, mercilessly, in endless oscillation. In the end, to be sure, death was their "final" solution for almost all the Jews of the Kovno Ghetto. But first came the torture of hope.

The Appointment

Five a.m., Tuesday, October 28, 1941.

Night still has its grip on the Kovno Ghetto. No one is sleeping. Doors begin to open. More and more doors. More and more shadowy figures slip into the darkness. They leave their doors open behind them. It is a sign to the Germans that no one is inside. Pinpoints of light begin to appear. Then more and more of them. Flickering candles make ghosts of figures hurrying in the night. Men, women, children, the old, the sick, the feeble, anyone who can walk or be carried--the entire ghetto is streaming toward a huge, open area...toward Democratu Platz...Democratu Square. They hurry as if they have an urgent appointment to keep there.

This is the way it was.

Josef Gar calls October 28, the day of the Great Aktion, "the blackest day in the history of the Kovno Ghetto."[9] Rabbi Oshry writes, "Kovno Jews--those who went through this ordeal and remained alive--will never forget it." Masha Greenbaum in her history *The Jews of Lithuania: 1316-1945* writes that October 28 is, in fact, the date "Lithuanian Jews all over the world chose...to commemorate the destruction of Lithuanian Jewry."[10]

The order had been posted: Everyone--everyone--was to be in the Democratu Platz by six in the morning. Anyone found at home after six would be shot. Along with everyone else, Di Tante, her husband Chaim, Fanny and Aharon, and Osya were in the Square by the appointed hour.

The nightmare was only beginning. Though it was still autumn, most accounts of that day mention a light, thin snowfall. The wait began before first light. It went on for two, some say three, hours. Then and only then did the German officers arrive.

Rauca, Jordan, Tornbaum--these are the names of the ghetto commanders I recognize in the accounts of that October 28. They will never again be simply names to me. The names have lodged themselves in my mind. SS Master Sergeant Helmut Rauca, the Gestapo man, was in charge of the Great Aktion. SA Captain Fritz Jordan, who was responsible for advising the German civil administrative authorities about Jewish affairs in Kovno, was there. So was SS Captain Alfred Tornbaum, the commander of the Third Division of German Police in Kovno. Together they held in their hands the fate of perhaps 28,000 Kovno Jews. A world away, back on the West Side of Chicago on October 28, 1941, I was a very young sophomore in Marshall High School, totally ignorant of them and the role they were playing in Di Tante's life and in all the other Jewish lives of the Kovno Ghetto--and, in a way, in mine.

The hour, the order for all the Jews of the ghetto to appear, the quick death promised for all who failed to come, the fears of the members of the *Aeltestenrat*, the talk of a "census" to separate the productive workers from the non-workers, the Lithuanian partisans in the Square--all the signs were ominous. And when Rauca appeared the signs must have turned grim, for his reputation as a killer preceded him. He had been the one in charge of the Intellectuals Aktion and other Aktions as well.

As he set to his "work" it became clear that a selection was underway, and in earnest. He stood on a platform and, says Rabbi Oshry, he ate his breakfast, a "white roll with butter," even smoking a cigar afterward, all the while motioning to the right or to the left as the Jews passed before him. Rauca, he says, "did his work very quietly, coldblooded and systematically."

The right, says Tory, meant death; the left, life. Rauca did his work "very deftly and nimbly, sedately, with a smile on his face, refreshing himself from time to time with a sandwich wrapped in waxed paper." And every half hour, he adds, Rauca would call out to a subordinate, "The count, the count, I must have the exact count...."

194

The Lithuanian partisans forced the doomed into the Little Ghetto. Those chosen for life remained in the Large Ghetto. Thousands stood waiting their turn. Screams. Tears. Husbands separated from wives...parents from children. Hunger and thirst...the gradual emptying out of the square...the growing darkness.... As the selection proceeded, writes Josef Gar, "A sorrowful wail carried over the huge square from family members forever separated from each other."[11]

My cousin Fanny remembers only Jordan, the man and his name. She does not mention Rauca and did not recognize the name Tornbaum when I proposed it to her.

In early August, 1941, Jordan had ordered the execution of twenty-six Jews guilty "of purchase of foodstuffs on the highway," and he had furthermore warned the *Aeltestenrat* that "for an offense committed by one Jew, ten Jews will be killed." Jordan had ordered the *Aeltestenrat* to elect a chairman. He had ordered the ghetto closed on August 15. Three days later he had ordered the ghetto to supply 500 Jews from "the educated classes" to appear for work in the Kovno archives--a deception that turned into the Intellectuals Aktion. He had ordered the *Aeltestenrat* to distribute the 5,000 "Jordan certificates" to skilled Jewish tradesmen, a trick to set Jews against each other in their attempts to acquire what they believed to be a "life pass," an exemption from all roundups and selections.

On that fateful Tuesday, says Joseph Gar, Jordan was at first interested only in the general process of the selection, not in the actual selection of people. But as the day wore on, according to Gar, he became jealous of his "colleague" Rauca and began to take an active part in it. Perhaps he saw Rauca tiring. "It was beginning to grow dark," writes Tory, "yet thousands of people remained standing in the square. Captain Jordan now opened another selection place; he was assisted by Captain Tornbaum. Rauca could count on this pair without reservation."

Fanny remembered Jordan well enough. He was young, tall, and very handsome in his uniform, she said, the very picture of a Nazi officer. But he was the very picture of death as he and another officer came down the rows to make their selections. Death was only a step away from the family during those seconds that Jordan and his fellow officer paused before them.

That other officer must have been Captain Alfred Tornbaum. His men were assigned, among other things, to patrol the fence outside the ghetto. Tory describes him as "the embodiment of a typical German gendarme. He expressed great interest in art, in philatelic collections, and in valuables in general. He was a sadist, fond of listening to Liszt's rhapsodies played by an artist, only to rob him afterward of his piano. He was a police dog, who forced women to undress, so that he could then conduct gynecological examinations on them while, at the same time, beating them severely. This police inspector who plundered and looted treasures from the Jews, repaying them with blows on all parts of their bodies; this broad-shouldered man in his gray uniform and shining boots, feared by his own subordinates; this Tornbaum...thought his rule over us would be indefinite...."

On August 19, 1941, only one day after the Intellectuals Aktion, Captain Tornbaum led a detachment of German soldiers into the ghetto and began two weeks of terrifying house-to-house searches, looting the ghetto of money, jewelry, gold and silver, electric appliances, coats, suits, furniture--anything of value. Beatings became routine. Tornbaum, says William Mishell, was a soldier "experienced in Gestapo tactics."

On October 28, during the Great Aktion, German police heavily armed with machine guns surrounded the ghetto fence. Battalions of armed Lithuanian partisans kept the selection in the Square itself under control. Captain Tornbaum commanded both the police and the partisans.

"The count, the count, I must have the exact count...," Helmut Rauca shouted. Well, the figures vary. Historians of the ghetto do not agree on the statistics. The Gestapo figure is that the selection left 14,000 Jews in the ghetto. Avraham Tory says 10,000 Jews were killed out of a population of 30,000. William Mishell puts the figure at 10,000 killed out of 28,000. Rabbi Oshry puts the figure at 10,000 killed out of 26,500. In the *Encyclopedia of the Holocaust* Dov Levin says 9,000 were killed, half of them children, out of a total ghetto population at 26,760. In *Hidden History of the Kovno Ghetto* Levin, Jurgen Matthaus, and Solon Beinfeld place the killed at 9,200. Matthaus says 4,200 children were killed. We will probably never know the exact number of all the Kovner who kept their first appointment on October 28, nor the exact number of all who kept their final appointment on October 29.

On October 30, the day after the massacre at the Ninth Fort, Elena Kutorgiene-Buivydaite--a Lithuanian doctor who hid Jews in her home in Kovno and supported the Jewish partisans and the Kovno underground--recorded in her diary what she knew of the Great Aktion:

> ...10,000 people have been taken out of the ghetto to die. They selected the old people, mothers with their children, those not capable of working. There were many tragedies: there were cases where a husband had been in town and on his return he no longer found either his wife or his four children! And there were cases where they left the wife and took away the husband. Eye-witnesses tell the tale: On the previous day there was an announcement that everybody must come at six in the morning to the big square in the ghetto and line up in rows, except workers with the documents which were recently distributed to specialists and foremen. In the first row were the members of the Council of Elders and their families, behind them the Jewish Police, after that the administration officials of the ghetto, after that the various work-brigades and all

the others. Some of them were directed to the right--that meant death--and some were directed to the left. The square was surrounded by guards with machine guns. It was freezing. The people stood on their feet all through that long day, hungry and with empty hands. Small children cried in their mothers' arms. Nobody suspected that a bitter fate awaited them. They thought they were being moved to other apartments....At dawn there was a rumor that at the Ninth Fort...prisoners had been digging deep ditches, and when the people were taken there, it was already clear to everybody that this was death. They broke out crying, wailed, screamed. Some tried to escape on the way there but they were shot dead. Many bodies remained in the fields. At the Fort the condemned were stripped of their clothes, and in groups of three hundred they were forced into the ditches. First they threw in the children. The women were shot at the edge of the ditch, after that it was the turn of the men....Many were covered [with earth] while they were still alive....All the men doing the shooting were drunk.[12]

And she concludes: "I was told all this by an acquaintance who heard it from a German soldier, an eye-witness, who wrote to his Catholic wife: 'Yesterday I became convinced that there is no God. If there were, He would not allow such things to happen.'"

The Airfield

The first few times I encounter Aleksotas in my reading about Kovno and the Kovno Ghetto the name means little to me. At first I learn that it is a suburb of Kovno, across the River Nieman. Then I discover a map that locates an airfield there, to the south of Kovno. But I am in search of the family, not of Aleksotas, and I pay little attention to it.

In time, however, the name begins to crop up more and more frequently on the printed page, and gradually, as I learn more and more, I become familiar with it. "Aleksotas," it turned out, referred not to the suburb itself but to the airfield the Germans took over there for the Luftwaffe during the war. At times as many as 4,000 workers, about half the ghetto work force, labored at the airfield, men and women both. The Aleksotas "workplace was both the largest and most difficult of all," writes the historian Dov Levin. "Thousands of Jews and Soviet prisoners of war worked there from early in the morning to late at night, exposed to the elements, in all sorts of weather. They were beaten and treated with sadistic ruthlessness. During the day they were given only one slice of bread and some thin broth. In addition to this the workers had to walk four hours to and from this work site."[13]

The Aleksotas brigades worked twelve hour shifts at the hardest labor of all--doing heavy construction work, loading and unloading cargo, making airfield repairs, hauling building materials. Small wonder, then, that ghetto inmates would do almost anything to avoid the Aleksotas brigades and try their utmost to get into one of the city brigades. When the Jewish Council--the *Aeltestenrat*--was unable to meet the required quota of workers for Aleksotas, the Germans would simply seize people on the street to fill the quota. In September, 1942, the absentee problem grew so serious that the Germans were forced to resort to a very different tactic. In his *Diary* Avraham Tory records that SA Col. Hans Cramer, city governor of Kovno, "threatens to halt food supplies to the Ghetto for a period of eight days if the Ghetto fails to provide the required number of workers for the airfield."

Work at the airfield was so heavy that to spare their parents children as young as thirteen would substitute for them in the Aleksotas brigades. The children--they were called "angels"--even substituted for strangers for pay.

Tory describes the plight of a teenager whose parents had been murdered at the Ninth Fort and who was being transferred from his job at a bakery to work at the airfield. At the bakery he would get an extra slice of bread and be warm in winter, but "from now on," writes Tory, "he will have to make do with *jusnik*--a thin, watery, altogether repulsive soup--and a meager food ration. He will not be able to buy food in the city as he has nothing to sell or trade; he has no money either. Nor does he have proper shoes to walk all the way to the airfield...." On March 2, 1942, Tory records, "The Council asked the Ghetto inmates to donate shoes and galoshes for the airfield workers."

Life at Aleksotas could be deadly too. Three weeks later Tory notes without comment that "Two workers, Nachman Shrak and Josef Fried, were shot dead in the airfield while buying groceries. Their bodies were brought to the Ghetto."

The more I learn about Aleksotas, the larger it looms and the more I see again the scene of the Great Aktzie and understand that fateful moment, late in the day of October 28, 1941, at Democratu Platz when the family's fate hung in the balance. Eight or nine thousand of all the Jews of Kovno--out of perhaps 30,000 who had gathered there early in the morning--have already been "selected" and driven into the Small Ghetto to await their fate the next day at the Ninth Fort. Di Tante and her husband Chaim are still standing in one row awaiting their turn in the continuing *selektzieh*. Fanny, Osya, and Aharon are in another. Capt. Jordan and another officer walk down the rows toward them. They approach the family. Closer. And closer. They reach Osya and stop. Directly in front of him.

All but dead from his fever, Osya somehow summons all his remaining strength, leaps to his feet in sudden life before those who hold his life in their hands, and almost shouts, "I am in the airport brigade! I work at Aleksotas!" Jordan and his fellow officer pass on. Fanya and Aharon support Osya on either side, lest he collapse. Osya is saved. The Great Aktzie takes its course.

Today I understand something of Aleksotas.

The Accursed

"The soil of Lithuania is soaked with our blood, killed at the hands of the Lithuanians themselves; Lithuanians, with whom we have lived for hundreds of years, and whom, with all our strength, we helped to achieve their own national independence. Seven thousand of our brothers and sisters were killed by Lithuanians in terrible and barbarous ways during the last days of June 1941. They themselves, and no others, executed whole generations, following German orders. They searched--with special pleasure--cellars and wells, fields and forests, for those in hiding, and turned them over to the authorities. Never have anything to do with them; they and their children are accursed forever." Driven to the extreme as he set down these words in his Last Testament, Dr. Elkhanan Elkes had no time left to tell his children anything but the truth.

Under the terms of the Nazi-Soviet Pact, Lithuania came under the control of the USSR in June, 1940. A year later, on June 22, the Germans attacked the Russians. The next day the Soviets began their retreat from Lithuania. The Germans entered Kovno on the 24th. Even before the German invasion the Lithuanian Activist Front (*Lietuviu Aktyvistu Frontas*) proclaimed its intentions in a flyer headlined "The Time Has Come to Settle Accounts with the Jews."[14]   Even before the Germans arrived, the LAF and others who called themselves "partisans" began to settle those accounts, terrorizing and murdering Jews in villages, towns, and cities throughout the country.

Initially, the Lithuanians saw the Germans as their liberators from the Soviets. In time they would be disabused of this notion. Meanwhile, however--never mind that the Soviets had destroyed the Jews as a functioning community--they saw Jews as pro-communist, and therefore as anti-Lithuanian. From the very beginning Lithuanian "partisans" were eager and willing executioners. Prominent among them were "the White Ribbons"[15] who wore on their left arm the white ribbon of the LAF. On October 15, 1941, SS Brigadier General

Walther Stahlecker, commander of *Einsatzgruppe A*, a mobile killing unit, reported to Berlin that in Kovno in "the first pogrom during the night of June 25/26, the Lithuanian partisans eliminated more than 1,500 Jews, set fire to several synagogues, or destroyed them by other means, and burned down an area consisting of about sixty houses inhabited by Jews. During the nights that followed, 2,300 Jews were eliminated in the same way."[16] Thereafter, though they sometimes acted on their own, they were primarily under German control.

William Mishell remembers: "The Lithuanian population was almost entirely Catholic, deeply religious, and the influence of the clergy was pronounced....There was absolutely no doubt that if the priests said just one word to discourage the population from committing crimes against the Jews, it would have a profound effect. What the partisans were committing was pure murder. It was not an act in defense of the country, no battle was raging. It was an act against defenseless people who, deep in their hearts, loved Lithuania but happened to be Jewish."[17]

In early July when an envoy from the Kovno Jewish community approached the Lithuanian finance minister Matulionis for help to put an end to the ongoing murders, he responded, "I am a practicing Roman Catholic; I--and other believers like me--believe that man cannot take the life of a human being like himself. Only God can do this. I have never been against anybody, but during the period of Soviet rule I and my friends realized that we did not have a common path with the Jews and never will. In our view, the Lithuanians and the Jews must be separated from each other and the sooner the better. For that purpose the Ghetto is essential. There you will be separated and no longer able to harm us. This is a Christian position." He refused to exert his influence. "The wrath of the people is so great that there is no way to stop these acts. When you leave the city for good and confine yourselves in the Ghetto," he offered, "things will quiet down." To Avraham Tory, who on July 8 recorded Matulionis's response to the Jewish plea for help, it was plain that "the assaults on the Jews express the will of the Lithuanian people."

Looking backward after the war, and recalling how the Germans had brought Jews from Germany, Czechoslovakia, and Austria "to spill their blood in the Lithuanian soil," Tory saw the Lithuanian people as marked "with the sign of Cain...for their conscious and persistent collaboration with the Germans in the murder of the Jewish people."[18]

On December 1, barely five months after entering Kovno, SS Colonel Karl Jaeger, the commander of *Einsatzkommando* 3, a sub-unit of *Einsatzgruppe A*, gave due credit for the success of *EK* 3 to the "co-operation of the Lithuanian partisans and the respective civil offices."[19] Jaeger described the "Aktions in Kovno itself, where a sufficient number of trained partisans was available," as "a shooting paradise" for them compared to Aktions in the countryside "where the greatest difficulties had to be overcome time and again.[20]

The record of the Lithuanians is grim. Like Dr. Elkes, Avraham Tory is unforgiving in his condemnation of the Lithuanians. On February 16, 1943, he writes in his *Diary*: "One may speak of feelings of hatred and revenge with regard to everything that has to do with Lithuania. One may speak of the curse with which, in his heart, each one of us curses this Lithuania, which with its own hands has exterminated Lithuanian Jewry. Curse upon Lithuania and upon its sons, who, during the most trying times for the Jewish people, stabbed them in the back."

Seeing Lithuanian national flags flying in honor of Lithuanian independence, he thinks of them as "hoisted on houses built with Jewish labor and sweat. Where are they now, the former owners of those houses, who for many years had been loyal Lithuanian citizens? These days Lithuanians live in Jewish houses; they use the Jewish furniture and wear the Jewish clothes. The Old City of Kovno is packed with people. Jewish houses and apartments have not remained vacant; but their rightful owners are not alive. The Jews who relate in their own unique way to all they have built and created are missing. What else does the future have in store for us?"[21]

A month later, on March 16, he adds, "All our Christian friends and acquaintances have forgotten us. We remain alone, isolated and forgotten."

In late March and early April, the Germans brought 2,000 Jews from villages in the Vilna district to the Vilna Ghetto, promising to send them to the Kovno Ghetto. Seeking to rejoin their families in the Kovno Ghetto, some Kovno Jews living in the Vilna Ghetto joined them. Another 3,000 Jews from the Vilna district also decided to join the train bound for Kovno. The train was barely underway when it came to a stop at the forest of Ponar, a few kilometers from Vilna. Lithuanian, Latvian, and White Guard Russian police under command of the Germans shot down all 5,000 Jews. Tory writes that "only a handful of the Lithuanian police refused to fire on innocent people." The Gestapo shot them immediately. "By their refusal to fire," he says, "these murdered policemen gained the world to come, and brought honor to their homeland, Lithuania," unlike the Lithuanians, Latvians, and White Guards who by taking part in the massacre had succeeded in "casting themselves out of the human family."

For Rabbi Oshry the Lithuanians left an indelible record, one that extends beyond the war. "The same fate that awaited the mass graves of the Jews throughout Lithuania also awaited the field where the Jews were murdered in the Ninth Fort next to Slobodka. There the remains of some 40,000 Lithuanian, German, Austrian, and French Jews had been buried. This grave was plowed under and planted in potatoes and grain. This produce, fertilized by the blood of our martyred brothers and sisters, was eaten by the Lithuanian peasants, the cruel murderers who had helped the accursed Germans annihilate these Jews and who had robbed them."[22]

Oshry survived the death of his hometown. He survived the Kovno Ghetto's fiery end. He survived the destruction of Lithuanian

Jewry. He was as unforgiving of the Lithuanians as Dr. Elkes and Avraham Tory.

The New Zealand Station
Feb. 7, 1991

We are in New Zealand. We've left Fanny and Abrasha far behind, twelve hundred miles behind. We spent last night at the home of George and Robin Harber, outside the town of Cambridge. Bed and Breakfast.

After dinner it was time to wander around the house a bit under the cool--not cold--eye of our host. In my imagination the living room *feels* English to me. Harber's ancestors came to New Zealand in 1856! They were lawyers, churchmen, soldiers. A great-great-grandfather was the Anglican Archbishop at Christchurch. Harber tells me he's entombed there in his very own sarcophagus. The dark paneled walls of the living room are rich with photos of soldiers in uniform, family members who died in World War I. As Harber leads me around the room, explaining what's visible, I imagine the Harbers as being like the long ago Englishmen who went to live "in the colonies." They still have feelings for the Mother Country.

The Harbers live in an area famous for its breeding "paddocks." This is New Zealand's Kentucky blue grass country. "We're world famous, you know, for our polo ponies and thoroughbreds," Harber says with a touch of pride. Harber himself formerly bred and trained polo ponies, even the one that threw him and nearly killed him a few years ago. I gather that that pony taught him the value of life as he had never known it before.

Today we had a good introduction to the Harber "station." What Australians and New Zealanders call a station is really a sheep ranch or a cattle ranch. By the standards of the huge stations in the Australian Outback the Harber station of thirty acres is a minor affair. The

Harbers have 127 sheep and twenty cattle. Harber uses his land to fatten the animals before shipping them off to market.

Harber put on a bit of a show for us. He demonstrated the whistles he uses. One whistle--and his border collie maneuvered the flock of sheep one way. Another whistle--and he moved them another way. His whistles cut into the clean, clear air, and from far off the dog worked the flock unerringly and inevitably toward us and into their pen.

I am from the city. I do not know cows. I do not know cattle or sheep. So I listen uneasily when he says, "I used to kill a cow or a sheep myself for our personal use. But I don't do that anymore. Now I send one to the butcher for slaughtering. The others I ship to the abattoir for the market." Those creatures I see out in his field: he considers them as nothing--as nothing more than so many kilos of wool, so many kilos of meat. Harber is no different from any other farmer, I suppose. He simply does not see them as living creatures. He has absolutely no feeling whatsoever toward them. They are objects of cold calculation. They signify to him only for what they will fetch in the market. I look off at them foraging in the field, fattening. They are already dead and cannot know it.

***

It is eight years since the New Zealand station.

When the mind works in counterclockwise fashion, sometimes terrifying connections lie in wait for you, like a beast in the jungle. I am searching for the Ninth Fort. And suddenly it leaps at me, a line from a report by SS Brigadier-General Walther Stahlecker to Berlin, January 3, 1942: "The first five shipments (expelled from the Reich), intended for Riga, have been sent to Kovno."[23] One thousand to a shipment. One thousand to a train load. Cold, matter-of-fact, calculating and calculated.

SS Colonel Karl Jaeger, commander of *Einsatzkommando* 3, a sub-unit of *Einsatzgruppe A*, had informed Stahlecker that he had shot 2,934 Jews at the Ninth Fort on November 25, 1941--Jews deported from Berlin, Munich, and Frankfurt: 1,159 men, 1,600 women, 175 children. The Jaeger Report lists 2,000 more Jews shot at the Ninth Fort on November 29--Jews from Vienna and Breslau: 693 men, 1,115 women, 152 children.[24]

The SS told the Kovno Jewish Council to prepare to receive the Riga shipments. And they told the Jews in the Riga shipments they were going to be "resettled" in the Baltic countries. All lies--but initially believed. When the Jews arrived at the Kovno train station, they were straightaway marched through Kovno directly to the Ninth Fort and their death.

The Jews in the November 25 transport were the first German Jews murdered in the Final Solution. With most of the Jews of Lithuania already murdered, the killing of the Jews in these two transports marked the beginning of the Ninth Fort as the killing ground for Jews shipped from other countries. Rabbi Oshry reports that beginning in December, 1941, "about 40,000 foreign Jews arrived in Kovno--German, Austrian, Czech, and French, mostly from Berlin, Frankfurt, and Hamburg."[25] They were debarked at the Kovno station and shot at the Ninth Fort.

"The fact is," Oshry writes, "the mass extermination of Jews began much earlier in the Ninth Fort than in Auschwitz."[26]   In other words, the Ninth Fort was Auschwitz before Auschwitz.

J'accuse

Emile Zola's "Open Letter to the President of the Republic" caused a sensation upon its publication and has ever since linked Zola's name to the Dreyfus Affair. Better known as *J'accuse,* the letter did the unthinkable: it accused French government officials and the French

Army of a cover-up.   According to Anatole France, with *J'accuse* Zola created "a moment in the conscience of Man."

Report to the Secretary on the Acquiescence of This Government in the Murder of the Jews caused no sensation--though it nearly did. It remains one of the least known American documents dealing with the Holocaust--and one of the most devastating. It was not published till years after it was written. But today, more than half a century after the event and in the light of what we now know about the history of the Holocaust, it has grown even more devastating--and bone chilling. It accuses American government officials of a criminal cover-up of murder. It reaches from the bureaucrats of the Visa Division, through the State Department, through the government to the very desk of President Roosevelt in the Oval Office. It is as powerful an accusation as has ever been leveled at the American Government.

Report to the Secretary... was intended for Henry Morgenthau, Jr., the Secretary of the Treasury, and presented to him by members of his staff early in January, 1944. It details the experience of three young lawyers--Joseph DuBois, Randolph Paul, John Pehle--with the head of the Visa Division in the State Department. Today their *Report* stands as an impassioned accusation of murder committed not simply by the bureaucrats in the Visa Department but by a government whose sins of omission and commission led as certainly to death as anything the Germans ever did.

The murder in its title was foreshadowed in the two international conferences that the United States and Great Britain organized to do something about the Jewish problem that Hitler was creating for them and for the conscience of the international community.   Both conferences failed. They were never intended to succeed. The first, at Evian in July, 1938, a little over a year before Hitler attacked Poland, was supposed to open the doors of immigration for the rescue of Europe's Jews. Anne O'Hare McCormick, columnist for *The New York Times*, saw clearly the reality at stake at Evian.   "It is a test of civilization," she wrote. "Can America live with itself if it lets Germany get away with this policy of extermination, allows the fanaticism of one man to triumph over reason, refuses to take up this gage of battle against barbarism?"[27] The Germans offered to give the Jews away free to the thirty-two nations assembled at Evian. There were no takers. "Jews available, cheap," mocked *Der Reichswart* on July 14. "Who wants them? No one!"[28]

The second conference opened in Bermuda on April 19, 1943--the very day the Warsaw Ghetto uprising began. The Bermuda Conference also gave lip service to the rescue of Europe's Jews. This time the British Foreign Office actually argued against rescue because of the "difficulties" involved in "disposing of any considerable number of Jews should they be rescued from enemy-occupied territory." Anthony Eden, the British Foreign Secretary, contended that there weren't enough ships and transport to handle all the Jews that might be rescued--this at a time when he surely knew Allied ships were carrying prisoners of war to the United States or were otherwise returning empty after delivering their cargoes to Britain. What Eden was really saying was that the murder of the Jews would have to--and should be allowed to--take its course. Not only was rescue not the first order of business at the Conference, it was never really on the agenda. The British government became a partner in crime: it, too, willfully "acquiesced" in the murder of the Jews. Jewish leaders at the Conference protested, "Unless action is undertaken immediately, there may soon be no Jews left alive in Europe." No one heard them.

Breckenridge Long, Assistant Secretary of State from 1940 to 1944, was in charge of the Visa Division and controlled refugee policy for the State Department. He and his staff did everything they could to close the doors to Jewish emigration to the United States. He deliberately withheld crucial cables from Europe. He lied to a congressional hearing. He and his staff were instrumental not only in cutting immigration quotas that could have been used to rescue Jews but they made sure that what quotas were left would go largely unfilled. Long himself wrote a memorandum (June 26, 1940) to State Department officials proposing a deliberate policy to thwart the rescue of Jews: "We can delay and effectively stop, for a temporary period of indefinite length the number of immigrants into the United States. We could do this by simply advising our consuls to put every obstacle in the way and to require additional evidence and resort to various administrative devices which would postpone and postpone and postpone the granting of visas."[29] Long implemented this policy as if he were a character out of Kafka. He, too, knew something about the torture of hope.

Stressing, first of all, that "This government, has for a long time maintained that its policy is to work out programs to serve those Jews of Europe who could be saved," the *Report* proceeded with its indictment: "...that certain officials in our State Department, which is charged with carrying out this policy, have been guilty not only of gross procrastination and willful failure to act but even of willful attempts to prevent action from being taken to rescue Jews from Hitler." It accused State Department officials of "concealment and misrepresentation." It accused them of "false and misleading explanations for their failures to act and their attempts to prevent action." It accused them of a cover-up. "The matter of rescuing Jews from extermination is a trust too great to remain in the hands of men who are indifferent, callous, and perhaps even hostile....Only a fervent will to accomplish, backed by persistent and untiring effort, can succeed where time is so precious." "Unless remedial steps of a drastic nature are taken and taken immediately," the *Report* declared, it was clear "that no effective action will be taken by this government to prevent the complete extermination of the Jews in German controlled Europe." The result would be equally clear: "that this Government will have to share for all time responsibility for this extermination."

Morgenthau received the *Report to the Secretary...* on January 16, 1944. Though he condensed it, he left it essentially unchanged, and what had been addressed to him he renamed as *Report to the President*. In it he said, "There is a growing number of responsible people and organizations today who have ceased to view our failure as the product of simple incompetence on the part of those officials in the State Department charged with handling this problem. They see plain anti-

Semitism motivating the actions of these State Department officials and, rightly or wrongly, it will require little more in the way of proof for this suspicion to explode into a nasty scandal."[30]

President Roosevelt averted scandal. Narrowly. Six days later he signed an executive order creating the War Refugee Board that took the rescue program out of the hands of Long and the State Department and managed to help save about 200,000 Jews. Too little and too late.

It is not Roosevelt's action but the *Report to the Secretary on the Acquiescence of This Government in the Murder of the Jews* that stands as a moment in the conscience of America.

The Problem Is

"The problem is," wrote Avraham Tory "that we are not dealing with people whose actions are guided by logic. We are dealing with wild beasts, with savages who are bent on killing, exterminating and destroying Jews. Mass murder is their raison d'etre."[31] On June 9, 1942, just weeks before the mass deportations began from the Warsaw Ghetto, Chaim Kaplan in his *Diary* also sought some motive to explain the slaughter already occurring and came to the same conclusion, that the motive of the Germans "is the motive of Haman: to destroy, to murder, to annihilate. These are the only reasons."

To face the Ninth Fort is to have to face a central question--if not *the* central question--of the Holocaust. The problem is: How do you deal with those whose reason is anti-reason? with those whom you cannot reach with reason because they are beyond reason?

When R. W. Thompson began his report of the liberation of Bergen-Belsen with "It is my duty to describe something beyond the imagination of mankind," his sentence announced one of the many themes that he and his fellow reporters touched upon in their first dispatches to England, themes that continue to occupy and beset the minds of historians, theologians, philosophers, and others who have wrestled with the Holocaust. What Thompson and the others wrote has never been stated more explicitly, more honestly, or more uncompromisingly.

The Germans--and their accomplices--did go beyond the imagination of mankind, in their conception and their execution of the Final Solution. Excess--excess beyond human limits--marks the Holocaust as unprecedented. Rabbi Ephraim Oshry, who survived the Kovno Ghetto to its fiery end, writes, "Yes, I am a witness of this destruction without peer in the history of our people." The Kovno Ghetto "was real Hell. Whoever has not lived under German rule cannot imagine it, cannot conceive what happened to us in Lithuania during the awful years between the German occupation and the liberation of Lithuania by the Red army on the first of August, 1944. Any comparison to the life of a dog or a wild animal misses the mark."[32] The Slobodka pogrom, he says, was only "a fitting prelude to the ultimate cruelty of the German annihilation. This unspeakable cruelty is unmatched in human history."[33] He writes, "It is truly impossible to imagine what happened in those days of December, 1941. Each day literally thousands of Jews were murdered... About 40 thousand foreign Jews were shot."[34] When Dr. Elkhanan Elkes, the leader of the Kovno Ghetto Jewish Council, writes his "Last Testament" (October 19, 1943) he knows that the vast majority of Lithuanian Jewry has already been "put to death in terrible ways by the followers of the greatest Haman of all times and of all generations."

Beyond the limit, yes. Beyond the imagination of mankind, yes. But then the problem is: What do you do about the guilt of the German people for such atrocity? Christopher Buckley of the *Daily Telegraph* wants "to find some clue to the problem of the German people." Even if one were to allow that "the German people, collectively, are guilty of nothing more than ignorance and negligence," he can only conclude, unflinchingly, "You are still faced by the fact that the German people, collectively, produced the men and women in requisite numbers to maintain this system." For Thompson, "The shock and horror of it all grows with each day. The extent of the Nazi crime slowly dawns on the mind with all its fearful frightening implications. Sadism, brutality, rape and murder--all the usual crimes of humanity against humanity pale to insignificance beside this conception of the German mind." Watching the SS guards, men and women, collecting the corpses and "riding with them on the trucks and piling them into the great burial pits," he sees they are "utterly without shame." Not only the guards, he maintains, but "the whole German race share the guilt."

The problem is: What is one to do with a German people that has completely altered the basis of civilized life? For Thompson Bergen-Belsen has completely altered "all normal standards." In erasing the "difference between the living and the dead," the camp has taken him into a completely foreign world, one "beyond human standards." That Joseph Kramer, the camp commandant, and his guards, men and women both, "are actually proud of this camp," that they see nothing wrong with it leads him to one conclusion: "In fact, these Germans are without hope. They are not as other men. The thing is satanic." Bergen-Belsen is "colossal evidence of the complete corruption of their race to the world." For Buckley "Belsen is the nearest thing I know to a spectacle of absolute evil. I have visited many battlefields in this war and Belsen is incomparably, immeasurably more terrible a sight."

The problem is: What do you do with those who embody absolute evil?

The problem is: What do you do with those who committed crimes so enormous that they exceed one's ability to put words to them because they are beyond words? Rabbi Oshry writes, "Were all the oceans ink and all the skies parchment, and every single person on earth a scribe, they could never relate with entirety all that our enemies--the accursed Germans--did to the Jewish people."[35] On July 31, 1942, a little more than a week after the first deportations from the

Warsaw Ghetto began, Chaim Kaplan writes simply, "My powers are insufficient to record all that is worthy of being written." Oshry's pain at his own inability is palpable: "There was once a shtetl Kupishok. Today it is no more. Such holy souls torn out by the roots! My *shprakh* [my language, my speech, my vocabulary] is too poor to bewail my hometown and tell what we possessed and what we have lost."[36] Writing to her "dear fortunate sons" only days before the destruction of the Kovno concentration camp, Shulamith Rabinowitz said, "We resent that we cannot give over to you all that we have experienced. You will probably know, but whatever you know and hear, the reality is a thousand times more terrible and painful. There are no words to relate this...."[37] After the liberation of Kovno, Oshry says, "One of the first things we were faced with were the remains of martyrs whose bodies lay abandoned in the streets and fields like ordinary fertilizer one avoided stepping on. It was a nightmare. Everywhere we looked we saw skeletons and single limbs, skulls and bones. The most wretched scene was inside the concentration camp known as the Kovno Katzetlager....Scorched bones and human hands could be seen protruding from these piles of ashes....It is hard to set down in writing the pathetic and horrible sights we saw while we collected these remains."[38]

The problem is that the Holocaust was unprecedented, that to touch upon any understanding of it at all, one has to understand, as Oshry wrote, "what we possessed and what we have lost." For which there is no *shprakh*.

The Thin Line

You can't understand the story of the Kovno Ghetto and the Ninth Fort--you can't understand anything about the Holocaust-- without somewhere along the line taking *nekomah* into account. *Nekomah*--revenge--isn't a subject much discussed by historians, theologians, and others who concern themselves with the Holocaust. But it's a reality--and it's a question. It's not that the subject doesn't come up in the testimony of witnesses to the Holocaust. It does. And because it does figure in their accounts, it can't be avoided or ignored, and shouldn't be. For some survivors, just remaining alive constituted *nekomah*--after a fashion. Some survivors saw *nekomah* not only in their sheer survival but in being able to offer their story as testimony. Others saw physical *nekomah* as the only direct way to repay the enemy for the suffering he had inflicted on them. However it expressed itself, *nekomah* was a powerful force.

Take Feinberg, for instance. Avraham Tory in his *Diary* of the Kovno Ghetto doesn't even record his first name. What he does record in a brief paragraph or two is that Feinberg "carries within him a deep and painful wound"--the heartbreak of seeing his wife and child taken captive by the Lithuanians and carried off to their death--and that he has escaped from the ghetto to join the partisans in the forest to "speak with the enemy in the language of force." "Now," says Tory, "Feinberg lives for one purpose only--revenge."

On Christmas Eve, 1943, sixty-four prisoners escaped from the Ninth Fort. Though little known today, theirs was one of the most spectacular escapes to take place during the Holocaust. They were part of a special brigade the Germans formed to exhume the thousands of corpses from the pits of the Ninth Fort and then to burn them. The Jews knew the fate that awaited them. They knew that they too would be shot and burned once they had completed their task. They knew their only hope was to escape from the Ninth Fort. And they knew no one ever escaped from the Ninth Fort. Incredibly, though, they tunneled their way out. Once free, they split into four groups, then struck out in different directions. Some were captured and killed. But some managed to return to the ghetto. Keeping their arrival secret, the ghetto underground immediately hid them. Then, washed clean of the smell of death that had clung to them, they waited for the opportunity to get back at the enemy. It came. Oshry writes that these men "joined the partisans with weapons in their hands in order to take *nekomah*."[39]

215

Avraham Tory, like all the Jews of the ghetto, could not help but be moved by the glow of the fires at the Ninth Fort and by the smoke from the burning corpses that hovered above it. In his *Diary* he writes that he hears his fellow Jews saying, "Our brothers are burning, our blood is burning." For him "the red strip in the sky, the new 'crown' over the Fort, whispered quietly the word 'revenge.'"

Tory saw his *Diary* as "material evidence--'corpus delicti'--accusing testimony" for the time "when the Day of Judgment comes, and with it the day of revenge and the day of reckoning, the calling to account." Before he escaped from the Kovno Ghetto, he placed his *Diary* and other documents in five crates and buried them in the ghetto. In each crate he also placed a copy of his will. In it he called down "Eternal shame on the Nazis and their collaborators--the Lithuanians, the Ukrainians, and the others!" and called out for "REVENGE! NEVER FORGET! NEVER FORGIVE!"

After his liberation from the ghetto, Rabbi Oshry returned to his hometown Kupishok, whose one hundred Jewish families were no more. He tells of encountering a Christian servant woman, a day cook, who lived near his grandfather's home, and of learning from her the fate of Reb Pertzovski and his eldest child, Eliahu Meir. He records how she gave him the boy's jacket--all that was left of him--and how he discovered in one of its pockets a slip of paper bearing the words: "They are taking us to our death. *Nemt nekomah.* Take revenge."[40]

Living under the bitter conditions of the ghetto, pious Jews would often find themselves in situations requiring them to act contrary to Jewish law. Doing what such Jews have always done in times of distress, they turned to rabbinic authority for advice, first to the chief rabbi of Kovno, Abraham Duber Kahana-Shapiro, then, after his death, to Rabbi Oshry. After the liberation of the Kovno Ghetto a survivor came to Oshry and asked him whether he might seek out the Lithuanian janitor of their apartment house, the murderer of his parents, brothers, and sisters, and exact justice "so that other Jew haters would learn a lesson and restrain their murderous instincts

216

against the Jews." Oshry recognizes this as "a problem faced by many people," that many German killers and "their Lithuanian butcher-accomplices" had escaped to other countries, gone underground, changed their identities, and escaped justice. "Were we bound to avenge as much of the shed blood as possible?" Oshry asks himself. And he answers: "I instructed the man to make every possible effort to avenge the murder of his family. Several weeks later he returned and told me that he had thrown a hand grenade into the janitor's house, killing him. I advised him to leave Lithuania immediately so that the murderer's relatives should not find him, and also because the Lithuanian government did not look kindly upon Jews who took justice into their own hands. The man followed my advice and left the country." [41]

Five years earlier, when Chaim Kaplan in the Warsaw Ghetto posed much the same question, though on a much larger scale, he could manage only an anguished single paragraph entry (April 12, 1940). Out of his anguish he asked, "Is there any revenge in the world for the spilling of innocent blood?" And out of his anguish he answered, "I doubt it. The abominations committed before our eyes cry out from the earth: 'Avenge me!' But there is no jealous avenger. Why has a 'day of vengeance and retribution' not yet come for the murderers? Do not answer me with idle talk--I won't listen to you. Give me a logical reply!"[42]

Two years later, on the night of May 30/31, 1942, a thousand British bombers struck Cologne. Dr. Emmanuel Ringelblum, the archivist of the Warsaw Ghetto, a man some regard as "one of the most important historians in the annals of the Jewish people,"[43] wrote in his *Journal* that the air raid "evoked great joy among the [Polish] populace....However, the Jewish jubilation was quite different from the general one. Day in, day out, in hundreds of cities throughout Poland and Russia, thousands upon thousands of Jews are being systematically murdered according to a preconceived plan, and no one seems to take our part. The bombing of Cologne, the destruction of thousands of buildings, the thousands of civilian victims, have slaked our thirst for revenge somewhat. Cologne was an advance payment on the vengeance that must and shall be taken on Hitler's Germany for the millions of Jews they have killed. So the Jewish population of tortured Europe considered Cologne its personal act of vengeance. After the Cologne affair, I walked around in a good mood, feeling that, even if I should perish at their hands, my death is prepaid!"[44] The Germans murdered Ringelblum, his wife, and son in March, 1944.

But it is Tadeusz Borowski who offers what is perhaps the most challenging view of the question of *nekomah*. His *This Way for the Gas, Ladies and Gentlemen*, a volume of short stories, is unquestionably one of the masterpieces of what has to be called Holocaust literature. In his Introduction to the book the critic Jan Kott says Borowski was "the greatest hope of Polish literature among the generation of his contemporaries decimated by the war."[45]

Kott points out that in the period immediately after the war over ten million uprooted people--prisoners from concentration camps, former prisoners of war, refugees, forced laborers--found themselves in territories liberated by the Allies. "Never before," he says, "was there such a thin line between the demand for vengeance and the call for justice...."[46] Borowski examines this thin line in a passage in the story "The People Who Walked On." It is a remarkable dialogue (p. 90) between the narrator, a prisoner in Auschwitz like Borowski himself, and a sympathetic Block Elder, a woman prisoner in charge of one of the barracks for women in Auschwitz:

> "Do you believe in life after death?" she asked me once in the middle of some lighthearted conversation.
> "Sometimes," I answered cautiously. "Once I believed in it when I was in jail, and again once when I came close to dying here in the camp."
> "But if a man does evil, he'll be punished, won't he?"
> "I suppose so, unless there are some criteria of justice other than the man-made criteria. You know...the kind that explain causes and motivations, and erase guilt by making it

appear insignificant in the light of the overall harmony of the universe. Can a crime committed on one level be punishable on a different one?"

"But I mean in a normal, human sense!" she exclaimed.

"It ought to be punished. No question about it."

"And you, would you do good if you were able to?"

"I seek no rewards. I build roofs and want to survive the concentration camp."

"But do you think that they," she pointed with her chin in an indefinite direction, "can go unpunished?"

"I think that for those who have suffered unjustly, justice alone is not enough. They want the guilty to suffer unjustly too. Only this will they understand as justice."

How *does* one answer the call for *nekomah* from the innocent, from those who have suffered unjustly, from those whose faith in reason proved useless, and therefore fatal, in the encounter with those who march to the drumbeat of anti-reason?

First Principles

The unanimous choice of the Kovno Jewish community's leadership, Dr. Elkhanan Elkes led the Jewish Council from the formation of the ghetto until April, 1944, when the Germans dissolved the Council.

Elkes was nothing if not an eyewitness to life and death in the ghetto. "The Germans killed, slaughtered, and murdered us in complete equanimity," he wrote in his Last Testament. "I was there with them. I saw them. I saw them when they sent thousands of people--men, women, children, infants--to their death while enjoying their breakfast, and while mocking our martyrs. I saw them coming back from their murderous duty, stained from head to foot with the blood of our dear ones. They sat at their table--eating and drinking, listening to light music. They are professional executioners."

The disaster for the Lithuanian Jews began on June 22, 1941, when the Germans launched Operation Barbarossa against the Russians. Lithuania immediately became the first great killing ground of European Jewry. Ten thousand Jews were killed in Kovno from the end of June and into July, before the establishment of the Kovno Ghetto. Lithuania is where the Holocaust began.

The Germans and their Lithuanian collaborators worked fast, so fast that by December 1, in a "Reich Secret Document," SS Colonel Karl Jaeger could report to Berlin, "I can confirm today that *Einsatzkommando* 3 has achieved the goal of solving the Jewish problem in Lithuania. There are no more Jews in Lithuania, apart from working Jews and their families."[47] According to his statistics 15,000 Jews remained in the Kovno Ghetto--with another 15,000 in Vilna, and 4,500 in Shavli.

The Germans began to evacuate the Kovno Ghetto in early July, 1944. They deported 4,000 Jews to camps in Germany, Elkes among them. Then, anticipating Russian advances, they began the destruction of the ghetto. They burned it to the ground, killing two thousand Jews who, fearing deportation, tried to hide in bunkers. When the Russians arrived in Kovno on August 1, 1944, they found only about ninety Jews alive in the ghetto.

Elkes did not see the final total destruction of the ghetto, but his eyes had already seen enough. In his Last Testament, in his moment of extremity, writing as one who knows a fundamental and incontrovertible truth and with a heart that must have been close to despair, he offered his children the only legacy he could: "Remember, both of you, what Amalek has done to us. Remember and never forget it all your days; and pass this memory as a sacred testament to future generations."

Out of his own brutal experience and the doom that hung low over him, he offered them what he himself no longer had, but what every father who is a father must, no matter what, offer his child if it is to survive: hope. In the end he turned to the story of Amalek in Deuteronomy. In the end he returned to first principles.

DEFINITIONS

DEFINITIONS

For Rina

The memories in these pages have accompanied me over a lifetime. As they have accumulated they have become connected in ways I never expected and taken shape in a story I never expected.

I did not intend to write any of these pages *for* you. Not one. And yet, in a strange way, they have turned out to be for you after all. You will even find yourself in many of them. And with a little imagination you will discover your own connection to the story.

The story starts back in the nineteenth century and, with luck, you will carry it forward with you far into the twenty-first. I don't know a great deal about its earliest beginnings. And I can't foresee its future. What I do know about is its middle, the twentieth century.

You re-entered this story when you rang our doorbell in Highland Park on September 20, 1998, *erev* Rosh Hashanah--that is, on the eve of the New Year 5759 according to the Jewish calendar. You first entered it in August, 1970, when you were born. Looking back, I find that by June of the following year I was already giving you a place in it. "Our family," I wrote in a letter, "--from Tante to Irina--is really extraordinary." Since then I have learned that our family is even more extraordinary than I had thought.

When I first saw you--in Vilnius in 1971--you were a toddler already insisting on occupying center stage. When I next saw you--in Israel in 1974--you were living with your parents in an apartment across the street from an orange grove in Rehovot. And the next time I saw you (and your younger sister) you were already a teenager living with your parents on Long Island. I don't know what I expected when you rang our doorbell in Highland Park. But what I saw was a grown young woman whose astonishing resemblance to my cousin--your grandmother--struck me speechless. In you, suddenly the whole story yielded still another charge of life.

225

I would like to think you came out of some sense of curiosity. When, out of my own curiosity and anticipation of a story, I ask friends or acquaintances of my generation where their parents came from, what I generally hear is the vague uncertain name of a *shtetl*, a little town somewhere in eastern Europe, little more, followed by awkward silences of embarrassment, regret, even sadness--acknowledgments of an essential failure of their curiosity. They know all too well of their irreparable loss--that the gaps in their knowledge mean that they must die somehow incomplete, that they have cheated themselves, failed in their duty to the past. If they offer an excuse it is "When you're young, who thinks of asking?" But deep down they know they have only themselves to blame.

So, as we sat around the dining room table, the September sun streaming through the window onto the white tablecloth and the blue china cups and saucers, my mind went racing, "...so this is Irina...a relative...she is related to me and I to her...a relative and yet she's almost a complete stranger...*what* does she know...how much does she *want* to know...how much can I tell her...how much *should* I tell her...*how* do I tell her...how much does she know of the stories of her parents, her grandparents, and her great-grandparents...not just their history but of their history *inside* history...how much does she know of her *own* history, the history that has brought her here?"

I looked at you and thought of asking, "Do you know what a rarity you are in this world? Do you know that at the beginning of the second World War about a quarter of a million Jews lived in Lithuania--and that only five percent of them survived the Holocaust? Do you realize--genuinely realize--that you are the remnant of a remnant of Lithuanian Jewry?"

I thought of how much more of "your" story I know than you yourself know, of how much more I know of it than your father knows or than he has told you. I thought of how in some ways I know more of the whole story than anyone else in it, even more than your grandmother knows. At the same time, I also thought of how little I know.

What I heard myself asking, though, was, "Did you know about Abrasha?"

"Yes, of course."

"Did you ever meet him?"

"I saw him in Australia when I went to visit my grandmother."

I hear your answer. What I do not tell you is that without him this story would not exist, that without him you would not exist at all. I did not tell you that I myself did not know this fact until after many years of living my own way into the story.

"And your grandmother--," I hesitated. "Did she tell you anything about the war...about her experiences during the war?"

"No. Nothing."

"Did you ask her?"

"Yes."

"And what did she tell you?"

"She wouldn't tell me anything. She said she didn't want to talk about it--but that maybe she would some day."

I wasn't surprised. Several years ago, writing to me from Australia, in Yiddish, Fanny said, "What do you want from my years? You know very well that I have never been a writer and that wherever possible I utilize the little dots.... You are the man of letters dealing with speeches and problems. How does it enter your head to make me a source of memories, to write memoirs and recall problems of my young years? This is an interesting matter for you. But what have I to do with this?"

Fanny's letter did answer some of my questions. But she ended it by saying, "Dear Yitzhak, you have opened for me a covered night. It hurts me very much to turn back to these times. You say we must not forget. I say I have not forgotten, but I will not talk or write about this anymore. Dear one, do not ask me anymore. I do not remember anymore. You asked. I have answered." She had every right to be impatient with me. But I thought it was better to risk her impatience than to lose anything of the story.

"Do you know about your great-grandmother...and Fima...the role she played?"

"That she raised my father? I know she was like a mother to him."

"So you know something about that, do you? You've thought about it?"

"Yes."

"And your father--," I could not help but ask, "did Fima tell you about my shoes? They were the best pair I ever owned, you know. I still remember them."

You looked puzzled. Shoes? What shoes? "No," you said.

"And the napoleon?"

Still puzzled, you said, "No, I don't know anything about it."

"What about the index finger? Do you know anything about the index finger?

"Index finger?

"Yes."

228

"I have no idea."

We were sitting side by side at the table, two long generations between us. Actually, a whole era separates us. World War One, the Depression, World War Two, the Holocaust, the USSR. They piled up on each other, overlapped each other, interfused each other in my time. Sometimes they are in the foreground of this story, sometimes they are in the background. Either way they are always a presence on stage. Though they belong to "my" time, not yours, they are part of your story too.

It is not only history that comes between us.

In my generation time and distance held mysteries. They still do for me even though times have changed. When the mailman delivered a letter from Europe, it was an event. Such a letter meant something. There was suspense in waiting for it, suspense in receiving it, suspense in opening it, in reading it, in devouring every morsel of news, tasting every word for its nuances of fear and hope, joy and sorrow. You could touch it, read it, put it away, pick it up again, read it again, feel it-- contemplate it. The stamp, the date, the handwriting--they all held meaning, they were all the more exotic because the envelope and its contents had survived unknown dangers of travel across time and distance.

Today, technology has forged a huge gap between us. I grew up at a time when time and distance were still obstacles. They created suspense and appealed to the imagination. The far away and long ago hold no mysteries for you and your generation. For you history is instantaneous. Your mail arrives in an instant, at the touch of a button. And Europe is only a few hours away. An event on the other side of the globe will appear on a screen in your own home at the very moment it is happening. Your generation "reads" screens: television screens, movie screens, computer screens. For your generation images *are* worth a thousand words. They have altered the very nature of thinking. Your generation "thinks" in terms of images that move so fast that the very notion of contemplation is all but obsolete.

Over half the people on earth were born after World War Two. They have no personal knowledge of the War or the Holocaust. How do we speak to them of these events? How does one write of past horrors, when each day's news brings fresh horrors that exceed those of the day before? Assassination, random killing, mass murder, "ethnic cleansing"-- death is an everyday affair in the newspapers, on television, on the movie screen. Current violence is so much a part of life that it no longer shocks us. But there is no escaping history--and certainly not the sheer horror of the blood-soaked history of the twentieth century.

There are things you should know about what it was like to have lived in this exceptional time. The horror began in 1914 with the first World War. With no firsthand experience of it--I was born eleven years later--that war remains an abstraction to me, in a way. Not so the Depression, World War Two, the Holocaust, the USSR--each touched my life, directly and indirectly. I knew well enough that I was alive and living in those days, but I did not know that I was *living* "history." I did not know I was living *inside* history. I did not know that these histories would take up residence in my very own history, that they would come to live inside me.

Abstractions can be very dangerous, Rina. You have to be wary of them because they are so all-encompassing that they drain the life and truth out of the way things really are. Six million--6,000,000--is an abstraction, an all too convenient one these days. What it stands for is the greatest single horror of the century, the greatest crime in Jewish history. Only telling a story can put life and truth back into an abstraction.

Chaim Dembovitz, your great-grandfather, and his son Aharon, your grandmother's brother, were two of the six million. To tell this story is to declare that they were not--are not--abstractions. I do not know how much you know about them. But their story is part of your story. Your father changed his name from Fima to Chaim in memory of his grandfather. In a way, they are part of my story, too. We are all related--to each other and to that horror.

Often, especially upon a first meeting, people will ask you, in all innocence, "Where do you come from?" And you have probably given the simple answer: "I was born in Vilnius" or "I come from Lithuania," and let it go at that. But after you read these pages you will realize that the question is more complex, more serious, more far reaching than it might ever have appeared to you. You will see that your answer contains other questions. Wherever you are when anyone again asks you where you "come from," you will know that your answer "Vilnius"--or do you answer Vilna?--even as you say it, is far from telling the whole story.

What you have in these pages is a cast of characters and a "plot" fit for a novel. You have known many of the major characters. Each of them has a history. At first you will read for the plot, turn the pages to learn "what happened," but you will make a mistake if you read only for the plot. There are documents in it too--so that, in a way, what you have here is also a documentary. This is a story that belongs peculiarly to the twentieth century. But it is no fiction. The twentieth century was no fiction.

This is a story about the mystery of relationship: the worlds that words like "father" and "mother" and "brother" and "sister" encompass. Also "Tante" and "Uncle." And "niece" and "nephew" and "cousin." "Husband" and "wife." "Grandfather" and "grandmother." "Great-grandmother." "Great-grandfather." It is about how the stories within them--their meanings and mysteries--shift depending upon who within a family is using these words and when and where. This is a story about relatives, about the links between relations, between generations. My father did not know Rina and Rina did not know my father. But Rina can and should know something of my father--of his connection to your life.

Because this is a story of generations and their relationships this is inevitably a story built from pieces of various times and different places. Like life itself. Certain times in it are chronological but not logical. Others are logical but not chronological. Like life itself. The events of the story occur at specific times and in specific geographic spaces. But they occur in inner time and inner space too. I have written these pages not only to reclaim these events for myself but for their own sake, not just because of history but in spite of it, too.

They occur when I lived in a world that was larger, far less accessible, than the one I live in now. They occur in a time when I still felt that anyone who came from "somewhere else" was somehow extraordinary. There was something mysterious in their not being from the "here" that I knew. There were stories in what they had left behind--and in what they had brought with them. And I wanted to hear those stories.

Without my father's story or mine or all the others your story, Rina, would not be the one you know, the one you think is yours. You do not--you cannot--have any memory of them. Though these pages were not written for you at first, they were written for you at last. They will remember for you what you cannot remember for yourself: where you came from.

Ancient History

On one of your grandmother's visits to us from Israel, Rina, she presented me with *Mariampole Lithuania*, a *Yizkor* book--a memorial book, a memory book.

Such books have an ancient history. They hark back at least to the Middle Ages. Back then they were called *pinkasim*. A *pinkas* was a record book kept year after year, an ongoing history of life in the Jewish community in a European town or city--a compilation of minutes of meetings, lists of community officers, stories of unusual events, sketches, memoirs, and other matters of interest. After the first World War and especially after the second, Jews who had emigrated from these *shtetlakh*, towns, and cities, as well as survivors of the

Holocaust, were driven by the Jewish mania for remembrance to publish such books to memorialize the Jewish communities they had left behind. They wanted their children, grandchildren, and future generations to know where they had come from. These books--they are often divided into sections according to language--are a rich source of wonderful stories, a gold mine for the historian. In the United States, South Africa, Israel, elsewhere in the world, these *Yizkor* books have brought back into life, albeit only on paper, a vanished world.

The first edition of *Mariampole Lithuania* was published in Tel Aviv in 1983, the second in 1986. Introducing it on a note common to all such books, the editor writes, "A full generation after its destruction we submit, with awe and reverence, this book describing the story of the Jewish community of Mariampole (Lithuania), from its inception until its tragic end." The editor is Avraham Tory.

The Hebrew section lists double-columned pages of victims of the Holocaust. Among them, though they were not from Mariampole, you can find the names of Chaim Dembovitz, your great-grandfather, and Aharon Dembovitz, your granduncle. As with most of the victims of the Holocaust, they lie in no cemetery. No gravestone marks their final resting place. Their only *matzeyveh*--their only gravestone--is on page 189 of the Mariampole *Yizkor* book.

On November 25, 1989, *The Jerusalem Post* carried the kind of story that could well have appeared in a Nuremberg *Yizkor* book--if such a book exists. It is about the return of Meier Schwarz, a professor of bio-technical engineering at the Jerusalem College of Technology, to Nuremberg, where he was born in 1926. He was twelve when he beheld the shell of the Orthodox Adass Yisroel Synagogue, all that remained of the synagogue after it was destroyed on Kristallnacht. When he sought out the site on Essenweinstrasse where the synagogue had once stood, he discovered no marker there, no plaque, no sign that it had ever existed. When he asked city officials why there was no plaque, they answered, "There never was such a building."

On January 6, 1992, *The New York Times* carried an account of a very different kind of visit. It was the story of Irving Balsam's encounter with a history class at St. Mary's High School. in Jersey City. Balsam was fourteen when the Germans invaded Poland on September 1, 1939. He told the class of his life during the Holocaust, how he became number 141938 at Auschwitz-- "I was robbed of my name," he said--and of how he was a prisoner of the Germans for four years. "My story," he said, "is not such ancient history. I was a teenager like you, the son of a tailor, living a happy life not because of material possessions--we were very poor--but happy because I belonged to someone, my family." And then of how the Germans robbed him of that family: they killed his mother and father, his two brothers, and his sister. "Even now," he told the class, "the passage of time has not eased the pain or the horror. I have children and grandchildren. But history never leaves me." When Balsam ended his story, a student asked him, "After all that suffering do you have any German friends?" "No" was all he said.

Every survivor of the Holocaust has had to deal with his experience in his own way. Some like your grandmother, Rina, have chosen silence. But your grandmother's silence, when you think about it, is just *her* way of saying that history never leaves her. Others, like Avraham Tory, Meier Schwarz, Irving Balsam--they know that the past is what gets lost, that you have to fight to save at least some of it, that you have to speak out against the silence that is deadlier to them than death itself. The *Yizkor* book, the names on page 189, all the names listed in all the columns of the murdered, the desire for a plaque, the need to speak to a high school class--all these belong to the Jewish mania for remembrance that has inspired all of Jewish history.

In 1999 in a book review for *The New York Times* Roger Cohen wrote, "For more than a half century now history has had Germany in its grasp, thanks to the enormity of Hitler's genocide. The Third Reich's industrialization of mass murder is as shocking to many young Germans descended from Nazis as it is to Jews descended from victims."[48] The Holocaust is as much in your history, Rina, as it is in

234

the history of a young German or, for that matter, as it should be in the history of a young Lithuanian. It is only fifty-five years since the end of the Holocaust. It is not "such ancient history." The Germans already know this. Perhaps the Lithuanians will too.

The problem for you, Rina, as for everyone, is that you never know until you know. That is, you never know anything--not really--until you know firsthand, from your own experience. You never know--really know--secondhand. Unless you are lucky and gifted with imagination. Perhaps then--but only then. So if you listen closely, you can hear your great-grandmother's voice in her letters. If you listen closely, you can hear something of your grandmother's voice in her letters and on the occasions I managed to capture her on tape. And Tory's voice. And other voices. But you have to listen. If, that is, you want to know something of what Dr. Elkes called "this unparalleled tragedy of our people."

Sometimes I think Americans want to have nothing to do with the past, unless it be on Memorial Day, when we remember our Civil War dead that we wanted not to have died in vain, or on what used to be called Armistice Day, when we once remembered the end of World War I that was to make the world safe for democracy. America was born looking ahead. Sometimes I think it has never looked back since then. At least it has never liked looking back, except maybe on July 4. The sort of thing you mainly hear from us is that the past is "the dead past," that we must let it "bury its dead," that one has to "close the door on the past," and then always, of course, "move on" and "put it behind us." That we *are* our past, that because we are our past it is never over, that it can't be suppressed--these are matters we seldom hear discussed--except, maybe, when the "dead" past crops up to shock us and show us that history has us in its grasp too.

I have lived a half century and more of ancient history. I have never found the past to be over and done with. Rather, I find that from time to time it keeps getting mixed up in the present, just as the present gets mixed up in the past. All the while, what I wanted to find out, how I went about finding out what I was looking for, why I went looking, and the meaning of what I went looking for--this ancient history--has never left me. It never leaves me.

The Starting Point

"I am the man who, with my own eyes, saw those about to die. I was there early in the morning of October 29, in the camp that led to the slaughter at the Ninth Fort. With my own ears I heard the awe-inspiring and terrible symphony, the weeping and screaming of 10,000 people, old and young--a scream that tore at the heart of Heaven. No one had heard such cries through the ages and the generations."

When Dr. Elkhanan Elkes wrote these words for his children in his Last Testament, he was writing about more than *di Groyse Aktzie*, the Great Aktion of the Kovno Ghetto. Though he had no name for it--no one did yet--Elkes knew he had entered *terra incognita*, a world completely different from anything he--or any Jews--had ever experienced before. He was writing about what the Jews would come to call the "Holocaust"--the murder of six million Jews by Germany and its accomplices in Christian Europe in the last four years of World War Two.

Rina, the Holocaust is part of your inheritance. If you ever want to think meaningfully about it--and you should--or to talk about it usefully, you have to start with what is fundamental. This definition is basic. Do not let anyone try to divert you from it.

And they will.

Sports reporters, opponents of abortion, African-Americans, Native Americans, politicians, and others saw soon enough the mileage to be gained by linking their words and causes to the Holocaust. And misappropriate the word they did--with a vengeance. A lopsided defeat on the football field became a holocaust. Abortion became a holocaust perpetrated against the "unborn." Slavery was a holocaust perpetrated by whites against blacks. Likewise the American treatment of the Indians. And so on. As the holocausts have multiplied and continue to multiply the original meaning of the term has gradually faded from memory. The Holocaust has turned into a metaphor that has not only diminished the meaning but demeaned it. When you hear someone speak of "the Jewish Holocaust," you know that, intentionally or not, he is reducing its uniqueness to one among many. Holocaust deniers would reduce it altogether--to a lie. The term has been popularly accepted in almost every way except in its original sense. Without the underpinning of its definition, Rina, you will find that honest discussion of the event itself is hopeless.

Universalists of every stripe have expanded the term beyond recognition--to include Jehovah's Witnesses, Gypsies, homosexuals, Russian prisoners of war, and Poles.

If you look into the facts, you will find that in 1933, when Hitler came into power, there were about 20,000 German Jehovah's Witnesses in Germany. In that year, according to the *Encyclopedia of the Holocaust*, "a convention of the Witnesses in Germany was still able to declare that essentially it had no quarrel with the National Socialist government, and in principle shared its hostile attitude toward Bolshevism and the church, and its anti-Semitism." The Nazis persecuted them only when they refused to make the Heil Hitler salute and to serve in the army. Even then, by signing a statement promising to cease their activities for their organization, they could have avoided the concentration camp. Jews had none of these options.

You will find that most pure blooded Gypsies were not killed. Hundreds of thousands of others of mixed blood and marked as "asocials" were murdered. But the Germans had no fixed policy to annihilate all Gypsies. Only Jews were slated for total destruction.

You will find that the Nazis also regarded homosexuals as asocials. The *Encyclopedia* records that about ten thousand were sent to concentration camps and that many died there. Before the war's end, however, some were freed to serve in the Wehrmacht. Nor did the

Germans make any effort to pursue homosexuals in the countries they occupied.

The Germans captured 5,700,000 Russian soldiers. You will find that of the 3,300,000 Russian prisoners of war who perished the overwhelming number died not in concentration camps but in POW camps and that they died from starvation, epidemics, exposure, arbitrary executions, and general mistreatment. They were not murdered *en masse*. The Germans put over 600,000 Russian POWs to work for them. A million more volunteered to assist the German armed forces. Almost another million were still in German camps at the end of the war. In any case, a prisoner of war is not a victim of the Holocaust; a prisoner of war is a victim of war. The Holocaust is about the German war against the Jews; the Holocaust is not about the German war against the Former Soviet Union.

The Germans killed three million Poles. They used murder and terror in an effort to destroy Poland as a nation. You will find that they wanted to subdue, control, and enslave its people--but not to wipe all of them off the face of the earth. The Poles--like the Jehovah's Witnesses, the Gypsies, the homosexuals, the Russian POWs--were victims of the war. Like the others they were often caught in the merciless machinery of the Holocaust. But only Jews were victims of the Holocaust.

The Wannsee Conference in Berlin on January 20, 1942, was called to put into motion "the final solution of the Jewish question." The conference applied only to the Jews. It formalized what was already underway: the Great Aktion took place at the Ninth Fort on October 29, 1941. The Final Solution was uniquely intended and ultimately designed for one purpose: to eliminate 11,000,000 Jews from Europe. It was to be the first step in the eventual eradication of all Jews from the whole world.

The political commentator George Will put it this way: "Yes, before the killing of Jews became systematic, the killing of the mentally retarded was systematic in Germany. Yes, the Nazis killed Gypsies and others. Yes, Mao and Stalin were much more prolific killers than Hitler....But we falsify and trivialize the Holocaust when we bend it to our convenience, making it a symbol--of general beastliness, or whatever. It was not a symbol; it was a fact....the Holocaust was directed murderously against particular victims--Jews. Their tragedy cannot be appropriated by others as a useful metaphor."[49]

"Treblinka," says Will, "is the starkest testimony to the radical evil that gives the Holocaust its stunning uniqueness, its apartness from all other human experiences. The radicalism was in its furious focus on Jews." And he fears anything having "the effect of diminishing the Holocaust, sinking it back into the stream of history by blurring its monstrous clarity.   That clarity is a function of the Holocaust's particularity: all the resources of a modern state were turned toward the destruction of one people, the Jews."[50]

There was no Wannsee Conference and no Final Solution for the Jehovah's Witnesses, the Gypsies, the homosexuals, the Russian POWs, the Poles. The Final Solution--in German it is the *Endlosung*-- was aimed at the Jews. In its scope, in its magnitude, in its purpose, in its relentless fury, in its unique target, the Holocaust was intended only for the Jews.

What you really have to ask is why so much effort has been expended to diminish the meaning of the term, to trivialize it, to distort it, to deny it, to expand it beyond recognition.   If you want to think meaningfully about the Holocaust, Rina, this is the question you have to pursue. But it will lead you into deep water.

The Defining Moment

Nowadays the term "defining moment" has become something of a cliché. It wasn't a cliché in the summer of 1943 when Avraham Tory arrived at a defining moment. He set the moment down in his *Diary* in words that are still as chilling as the day he wrote them.   Life in the

Kovno Ghetto, he wrote, is "without precedent not just in Jewish history, but in universal history as well."

The Holocaust as a field of historical study is unprecedented. "Holocaust literature" is an unprecedented genre. Never before has there been such testimony and documentation for a murder. Barely half a century after the Holocaust the bibliography of the Holocaust is as unprecedented as the event itself. You would think, therefore, that, no matter what, Tory's statement--and all that it implies--would go unchallenged. Within the Jewish community, however, there are those who fear that the Holocaust has usurped the center of Jewish life and become a priority undercutting other Jewish causes and issues, that it has emphasized Jewish victimization and teaches negative lessons to the young. And they point especially to the proliferation of Holocaust museums and memorials to make the case that the Holocaust has become a Jewish obsession. Some members of the rabbinate are deeply concerned that the Holocaust is turning into a secular religion and becoming a sort of substitute Judaism. They have good reason to be concerned. Rather than address the question of God's ways toward the Jew during the Holocaust they prefer to see the central place that the Holocaust has taken in the Jewish world as an encroachment upon their territory.

In the academy, Irwin Weil, a professor at Northwestern University, voices a typical complaint. He admits to "deep feelings about what the Nazis destroyed in World War II," but insists that the Holocaust is "not the most memorable event in Jewish history. Shall we forget Jewish medieval philosophy and history? Forget the beautiful verse of the Bible? Ignore Jewish culture and the music of Jewish services?...If the Jews let the Holocaust become the most important event in Jewish history, Hitler has won."[51]

Elie Wiesel is the last person in the world who would give Hitler any kind of a victory. But for him there is no question of the centrality of the Holocaust. He sees the Holocaust as incomparably "the most important event in Jewish history and in human history." For him the

Revelation at Sinai is the only possible comparison to the Holocaust, and then only because it is the anti-Sinai. The Holocaust is "even more important than the rebirth of Israel." Moreover, it demands "a new philosophy of Jewish existence," a re-examination of man's "relationship to his Creator, to society, to politics, to literature, to his fellow man, and to himself." Everything--everything--in the Jewish future, he declares, will have to "be seen in the light of the fiery shadow of the Holocaust." What could be more central?

Wiesel is far from alone in his view of the Holocaust as the unique defining event of our time. The German philosopher Karl Jaspers, for example, maintains that anyone who "plans the organized slaughter of a people and participates in it, does something that is fundamentally different from all crimes that have existed in the past." The Jewish philosopher Emil Fackenheim calls the Holocaust "a horror like no other...even now nobody really knows how to live with it." In his opening statement at the Nuremberg trials Justice Robert H. Jackson said, "History does not record a crime ever perpetrated against so many victims or one ever carried out with such calculated cruelty." Learning of the final disaster that had befallen Hungarian Jewry, Winston Churchill wrote that "this is probably the greatest and most horrible crime ever committed in the whole history of the world." In *The Holocaust and the Historians* Lucy Dawidowicz wrote "Never before in human history had a state and a political movement dedicated itself to the destruction of a whole people." In *The Rise and Fall of the Third Reich* William L. Shirer wrote, "This burning hatred, which was to infect so many Germans [in the Third Reich]..., would lead ultimately to a massacre so horrible and on such a scale as to leave an ugly scar on civilization that will surely last as long as man on earth." The political commentator William Pfaff wrote in *The New Yorker* (December 7, 1987) that "A Jew, any Jew--also any German, any European, any American, any citizen of Western civilization--must look at himself today in a way that he never could have if the Holocaust had not taken place." For the political commentator George Will, "The Holocaust was not just the central event of the 20th century; it was the hinge of modern history." In his Foreword to Elie Wiesel's *Night* Francois Mauriac saw the Holocaust as marking "the end of one era and the beginning of another." In her Introduction to Gideon Hausner's *Justice in Jerusalem* the historian Barbara Tuchman writes that the Holocaust deals "not simply with Germans and Jews, with war crimes and unimaginable atrocity but...fundamentally with the human soul....what we are confronting here is the soul of man in the twentieth century." The Holocaust, she says, "inflicted a moral damage on mankind. It horribly scarred man's image of himself, with effects that society is now showing."

Each of these statements is an attempt to define the defining moment. Follow any one of them, Rina, and it will take you far out and in deep. But I recommend still another one to you. It appears in a work of fiction that isn't even about the Holocaust, not directly anyway. It appears in "For Esme--with Love and Squalor," one of the best short stories J. D. Salinger ever wrote. It's a love story and a war story both.

The narrator-hero is a veteran who has experienced the war firsthand from the D-day landing through and beyond V-E Day. Billeted in the home of a minor Nazi official, a woman he has himself arrested, he chances upon a book belonging to her. The book and an inscription in it stun him. Every time I reach this point in the story its author's name and the title of his book leap from the page to define for me--beyond Salinger--the central truth that Tory and the Tante and her family lived.

The author was Dr. Paul Goebbels.

He called his book *Die Zeit Ohne Beispiel--The Time without Example.*

The War

Rina, to begin to know where you "come from," you have to understand the war.

"Slaves of the Jews" is as good a place to start as any.   It's an article that appeared in the July 7, 1943, issue of *Ateitis* (*Future*), a Lithuanian newspaper published in Kovno by pro-Nazi Lithuanians. SS Colonel Lenzen, governor-general of the Kovno district, wrote it. Avraham Tory recorded parts of it in his *Diary*.

"The Jews," Lenzen wrote, "are the source of all evil. Everywhere they go, they bring trouble and destruction in their wake. The Jews are to blame for the outbreak of the Second World War. The culpability of the Jews for the war is the cause of the German decision to remove them from all spheres of life.   There is no difference between the Jews in the Kremlin in Moscow, the Jews on Wall Street, the Jews of the English plutocracy, and the Jews from the Kovno Ghetto."[52]

Whether or not your grandmother or your great-grandmother ever saw his words, they heard them often enough in one form or another, as had other Jews in Kovno.   They were the party line in Kovno and everywhere--in the Warsaw Ghetto, for example, where Emmanuel Ringelblum recorded them in early October, 1940: "The Jews wanted the war; the Jews are responsible for the war.   That's the slogan repeated by the Others, even the best of them, in every conversation."[53]

More explicit were the words Reichsfuhrer Heinrich Himmler, the head of the SS, spoke to his senior SS officers at Poznan in Poland, on October 4, 1943.   Though theirs was to be "an unwritten and never-to-be-written page of glory in our history," their goal, he said outright, was "the extermination of the Jewish people."   "We had the moral right," he declared, "we had the duty towards our people, to destroy the people that wanted to destroy us."

On January 30, 1939--the sixth anniversary of his rise to power-- Hitler told the Reichstag, "Today I will once more be a prophet: If the international Jewish financiers...should succeed in plunging the nations once more into a world war, then the result will not be the

Bolshevization of the earth, and thus the victory of Jewry, but the annihilation of the Jewish race in Europe!"

He returned to this theme often enough. Prophecy turned into a war. The Jews were responsible for the war; therefore the Jews were the enemy; therefore the war against them was justified. Hitler, Himmler, Lenzen, the Germans, and their accomplices devoutly believed their own propaganda, spread it across Europe, and went to war for it. To judge from the perspective of their own propaganda, World War II was--more than anything else--a war against the Jews.

In a military sense the war against the Jews was no war at all. A war means adversaries, enemies equipped and prepared to do battle to kill each other. The Jews of Germany and in the rest of Europe were an unarmed, defenseless civilian population. When it launched its direct attack on the Jews, Germany had its police, its soldiers, its generals to throw into the "battle." It had bullets and bombs, flame throwers and grenades. It established, operated, and maintained ghettos and labor camps, concentration camps and death camps. It had firing squads and it had gas chambers. And defying the rules of warfare, it gave no quarter to the Jews it relentlessly pursued, trapped, and captured: it executed six million Jewish captives. The "war" was a completely one-sided affair, so fanatic, malevolent, and implacable that it continued long after the war against the United States, Great Britain, and the USSR was already lost, continued, in fact, until the very last day of that other war.

Adolf Hitler finished his Political Testament at four o'clock in the morning on April 29, 1945. Twenty-four hours later your great-grandmother's Haman committed suicide. His very last command from his bunker in Berlin was for Germany to continue the war against the Jews.

Because they were Jews

Rina, you have to be careful. Over and over again, you will encounter it in popular articles, read it in museum explanations, hear it in conversations among your friends and acquaintances. It has been repeated so often that it has been taken for granted as self-evident and undeniable--so obvious historically that it needs no further comment. "The Holocaust happened to the Jews," so the explanation goes, "just because they were Jews" --"just" in the sense of "only" or "solely" and "for no other reason" than that they were born Jews.

Just because they were Jews? Don't you believe it.

A crime requires a motive. The Holocaust was a crime. It was six million crimes. It was murder on such an unprecedented scale, executed with such relentless violence and ferocious brutality, and carried out with such fiendish determination to the very end of the war that, clearly, the motive behind it must have reached far beyond "just because they were Jews."

You can't consider the motive behind the Holocaust without recognizing its specificity. The Jews were not accidental victims--they were the chosen, selected enemy. Whatever threats the Nazis saw in their other victims, they did not see in any of them the moral-philosophical threat--and therefore the mortal threat--they perceived in the Jew. Not one of the others possessed the vision of life that animated the Jew. Nor had any of them--as a people--made so central a contribution to Western Civilization.

The Jews were the specific target. They were on Hitler's mind in his early manhood. They were on his mind when he wrote *Mein Kampf.* They were on his mind in the last few hours of his life. German Jews were the specific target of the Nuremberg Laws. They were the specific target of Kristallnacht. Wannsee and the Final Solution were specifically aimed at one target, one people: the Jews. And none other. Half of Germany's Jews escaped Germany in time:

some before Hitler came to power, some as soon as he came to power, and the rest while the exit doors remained open. All the Jews who fled realized they were the specific target. So did many who did not have the means to escape when the opportunity was still there. And so, sooner or later, did all the rest who remained after the doors were closed.

Only because they were Jews? *Exactly* because they were Jews.

You can't consider the motive without recognizing the totality of the Holocaust. The Germans and their accomplices targeted every last Jew anywhere and everywhere in a vast, relentless manhunt. They allowed no surrender, gave no quarter. They took no prisoners--except sooner or later to execute them. Lithuania was a foreshadowing. The Germans imprisoned 30,000 Jews in the Kovno Ghetto. They murdered thousands of them at the Ninth Fort, more thousands at the Seventh Fort and the Fourth Fort. The Germans and their Lithuanian accomplices captured and executed almost all of Lithuanian Jewry. Their pursuit of the Lithuanian Jews--and the millions of other Jews elsewhere--was so extreme, radical, and fanatic that their motive had to be something more than "just because they were Jews." Scholars and laymen have not been exactly shy about offering racial, social, and political motives for the Holocaust. But the Holocaust was of such an unprecedented magnitude that the usual motives simply don't satisfy.

On November 13, 1940, as he saw the walls of the Warsaw Ghetto go up, Chaim Kaplan wrote in his diary, "Is this not a dream? No, it is bitter, tragic Jewish reality. It is the fate of an entire people." On June 9, 1942, less than two months before his last entry, he wrote, "...never before in history has any tyranny ever allowed itself to proclaim publicly that it is preparing to annihilate an entire people." Others were trapped in the machinery of the Holocaust and destroyed by it. But whatever threats the Nazis saw in their other victims, they never planned, mounted, or launched an attack so massive as to eradicate them totally. Only the Jews were to be wiped from the face of the earth. If the Jews and their vision were supposed to be a beacon to the nations, then the German goal was to extinguish their light--totally. They were determined to annihilate an entire people. Totally.

Just because they were Jews? For no other reason?

You can't consider the motive behind the Holocaust without asking the inescapable question: *why* the Jews? Inescapable--but hardly anyone ever asks it. Asked or not, it remains the key question. And, no matter what, it never goes away.

What, in fact, was "the Jewish Problem" that it required 6,000,000 murders in an attempt to solve it--that it demanded not only a solution but a bloody Final Solution? What impelled the Germans and their all too willing accomplices to carry out the Holocaust? What drove the Germans to continue the Holocaust even *after* they knew they had already lost the war? The real question of motive remains: *why* the Jews?

"Tzu makhen ah bessern velt." In the days when I still asked my mother, "Why be Jewish? What's the point of all this suffering?" this was the answer she gave me. No matter what their own suffering, this was the answer that my mother and father lived every day of their lives, Rina. And by living it, they transmitted it to my brother and me. They expressed it in Yiddish. "To make a better world" is the exact, word-for-word translation. But the Yiddish contains a whole universe inaccessible to the word-for-word English translation: a whole moral-philosophical-historical universe of values.

Tzu makhen ah bessern velt. What it meant, Rina, was that the Jew--by definition--was committed to work for a better world, to work for social justice, for a civil society. He took on a code of laws, commandments, that set forth, among much else, the moral basis for the conduct of men toward each other and so pointed to the possibility of a civilized life within the Jewish community. But the Jew also understood that if social justice was good for his own community, it ought to be good for the larger society in which he had to live. Moreover, he understood that he really had no choice except to work

247

for social justice in that larger society if he was to have any hope of living within it with some measure of peace and security.

Early on, the Jew arrived at the idea of a better world--better than the one in which he found himself--and at the idea of making progress toward it, or at least at the possibility of making progress toward it. And he has clung to it ardently, long, and tenaciously. And with hope. Always with hope--hope that he embodied in the messianic vision or that the messianic vision embodied in him. Somehow, in one form or another, he has managed to get word of it out into the Western tradition, even seen it work its way into the very history of Western Civilization.

The Nazis, however, had something very different in mind for the world. They had one major goal: to create a New Order, a new world order. Instinctively, they recognized the Jewish vision as a vital denial of the New Order and therefore an obstacle to it. If the power of the Jewish idea had survived because the people who believed in it for thousands of years had survived and still believed in it, then the only way to be rid of the threat was to rid the world of the people who had originated it and kept it alive and vital. Instinctively, they recognized the Jew as their anti-world, their antithesis, their mortal enemy. Here was motive enough for the Holocaust. Instinctively, they understood there could be no room for the Jew in their New Order. Germany had to be made *Judenrein*. Europe had to be made *Judenrein*. The world had to be made *Judenrein*.

Yes, you have to say it: the Jews were victims of the Holocaust "just because they were Jews." But make no mistake about it, Rina: the crime was committed not simply because they were Jews but *precisely* because they were Jews.

When you consider the motive behind the Holocaust, you have to recognize that Hitler, Germany, and the Nazis--and their accomplices--were in line with centuries long historical tradition. At many and various times and places the Catholics hated the Protestants, and the Protestants hated the Catholics. But on one issue they agreed:

248

they both hated the Jews. In the twentieth century the Nazis hated the Communists, and the Communists hated the Nazis. But on one matter they agreed: they both hated the Jews. What was it about the Jew that could bring Catholic and Protestant, Nazi and Communist into agreement about the Jew and make him their specific target? What they all saw and understood was that the Jewish vision was incompatible with their own, the antithesis of their own.

The Christian vision was, as it continues to be, a messianic vision. The Communist vision, though it eliminated God, was also fundamentally a future oriented messianic vision. The Nazi vision was a messianic one, as well. *"Ein Volk! Ein Reich! Ein Fuhrer!"* was supposed to culminate with *"Heute Deutschland! Morgen die Welt!"* If "One Folk! One Reich! One Fuhrer!" meant that "Today Germany" was theirs, it also meant that "Tomorrow the world" was destined to be theirs, too. All theirs.

When you consider the motive behind the Holocaust, you have to consider the precarious place of the Jew in the history of the West. As the historian Barbara Tuchman put it (in her introduction to Gideon Hausner's *Justice in Jerusalem*), "An old and enormous paradox lies buried here: that the Western world should have adopted for itself the religious and ethical system formulated by the Jews while periodically practicing or acquiescing in attempts to destroy them." Christianity, Communism, and Nazism saw danger not so much in the Jew's relationship to God as in his emphasis on man's relationship to man, on right conduct that would lead *tzu ah bessern velt.* All three saw the Jewish vision of life as a deadly contradiction to their own. At one time or another each believed that it could destroy the Jewish idea by eliminating the people who embodied it. You could kill the message by killing the messenger, and the Christians and the Communists experimented with various ways of killing the messenger.

But it remained for the Germans to go to actual full blown warfare against the Jews. Their war was a war against what the Jew stood for. It was never a war against an armed enemy. Nazi logic was simple. To defeat an idea totally all you had to do was murder all those who held

249

it. The Holocaust was specific to the Jews. It was an ideological matter, a crime ultimately designed to destroy an entire people, first in Europe, then everywhere in the world.

The Holocaust did not come into being overnight. The Holocaust was almost two millennia in the making. The preparation took time. It began with the central charge that the Jews killed Christ. The motive grew and flourished in various places at different times. It took many shapes and forms. It became historical. But there was a common line: exile, expulsion, crusades, Chmelnitzkes, pogroms, trials, massacres, abductions, forced conversions, torture, every conceivable--and inconceivable--violence. No other people has over so long a time and in so many different places undergone such persecution and still so stubbornly and mysteriously managed to survive.

But when the Holocaust came, it came swiftly. The Germans and their accomplices murdered 6,000,000 Jews in four years. The Germans had the willing cooperation of Lithuanians, Latvians, Estonians, Hungarians, Dutch, Rumanians, Croatians, Russians, Poles, and many others. The Holocaust these executioners perpetrated was no primitive reversal of civilization. The Holocaust was the historical end-of-the-line result, the logical outcome of an unappeasable anti-Semitism. And the Germans, Catholic and Protestant, were nothing if not masters of its logic.

The Holocaust was the implicit made explicit. When Hitler said, "Christ has been the greatest pioneer in the struggle against the Jewish world enemy....The task which Christ began but did not finish I will complete,"[54] he was in the realm of the ultimate. Everything else--almost two thousand years of preparation--was penultimate.

"Just because they were Jews," Rina? Only because they were Jews? For no other reason than that they were born Jewish?

Don't you believe it.

The Bone

Whenever I heard my mother say, *"Mir shteyen zey vi ah beyn in haldz,"* I knew instinctively what she meant. I understood immediately. No need for her to elaborate. My mother would never have thought of herself as defining the Jew in history, but that is what she was doing. It was history as she had heard it, seen it, knew it. It was Jewish history almost two thousand years old; it was Jewish history up-to-date.

"We are like a bone in their throat" is what her Yiddish said. "We" were the Jews. Most often "they" were the Christians. But frequently enough "they" were also the Russians under the Tsar, or the communists under Stalin, or the Germans under Hitler. It is a fundamental definition, Rina. And you have to understand it if you are to understand certain essentials about the Holocaust.

In 1978 the Protestant theologian Franklin H. Littell asked, "How could it happen that 6,000,000 Jews were murdered by baptized Christians in the heart of Christendom, with the leaders of the so-called Christian nations either perpetrators or spectators?"[55] It's a key question, and you have to follow it wherever it leads.

This is how it happened.

You have to go back almost two thousand years to the Gospels, a word that itself means "good tidings" or "good news." The Gospels were "good news" for the Christians. But they have been bad news for the Jews ever since. Telling and retelling the story of Jesus, the Christians made the initial charge: that the Jews killed Christ. And with it, though they could not have known it, they set the direction and tone of Western civilization. Wander almost anywhere around Europe and you will see the undiminished power of the Crucifixion--in sculptures in wood, metal, marble, and stone, in marketplaces, at roadside shrines, in churches and museums. In paintings and in stained glass.

But most of all that power resides in the words of the Gospels, in the words, for example, of the Gospel according to Matthew. Matthew does not take it upon himself to point the finger of blame at the Jews for the death of Christ. He has the Jews themselves do it for him. When he has them say, "His blood be upon us and on our children," he has them acknowledging in their own words not only their own guilt but accepting it for all their descendants as well.

Ever since they were created the Gospels have had a life of their own among believers. But no matter how much progress Christian churches have made since the Holocaust in their attempts to qualify, modify, and reinterpret the teachings of the Gospels, the texts remain an unaltered source of anti-Semitism except among the more enlightened. Guilt by association has kept the charge against the Jews alive to this very day. And every other charge leveled against Jews--no matter how transformed by economics, politics, religion, or culture-- can, one way or another, be traced back to it. For the unenlightened Christians and even for the more sophisticated the stubborn Jewish rejection of Christ remains a bone in the throat.

The message of the Gospels was clear and unmistakable. The Holocaust did not come out of thin air. What has been called "the longest hatred" became a basic premise, a vital part of the European Christian tradition. Generation after generation, church, school, and home taught the essential story: the Jew as Christ-killer. Accepted, taken for truth, unquestioned, it was widespread, powerful--and deadly. The Jew was forever suspect, forever guilty as charged, forever the enemy. Once he was labeled the Christ-killer, any evil could be attached to him. He was guilty of poisoning the wells, guilty of the ritual murder of Christian children, guilty of a conspiracy to rule the world. Over the centuries, at various times in various places, the Jew was the obvious enemy and therefore fair game: he could be kidnapped for ransom, sold into slavery, forced to choose between baptism and death, expelled from city or country; his property could be confiscated, his home and synagogue looted; he could be the target of Crusade and Inquisition, of pogroms and mass murder. Hatred of the Jew was ingrained in daily life. It was embedded in literature: in the story of Hugh of Lincoln in Chaucer's "The Prioress's Tale," in Shakespeare's Shylock, in Dickens's Fagin, in the Oberammergau Passion play produced almost every ten years since 1634. It was in cartoons, newspapers, folk tales, nursery rhymes. In time it became natural, second nature, as natural as the air the Christians breathed. Anti-Semitism was in the nature of things.

By singling the Jew out as the Christ killer the Christians unwittingly put into motion the law of unintended consequences: they actually created "the Jewish Problem" with which they have saddled themselves for two thousand years. The Jews didn't create the Jewish Problem: the Christians did. It's their problem. And Western civilization has been indelibly marked ever since by their efforts to solve it. Ever since then *mir shteyen zey vi ah beyn in haldz*.

Judaism could very well have existed without Christianity, but not Christianity without the Jews. In the beginning the Church actually needed the Jews precisely for their uncompromising rejection of Christ. The Jews provided a necessary obstacle, a challenge to be met and overcome, a made-to-order opportunity for the Church to assert its own superior truth. But ever since then, in its continued rejection of Christ, in its continued refusal--no matter what--to convert, in short, in its stubborn refusal to go under, the hard core of Judaism has also proved an obstruction to Christianity, long after and far beyond its original usefulness as a negation of the Church. Ever since then *mir shteyen zey vi ah beyn in haldz*.

What happened was that almost two thousand years of Christian history culminated in the Holocaust. What happened was that "baptized Christians in the heart of Christendom"--Germans and their collaborators throughout Europe--killed six million Jews while other baptized Christians looked on or turned their eyes away.

What happened was that most Christian nations in the West not only stood by but for the most part actually stood in the way of rescuing or aiding the Jews. At Evian and Bermuda America and Great

Britain--leaders of the democratic West--led international conferences designed to save Jewish refugees, then turned them into fiascoes. Though within range of Auschwitz and the railroad lines leading to it, American and British planes somehow never managed to bomb them, not even symbolically. And France--the France that had proclaimed liberty, fraternity, and equality, that had been the first to emancipate its Jews, that had been a bastion of the democratic West--France for its part, actively assisting the Germans, managed to send over 70,000 Jews to their death, one-third of them French citizens.

What happened, says the Jewish theologian Eliezer Berkovits, is that the Holocaust exposed "a morally and spiritually bankrupt civilization and religion."[56]

***

Mir shteyen zey vi ah beyn in haldz. "We" were always the Jews. For my mother we were sometimes the bone in the throat of the Russian Empire.

I never heard either of my parents speak, in Yiddish or in English, of the Pale of Settlement. As a child I never knew that Lithuania was in the Pale or that they had been born in it. I never really knew what it was. Most of the time when I encountered "the Pale," it was the mystery word in the phrase "beyond the Pale." I guessed "beyond the Pale" meant "beyond the limit" or "beyond the boundary" or "beyond the fence," but I was never sure what it meant in the context of Russia and Jews.

The fact is that by the end of the nineteenth century over 5,000,000 Jews--ninety-four percent of the Jews in Russia--lived in the Pale, in territory taken from Poland a hundred years earlier. From the beginning most of the Jews simply did not belong. They were alien in dress, customs, diet, language, culture. But most of all they were alien in religion. By their sheer numbers they stood "in the way" of the throne. By the sheer strength of their faith they stood "in the way" of

254

the Russian Orthodox Church. To the mid-eighteenth century Empress Elizabeth the Jews were, above all, 'the enemies of Christ." A bone in the throat.

Catherine the Great, Elizabeth's successor, hit upon the Pale of Settlement as the solution to Russia's Jewish problem. To be rid of the Jews all you had to do was simply restrict them to where almost all of them already lived--in the western part of Russia, from the Baltic to the Black Sea, an area that amounted to only four percent of the empire. In effect, Catherine turned the Pale of Settlement into a huge ghetto. She must have believed out of sight really meant out of mind. A little over a century later the Jews were, if anything, even more in sight and in mind than ever--so much so that Konstantin Pobedonostsev, advisor to Nickolas II, looked forward to an even more radical solution to the Jewish problem: that one-third of Russia's Jews would be forced to emigrate, one-third would be converted, and one-third would die. The goal never changed: to be rid of the Jews. To get them out of the way, to get them to go away, to transform them into non-Jews, to starve them, to kill them. Anything to get rid of them.

Joseph Heller's novel Catch-22 had the perfect word for it: what the Tsars and the Church wanted most of all was to "disappear" the Jews, no matter how.

***

Mir shteyen zey vi ah beyn in haldz. For my mother the Jews were also a bone in the throat of the Communist Empire.

Both my parents left a Russia still ruled by the Tsars. They were among Pobyedonostsev's third that were to be forced or encouraged to emigrate. When the 1917 Revolution ended the Tsarist regime, the Romanovs left behind a Russia securely locked into the centuries-old anti-Semitism that they and the Russian Orthodox Church had successfully exploited. They also left behind their Jewish problem.

But Communism was now the new religion. And the Jews proved as much a bone in the throat of its true believers as they had been in the throat of the Tsars and the Russian Orthodox Church. Even more so. What the communists wanted was exactly what the Tsars wanted: that the Jews be absorbed into the general Russian population. Rejecting the idea of a nation within a nation, they simply denied the Jews their nationality. At the same time, however, they saw the Jews as enough of a nationality to want to destroy that nationality. More important, they must have understood that the Jewish messianic vision was incompatible with their Communist messianic vision and a threat to it. And, in fact, they saw no other course of action than to "disappear" the Jews.

The communists were more vicious than the Tsars. For most of the years of its existence the USSR did all it could to deprive the Jew of his difference, of his Jewishness, of his Jewish identity. Stalin and his successors suppressed Hebrew, undermined Yiddish. They shut down schools and synagogues, closed newspapers, theaters, community organizations. They were determined to de-Judaize the Jew, to put an end to his culture and his history. Like the Tsars, they wanted to "disappear" the Jew into the larger whole.

Under Stalin, anti-Semitism took the form of outright murder. Accused of being "spies" and "traitors," prominent, and not so prominent, Jews simply disappeared into the night after they answered the dreaded knock on the door. Stalin's secret police executed Jewish intellectuals--writers and poets. Hundreds of others--artists, musicians, actors--simply vanished into concentration camps. The communists took the same tack as the Germans during the Intellectuals Aktion in the Kovno Ghetto. They cut off the head of the Russian Jews, to deprive them of the leaders of their culture and hasten their disappearance into the masses.

Stalin's anti-Semitism had especially disastrous consequences for the Jews during the Holocaust. His press did not report the German war against the Jews. It made no distinction between Jewish and non-Jewish victims of the Nazis. Kept in the dark, Jews in the west were

256

totally unprepared for the German onslaught. Had they known what was happening, thousands might have escaped the Nazis. The Soviets refused to acknowledge the Holocaust during the war. They refused to acknowledge it after the war. According to them, no Jews ever died at the hands of the Nazis: only "Soviet citizens." Soviet propaganda simply converted Jewish victims to "victims of Fascism." Nazi crimes against the Jews were transformed into "crimes against the Soviet people." During the war--in more than one way--Stalin disappeared the Jews.

Whether it was based on his years of study for the priesthood or on his political ideology, or on both, Stalin's anti-Semitism drove him to the very last days of his life. In his last years, still ruling by terror, he trumped up the Doctors' Plot, accusing a group of doctors, mostly Jews, of conspiring to murder Soviet party leaders and generals. His aim was to incite public anti-Semitism, even pogroms, as a pretext to deport large numbers of Jews to Siberia, where, rumor had it, concentration camps were being built to hold as many as 250,000 Jews. Only his death in March, 1953, cut short his last attempt to disappear the Jews.

***

Mir shteyen zey vi ah beyn in haldz. "We" were the Jews, and "they" were the Germans.

The German killers and their accomplices grew up in a Christian world which for centuries had relentlessly driven home the Christian story of Jewish guilt--that from the very beginning the Jews were guilty as charged. They absorbed the story and its lessons all too well.

The Nazis, the Germans behind them, and all their collaborators saw--however dimly--that the Jews were a people whose ideas and values--whose concepts of law, morality, conscience, and social justice--were a philosophical threat, a spiritual threat, a mortal threat to them and their own vision of the world.

At the same time they could look back on centuries of Christian efforts to overcome the Jews. The Christians had tried everything: expulsion, pogrom, the stake, Crusade, the ghetto, blood libel, imprisonment, confiscation of property, the yellow badge, the burning of the Talmud, massacre and mob action. Nothing had convinced them. No matter what, the Jews had rejected Christ and his story. Despite every persecution, despite history itself there was still no conversion of the Jews.

The Germans knew full well that the Jews were no physical threat. But just as clearly they saw the Jews as the enemy they had been ever since the Gospels. And the Germans drew the logical conclusion from their major premise. Since all efforts to overcome the Jews through the Christian centuries had fallen short, they would be the ones to solve the Jewish problem. They had the Final Solution for it--and it would be absolute, irrevocable, total. They arrived at the one last way to achieve the conversion of the Jews: death itself. And first of all for European Jewry. They had the means, they had the will, and they had the opportunity. And, most of all, they had the imagination. Death was the way to disappear the Jews, once and for all.

And they came close. The Germans and their accomplices came very close. They literally disappeared six million Jews in fire and smoke, in mass graves, in unmarked graves.

But the bone in their throat remains.

***

Mir shteyen zey vi ah beyn in haldz. My mother's words applied to Christianity, to Catholic, Protestant, Russian Orthodox, to the Tsar and the Communists, to the Germans. All gave the Jew the highest priority in their individual scheme of things. And my mother's words apply as well to the Jews in Jewish history who cannot bear to be Jews, to the non-Jewish Jews, to universalist Jews, to the assimilated Jew--all of whose various denials of the bone only affirm its existence for them.

The nature of the bone in the throat--this bone, at least--is that it is lodged so peculiarly that it can't be swallowed and it can't be coughed up. It just remains lodged there. It can't be eliminated. To be sure, this is not a good position for the bone. But it is not a good position for the throat either.

The Offer

How did Di Tante and her family live through the Kovno Ghetto? Surely you have asked yourself this question, Rina. I know I have--a thousand times. But the question is misleading. You can't really explain how Di Tante and her family "lived through" the Kovno Ghetto without first asking how they lived through the weeks before they entered the ghetto. I do not know exactly when the family entered the ghetto, but what they must have faced at every turn between the German takeover of Kovno and the day the ghetto gates closed on them makes it difficult to understand how they got through at all--all of them. Each day hung on chance, on not being in the wrong place at the wrong time.

The Slobotkeh pogrom in June was only the beginning. In the days that followed, into early July, the Lithuanian partisans arrested thousands of Jews. The historian Joseph Gar writes that at the beginning of July alone "Seven to eight thousand Jewish men were machine-gunned to death [at the Seventh Fort]... and buried in mass graves dug by Soviet prisoners of war."[57] Not only did the Lithuanians carry out the massacre, says Gar, they organized it together with the Gestapo.[58]

On July 4,[59] with the Lithuanian massacres of the Jews at the Seventh Fort very much in the foreground, the Gestapo called a five member Jewish committee to Gestapo headquarters. Avraham Tory describes the meeting in the July 7 entry in his *Diary*. Seated on a sofa, the Jews standing before him, the Kovno Gestapo commander summarized the Jewish position: "Total disorder and general unrest prevail in the city. I cannot allow this situation to continue. I will issue orders to stop shooting. Peace and order must return to the city. The Lithuanians have announced that they no longer wish to live together with Jews; they demand that the Jews be segregated in a Ghetto." Then came his proposal: "The choice is up to the Jews--either the present situation with the disorder and the bloodbath, or leaving the city and moving into the Ghetto." It was an offer the committee could not refuse.

Three days later the Military Commander of Kovno and the mayor of the city issued "Order No. 15": the Jews were to begin the move on July 15 and to complete it by August 15.

Rabbi Ephraim Oshry says July 15 "marks the beginning of the tragic end of Lithuanian Jewry."[60] The Jews, he writes, "were forced into the ghettos like animals being penned prior to slaughter. They went on foot--men, women and children. As they went they were abused. Every day the march of the dead went on from Kovno to Slobodka." [61] Whether they entered the ghetto early or late, Di Tante and her family must have been part of this scene.

As the deadline drew near, Jews filled the streets of Kovno bringing what possessions they could from their old homes in Kovno to their new ones in the Slobodka Ghetto. On August 7, as if to hasten the move, the Lithuanian partisans suddenly rounded up 1,200 Jewish men and took them to the Yellow Prison in Kovno. They released about 150 and executed the rest.[62] Nor is it known where they were killed. William Mishell says August 7, 1941, has gone down in ghetto history as "the Black Thursday Massacre."

Twenty-five thousand Kovno Jews were forced into Slobotkeh, the poorest and most run-down section of the city, joining the five or six thousand Jews already living there. Most Jews went into the Big Ghetto, the remainder into the Small Ghetto. The Jews themselves put up the barbed wire that surrounded each ghetto and built the wooden footbridge that controlled the only access between them.

On August 15 the Germans closed the gates of the Kovno Ghetto on about thirty thousand Jews, sealing them off from Kovno and the world to await their fate--Di Tante and her family among them.

The Maze

Rina, if you are ever to know where you "come from," you have to try to understand what your grandmother went through during the Kovno Ghetto. You have to try to understand the impossible. There is only one way for you to do this: you have to try to imagine.

You have to try to imagine the constant threat to life in the ghetto--day by day, hour by hour, minute by minute. You have to try to imagine the terror of hunger, malnutrition, illness, exhaustion, abuse, mistreatment. You have to try to imagine the sudden round-up, a beating, a robbery, a random shooting, a house search, forced labor, a public hanging. You have to imagine the Aktions that stripped the Jews of their clothes, their furs, their books, their valuables. You have to try to imagine the selections. And the Aktions that were mass murder: 3,000 shot at the Seventh Fort, 1,000 at the Fourth Fort, 500 more at the Fourth Fort, 1,000 at the Ninth Fort, 2,000 at the Ninth Fort, 10,000 at the Ninth Fort. And thousands more at the Ninth Fort.

Dr. Elkes led the Jewish Council throughout the entire existence of the Kovno Ghetto, from the summer of 1941 until the fall of 1943, when the Germans turned it into KL Kauen--*Konzentrationslager* No. 4. Elkes tried to do the impossible--to keep the ghetto alive. The Germans he faced daily were not only masters of murder but masters of psychological warfare. The bullet was their ultimate choice but first they assaulted the ghetto with a fiendish array of lies, rumors, promises, deceptions. Elkes understood only too well their desire to crush the spirit before they destroyed the body.

261

The German method was to keep the Jews off balance. At every turn they confronted the Jewish faith in reason with the power of unreason. "They do not tell you things clearly," Avraham Tory writes in his *Diary*, "except when they curse you and scream at you. It is therefore imperative to assess their mood properly before they open their mouths. We must understand that, from their point of view, our situation must always remain unclear; we are not to be allowed to understand anything, even if our lives are at stake. Anything that happens to us must occur like a bolt from the blue. We are to remain always in a state of anticipation, without understanding what is going on around us."[63]

"The murderers' goal," Rabbi Oshry writes, "was to bring confusion into the lives of the Jews and to cause them the greatest despondency in order to make annihilating them all the easier."[64] To humiliate and dehumanize the Jews of the ghetto, he says, "...the German murderers brought suffering upon the dead as well as upon the living. They decreed that the ghetto Jews themselves must be responsible for their own dead and must bury them in the part of town reserved for sewage and garbage disposal."[65]

"Who can find his way in this maze," Dr. Elkes said in a moment of despair, "who can distinguish between truth and fiction, between good and evil?"[66] In the Kovno Ghetto, as elsewhere--what the Germans did was to go beyond the imagination of mankind--and take the Jews there with them. Dr. Elkes did not escape the maze.

Your grandmother did, Rina. It is where she refuses to take you.

The Cherry Orchard

The Polish Nobel Prize winner for literature Czeslaw Milosz says somewhere that "Language is the only homeland." He has it right.

DEFINITIONS

When I was a very young child, Rina, the only language I heard was the Yiddish of my parents, the Yiddish that was their homeland. It was a Lithuanian Yiddish, and I simply lived in it with them and grew up in its presence. When I was in grammar school they sent me off after school hours to the Workmen's Circle *shuleh*, a school where I learned more formally to read and write Yiddish and had my introduction to Yiddish literature and Jewish history. But I had no concept of "homeland." I did not know that I had already inherited a homeland from them, that Yiddish--its tragedy and its comedy--would bind me to them forever, beyond even their deaths. I did not know that one day on the other side of the ocean it would bind me to Di Tante and your grandmother as well.

How do I explain what it means to me today--today, more than a half century after the Holocaust—*tzu heren ah Yiddishn vort?* How do I explain how the heart leaps up when in the middle of my daily English world I hear an unexpected Yiddish word--a phrase, a sentence, a proverb? It's the feeling Wordsworth had when wandering lonely as a cloud he came suddenly upon a field of golden daffodils.

Tzu heren ah Yiddishn vort means that you hunger for the Yiddish *shprakh*, for the Yiddish language, for the *tam*, the taste of it, that you long for it like an exile possessed by an incurable homesickness. Decades have slipped away, neighborhoods have changed, my parents and their friends have died, new Jewish generations know Yiddish only vaguely if at all. In Europe where once millions spoke Yiddish there is now dead silence. So to hear a word of Yiddish now summons life, a time when the *shprakh* was still vital, when its words were still connected to life, and life, no matter how bitter it might be, was bearable because you could laugh in Yiddish.

In his novel *The Testament* Elie Wiesel writes that Yiddish is a "A language unlike any other, it tells of sorrows and joys unlike any others, it's a very rich language given to a very poor people." He has it right. Lovers of Yiddish will even tell you "*ahz Gott shraybt Ivrit ober ehr redt Yiddish*"--that God writes in Hebrew but He speaks in Yiddish: which means that when you speak Yiddish, maybe you are also a little closer

263

to God. They will also tell you *"ahz Ivrit redt men; Yiddish redt zikh"*--
which means that you may speak Hebrew well enough but that you
don't have to try to speak Yiddish: it simply speaks by itself out of you,
for you. "I know Hebrew perfectly well," Mr. Volpiansky told me in
Israel, "but when I speak from the heart it is in Yiddish."

Yiddishkayt is the quality of Jewishness characterizing the best of
Yiddish-speaking Ashkenazic Jewry. *Yiddishkayt* draws its values from
the primary call for morality: to make each Jew into a better human
being and to make a better world, too. *Yiddishkayt* is a special way of
looking at life. *Yiddishkayt* is stored deep within the Yiddish word,
inseparable from it, and concentrated in it like a poem. The *tam*, the
taste, of *Yiddishkayt* is uniquely embedded in the very words of Yiddish.
Yiddishkayt is in the language that is the only homeland. Isaac Bashevis
Singer was defining *Yiddishkayt* when he told his Nobel Prize audience,
"To me the Yiddish language and the conduct of those who spoke it
are identical."

Yiddishkayt lies deep in the story of the traveler who very early one
morning came to a *shtetl* somewhere in the Pale and saw an old Jew
hurrying in his direction. The traveler stopped him and asked him why
he was in such a hurry. "I am going to my work," he answered.
"Where is that?" the traveler asked him. Pointing, the old Jew
answered, "Do you see that tower over there? I am going to the top of
it." Puzzled, the traveler asked him, "But what do you do up there?"
"I look for the Messiah--to greet him when he comes," he said. "And
the town council pays you?" "A ruble a month," he answered. "Only
a ruble a month?" "Yes," he answered, "but it is steady work."

My mother was not religious. She never believed in the *meshiakh*.
Yet "....*ahz der meshiakh vet kumen*"--when the Messiah will come--was
among her more ironic comments on life. The *meshiakh* did not speak
to her, nor did she speak to him, but when she spoke of him she had
her reasons: she knew numberless occasions when he would have
done well to put in his appearance and finally set things right for the
Jews. But even if she could ever have somehow believed in him, he
had tarried far too long--and she would have told him so. If ever the

time had been ripe for him to appear, it was during her own time in Jewish history. But this time he had not only failed again but turned himself into a symbol for failure.

Like many a skeptical Litvak, she saw no sense in serious talk about him, but she could not simply discard him totally either. He was, after all, an inescapable part of the language--and baggage--of *Yiddishkayt*. He retained a certain wry usefulness for her: the difference between his promise and the reality of things was made to order for irony. She would have laughed at the story of the old Jew hurrying to the tower, but she would have understood all too well--and gently--the Jewish sadness, the Jewish pity, the Jewish tragedy and comedy of his task. She would have understood the hope that was the essential meaning of his *meshiakh*--and, all too well, its essential hopelessness.

Both my parents gave religion a wide berth. Except in jest they never gave the *meshiakh* much thought, not even the benefit of the doubt. You could never have convinced them that Jewish hope lay in the *meshiakh*. Whatever hope they did have was unencumbered by the *meshiakh*. It lay, purely and simply, in the ideal of working for "a better world." In spite of all the truth they knew about life, they lived the message of their *Yiddishkayt* to the end.

Maybe the existence and ubiquity of the saying *ahz es iz shver tzu zayn ah Yid*--that it is hard to be a Jew--is due to the fact that the Jew has waited too long for the Messiah. Like *ahz der meshiakh vet kumen*, the saying comes with a long life of its own, of countless physical and spiritual realities: sweatshops, strikes, hunger, expulsions, pogroms, quotas, the burning of books, the death of innocents--the list of cruelties suffered and hardships endured is endless. The burden of being a Jew, the burden carried by the Jew, has often been all but unbearable. It too comes with the territory. You could trace the burden to God himself. It is so heavy that a Jew once said, *"Gottinyu, Ikh bet dir, probir nit oystzugefinen vi lahng Ikh ken oyshaltn."* "Dear God,' he said, "I beg you, do not try to find out how long I can hold out."

The truth is that my mother and father placed the burden on my brother and me just as their parents had placed it on them. They did not ask our permission. Nor did we know they were doing it. Maybe they didn't even know they were doing it. It weighed a lot, but neither of us could have shaken it off, even if we had tried. We, too, had to discover it came with the territory. And we, too, willingly accepted the burden of its tragic--and sometimes comic--outlook on life.

The proverbs, the sayings, the stories of *Yiddishkayt*--all of them are in Yiddish, in words that reveal the spirit and vision that have animated the people. "In its millennial lifetime," the historian Lucy Dawidowicz wrote, "Yiddish became the most widely spoken of any of the Jewish languages in all of Jewish history."[67] Until the outbreak of the second World War world Jewry was ninety-five per cent Ashkenazi or of Ashkenazi descent, and for the most part Yiddish was its language. Yiddish was flowering like a cherry orchard in the spring. And then the Communists and the Nazis and their accomplices cut down the cherry trees and burned them. The Communists destroyed printing presses, shut down Yiddish schools, theaters, and cultural centers, imprisoned and assassinated Yiddish poets and intellectuals. They did everything they could to kill the Yiddish language in order to destroy its speakers as a people. The Germans and their followers chose the opposite strategy. They decided to kill off the Jewish people directly--men, women, and children--and kill the language at the same time. The Holocaust alone cut down two-thirds of European Jewry. The largest number were speakers of Yiddish.

In his Nobel Prize speech, Isaac Bashevis Singer acknowledged that the Holocaust had struck the Jewish people with "the worst blows that human madness can inflict" but, he insisted, "Yiddish has not yet said its last word." And speaking in the Yiddish that was his homeland, he accepted the Swedish Academy's award as "a recognition of the Yiddish language--a language of exile, without a land, without frontiers, not supported by any government, a language which possesses no words for weapons, ammunition, military exercises, war tactics, a language that was despised by both gentiles and emancipated

266

Jews." Yiddish, he offered, "is the wise and humble language of us all, the idiom of the frightened and hopeful humanity."

Yiddish was not Primo Levi's homeland. An assimilated Italian Jew, he did not understand Yiddish at all when he first heard it from the Polish Jews he encountered in Auschwitz. Auschwitz awakened him not only to Yiddish but to a consciousness of his Jewish identity. A chemist by profession, Levi never intended to be a writer, but Auschwitz awakened the writer in him too. The Yiddish proverb *Ibergekumeneh tsores iz gut tsu dertseylen*--"Troubles overcome are good to tell"--became the theme that, directly or indirectly, runs through all his work. It is the motto for *The Periodic Table*. It appears again in his novel *If Not Now, When?* a story of Jewish partisans operating behind German lines on the Eastern front during World War II. Before he began work on the novel, he studied Yiddish and read firsthand partisan accounts in Yiddish in order, he said, to learn "how one reasoned, how one thought, how one wrote in Yiddish."[68] *Survival in Auschwitz* and *The Reawakening*, his first two books, also tell of troubles overcome. So do many of his speeches and interviews. That troubles overcome are good to tell is even in his very last speech. In November, 1986, addressing an international conference of ex-deportees on "The Duty to Bear Witness," he said, "Among us ex-deportees it is pleasant to sit back and tell the tale of our now distant adventures to the people around us," but he had to admit that telling the tale of *Ibergekumeneh tsores* to others, especially the young, "doesn't do much good."[69] No matter. Though Yiddish was not his homeland, Primo Levi--ex-deportee--traveled there and returned from the Holocaust universe with tales to tell that refuse to be ignored.

Yiddish was not Aharon Appelfeld's homeland either. He describes himself as coming from "a half-assimilated family, whose Jewish values had lost their content, and whose inner space was barren and haunted."[70] His parents spoke German, scorning the Yiddish of Eastern European Jewry. The Holocaust awakened him, too, to his Jewish identity. "The caldron of the Holocaust," he says, "has drawn me very close to the Jewish people. My three years in the camps were fundamental to my self-understanding."[71] In the Yiddish-speaking prisoners in the camps he found an authentic Jewishness he had never known before. After the war and his wanderings in a war-torn Europe and "a belated childhood in Israel," he entered Hebrew University, where he specialized in Yiddish literature. "Yiddish," he says, "was for me a special vehicle into my past and myself....I chose to live in the religious quarter of Jerusalem--in Mea Shearim. I studied Yiddish and the Bible and surrounded myself with Jews who did not hate themselves."[72]

The great theme of Appelfeld's fiction is the spiritual emptiness of the assimilated Jew who did hate himself--and paid the price of his alienation from the Jewish tradition. The Holocaust "is the great Jewish experience, also a non-Jewish experience, and if it is not assimilated as it ought to be," he warns, "one day we will be like grown-up children who have been deprived of a basic truth of life."[73] Appelfeld's novels of the Holocaust center on the emptiness of the assimilated Jew's inner space. At the same time they center on the Holocaust as the great Jewish experience that has the power to restore Jewish values to Jewish inner space.

Elie Wiesel's *Night*, his memoir about a child who entered the Holocaust universe and became "an old man in one night," is the book that--more than any other--brought the Holocaust to the consciousness of the world. It was his first book. He wrote it as "a kind of testimony of one witness speaking of his own life, his own death." Originally called *Un di Velt hoht Geshvign--And the World was Silent*--he wrote it in Yiddish, "as a tribute," he says, "to the language which was mine, the language of my childhood," and "to the people who spoke Yiddish, to the culture which vanished."

Dovid Bergelson, one of the Yiddish writers assassinated in 1952 by Stalin's secret police, also had it right in his short story *"An Eydes"*-- "A Witness."[74] Written in Yiddish, it tells of a mysterious Jew, a man in his sixties, a tinsmith from western Ukraine and the only survivor, he says, of more than a million from the death camp below Lvov. His clothes in rags, his shoes worn out, to all appearances he is a ghost of a man. He appears in a town in Russia where he encounters a young Jewish woman, also the lone survivor of her family. "I am *an eydes*--a witness," he says. He tells her his story and she writes it down, translating his Yiddish into Russian as he speaks. He insists that she make no mistakes. When she reads his story back to him, she asks if her translation is accurate.

"Yes," he answers uneasily. Then, with a shrug, he says, "You ask me my opinion? What can I tell you? The suffering was in Yiddish."

In the end his friends fear for his life. "How can I die?" he says. "I am a witness after all!"

If you are to know any single truth about the Holocaust, Rina--about what Di Tante and your grandmother and the family went through and about what the Kovno Jews went through and about what all of Lithuanian Jewry went through, it's that the suffering was in Yiddish.

The Poster

Pick up almost any history of the Holocaust, Rina, and sooner or later you will run into "the Jewish Problem." Gerald Reitlinger's *The Final Solution*, an early history of the Holocaust, opens with it. Lucy Dawidowicz's Introduction to her *The War Against the Jews, 1933-1945* opens with it. The first pages of Raul Hilberg's *The Destruction of the European Jews* deal with it. And so on. The "Jewish Question" and the Holocaust are inseparable--inseparable because one led to the other.

Raul Hilberg writes that "The Nazi destruction process did not come out of a void."[75] But Hitler and the German Nazis didn't discover the Jewish Problem and the Jewish Question: Christianity did--by creating them. And for most of the last two thousand years it has been tireless in its efforts to answer the question and solve the

269

problem. Conversion, expulsion, segregation, Crusade, pogrom: it has been tireless in its efforts to eliminate the Jews.

The Holocaust, Hilberg says, emerged "from a slow and steady growth of anti-Jewish action and anti-Jewish thinking. The process began with the attempt to drive the Jews into Christianity. The development was continued in order to force the victims into exile. It was finished when the Jews were driven to their deaths. The German Nazis...did not discard the past; they built upon it. They did not begin a development; they completed it."[76] For Hilberg the end was in the beginning: the past was prologue.

When Hitler took his turn at the project, he marshaled a propaganda machine that never stopped hammering away at *Die Judenfrage*: "the Jewish Question," "the Jewish Problem." He was the architect and leader of a crusade. First and last, he was on a central mission: to destroy the Jews. He found apostles and volunteers almost everywhere. He offered his anti-Semitic propaganda for sale almost everywhere in Europe and he found ready buyers almost everywhere. He had a ready-made lie that went far back in history--that the Jews were the root of all evil. And he had a ready-made audience historically prepared to believe it. All he had to do was repeat it often enough to turn it into a truth that could be acted upon. His anti-Semitic propaganda opened the gates for him to much of Europe. And the Holocaust, when it came, was a blitzkrieg. "The operation was over," says Hilberg, "before anyone could grasp its enormity, let alone its implications for the future."[77]

From the beginning of his political life, but long before he came to power, Hitler cast the Jews center stage as villain. In *Mein Kampf* he already saw the future in terms of a crusade and saw himself as hero leading a Christian-based holy war against them: "...I believe that I am acting in accordance with the will of the Almighty Creator: by defending myself against the Jew, I am fighting for the work of the Lord." Jesus had set out on the path: he would follow it to the end. In speech after speech after he came to power he threatened the Jews and prophesied their destruction. The Final Solution to the Jewish problem was a sacred mission for him. The *Endlosung* was to be the answer, once and for all, to the Jewish question.

The Swiss Catholic theologian Hans Kung says straight out not only that "Nazi anti-Semitism would have been impossible without two thousand years of Christian anti-Judaism," but that the Holocaust "was not racial. It was religious." And he asks, "is not the case of the Austrian Catholic Adolf Hitler the most abysmal example of this? Even now many people do not recognize the religious roots of his anti-Semitism."[78] Christianity's past was the prologue to Hitler and the Holocaust.

Once Germany closed off any chance for its Jews to emigrate, the war against the Jews began in earnest. Such a war had never before been proposed, organized, and executed by a civilized government against its own citizens, at least not in modern times. The Germans carried the war into every country they invaded or occupied. And they found accomplices almost everywhere.

The Holocaust was a search-and-destroy mission, single-minded, endless in its ferocious brutality. Hitler and the Nazis pursued the Jews across much of Europe--and with such intensity that the Jews could find almost no place to hide. At the Wannsee Conference (January 20, 1942) the Nazis looked forward to the murder of 11,000,000 Jews in Europe. In its scale the Holocaust was to be no pogrom: it was to be total, absolute, final annihilation. The Jews were to be robbed and tortured. But sooner or later they were to be beaten to death, starved to death, worked to death, burned to death, shot to death, gassed to death. The German slogan "Today Europe, Tomorrow the World" signaled a New Order, one that promised to eliminate all Jews on earth. Forever.

Hitler and the Germans intended to destroy an entire people, a whole culture, a civilization. They intended total destruction. Not for him and his henchmen those inconclusive, half-way measures that had been tried in past centuries. This time there would be no survivors. "All of us [survivors]," Primo Levi told an interviewer, "are, by definition, exceptions, exceptions because in the Lager you were destined to die. If you did not die it was through some miraculous stroke of luck: you were an exception, a singularity, not generic, totally specific."[79]

In their pursuit of the Final Solution, the German priority was death--death for the Jews. Even when the German war effort against the Allies was in desperate need of Jewish manpower and skills, the Germans were relentless. Hitler's priority remained even after he had already lost that other war. In the end, consumed by hatred of the Jews, Hitler and his executioners uprooted thousands of Jewish communities and murdered two-thirds of European Jewry, one-third of the world's entire Jewish population.

What concerned Hitler as his end drew near--as the Russians drew near--was not so much the war against the Allies as the war against the Jews. It never left his mind. In his very last hours Hitler was still obsessed with the Jew. He who had poisoned the world with hatred against the Jews devoted the very last words of his Political Testament to one final diatribe against "the universal poisoner of all peoples, International Jewry." From first to last the Jews were a bone in his throat.

On a bright summer's day in 1971 I was down where the sun does not reach--down in the archives of Yad Vashem in Jerusalem. Librarians, historians--researchers all--were quietly about their business. A curator was showing me one of the small diaries Adam Czerniakow, leader of the Warsaw Ghetto Jewish Council, kept until July 23, 1942, the day he chose suicide rather than meet the German demands for daily quotas of Jews for the deportations they had begun the day before. I turned some of the pages, astonished at their very existence. Moments later I turned a corner in the room and the poster--as if it were yesterday--screamed at me in German: "Adolf Hitler speaks in the name of Germany."

272

In Germany it had probably hung on a factory wall. Now, reminder and trophy, it spoke from a wall in the archives of Yad Vashem. Maybe there was some small justice in that.

But the truth is that the death transports from the Warsaw Ghetto and the death marches to the killing fields of the Ninth Fort just outside the Kovno Ghetto were statements made in the name of the German people.

The deeper truth, Rina, is that Hitler's Final Solution to the Jewish Question and the Jewish Problem has a long and deadly past history-- that Hitler spoke in the name of more than Germany.

The Yerusha

In Yiddish the word is *yerusha*. It means "inheritance" or "legacy." Ordinarily, the word refers to money or property. However, in your case, Rina, it refers to something far less tangible but far more real. It refers to the unique 3,500 year old Jewish history you automatically inherited at birth. More immediately, it refers to the twelve year history of the Third Reich, and even more specifically to the 1941-1945 period of the Holocaust. You had no choice in the matter. That's the nature of your particular *yerusha*: it's not yours for the asking, it's not yours for the wanting, it just is. All yours.

A *yerusha* always comes with questions attached. Sooner or later, you have to ask them. They are normal enough: Who gave it to me? Why? What exactly did I inherit? How will I look upon it? How will I treat it? What should I do with it? What will I do with it? Do I pass it on? Why should I pass it on? What part of it will I pass on? How will I pass it on? To whom? Into what future? These questions raise questions, always more questions. They fly at you from all directions. But make no mistake about them, Rina: they all eventually come to rest on the meaning for you of where you come from.

Your father is the child of survivors of the Holocaust. He belongs to the first generation after the Holocaust. You belong to the second. A German your age also belongs to the second generation after the Holocaust. He can't escape his *yerusha* either. He is the grandchild of the generation that provided the killers, their helpers, and the bystanders. Like it or not, he has no choice in the matter either. And sooner or later he, too, will have to look back to see where and what he comes from. He has to ask the same questions as you. If he refuses to ask them, never mind. History itself will not let him off. The Holocaust is in his inheritance as well. If the Jews are forever destined to have the Germans in their history, the Germans are now forever destined to have the Jews--"the Jewish Problem," so to speak--in theirs.

The question is: what are the children, the grandchildren, the great-grandchildren of Germany's Holocaust generation to do with the *yerusha* they have inherited? What are they to do when they learn, as learn they must, that their ancestors went "beyond the imagination of mankind"--and not only in Bergen-Belsen? What are they to do with the indictment that "These Germans are without hope. They are not as other men. The thing is satanic."

It isn't enough for the children of the killers or the grandchildren or the great-grandchildren to say, almost as if they sensed a failure of responsibility on their own part, "We were born after. We had nothing to do with the Holocaust. You can't blame us." Even more disturbing are the voices that rally to their defense shouting: "They were born after! They had nothing to do with it. You can't blame them. The Holocaust is not their problem."

It is true. They were born after. True, they had nothing to do with it. You can't blame them for the Holocaust. I have to admit it: the chronology is self-evident.

But you can blame them. You can blame them, first of all, for denying any link to the killers. Their very denial of any link links them to the killers.

274

Niklas Frank was only seven in April, 1946, when the first Nuremberg war crimes tribunal found his father Hans Frank guilty and sentenced him to hang. Because he barely knew his father, Niklas Frank could easily have disavowed his link to him. He could have denied his *yerusha*. Instead he was obsessed by it. Desperate to tear his father out of his life, he indicts him in his book *In the Shadow of the Reich*, judges him, convicts and sentences him, and finally executes him a second time.

Among the first to join the Nazi party, Hans Frank was Hitler's defense attorney in over a hundred trials and rose to become the Governor General of German-occupied Poland. Niklas's research into his father's letters, speeches, and the 42 volumes of his diary, as well as his pursuit of interviews, eyewitness accounts, and other sources, reveals his father as a common liar, a thief, a black marketeer, a fool, and a hypocrite, but a man, he charges, who, in the end, "helped like a good German to pave the way for the mass extermination of human beings."

"Did you never pause," he asks him, "never stop, never weep from the sheer horror of being you, and of what you did?"

Niklas Frank saw a postwar, post-Holocaust German society shot through with former Nazis very much like his father and fatally flawed like him. He condemns the judges, lawyers, merchants, businessmen, bankers, professors, legislators, priests who after the war "all went home," where "With no memory, no regrets, no real human emotions, they simply went back to work."

"Millions of gallows," he says, should have been "erected along the autobahns" for all those who had no "right to go on living." Niklas Frank considers himself luckier than "the silent majority of my generation," the children of those millions of Nazis who escaped the gallows. The hangman had at least spared him from being fatally poisoned by "the same garbage filled with deceit and cowardice, with bloodthirstiness and inhumanity" that his own father had mouthed.

275

Part way through his trial Hans Frank startled the courtroom by confessing, "A thousand years will pass and this guilt of Germany will still not be erased!"[80] Ever since then his confession has been held up and quoted as the definitive judgment of the Third Reich--and by one of Hitler's very own.

What has been overlooked, however, is his retraction. In his final words to the judges before they adjourned to consider their verdict he said: "In the witness stand I spoke about the one thousand years that could not erase the guilt from our nation on account of Hitler's behavior. However, not only the fact that the behavior of our enemies toward our people and our soldiers has been so carefully excluded from the proceedings of this Tribunal, but also the gigantic mass atrocities of the most horrible kind, which, as I have now learned, were committed against Germans, above all in East Prussia, Silesia, Pomerania, and in the Sudetenland by Russians, Poles, and Czechs, and are still being committed--all this has completely canceled out, even today, any possible guilt on the part of our people and our nation."[81]

Niklas Frank's book is a fierce, unrelieved condemnation of his father and the *yerusha* his father left him. But Frank condemns his father even more bitterly for the legacy he left Germany in his final statement, which, he says pointed "the way for our next generation to deal in its own special way with overcoming the past, our celebrated *Vergangenheitsbewältigung.*" Frank will have none of it. He rejects any German attempt to master a past that cannot be mastered, any attempt to erase the link to the guilt of a thousand years.

The ultimate power of Niklas Frank's book goes beyond the recognition that the redemption of Germany can take place only when its children acknowledge and confront their *yerusha.* It lies in the recognition that the redemption of Germany can begin only with repudiation, a repudiation beyond any and all family ties, a repudiation of all the killers spawned by the Third Reich. Total repudiation.

276

The Word Game

Whatever you do, Rina, do not let yourself be taken in by those who play the word game.

You hear the words over and over again: condemnations of "man's inhumanity to man," appeals to "the conscience of mankind," "the conscience of the world," "the brotherhood of man." Once, perhaps, they sounded strikingly original, genuinely meaningful. Now they are clichés, words emptied of whatever meaning they may have had, words so commonplace it's hard to believe they're taken seriously anymore.

But they still have considerable mileage in them, especially for anyone looking for a shorthand way to gain instant support for any position he may hold. Most people who hear these words accept them without question. And why not? The words always sound good enough.

Well, the sound may be good. But sense is quite another matter. The fact is, Rina, that these words are only abstractions. They are cover-ups hiding the truth. They block questions, definition, discussion. Whether willfully manipulated by the speaker or unwittingly granted by the listener, they divert us from the truth and deprive us of it.

What you will most often hear is that the Holocaust is just one more self-evident example of "man's inhumanity to man." Make no mistake about it: the Holocaust was not an example among other examples. It was not an example of anything. It was itself. And only itself.

"Man's inhumanity to man" is the worst of all the cover-ups. It is a generalization whose every word is a lie. The "inhumanity" of the Holocaust--what was it? Inhumane treatment? The word is an out-

and-out cover-up for murder, for atrocity piled upon vicious atrocity: bloody tortures, mass executions, merciless cruelties. "Man's" inhumanity? Guilt can't be placed on nameless "man"; if you are honest you place it specifically where it belongs. The Germans perpetrated the murder of Lithuanian Jewry. Lithuanian collaborators helped them every step of the way. And both operated with the widespread acquiescence of the Lithuanian public at large. Inhumanity to "man"? Again nameless, anonymous "man." "Man" this time is a cover-up for the execution of nearly the whole of Lithuanian Jewry. You would never know that specific Jews, nearly a quarter million Lithuanian Jews, fell into the black hole of "man's inhumanity to man."

But the real question you have to ask, Rina, is: Why this pervasive drive to generalize and universalize the Holocaust? There are answers, of course.

Slobotkeh? The Ninth Fort? The Kovno Ghetto? The Lietukis garage? By his very nature the universalist--Jew or non-Jew--must reject any threats to his self image. The hard truths and difficult questions posed by the specific facts of the Holocaust represent precisely such a threat. He knows that at all costs he must avoid the *why* of the Holocaust.

But how do you evade six million murders? The trick, it turns out, is to re-define the Holocaust in the universal terms of "man's inhumanity to man"--no Jews allowed. Never mind that there would never have been a Holocaust without the Jews. By generalizing the Jew to extinction the universalist de-Judaizes the Holocaust. He disappears the Jews from the Holocaust. His logic is obvious--no Jews: no Holocaust. If there's no Holocaust there's no reason to confront the *why* of it. If there's no Holocaust there's no reason to consider Christian guilt for it. All the universalist has to do is assert "Man's inhumanity to man" and he has put into play a sure-fire strategy to head off and stifle any serious question about the Holocaust.

You have to ask: *Why* the refusal to specify killer and victim? They had names. Germans and Lithuanians were the killers and

278

Lithuanian Jews were their victims. The universalist has no stomach for probing the facts of the Holocaust. "Man's inhumanity to man" provides him with the perfect out: all men are guilty. It's the perfect cover-up. The logic is obvious: if all men are guilty, no one is guilty. Where there's no one to blame because everyone is to blame, guilt ceases to have meaning. Destroy the whole idea of guilt and you no longer have to confront either the desperate issues of the Holocaust or its challenge to your worldview.

During the Holocaust Jews in the ghettos and concentration camps clung stubbornly to their faith in "the conscience of the world." They believed in it--and lost. The universalist Jew believed in "the brotherhood of man"--and lost. Like the children of the Enlightenment that they were, Jews believed in the idea of progress-- and lost. They believed in the decency, democratic values, and good conscience of the Allied nations--and lost. Their hope that the "civilized" world would come to their rescue turned into ashes. It was nothing but a bitter delusion. "Our fate has not yet been finally decided," Abraham Tory wrote in the Kovno Ghetto. "We do not know which nation will be prepared to come to help us. It seems that strangers will not rescue us. All this talk about a war on behalf of the whole of humankind is just talk. Everyone fights for himself, for the sake of his own future. This is why our future is shrouded in darkness."[82]

In the February 28, 1941, entry in his journal Emmanuel Ringelblum, historian of the Warsaw Ghetto, records the story of a German police chief who stopped a Jew because he was on the street without his armband. When the Jew claimed he had lost his armband, the officer screamed back at him, "*Sie, Jude, Sie haben das zwanzigste Jahrhundert verloren!*" "You, Jew, you have lost the twentieth century!"[83]

That scream silences all the abstractions and universals that cover up the Holocaust. Yet the abstractions and universals that failed the Jews during the Holocaust have a way of coming back to life whenever the Holocaust turns up in general conversation. The belief in them is as deadly to the truth now as it was then.

Beware of the word game, Rina.

The Numbers Game

Rina, whatever you do, do not be taken in by the numbers game.

In the beginning was the word. Originally, the Holocaust meant the murder of 6,000,000 Jews by the Nazis and their accomplices. But historical truth seldom stands in the way of men determined to subvert it. Hitler wasn't wrong when he said if you tell a big enough lie long enough, people will come to believe it. Rina, what you have to do is become aware of how and why numbers have been--and continue to be--manipulated to distort the historical truth of the Holocaust.

At first, as I say, it was six million Jews--and no argument, or hardly any. But a quarter of a century after the Holocaust it was clear that the numbers game was well underway. On April 24, 1979, the Rotunda of the United States Capitol was the scene of ceremonies to commemorate victims of the Holocaust. In referring to the Holocaust, President Jimmy Carter spoke of "the sheer weight of its numbers--11 million innocent victims exterminated--6 million of them Jews." Vice President Walter F. Mondale echoed him: "Today we bear witness not only to the unanswered cries of the eleven million, but also to the duty they confer on us...to banish bloodshed from the annals of our children's future." President and vice president were not the first to cite these numbers, but in voicing them they gave credence to false weight.

As in all matters dealing with the Holocaust, you have to go back to basics. And nothing is more basic than Professor Roy Eckardt's position that the Holocaust "divides humankind into two camps: those who take the *Shoah*-event with absolute seriousness, and those who do not or will not."[84] Where President Carter had at least mentioned that

280

there were 6,000,000 Jews, and by implication 5,000,000 others, by the time his and America's vice president had finished speaking, the Holocaust had become 11,000,000, with nary a Jew mentioned. Almost in the blink of an eye the Jews were "disappeared" from the radar screen of history--and from "the conscience of the world." As you can see, even among the highest leaders of the land absolute seriousness--at least with respect to the Holocaust--is hard to come by.

Elie Wiesel saw the danger. On that very same day, at a meeting of the President's Commission on the Holocaust, he stated that what had once been 6,000,000 would give way soon enough to "the progression: six million plus five, then eleven including six, and then only eleven." The Communists, for their part, insisted that 20,000,000 Russians had also perished at Nazi hands in the Great Patriotic War. And if you included 20,000,000 more victims of the war, you had a total of 50,000,000 or so.... And there you'd have it at last: 6,000,000 lost and blurred into 50,000,000--the final obliteration of the Jews.

One could even go so far as to include German soldiers and the SS among the "others," a feat which another president, Ronald Reagan, managed to accomplish at the White House on April 18, 1985--only a year after George Orwell's 1984--when he defended his visit to the Bitburg cemetery in Germany: "I think that there's nothing wrong with visiting that cemetery where those young men are the victims of Nazism also, even though they were fighting in the German uniform....They were victims, just as surely as the victims in the concentration camps."[85]

Simon Wiesenthal took a somewhat different tack in the numbers game. He was among the earliest to urge that 5,000,000 non-Jewish victims of the Nazis be included in the Holocaust. But he was speaking to Jewish audiences--not to national and international audiences. He warned American Jews that their Christian neighbors didn't like being excluded from the Holocaust. And that it wouldn't be good for the Jews if they were. At one stroke he, too, transformed 6,000,000 murdered Jews into 11,000,000 anonymous dead.

It all depends on the direction you want to take--and why. You can start off with 6,000,000 Jewish dead. Then you can add 5,000,000 "others." Then you will have 11,000,000, of whom 6,000,000 are Jews. Then you can have 11,000,000 victims. And you can add 20,000,000 Russians, making 31,000,000 victims. And then another 20,000,000, making a total of 51,000,000 killed in World War Two.

Or you can start with 51,000,000--then subtract 20,000,000 killed, another 20,000,000 Russians victims, then those 5,000,000 "others," and you can get down to the 6,000,000. And in the end, Rina, you can discover Chaim Dembovitz and his son Aharon.

The deeper question you have to ask, though, is why there is such an eagerness to play the numbers game. Why--even among some Jews--the need to submerge 6,000,000 into 50,000,000?

As in any game, everything depends on who is playing, what the stakes are, and what the winner expects to gain.

According to Communist logic, since there was no Holocaust--for they acknowledged none--no Jews were killed in it. And they could, and did, lump all Jewish victims and non-Jewish casualties into one category: "victims of Fascism." Not till demonstrations by Jews inside the USSR and abroad, and long after the war, was there a monument specifically memorializing the Jewish dead at Babi Yar. Another example: Ilya Ehrenburg and Vasily Grossman compiled and edited *The Black Book*, a collection of documents recording the destruction of 1,500,000 Soviet Jews. In 1948 Soviet officials destroyed the printing plates, and the book never saw the light of day in the USSR. Soviet policy was to de-Judaize the Russian Jews, to deprive them of their national identity, to force their assimilation, to submerge them in the larger Russian public--and so to rid the USSR of a major irritant on the body politic, a people that by religion, language, and philosophy was diametrically opposed to Communist ideology. By de-Judaizing the Holocaust the Communists were continuing their relentless drive to universalize the Jew out of existence and into the larger "humanity" of the Soviet Union.

Christianity had its own logic and its own reasons for playing the numbers game. Weren't three million Poles--priests among them-- killed by Nazis? And millions of other Christians? The Holocaust did not belong to the Jews, so the argument ran. To make the Holocaust all-inclusive--in other words, to de-Judaize it--would mean that guilt for it could be lifted off Christian shoulders. Moreover, the guilt could then be spread far and wide, diluted beyond recognition: the perfect cover-up. In a way, Wiesenthal wasn't far off the mark when he warned Jews against incurring Christian wrath for excluding their Christian neighbors. What he didn't say was that to de-Judaize the Holocaust would actually mean to de-Christianize Christian guilt for it as well. What he didn't say was that to de-Judaize the Holocaust would divert the world from looking for the *why* of the Holocaust.

In the early years after the war historians rarely mentioned the 6,000,000. For the most part authors of school textbooks and histories of World War Two simply ignored the Holocaust: it was as though the six million had never existed. Sometimes they relegated the figure to a footnote. In some cases they touched upon the Holocaust in a paragraph or so, perhaps a page. Otherwise they treated it as a minor incident amid the general, universal suffering of World War Two and its fifty million dead. Purposefully or not, the war against the Jews--the death of six million Jews, two-thirds of European Jewry--didn't count in the larger scheme of things. In some ways, the early historians were guilty of the worst cover-up of all--especially in the light of the immense amount of work that has been published since their silence.

Neo-Nazis and anti-Semites of every stripe play the numbers game too. They deny the 6,000,000 figure as a hoax, distort the number or minimize it or question it. They have laid the groundwork for the version of the Holocaust they want to send into the future. And they have their reasons as well--the reasons that every anti-Semite harbors, the reasons that the Nazis had: the destruction of the Jews.

But in a category all their own are the Jews who, wittingly or unwittingly, play the numbers game. In many instances they are uncomfortable with the Holocaust because they are uncomfortable with being Jewish. They have questions: "Why talk about it?" "Why do we keep on talking about it?" They have answers: "We have heard enough already." "Others were killed too. We're no different." Underneath, they hate having been born Jewish. They are the ones who are uncomfortable with the numbers game. They have no concept of the absolute seriousness with which one must consider the Holocaust. And they want none.

The pure Jewish universalists are another matter. Their discomfort with the figure of 6,000,000, the vehemence with which they deny its significance is, in fact, a clue to the threat it holds for them and their vision of the world. Most often assimilationists, they will brook no distinctions: all death is the same, that of Jews in the Holocaust--6,000,000 or not--was no different from the death of any other victim of the Nazis. Never mind that the Nazis were perfectly specific about the Jews and purposely singled them out for suffering and execution. The assimilationist does not--will not, cannot afford to--make any distinctions, lest his world view collapse. In his own way he, too, has to de-Judaize the Holocaust in order to avoid questioning the why of it. To merge the Jewish dead with all the other dead--just as he would merge the living Jew with the majority society--is to relieve him of any need to investigate the Holocaust. Better, and safer, to be a non-Jewish Jew absorbed and lost in the mainstream Christian community than to align oneself in any way with the 6,000,000 Jewish dead.

The universalist, Jew or otherwise, opts for the most all-inclusive numbers--so that numbers lose all meaning. The non-Jewish universalist does so out of hatred for Jews. The universalist Jew does so out of hatred for himself.

Hillel the Elder, the great first century Jewish teacher, left us something of a puzzler when he said, "If I am not for myself, who is for me? And if I am for myself, what am I? And if not now, when?"

The Jewish universalist finds his rationale in "If I am for myself, what am I?" But if twentieth century Jewish history proves anything, it proves that adherence to this belief is the Jewish universalist impulse gone mad. If twentieth century Jewish history demonstrates anything, it demonstrates the truth of the first part of Hillel's statement: "If I am not for myself, who is for me?" And of his conclusion as well: "And if not now, when?"

Whatever you do, Rina, do not be taken in by the numbers game.

The Warehouse

The Germans deported your grandmother from the Kovno Ghetto to Vaivara and then to Kivioli in Estonia. They put her to work in a warehouse. She sorted clothes that the Germans delivered there--clothes that came from all directions, clothes of all sizes, clothes for men, for women, for children. Clothes of Jews they had shot.

Their usual method was to march the Jews or take them by truck to a forest or some other killing ground, force them to undress, then shoot them down in pits that had been dug for mass graves. The Germans would collect the clothes and take them to the warehouse to be cleaned, repaired, and prepared for shipment back to Germany--to be given a second chance at life.

Bullets worked well enough. But later, in Poland, when the number of captive Jews grew out of hand, this method of murder proved inefficient. The Germans discovered that gas was a far better method of execution. Not only was it a less bloody affair, but gas chambers permitted mass production of murder. And gas had the added advantage that it permitted the recycling of the whole human being, not just the victim's clothes. The Germans recycled hair, mined gold from the teeth of corpses, collected eyeglasses, prosthetic devices, luggage, shoes, wedding rings, watches--all to be shipped back to Germany for re-use.

William L. Shirer records how at the Nuremberg trial Rudolf Hoess, commandant of Auschwitz, affirmed the success of gas: "The Camp Commandant at Treblinka told me that he had liquidated 80,000 in the course of half a year....He used monoxide gas and I did not think his methods were very efficient. So when I set up the extermination building at Auschwitz, I used Zyklon B, which was a crystallized prussic acid which we dropped into the death chamber from a small opening. It took from three to fifteen minutes to kill the people....Another improvement we made over Treblinka was that we built our gas chambers to accommodate 2,000 people at one time, whereas at Treblinka their ten gas chambers only accommodated 200 people each."[86]

The poet H. Leivick memorialized Treblinka in two volumes of Yiddish poetry called *In Treblinka bin Ikh nit geven--In Treblinka I Was Not*. I was not "there" either. But when I hear talk of apologies offered and forgiveness asked for the Holocaust, I can't help but wonder what in the world those who are apologizing really know of bullets and gas and warehouses full of clothes of the dead. I can't help but wonder who is asking forgiveness and why. What in the world do these petitioners know of the unspeakable? the unimaginable? To whom are they apologizing? Of whom do they ask forgiveness? Who has the right to accept apology, the power to grant forgiveness? Only the dead. And they are out of reach, far beyond apologies and forgiveness.

Did the victims say "I forgive you" to their murderers? Did they say "I forgive you" before they were murdered? As they were being murdered? Immediately afterward? Would they say "I forgive you" to their murderers today? Would they want to be included with those 5,000,000 "others" in a holocaust of 11,000,000 and find themselves among those who all too often were anti-Semites and themselves killers of Jews? Would they willingly accept this final agony, this final injustice to them--their worst nightmare--that their story would be forever lost among millions of anonymous dead, their enemies among them?

Never.

Somebody has to say it.

Oat-cakes

Sometimes, Rina, if you read enough, and if you are lucky, you will run across a passage in a book, or somewhere, that you will recognize instantly as perfection itself. It will stun you with its clarity, with both its beauty and its truth. I wish you the unique joy of such moments.

One of these moments occurred for me when I reached the last three pages of a book called *Wake Up, Stupid* by Mark Harris. It is an epistolary novel--a novel consisting of letters. It was published in 1959, eleven years before you were born. To my mind, it is a small classic, serious in the way that only very funny books can be. My own copy of the book has fallen apart. But I will never part with it, not even on "temporary loan" to a good friend.

It is about Lee Youngdahl, a young college English teacher up for tenure but in considerable hot water with some members of the Tenure Committee and the Administration. The Committee has its reservations about recommending him because, among other things, as it reports, "he behaves contrarily to demands of a democratic learning experience by shouting at a student, 'Wake up, stupid!'" It is a shout that has always endeared Youngdahl and the book to me.

The last letter in the novel is one that Youngdahl writes to his dear friend and fellow English teacher Harold Rosenblatt. Both of them share a deep interest in James Boswell and Samuel Johnson and their times, so much so that Youngdahl, in high spirits, is moved to send him a box of oat-cakes and the story of how he came upon them:

I discovered the shop while strolling one night with a theater associate. Dashing within, I told its proprietors, a Mr. and Mrs. Dunnichen, "I must taste an oat-cake."

"Oh Sir," said Mrs. Dunnichen, "we haven't made oat-cakes in years. The tradition, Sir, has died with the passing of the New-York Scotch."

But we can make an oat-cake yet," said her husband.

"Make me one," I said.

"Oh Sir," said she, "we couldn't make one."

"Make me three boxes then," said I, "a box for my wife, a box for me, and a box for Harold."

She assured me that her oat-cakes were genuine, prepared in the manner of her mother before her, backward in time to the generation of the mother of James Boswell. "When we first set up to make oat-cakes here," she said, "they were in demand."

"But then, Sir," said her husband, "to suit the changing taste we took to making English muffins."

"Or what they call hereabouts English muffins," said his wife.

"For they aren't rightly English," he said.

"Nor rightly muffins neither," said Mrs. Dunnichen.

"It is this city," I said. "It is a whoredom."

"Not at all," said Mrs. Dunnichen. "There's whores in every city, in every age, and now no different."

"Somebody somewhere," said Mrs. Dunnichen, "will always be keeping high the tradition of oat-cakes."

"Somewhere," said her husband, "somebody will always go on calling things by their right name."[87]

What, you may well wonder, do oat-cakes have to do with the Holocaust? Nothing. And everything.

PERSPECTIVE

A Primer

Rina, five years before you were born the Catholic Church took its first step toward dialogue and reconciliation with the Jews. Many Jews have hailed the steps since then, especially those taken by Pope John Paul II, as the beginning of a new era in Catholic-Jewish relations and in Christian-Jewish relations. The events I talk about here all occurred after the Holocaust and did not directly affect the family. But you have to know something about these "new" relations in order to have some idea of what was happening to your great-grandmother and her family during the "old" ones.

The new reflect the old and illuminate them too. Context is everything. The Holocaust was intimately involved in all of them--and if you "read" them accurately, you will discover something of the Christian context--the European Christian climate and atmosphere-- within which Di Tante and your grandmother lived--and within which almost all Lithuanian Jews were murdered. This primer isn't complete, but it will give you an essential perspective from which to understand what happened to Di Tante and her family--and why.

Nostra Aetate

Pope Pius XII kept his silence even after World War Two ended. The Church could not very well afford to admit to itself, let alone to anyone else, the connection between its Jewish Problem and the Holocaust. But twenty years later, under the influence of Pope John XXIII, the Church sensed it was time to speak. In 1965 the Second Vatican Council broke the silence with *Nostra Aetate*--"In Our Time"-- its "Declaration on the Relationship of the Church to Non-Christian Religions." The Declaration contained the Church's first official attempt in modern times to address its Jewish Problem. *Nostra Aetate* does not mention the Holocaust, but the Holocaust is there all the same. You can be sure there would have been no *Nostra Aetate* for the Jews if there had been no Holocaust. Nor without *Nostra Aetate* could there have been the Vatican's historic 1998 centerpiece document "We Remember: A Reflection on the Shoah."

Nostra Aetate was a signal that times had changed. But it was not simply that times had changed: it was that the Holocaust had happened--and forever changed the times. The Vatican had to recognize that the Jewish people had entered a new era, and that if the Jews had entered a new era, so too had the Church. Like it or not, after World War Two the Vatican had to realize, more than ever, that the Holocaust had so bound the Church to the Jews that it would forever afterward have to take the Holocaust into account in its relations with them.

Nostra Aetate's assertion of the "spiritual bond" between Catholics and Jews, its call for "mutual respect and understanding," its condemnation of discrimination and anti-Semitism, and its anticipation of "brotherly dialogues" spoke words approaching the Third Millennium that the Church had not uttered during the first two millennia. Ever since its publication many Jews have hailed *Nostra Aetate* for having absolved Jews of the charge of having killed Christ, the very accusation that from the beginning has fueled Christianity's anti-Semitism. *Nostra Aetate* seemed about ready to end almost two thousand years of Christian antagonism toward the Jews.

But what Christianity and the Church had constructed for almost two thousand years was not about to be torn down in less than twenty. The record was bad, and contrary to what many Jews and Christians believe--and would have us believe--it still is.

Many Jews think--or want to think--that *Nostra Aetate* absolves all Jews of deicide. *Nostra Aetate* wants no misunderstanding on this count. "True," it says, "authorities of the Jews and those who followed their lead pressed for the death of Christ." Plenty of blame and guilt still there. Then its authors add "still, what happened in his passion cannot be blamed upon all the Jews then living, without distinction, nor upon the Jews of today." "Cannot?" But it has been and continues to be. Moreover, by condensing the Gospel story into just five seemingly neutral words--"what happened in his passion"--the authors glide quickly over the fundamental, unavoidable anti-Semitism of the story that can be, and was, blamed upon *some* Jews, Jews "then living," but living *with* "distinction" from other Jews. As for the Jews of today, well, they are off the hook, unless they still happen to be tainted just a bit with guilt by association. But make no mistake about it, Rina: *Nostra Aetate* offers no total absolution for all Jews of the charge of killing Christ. As one observer noted, *Nostra Aetate* "limited, but did not render null and void, the guilt of the Jews in killing Jesus."[88]

Nostra Aetate maintains that "the Jews should not be presented as repudiated or cursed by God, as if such behavior followed from the holy Scriptures." "Should not be?" But they *were* so presented. By whom, after all? How did this happen? Over the centuries did the passion plays--like Oberammergau's--emerge from a void? Why were they performed? Where did repudiation and curse come from if not from the Scriptures? Who objected to such presentations? Condemned them? Or prevented them? If not "as if" they were derived from the Scriptures, then how and where did they originate? And why, after all, did it take so many centuries for the Church to note the misrepresentation of the Jews--and then only *after* the Holocaust?

To be sure, the Declaration "deplores the hatred, persecutions, and displays of anti-Semitism directed against the Jews at any time and from any source." And, to be sure, Pope John Paul II and the Vatican are against anti-Semitism. And, yes, since *Nostra Aetate* "anti-Semitism" holds a central place in their vocabulary. But nowhere in their major statements about it does one sense that they genuinely "have" its meaning in their bones or see its fundamental connection, beyond abstractions, to the Holocaust--not, at any rate, in the way the Jewish philosopher and theologian Eliezer Berkovits defines it. "What really stands between us," he says of Christian and Jew, is "not creed and dogma, but first of all, a river of tears and blood running through the centuries. The crime against the Jewish people is the cancer at the very heart of Christianity. Anti-Semitism is a mild word to describe it. It covers up much more than it reveals. What we are dealing with is neither prejudice nor dislike of fellow human beings; it is not even hatred in the normal sense of the word. None of these can explain the sadistic passion with which Jews have been persecuted, entire communities mercilessly annihilated, generation after generation, almost through the entire course of Christian history, ever since, with the help of Constantine's sword, Christianity became triumphant."[89] In Berkovits's terms, neither pope nor Church is willing or able to face the specific truth at the core of "anti-Semitism."

The fact is that anti-Semitism was built into Christianity through the Gospels: through the centuries anti-Semitism *became* Christian tradition, an attitude ingrained in Christianity. Anti-Semitism is central to Christianity: it's a given. To eliminate anti-Semitism--to eliminate the Gospels from the Christian tradition--would be to put an end to Christianity. The Church simply has to retain the attitude out of self-preservation.

For Berkovits, *Nostra Aetate* does not at all represent a full-faith effort by the Church to address its Jewish Problem--not in the light of the Holocaust. A year after the appearance of *Nostra Aetate* Berkovits writes: "To be told after sixteen centuries of oppression and persecution in Christian lands by those responsible for these acts of inhumanity that the Jews are not a people accursed by God is an offense not so much to Jews as to God."[90] For him the record of the Church was not just as bad as ever. It was worse.

Archbishop and Pope

Though *Nostra Aetate* seemed to suggest a change of direction in Catholic-Jewish affairs, the Church's underlying theological attitude toward the Jews remained fundamentally unaltered. Jews saw no change of direction in Pope Paul VI's beatification of the Franciscan Maximilien Kolbe. Many felt that Kolbe's record was questionable, that as the general editor of a major Polish journal he had demonstrated anti-Semitic leanings, in its publication, for example, of the *Protocols of the Elders of Zion*. But Pope Paul VI had justification enough for beatifying him: Kolbe had voluntarily offered his life for a fellow prisoner at Auschwitz.

Far more important--and what those Jews who objected to Kolbe should have taken note of--was a speech in which the Archbishop of Krakow, the future John Paul II, recognized the deeper possibilities in the beatification of Kolbe. On Vatican Radio on October 20, 1971, he said, "The Church of Poland sees the necessity of a place of sacrifice, an altar and a sanctuary, precisely in Auschwitz. This is even more necessary after the beatification of Father Maximilien. We are all convinced that in this place of his heroic immolation, a church should be erected, in the same way that since the first centuries of Christianity, churches were built on the tombs of martyrs, beatified people and saints."[91] John Paul's speech foreshadowed his own canonization of Kolbe in 1982. But, more important, his words also laid claim for the Church to what he called "the Golgotha of the Auschwitz camp."[92] For him Auschwitz was the site of Christian martyrdom. What Auschwitz--and the Holocaust--meant to the Jews was of no concern to him.

Eight years later he enlarged the Church's claim to Auschwitz. He now called Auschwitz "this Golgotha of the modern world."[93] Henryk

Grynberg, novelist, poet, and chronicler of the fate of Polish Jewry during the Holocaust, points out: "When Pope John Paul II made his celebrated visit to Auschwitz in 1979, he enumerated some twenty languages in which the commemorative plaques were written. He referred to the inscriptions on these plaques as 'languages of the victims of this Golgotha' and went on to say that these plaques 'testify to the losses suffered by the nations.' But in fact those plaques testify only to the different *languages* spoken by the victims, who were predominantly of *one* nationality--Jewish."[94] The Israeli diplomat Sergio Minerbi, going still further, states that John Paul "stood before the inscription in Polish and spoke about remembering the six million Poles who had perished,"[95] disappearing 3 million Jews into six. For the newly elected pope Auschwitz was an opportunity not only to misrepresent the Holocaust but to appropriate it.

Convent and Cross

The convent that a group of Carmelite nuns established in 1984 in an old theater building just outside a wall of the Auschwitz concentration camp wasn't quite the church John Paul II envisioned for Father Kolbe, but it would do. Jews, however, objected to a convent at Auschwitz. Nuns offering prayers for over a million Jews killed at Auschwitz? Or for the Poles executed there? Soon enough, the convent touched off an inevitable controversy between Jewish community leaders and Church and government authorities. Church authorities permitted the dispute to fester for more than a decade. They reached an agreement with the Jews to remove the convent, broke the agreement, then added one delay after another to frustrate any resolution of the situation. Tensions grew. Anger escalated into so bitter a confrontation that it threatened not only Polish-Jewish relations but worldwide Catholic-Jewish relations.

In 1988 Jewish objections to the convent extended to the erection there of the cross Pope John Paul had used during Mass at Auschwitz in 1979. The confrontation grew deeper when Polish Catholic extremists responded by planting three hundred crosses protectively around the "papal" cross. Charge led to counter-charge and further deepened the controversy. By the time John Paul II and government officials finally intervened the damage was done. The crosses were removed and the Carmelites relocated outside of Auschwitz, but the dispute left dialogue and reconciliation in shambles. Jews, for their part, were wounded by the attempt to use convent and cross to appropriate for Christianity not only the greatest Jewish memorial of the Holocaust but the Holocaust itself.

The Great Synagogue of Rome

Pope John Paul II made an unprecedented visit to Rome's Great Synagogue on April 13, 1986, and spoke words that no pope had ever spoken before, let alone from inside a synagogue. He devoted much of his speech to the meaning of *Nostra Aetate* for Catholic-Jewish relations. He spoke of his abhorrence of the Holocaust, of his opposition to anti-Semitism, of his friendship for the Jewish people, and of the bond of brotherhood between Catholic and Jew. "With Judaism," he declared, "...we have a relationship which we do not have with any other religion. You are our dearly beloved brothers, and in a certain way, it could be said that you are our elder brothers." No Jew on first hearing such words could have been less than astonished and hopeful. And, in fact, they remain among the most frequently cited in his favor.

If Church and pope know the value of timing, they know still more the power of their language. When John Paul addressed Jews as "our dearly beloved brothers" and as "our elder brothers," he knew exactly what he meant--and exactly what he wanted his audience to think. His language was persuasive. Who, after all, could be against brotherhood? To Jews impressed by the pope's sheer physical presence and by his eloquence it seemed that the Church had indeed reached a turning point in its attitude toward the Jews.

Caught up by hopes for brotherhood, Jews heard the plain meaning of his words. Carried away by the idea of a change in the

Church's attitude, the Jewish world was deaf to the theological connotations locked into the vocabulary of the Church.

In his statement *Tertio Millennio Adveniente*--"As the Third Millennium Draws Near"--in November, 1994, Pope John Paul explained a vocabulary from which neither he nor the Church has ever deviated. "In the history of the Church," he said, "the 'old' and the 'new' are always closely interwoven. The 'new' grows out of the 'old,' and the 'old' finds a fuller expression in the 'new.'" Thus, the New Testament is the "fuller expression" of the Old Testament. And to be a younger brother is to achieve a "fuller expression" than an "elder" brother. "In a certain way, it could be said that you are our elder brothers" said the pope. Yes, "in a certain way, it could be said," but he carefully left unsaid the theological significance of what he meant by "a certain way" or "it could be said." He knew--as those who accepted his words at face value did not--that his vocabulary expressed the age-old theme of supersessionism while it retained and covered up the very basis of the anti-Semitism he professed to abhor. Nor would it have done to expose how this theme--and its ramifications--undercut much of what he said in the rest of his address at the synagogue. Though his words appeared to indicate a change in the attitude of the Church, and were intended to do so, the reality was that the record of the Church remained what it had always been.

The Liar

The Waldheim affair offers another example of the record.

Unaccountably, no one in authority during Kurt Waldheim's two terms as secretary general of the United Nations saw fit to look into his wartime record. Investigative reporters did look into it, though, when he campaigned for the Austrian presidency in 1986. Waldheim had let it be known that he was wounded on the Russian front in 1941, and that after his medical discharge--from 1942 to 1945--he had studied law in Vienna. Alert to the three year blank in his record during the war years, they sensed a cover-up. It turned out that he had lied--that he had spent those years as an intelligence officer serving under Alexander

Lohr, a Nazi general, and that he had served in the Balkans with a Wehrmacht unit that had rounded up and deported over 48,000 Jews from Salonika to Auschwitz. In 1945 Yugoslavia executed Lohr for war crimes.

Western European governments knew Waldheim's record was bad--and shunned him. The United States knew his record was bad--and barred him from the U.S. The Austrians themselves knew that his record was bad--and elected him. Only John Paul II and the Vatican did not seem to know how bad his record was: on June 25, 1987, the pope received him on a state visit to the Vatican.

The American Jewish leadership exploded and threatened to boycott the pope's upcoming visit to the United States. Seeing a disaster ahead for Catholic-Jewish relations, and for the Church's public relations generally, the pope defused the threat by promising the Jewish leaders that the Vatican Commission for Religious Relations with the Jews would soon publish a document dealing with anti-Semitism, the Church, and the Holocaust. Somewhat mollified by the promise, and having long hoped for such a document, the Jewish leadership took the pope at his word.

It had no idea that "soon" would stretch into eleven years of waiting for "We Remember: A Reflection on the Shoah" to arrive. Nor could it foresee that in June, 1988, exactly a year after the pope first met with Waldheim at the Vatican, the two would meet again in Vienna. Or that John Paul II would confer a Papal knighthood on Waldheim only six months after establishing diplomatic relations with Israel in 1994 and while the Commission's Holocaust document was still a promise. Even the pope's timing carried a message.

Saint Teresa

Edith Stein was another test case of Church attitudes and intentions.

Pope John Paul II oversaw more beatifications and canonizations than any other pope in the history of the Church. The Jewish world community recognizes well enough that such matters are strictly the concern of the Church. Nevertheless, John Paul's beatification and canonization of Edith Stein proved a double shock to Jews for whom the Holocaust was still a vivid memory. Shock turned into a controversy so bitter that it, too, threatened to rupture Catholic-Jewish relations.

Stein, a Jewish woman who converted to Catholicism in 1933, became a Carmelite nun--Sister Teresia Benedicta a Cruce--Teresa, Blessed of the Cross. She was murdered at Auschwitz in early August, 1942. John Paul considered her a martyr for the faith. He beatified her on May 1, 1987, and elevated her to sainthood on October 11, 1998.

To the worldwide Jewish community Edith Stein died only because of her Jewish origin--not because she was a Catholic, or a nun, or because she was a martyr for the Catholic faith. Jews were outraged at what they saw as the Catholic exploitation of her death.

Their worst fears could only have been confirmed by the words Pope John Paul used to support his case. In his homily in 1987 on beatifying Stein he saw "her life and her cross itinerary" as "intimately linked to the destiny of the Jewish People." In canonizing her eleven years later, he termed her a "Catholic Jew," never mind that at the Rome synagogue in 1986 he had said, "...each of our religions...wishes to be recognized and respected in its own identity, beyond any syncretism and any ambiguous appropriation." If in one breath he cited her as "this eminent daughter of Israel," in the next he saw her completely fulfilled as a "faithful daughter of the Church." Her "experience of the Cross," he said, enabled her "to open the way to a new encounter with the God of Abraham, Isaac and Jacob, the Father of our Lord Jesus Christ." He saw her death as a symbol of Catholic martyrdom in the Holocaust. He saw her life as an example of traditional Christian doctrine: that the future of the Jewish people still lay in Christ and the Cross.

The conversion of the Jews, however, has never been very high on the Jewish agenda. That after *Nostra Aetate* it still held a special place for John Paul on the Catholic agenda jolted the Jewish world. To Jews, sainthood for an Edith Stein represented still another effort by the pope to Christianize Auschwitz and the Holocaust and to appropriate them for the Church. He actually chose the day on which she was probably killed as the Holocaust remembrance day for Catholics. August 9 became a day for them to "remember the Shoah...to which millions of our Jewish brothers and sisters fell victim"--never mind that the Christian "brothers and sisters" of the Jews had failed to do what family members are called upon to do when brothers and sisters are in mortal danger. After using Stein to advocate the conversion of the Jews, the pope somehow found the courage--Jews would say *chutzpa*-- to end his homily with the hope that "her witness [would] constantly strengthen the bridge of mutual understanding between Jews and Christians." In the uproar that followed her canonization, his hope for a "bridge of mutual understanding" all but came crashing down. A church spokesman hurriedly delivered a special "advisory" to counteract Jewish concerns about the pope's words, too late, though, to undo the severe damage they had done to dialogue and reconciliation.

The Mask

In 1998 the Vatican kept its promise to speak about the role of the Church during the Holocaust. Under its president Cardinal Edward Cassidy, the Vatican's Commission for Religious Relations With the Jews finally released its statement "We Remember: A Reflection on the Shoah." It was the first official statement of the Church on the Holocaust--and it remains its centerpiece gesture toward reconciliation with the Jews. It illuminates all the gestures that preceded it--and all those that were to follow it. It was the Vatican's version of what post-Holocaust Germany called *Vergangenheitsbewältigung*, a coming to terms with the Holocaust.

What "We Remember.." remembers--and wants us to remember--is its own version of history. Well aware of the primary truth--that the Holocaust had come as the culmination of two thousand years of the Christian experiment and that its stunning horror had put Christianity and the Church on trial--the Vatican resorts to a classic defense: it simply denies outright both guilt and responsibility. Moreover, it claims that the charges against it do not apply and points its finger at where it insists they do apply.

The document's fundamental strategy is to shift the spotlight from the role of Christianity and the Church during the Holocaust to the "neo-pagan regime" of the Nazis. "We Remember..." admits that some Christians--bad Christians, to be sure--bear some guilt for their part in the Shoah. But it insists they were guilty of an anti-Judaism based on "sentiments of mistrust and hostility," not on anti-Semitism. Without disavowing them, it calls them the "spoiled seeds of anti-Judaism." Cardinal Joseph Ratzinger attempted to explain the Church's position in a front page article in *L'Osservatore Romano* (December 29, 2000). "It cannot be denied," he offered, "that a certain insufficient resistance to this atrocity on the part of Christians can be explained by the inherited anti-Judaism in the hearts of not a few Christians."

In shifting blame for the Shoah from ancient Christian anti-Judaism to modern twentieth century Nazi anti-Semitism, in shifting blame from inside Christianity to roots "outside of Christianity," "We Remember..." denies and falsifies history--the Church's own history--of the anti-Semitism it invented, imposed, and perpetuated. The Jews, writes Eliezer Berkovits, "are able to survey the Christian performance from the beginning of the Christian era to its end. We have been there all the time, we alone know what it has meant."[96] It is inconceivable that the performer, who was also there all the time, was unaware of what his performance meant--at least to him and his audience. At the very least, the Nazis and their collaborators, performers or products of that performance, acted on a Christian stage in a Christian world.

"We Remember..." asks, "Did Christians give every possible assistance to those being persecuted, and in particular the persecuted Jews?" And it answers, "Many did, but others did not." It shifts the focus from Christians who sinned during the Holocaust to those who saved Jews. The trouble is that the question is badly put. The Shoah is not about all "those being persecuted" and only "in particular" about the persecuted Jews. Intentionally or not, the authors of "We Remember..." blur the salient point that the Shoah is about the murder of six million Jews. The more relevant and precise question that "We Remember ..." does not wish to ask is: "Did Christians give every possible assistance to the persecuted Jews?" The answer that "many did, but others did not" is quite simply a complete reversal of history. The truth is that some did but most did not. The ostensible purpose of "We Remember..." was to answer this question. Why should the Vatican propose "We Remember..." at all if not to answer it with total honesty? If, in fact, the Vatican honestly believes it has given the right answer, then there is no point to "We Remember..." at all. And everything else in the document becomes pointless.

"We Remember..." shifts its focus from Pope Pius XII who, it says, saved a great many Jews during the Holocaust, to the guilt of the Allied nations that closed their borders to the Jews and did not. It shifts from any questions about his silence before, during, and after the Holocaust to his role as a savior of Jews. It ignores any possible guilt of the Church as an institution in order to place whatever blame it must on Christians who had sinned. It argues not for crime and punishment, but for crime and forgiveness.

At first glance, as the document's title suggests, the Vatican Commission seems to be addressing an exclusive audience of Catholics and Jews. The truth is that it has an ever more inclusive audience in mind. It enlarges its audience from "our brothers and

302

sisters of the Catholic Church throughout the world" to "all Christians," then to "all men and women of good will" until finally it calls out for "the attention of all humanity." Instead of exploring and explaining to its adherents its own role during the Holocaust, the Church distributes among a universal audience the burden of whatever guilt and responsibility is attached to the Holocaust. And its own burden effectively disappears.

To discover the thinking behind "We Remember..." you have to disentangle its ideas, organize them, and, yes, italicize them, as the document itself does not. "We Remember..." begins with the specific event of the Shoah but gradually shifts far beyond it. The Commission "deeply regret[s] the errors and failures" committed during the Shoah by "sons and daughters of the Church." Thereafter, it "deplores the hatred, persecutions and displays of anti-Semitism directed against Jews at *any* time and from *any* source." It "repudiates *every* persecution against a people or human group, *anywhere* at *any* time." It notes the obligation of the Church "to become more fully conscious of the sinfulness of her children during *all* those times in history" when they "indulged in ways of thinking and acting which were truly forms of counter-witness and scandal." The Church asserts "her deep sorrow for the failures of her sons and daughters of *every* age." The added italics make it abundantly clear that "We Remember..." is not concerned with a full, direct confrontation with the specific Shoah and the specific role of the Church in it. It is concerned with the universality of sin precisely to avoid that confrontation.

In one sentence "We Remember..." asks all Christians to join Catholics to meditate on "the catastrophe which befell the Jewish people." In the very next it shifts to Pope John Paul's statement that the Shoah "has become a symbol of the aberrations of which man is capable when he turns against God." Once more "We Remember..." leaps from the specific to the general, from the particular to the universal, from the Shoah as a unique event to the Shoah as a symbol. The Shoah, however, is not a symbol: it does not stand for anything else. To treat it as an "aberration" by a universal "man" in an abstract theological conflict with God is to deny that it was a concrete crime, six

303

million crimes, against flesh-and-blood Jews committed by willing, flesh-and-blood Germans and their actual, willing collaborators at a place like the Ninth Fort. No mention of Auschwitz or Treblinka either. Again "We Remember..." evades the exact event in order to avoid the issues raised by the precise role that the Church and Christianity played in the Shoah.

The Vatican Commission for Religious Relations With the Jews had one major purpose: to offer Catholics and Jews the Church's thinking on the Shoah. However, before "We Remember..." ends, it remembers "the massacre of the Armenians." It remembers "the countless victims in Ukraine in the 1930's." It remembers "the genocide of the Gypsies." It remembers "similar tragedies... in America, Africa and the Balkans." It remembers "the millions of victims of totalitarian ideology in the Soviet Union, in China, Cambodia and elsewhere." Nor does "We Remember: A Reflection on the Shoah" forget to remember "the drama of the Middle East, the elements of which are well known."

By intentionally reducing the Holocaust to one of many "similar" catastrophes "We Remember..." contradicts its own call for reflection "on the significance of the Shoah," the very subject it has chosen to remember. It implies comparisons to the Holocaust that simply do not exist. With its "reflection" on John Paul's comment that "many human beings are still their brothers' victims," "We Remember..." completely submerges the Holocaust in the universalist cliché of man's inhumanity to man. Instead of focusing on the centrality of the Shoah for both Catholics and Jews "We Remember..." finally loses itself and the Holocaust within a universal meaninglessness. When man's inhumanity to man becomes the root cause of the Holocaust, all charges against Christianity and the Church for their role during the Shoah simply vanish.

Had the Jewish community been alert to Pope John Paul's remarks in Rio de Janeiro less than six months before the publication of "We Remember..." it might have foreseen the direction he and the document would take. Responding in Rio de Janeiro to questions about its forthcoming publication, he told reporters, "One mustn't forget there were other holocausts."[97]

If so, what possessed the Vatican Commission to go out of its way to write a document on the Shoah and not a "We Remember: A Reflection on the Armenian Massacre"? Why didn't it reflect on the Ukrainian tragedy? Or on any of the other tragedies it remembers? If the Shoah was only one of many Holocausts, why did the Vatican undertake "We Remember..." at all? In agreeing that there were other Holocausts beyond the Shoah, both the Commission and John Paul ignored the centrality of the Holocaust to the Jews as well as its centrality with respect to Christian-Jewish and Catholic-Jewish relations. Or they understood its centrality all too well and avoided it in order not to reflect on it. If so, the digressions to all the other Holocausts were not digressions at all but a maneuver to diminish the staggering immensity of the Shoah and thereby relieve the Church of any great guilt or responsibility for it.

The very word "Shoah" in the title of this document, its early reference to the Holocaust as the "worst suffering of all" ever to befall the Jews, and its appeal to "our Jewish friends...to hear us with open hearts," offered not once but twice, as well as assorted expressions of sympathy, sorrow, and regret: all seem clearly intended for Jewish consumption, a prologue to what Jews were hoping at last to hear from the Church. But its title was only a mask for the defense of the Church, a defense that makes every possible effort to sever the Church from any connection to the Shoah. What "We Remember: A Reflection on the Shoah" asked Jews to hear with open hearts was not an apology but its opposite: a deliberate defense of the Church--and Christianity. Nor does it ever stray from this defense. It had no intention to face the Holocaust or to come to terms with it. What had the appearance of being offered in good faith turns out to have been an exercise in bad faith.

Jubilee

The Vatican Commission responsible for 'We Remember: A Reflection on the Shoah" in large part draws its words and ideas from the writing and speeches of Pope John Paul II.

"We Remember..." begins with a major premise: the Pope's generalization that it is the Church's obligation to "become more fully conscious of the sinfulness of her children during all those times in history" when they fell short of "the spirit of Christ and his Gospel" and "indulged in ways of thinking and acting which were truly forms of counter-witness and scandal." "We Remember..." relegates the Shoah to its minor premise--useful only as an example: that there were Christians during the Shoah, whose "spiritual resistance and concrete action...was not that which might have been expected from Christ's followers." Christians, that is, who at the very least were bystanders and for whom "this heavy burden of conscience of their brothers and sisters during the Second World War must be a call to penitence." Like John Paul, "We Remember..." regrets "the errors and failings" of these "sons and daughters of the Church."

And "We Remember..." concludes with a restatement of its major premise--the generalization that "the Catholic Church desires to express her deep sorrow for the failures of her sons and daughters of every age."

In a letter to Cardinal Cassidy accompanying the publication of "We Remember..." the pope gave his whole-hearted approval to the document. Only once does he mention the Shoah: to acknowledge it as "an indelible stain on the history of the century that is coming to a close" and say it must never happen again.

Then he turns to what interests him most: the Jubilee, "the beginning of the Third Millennium of Christianity." It interests him because it holds the promise of the Jubilee joy of "the forgiveness of sins and reconciliation with God and neighbor." It is a time, he says, when the Church calls upon its sons and daughters "to examine themselves on the responsibility which they too have for the evils of our time" and "to purify their hearts, through repentance of past errors and infidelities."

Pope John Paul's letter does not directly mention the Shoah as being among the past errors, infidelities, and evils of our time. Nevertheless, for him as for the Commission, the problem is to come to terms with the Holocaust. Neither is concerned with memory or justice or reflection upon the "indelible stain" of the Shoah. What both are concerned with is purification, repentance, forgiveness: the removal of the indelible stain.

Which--by definition--cannot be removed.

Flexibility

In 1944 Italian partisans exploded a bomb killing 33 German soldiers. Hitler ordered ten hostages executed for each dead soldier. SS Col. Herbert Kappler, head of the Gestapo in Rome--a man who had sent 1,007 Italian Jews to Auschwitz a year earlier--selected 335 Italians, including 78 Jews, and had them executed in the Ardeatine Caves near Rome. After the war an Italian military tribunal tried him as a war criminal and sentenced him to life imprisonment. In 1977, when he was dying of cancer, his wife managed to smuggle him out of the hospital and into West Germany. *L'Osservatore Romano,* the Vatican's daily newspaper, observed that it was "understandable" that Kappler's guard had, in fact, looked the other way. He died shortly afterward at age 70. Two hundred mourners attended his funeral.

Referring to the executions and "those who felt most directly joined to the victims by blood or spiritual solidarity: relatives, survivors, supporters of an atrociously trampled-on civil law and above all the members of the Jewish community," a front page editorial in *L'Osservatore Romano* declared, "A large number of those involved seem to have lacked the moral strength to overcome themselves and forgive....It is here that, as Christians and citizens, we feel we cannot praise that final inflexibility." The basic issue, it said, was whether "even the worst, most inhuman and hateful persecutor should not be given the chance of a final conversion, the right to a liberating redemption and, in any case, to human mercy." [98]

According to the report on the Kappler funeral, one of the mourners at the graveside cried out, "You acted on orders. You did what every German officer would have done." Several others gave the Nazi salute.[99]

The Hinge

On October 31, 1997, Pope John Paul II spoke at a symposium on "The Roots of Anti-Semitism in the Christian Milieu" and reaffirmed his position--harking back to *Nostra Aetate* and to his speech at the Great Synagogue in Rome--that "in the Christian world--I do not say on the part of the Church as such--erroneous and unjust interpretations of the New Testament regarding the Jewish people and their alleged culpability have circulated for too long, engendering feelings of hostility towards this people." The same passage reappeared five months later in "We Remember...."

In the Rome Synagogue Pope John Paul wisely chose not to explain the crucial theological implications of his references to Jews as "our dearly beloved brothers" and as "our elder brothers" or to explain their implications for Catholic dialogue and reconciliation with the Jews. Nor did he clarify what he meant by his aside "I do not say on the part of the Church as such." "We Remember..." doesn't either.

"As such" or "the Church as such" are puzzling locutions when you first encounter them. Far from innocent, they are a key to much that puzzles Jews about the pope and the Vatican in their relationship to the Jews. "As such" enabled the pope to make the crucial distinction he needed between those, Christians or otherwise, who live in "the Christian world" and "the Church as such," that is, the Church as an institution. "As such" is the hinge upon which he unfailingly hung the defense of the Church.

To understand "as such" one must go forward to December, 1999, when the International Theological Commission under its President Cardinal Joseph Ratzinger produced "Memory and Reconciliation: The Church and the Mistakes of the Past," a document which itself looks back to the 1960s and the Second Vatican Council. As "Memory and Reconciliation" puts it: "From a theological point of view, Vatican II distinguishes between the indefectible fidelity of the Church and the weaknesses of her members, clergy or laity, yesterday and today." By its very nature the Church as such, in and of itself, is forever faultless. Thus, the Church cannot be responsible for the erroneous and unjust interpretations of the New Testament that have spread "in the Christian world" and created hostility toward the Jews. Its sons and daughters might be guilty of sin, but not the Church "as such."

Father Jean-Louis Brugues, a French member of the committee that wrote "Memory and Reconciliation," reportedly said on its initial French publication, "We are not responsible for errors we did not commit..... We have had to find a way to liberate and purify memory without talking about responsibility"[100] No apology here. The Church, by definition, is an institution immune to responsibility or guilt. It has no choice: to admit either is to initiate its collapse. Nor was Cardinal Edward Cassidy unaware of the danger lurking in the document. "The greatest difficulty," he said, "was the fear that if you say the Church has been wrong in the past, then it can be wrong today and tomorrow."[101]

Even after the disappointment that many Jews voiced after the publication of "We Remember...," other Jews still managed to look forward to an apology from the Church for its role during the Holocaust.

General Audience

During his General Audience in Rome on March 1, 2000--three weeks before his trip to Israel--Pope John Paul said, "The Beatitudes are the evangelical completion of the Law of Sinai. The Covenant made then with the Hebrew people finds its fulfillment in the new and eternal Covenant established in Christ's Blood. Christ is the New Law, and in Him salvation is offered to all nations."[102]

Day of Pardon

"Memory and Reconciliation: The Church and the Mistakes of the Past" was issued on March 7, 2000. Five days later Pope John Paul celebrated the Day of Pardon Mass at St. Peter's Basilica in Rome. With the newly released statement very much on his mind, he asked God's forgiveness for the Catholics who had committed sins throughout history. For many this was an unprecedented moment in the history of the Church.

The pope invited everyone "to make a profound examination of conscience." The Jubilee, he reminded his audience, was a time for "purification of memory." Endorsing "Memory and Reconciliation" in his homily, "The Church," he said, "strong in the holiness which she receives from her Lord, should kneel before God and implore forgiveness for the past and present sins of her sons and daughters." This first Sunday of Lent, he said, "seemed to me the right occasion for the Church...to implore divine forgiveness for the sins of all believers."

Though "Memory and Reconciliation" did not especially have a Jewish audience in mind, its very subtitle--"The Church and the Mistakes of the Past"--might well have given Jews hope for the long awaited apology of the Church for its role in the Holocaust. One section of "Memory and Reconciliation" did, in fact, take up the issue of the Shoah, but it repeated only what the Vatican had already said in "We Remember...."

It was a day for the confession of sins, a long catalogue of sins, even for sins committed against the Jewish people. Cardinal Edward Cassidy did say, "Let us pray that, in recalling the sufferings endured by the people of Israel, Christians will acknowledge the sins committed by not a few of their number against the people of the Covenant...." And the pope did acknowledge being "deeply saddened" by the actions of

Christians who brought suffering upon Jews. But neither made specific apology for the Vatican's record during the Holocaust. Not for its neutrality during the war nor for its refusal to make a direct, unequivocal condemnation of the Holocaust. Disappointed as they were, many Jews were again willing to give the Pope the benefit of the doubt--that he would take the opportunity of his upcoming visit to the "Holy Land" to make that apology.

Yad Vashem

On March 23, 2000, Pope John Paul went to Yad Vashem, Israel's Holocaust memorial. It was the perfect stage for an apology. He re-kindled the Flame of Remembrance, placed a wreath before it, embraced a survivor he knew from boyhood. No one could miss the symbolism of these gestures: the Shoah meant something to him.

The words the Pope spoke probably meant something to those Israelis who were hearing them for the first time, though they were words he had repeated often enough on other occasions. They were drawn from *Nostra Aetate*, "We Remember...," and other similar sources: "How could man have such utter contempt for man?" "The Catholic Church...is deeply saddened by the hatred, acts of persecution and displays of anti-Semitism directed against the Jews by Christians at any time and in any place." "The Church rejects racism in any form...." "Let us build a new future in which there will be no more anti-Jewish feeling among Christians or anti-Christian feeling among Jews.

The pope paid "homage" to the murdered millions. He "deplored" their murder. He expressed "solidarity" with the victims. But he did not speak of the silence of the Church while they were being killed. At Yad Vashem, the very place where he might properly have offered the apology for the Holocaust that Jews hoped to hear, he offered none.

The Kvitl

On March 26 Pope John Paul, a frail figure in white robes, stood before the Western Wall, the Kotel, the holiest of Jewish holies, and with Jerusalem, all Israel, and the world for his audience, he offered the same prayer he had given eleven days earlier on the Day of Pardon: "God of our fathers, you chose Abraham and his descendants to bring Your Name to the Nations: we are deeply saddened by the behavior of those who in the course of history have caused these children of Yours to suffer, and asking Your forgiveness we wish to commit ourselves to genuine brotherhood with the people of the Covenant." Then, in a dramatic gesture that could only have moved the heart of every Jew who saw him, even the most skeptical one, he took the note--the *kvitl*--on which his prayer had been typed and inserted it between two stones of the Wall. In one astonishing stroke he seemed to link himself to every Jew who had ever placed a *kvitl* in the Wall to request something of God. His *kvitl* was also his last best chance to offer the apology for the Shoah.

He did not take it.

The pope addressed his prayer to God. He meant for Jews to hear it as well. But his prayer spoke about the "descendants" of Abraham, about God's "children," and about "the people of the Covenant"--but never about Jews as such. He spoke about being "deeply saddened"--but by what? By "the behavior of those who in the course of history" caused the Jews "to suffer." What suffering? Spiritual suffering? Murder? Was the Pope referring to the Shoah without referring to the Shoah? Was he referring only to the Shoah? "Behavior?" Which? Whose? "Those?" In the "course of history?" In the ordinary, normal, natural "course of history?" Did Christians, Christianity, and the Church have anything to do with the course of history? When? He asked forgiveness of God, but for what? For whom? These glaring omissions created uncalled for ambiguities. The occasion warranted something better.

312

Many assumed that the pope's *kvitl* made an apology to the Jews for the behavior of the Church during the Shoah. It made no such apology at all. Instead the pope's *kvitl* asked God's forgiveness for the Church's Christian sinners! The *kvitl*, signed and delivered, was a breathtaking reversal. It was the work of a master magician. In the shadow of the Western Wall it was a pure stroke of *chutzpa*.

The Sleepers

Throughout most of his papacy John Paul II was liberally praised by Jews and Catholics as an unparalleled spokesman for dialogue and reconciliation. In Vienna in June, 1998--shortly after "We Remember: A Reflection on the Shoah"--he declared, "Reconciliation with the Jews is one of the fundamental duties of Christians in Europe."[103] And again, at Yad Vashem in March, 2000, "We must work for a new era of reconciliation and peace between Jews and Christians."[104] The same at other times in other places.

And, yes, since *Nostra Aetate* the Vatican and its various commissions have taken steps toward improving relations with the Jews. Yes, changes have been made in textbooks, in the liturgy, in the teaching and preaching within the Church in "the correct way to present Judaism." Yes, the many statements of repentance and the expressions of sorrow and regret over the Holocaust and the frequent denunciations of anti-Semitism have created a climate conducive to dialogue and reconciliation between Catholic and Jew. Yes, John Paul's Day of Pardon Mass, his speech in the Hall of Remembrance at Yad Vashem, his appearance at the Western Wall: all were unique and memorable events.

But these steps have also been met with a full measure of sharp skepticism. So much so that an exasperated Cardinal Cassidy charged that the Jewish responses are "often so negative that some now hesitate to do anything at all for fear of making the situation worse."[105] In agreement, some in the Jewish community have deplored the failure of the Jewish community leadership to credit Catholics with the changes

313

they have made in their thinking and teaching about Judaism. They have accused Jews of "sleeping through a revolution."[106] Why, they complain, can't Jews take "Yes" for an answer? Weren't all the pope's various apologies enough?

But "apology" is precisely the crucial word. John Paul made apologies that sounded so much like apologies and looked so much like apologies that some accepted them *as* apologies. But they weren't apologies--not *the* apology. Only two days before the pope spoke at Yad Vashem, the columnist John Leo found himself still hoping to hear the specific apology--but he did not sound very optimistic about his chances either. "The Catholic Church," he wrote, "has been apologizing for its faults and sins for many years now, particularly for its treatment of Jews. By one count, Pope John Paul II alone has made more than a hundred confessions of Christian failure."[107]

The Church has made apologies galore--for its sinful followers but not for the Church itself. Apologies, yes. But not *the* apology. The Church understands this distinction far better than do the Jews who are willing and eager to accept at face value all the Church's overtures toward the Jews. All along the pope was aware of the intense Jewish desire for a genuine sign that the Church had a genuine understanding of the Holocaust--a desire concentrated in all that *the* apology represented. And all along his words and gestures were always calculated to stop short of any specific and unequivocal apology. The agenda of the Church has no room for the admission of error.

It could not be otherwise. By definition the Church is sinless. The fact is, the Church is not, has never been, and cannot be in the business of apologizing for itself. On its surface "We Remember: A Reflection on the Shoah" was designed to promote Catholic-Jewish relations. But its core agenda remained the defense of the Church. And its defense precluded any apology.

There has been no revolution.

Pope John Paul's Rome Synagogue speech, the canonization of Edith Stein, the Carmelite convent, the papal cross, the Waldheim scandal, the silence of Pius XII, "We Remember...," the pope's Day of Pardon remarks, his Yad Vashem statement, his Western Wall prayer: each was a test case for the Church, and each in its own right required an accurate reading of the message the pope and the Vatican were sending to the Jews. The Holocaust links them to each other. The Holocaust is their common denominator. But most important is that each served the timeless, fundamental, unalterable agenda that governs pope and Vatican: to assert the Church and to defend it--without apology.

There has been no revolution. *The* apology--and all it entailed-- would have been a revolution. Revolutions turn things upside down. The Church is not in favor of revolution.

The real sleepers are the wishful thinkers, deaf, asleep, and unable to decode the agenda of the Church. The real sleepers are the wishful believers blind and unable to take an accurate reading of the central agenda of the Church. The handwriting was on the wall of the Vatican all along: No Apology. Pope John Paul II himself had written it there.

The Balance

John Paul sounded the note of reconciliation frequently enough, especially during his visit to Israel. At Yad Vashem, echoing "We Remember...," he said, "Let us build a new future in which there will be no more anti-Jewish feeling among Christians or anti-Christian feeling among Jews."

If he did not offer the long awaited apology for the role the Church played during the Holocaust, these words called for change, for a new relationship between Catholic and Jew, between Christian and Jew. Considering the long history of the old relationship and its culmination in the Holocaust, who in his audience there or elsewhere could have quarreled with the call by pope and Vatican for "a new future?" And, yes, what Jew upon first hearing such words would not *want* to believe in them? Their very balance within the sentence persuades.

And misleads.

You have to take a careful reading of the text. The parallel structure of this key sentence emphasizes the equivalency the pope and the Vatican intended to convey. Except that there is no equivalency of meaning. The pope balanced "anti-Jewish feeling among Christians" against "anti-Christian feeling among Jews" as if they were of equal weight. It is false--and a sleight of hand--to suggest that they are.

Feelings have causes in historical facts. Did the anti-Christian feeling of the Jew cause the anti-Jewish feeling of the Christian? What damage, after all, have Jews done to Christianity that should give Christians cause to deplore Jews for their anti-Christian attitudes? If anything, the murderous hostility of Christianity toward the Jews, culminating in the Holocaust, caused the anti-Christian feelings among Jews in the first place.

The pope and the Vatican had their reasons for trying to persuade us to accept a false balance of ideas, this equivalency--that Christians and Jews are guilty in equal measure for the negative feelings they may hold toward each other. They are not good reasons. What apology could emerge from so false a concept of history?

Forty-seven Questions

The failure of "We Remember..." to offer a full apology for the role of the Church during the Holocaust ignited a controversy so huge that, more than any of the others, it threatened to engulf Catholic-Jewish relations. Its defense of Pope Pius XII only made matters worse.

Ten days after its formal publication Cardinal Edward Cassidy hastened to ward off disaster. Recalling an all but forgotten set of eleven volumes of documents dealing with the Vatican's wartime activities, he proposed that an independent team of scholars review them in order to resolve the issues that had been raised by "We Remember...."

These documents had a history of their own. In 1963 Rolf Hochhuth attacked Pius XII in his play *The Deputy*. A year later Pope Paul VI authorized their compilation in order to defend him. Between 1965 and 1981 the Vatican published the eleven volumes of *Minutes and Documents of the Holy See Relative to the Second Word War*. Pierre Blet, one of the original four Jesuit historian priests who prepared these volumes, added a twelfth, his *Pius XII and the Second World War: According to the Archives of the Vatican*. First published in French in 1997, it was a guide to the first eleven volumes and, Blet said, contained their "essence and... conclusions."

In October, 2000, after a year long study of all these works, the International Catholic-Jewish Historical Commission, a committee of six recognized historians--three Roman Catholics and three Jews-- presented their Preliminary Report.[108] Unable to resolve the issues "We Remember..." had raised, they came up, instead, with a list of forty-seven carefully phrased questions that they said needed answering before they could continue with their project. Actually, the forty-seven questions contained questions within questions.

What the historians had discovered was that the documents in the eleven volumes had been selected and edited by the Jesuit historians in ways that made them fundamentally unreliable and useless for any definitive research. Missing, they reported, were the "records of day-to-day administration of the Church and the Holy See," including such vital items as "diaries, memoranda, appointment books, minutes of meetings, draft documents and so forth that detail the process of how the Vatican arrived at the decisions it made." One volume alone cited seven hundred documents without publishing them. "It is plain," they said of the entire collection, "...that important pieces of the historical puzzle are missing ...." Their Preliminary Report stated not only that "a scrutiny of these volumes does not put to rest significant questions about the role of the Vatican during the Holocaust," but, worse still, that "the published documents themselves raise questions to which they do not provide answers."

In order to get answers to their questions--to learn how and why the Vatican had arrived at its policies and actions--the committee requested access to unpublished documents in the Vatican archives. On June 21, 2001, nine months later, Cardinal Walter Kasper (who had succeeded Cardinal Cassidy as the president of the Holy See's Commission for Religious Relations with the Jews) gave an interview in which he accused the commission of failing "to do what it was charged to do--to read the Vatican's 11 published volumes on Pius' pontificate. They must read the 11 volumes. They have never done the work they were asked to do in a proper way."[109]

That same day he sent a letter to the joint Historical Commission saying that for certain "technical reasons" the Vatican archives from 1923 onward were closed to them. At the same time, however, he insisted on a final report based on the materials available to them.

A month later the five members of the Commission (one had resigned after the completion of the Preliminary Report) replied that since they had been refused access to the archives they could not continue their work, and they suspended their project.

In August in a communique from the Commission for Religious Relations with the Jews, Cardinal Kasper said "the Holy See is ready to consent to the access of the Vatican's Secret Archive as soon as the reorganizing and cataloguing work is concluded....The Catholic Church is not afraid of the historical truth."[110] But he set no date for releasing them, not even a potential one.

The Historical Commission died a noisy, contentious death. Deciding to resign, Robert Wistrich, one of the Jewish historians, contradicted Cardinal Kasper, saying he *had* read all twelve volumes and found them "a damning indictment of insensitivity and moral failure, of indifference to the humiliations and suffering of the Jews under anti-Semitic laws and of a refusal to even consider any rupture with Nazi Germany."[111] For him "the attempt to present Pius XII as a kind of hero of the resistance" was nothing less than "a form of Catholic revisionism which...has nothing to do with historical truth, but more to do with the internal political agenda of the Church."[112] Wistrich said the failure of the Commission marked the lowest point of Catholic-Jewish relations since *Nostra Aetate*.

Upon the publication of "We Remember..." Cardinal Cassidy called it "a teaching document" for the Church. "Nothing," he said at a news conference, "is closed with this document."[113] Cardinal Cassidy had no idea he was opening a Pandora's box with his initial proposal for the Historical Commission.

Afraid of the historical truth or not, the Vatican has kept the relevant archives closed, a decision that remains a standing reminder of the limits the Church imposes on the spirit of dialogue and conciliation that the Vatican, Pope John Paul II, and Jewish sources as well, have so often and so highly touted.

Closed archives do not constitute closure. Open ones don't either, for that matter.

Calculations

On June 7, 1979, Pope John Paul II stood before the memorial inscribed in Hebrew at Auschwitz. It was "not permissible," he said, "for anyone to pass by this inscription with indifference." In November, 1986, at a meeting with representatives of the Jewish community in Sydney, Australia, he called the twentieth century "the century of the Shoah." In January, 1993, he told a group of Anti-Defamation League representatives that "the Holocaust was the greatest trauma, the greatest tragedy of our century."[114]

Over time these words and others like them sent Jews a message: not only that the Church recognized that the Holocaust had opened an abyss between itself and the Jewish community but that it understood and cared about the great tragedy that the Jews had suffered. And when under Pope John Paul II it began to seek dialogue and reconciliation with the Jews, a route first proposed by *Nostra Aetae*, it seemed that the Church intended to come to terms with the Holocaust.

Initially, Jewish leadership took heart from John Paul's overtures and efforts in this direction. In fact, from the beginning of his papacy he captured the imagination of many in the Jewish community not only by his words but by the sheer drama and symbolism of his efforts. He was, after all, the first pope to visit Auschwitz--the first pope to pay his respects before its memorial to the six million. Many Jews sensed in him the dawn of a new era in Catholic-Jewish relations.

Had they been more wary, they might have had second thoughts. They might have recalled that on March 12, 1979, in Rome, only three months before his June visit to Auschwitz, he had addressed a group of representatives of Jewish organizations and said, "I am...happy to evoke in your presence today the dedicated and effective work of my predecessor Pius XII on behalf of the Jewish people."[115]

Was the pope unaware of his audience's feelings toward Pius XII and his record before, during, and after the Holocaust? Or was he indifferent to their feelings? Or unable to imagine them? Or did he mean to say exactly what he wanted to say, no matter what his listeners felt?

Jews have a stake in understanding their "modern" relationship to the Church, particularly since 1965. To do that they have to take an accurate reading of the record since then. For their own sake they have to decode the real message inside the tests, the texts, the gestures that have marked the Church's efforts toward dialogue and reconciliation.

Assuming the pope really meant that it was not permissible for anyone "to pass by" the memorial to the six million "with indifference," what message was he conveying in 1979 and again on the fiftieth anniversary of the end of the Second World War,[116] when he recalled remarking at Birkenau, "I kneel at this Golgotha of the modern world." Golgotha is not a common word in the Jewish vocabulary or in Jewish memory. Its meaning for a Jew is not the same as for a Christian. Was the pope unaware that by using the term he was effectively removing the Holocaust from the realm of Jewish history and experience and defining--even re-defining--"the greatest tragedy" of the twentieth century in strictly Christian terms?

Was the Church unaware that Jews would interpret the establishment of the Carmelite convent at Auschwitz and "the War of the Crosses" that followed as further evidence of the Christian effort to appropriate the Holocaust? Did the pope and the Vatican care?

What message was Pope John Paul II sending by turning a converted Jew into a Catholic martyr and saint? By proposing that each year Catholics should memorialize the death of six million Jews by observing the date of a converted Jew's death? Was he unaware that by stressing her conversion to the Cross he was asserting that the age-old mission of the Church to the Jews was alive and well? Did he care that Jews saw his elevation of Stein to sainthood as only one more example of traditional Christian triumphalism? Was he unaware of the juxtaposition between the publication of "We Remember... " and his canonization of Stein only seven months later?

Did the pope care about Jewish reaction to his beatification of Alojzjie Stepanic, eight days before the canonization of Stein? Was he disturbed by what many Jews thought of this Croatian cardinal who, as the Archbishop of Zagreb and the Primate of Croatia, had supported the Catholic, pro-Nazi Ustache regime of Ante Pavelic, a war criminal responsible for the slaughter of at least 350,000 Serbs and 30,000 Jews? Or did he and the Vatican have their own calculations?

If Pope John Paul II truly understood the Holocaust as "the greatest trauma" of the twentieth century, an event not to be treated with indifference, how could he receive a Kurt Waldheim at the Vatican--a Nazi decorated by Ante Pavelic? How could he promise Jews a "We Remember..." to make amends for granting this first audience, then exactly a year later meet with Waldheim again? How in January, 1994, only six months after the establishment of diplomatic relations with Israel could he confer a high Catholic honor--a knighthood--on Waldheim? Were John Paul and the Vatican indifferent to these contradictions? Unaware of them?

"We Remember..." is only fourteen pages long, yet it took eleven years to complete. It is difficult to believe that the Vatican's centerpiece exploration of the Holocaust was other than a calculated document. With respect to its version of history, its intended audience, its very vocabulary, even its numerous footnotes, it had to be thoroughly calculated, as much for what it omits as for what it includes. In either case could the Vatican and Pope John Paul II have been unaware of the questions it would raise in the Jewish community? Or been indifferent to them?

If at first the Vatican was unaware or indifferent, it was neither deaf nor blind to what the outcry in the Jewish community might portend. It knew what it had to do: it had to cut its potential losses. It made a calculated decision. It refused to open its archives. It would not answer the persistent questions that "We Remember..." raised, at least not for the time being. The cost in continued controversy and ever widening suspicions of cover-up was more acceptable than the damage that could result from opening the archives.

When dialogue and reconciliation come face to face with the defense and welfare of the Church there is no question where the

Church stands. At first its words or actions may be difficult to read--apparent indifference, for example, turns out to be a calculated indifference. But once they are decoded they reveal the calculations that govern the priorities of the Church. In every test case the choice is the same. The Vatican's archive test case is the most explosive and most revealing of all because it touches each of the others and illuminates their place on the Church's governing agenda for the Jews.

For all the talk of dialogue and reconciliation--so appealing to susceptible Jews and Catholics alike--the Church's agenda after 1965 was in essence no different from what it had always been.

Conscience

On January 26, 1987, an outraged American Jewish Congress sent Pope John Paul II an immediate Open Letter via *The New York Times* to protest his first audience with Kurt Waldheim. "It is the fact," the letter said, "that you and the Vatican see Kurt Waldheim as just another head of state. Sadly this indicates to us that despite the Church's pronouncement on this subject, the significance of the Holocaust and the uniqueness of the evil it represents is not really part of the consciousness of the Church."

The American Jewish Congress statement regarding the Waldheim affair could just as well have applied to all the cases involving the Holocaust. Each tested the consciousness of the Church--and found it wanting. Without consciousness there is no possibility for conscience. The AJC statement would have been more accurate if it had said that the significance of the Holocaust and its unique evil played no role in the conscience of the Church.

Silence

Where does the Church stand--where does Christianity stand--on the question of Jewish survival? Where do they stand on Israel's survival? These are bottom-line questions governing Catholic-Jewish relations and Christian-Jewish relations generally.

Silent against anti-Semitism during the Holocaust, the Church and Christianity in general remained silent afterward as well. The Catholic Church did not really speak up until its 1965 declaration of *Nostra Aetate*. And since *Nostra Aetate*--despite the Church's follow-up efforts, which seemed to hold some promise--it has not spoken out with power, loud and clear for all the world to hear, at least for all Catholics to hear and take action. It has done nothing to protest and oppose the unprecedented rise and spread of anti-Semitism in Europe and elsewhere. Nor have authoritative voices of Christianity been especially successful in reaching the pews with their opposition to anti-Semitism. A half century after the Second World War Chaim Herzog, the sixth president of the State of Israel, made a grim discovery. "Amid a resurgence of anti-Semitism," he wrote, "especially in post-Communist Eastern Europe, extreme manifestations of this scourge have spread in areas where there are few Jews. I have discussed this strange phenomenon with many East European leaders and all have blamed the influence of the Catholic Church."[117]

Catholic and Jewish circles widely credit the Vatican and Pope John Paul II for the recognition of the State of Israel in January, 1994. What has been largely ignored since then is that the Vatican was the last major state to recognize Israel, that it took 46 years to do so, and that the Vatican and John Paul conferred public recognition upon Yasser Arafat and offered him support long before they formally recognized Israel.

Church policy toward the State of Israel has a long history. Its roots stretch back to the beginning of Christianity and reach to yesterday. Hark back a century--to 1904--and you can hear Pope Pius X telling Theodor Herzl point blank: "The Jews have not recognized our Lord, therefore we cannot recognize the Jewish people."[118] For him Jewish survival in history was still a standing, living contradiction to the claims of Christianity. "The Jewish faith was the foundation of our own," he conceded, "but it has been superseded by the teachings of Christ, and we cannot admit that it still enjoys validity."[119]   John Paul II could well have spoken these words himself.   "I know, it is disagreeable to see the Turks in possession of our Holy Places.   We simply have to put up with it," Pius X told Herzl.   "But to sanction the Jewish wish to occupy these sites, that we cannot do."[120]   Christian anti-Judaism and anti-Semitism--they go inseparably hand in hand-- have not been a matter of hating Jews "just because they are Jews" but because Jews are what they have always been: a bone in the throat of Christianity.

The Holocaust did not change the Church's mind.   It remained true to its historical anti-Jewish agenda.   From Pius X, through Pius XII and Paul VI, down to John Paul II the goal remained to deny recognition to the State of Israel, under John Paul II as under his twentieth century predecessors.

In 1948 the Christian world stood silent when five Arab armies attacked Israel.   No matter that the ashes of the Holocaust still smoldered, the Christian world stood by as the Jewish state fought for its very life.   It stood silent as the Jews seemed on the verge of a Holocaust after the Holocaust.   Pius XII was as silent in 1948 as he had been during the Holocaust.

In June, 1967--two years after *Nostra Aetate* had presumably reversed two millennia of anti-Semitism and anti-Jewishness--the Church and Christianity again remained silent in the face of war between Israel and Egypt, Syria, and Jordan.   Frank E. Talmage of the Department of Near Eastern Studies, University of Toronto, stated that the crisis was marked by "the failure of most of official North American Christianity to respond to it....it appeared as if the churches had reacted to the possibility of a second Holocaust as if the first had never happened."[121]

The same silence met the crisis before the 1973 Yom Kippur War, when Holocaust again threatened Israel.   And twenty years later, after having witnessed the unrelenting hostility of the Arab states surrounding Israel, Eliezer Berkovits and his son Dov wrote, "The international situation is not much different today from what it was during the Holocaust. Indeed, is the Holocaust yet over? Not much is needed for the Arab nations to reach a new resolve to drive the Jewish state into the sea."[122]

The Church has often enough declared its spiritual solidarity with the Jews. But in the world of practical politics it has remained silent in the face of the Arab denial of Israel's right to exist, silent in the face of Arab commitment to the destruction of the state, silent, once again, in the face of the possibility of Holocaust. It did not respond to Yasser Arafat's threats against Israel, nor has it responded to the deadly antagonism expressed by most Arab states toward Israel. Meanwhile, joining forces with those in opposition to Israel, the European Christian political community has turned actively hostile toward Israel.

And the churches? They have remained deadly silent, once again as though the Holocaust had never taken place. How, asked Gerhard Riegner--who first transmitted news of the Holocaust to the Western allies-- "How can one affirm constantly in the theological statements that the destiny of the people of Israel is of deep concern to Christians, and then forget this when it comes to delicate current political problems?"[123] Schneir Levin was more blunt. He said outright that if its words were to have any meaning, Christianity would have to take a stand, that "the Roman Catholic, Anglican, Lutheran, Baptist, and other churches" would have to take "an active pro-Israel stance in relation to the ever present Arab threat to Israel's existence." What was necessary, he said, was "a change of heart," the very opposite of what they had shown "in 1948, in 1967, in 1973, and to this very day."[124]

On March 3, 1943--Anne O'Hare McCormick, the foreign affairs columnist for *The New York Times*, wrote that the Madison Square Garden rally for the rescue of Jews had exposed "the shame of the world." "There is not the slightest question," she said, "that the persecution of the Jews has reached its awful climax in a campaign to wipe them out of Europe. If the Christian community does not support to the utmost the belated proposal to rescue the Jews remaining in Europe from the fate prepared for them, we have accepted the Hitlerian thesis, and forever compromised the principles for which we are pouring out blood and wealth."[125]

In 1948 Albert Camus--journalist, playwright, novelist, hero of the French Resistance, future recipient of the Nobel Prize for Literature-- was already the voice and conscience of his generation. That year he told the Dominicans at the Monastery of Latour-Maubourg that Pius XII and Christianity had failed. "During those frightful years of the war," he said, "I waited for a great voice to speak up in Rome....It seems that that voice did speak up. But I assure you that millions of men like me did not hear it and that at that time believers and unbelievers alike shared a solitude that continued to spread as the days went by and the executioners multiplied." And he added, "What the world expects of Christians is that Christians should speak out, loud and clear, and that they should voice their condemnation in such a way that never a doubt, never the slightest doubt, should rise in the heart of the simplest man. That they should get away from abstraction and confront the blood-stained face history has taken on today."[126]

What Anne O'Hare McCormick called the shame of the world in 1943 was its silence. Camus heard that silence too. Into the first years of the twenty-first century--in the light of the Holocaust--that shame is now more shameful than ever.

Writing in the *Forward* A. James Rudin, interreligious adviser for the American Jewish Committee, could still see *Nostra Aetate* as beginning "the initial, hopefully irreversible steps toward a remission of the anti-Semitic cancer that has plagued it for so long," but he had to admit, "Achieving a full cure remains for the future."[127] Anti-Semitism has, in fact, resurfaced and metastasized more virulently than ever before--from the Christian world into the Islamic world, from Old Europe to the Middle East and beyond. Alert to the usefulness of the

327

terminology--and the propaganda--that has worked for Christianity for a thousand years and more, the Islamic world has appropriated both with a vengeance. And the Church and the Christian world have met this "development" with silence--a silence that bespeaks appeasement, acquiescence, and realpolitik.

Pope John Paul II visited Damascus May 8, 2001, little more than a year after his visit to Israel. In his speech welcoming the pope to Syria President Bashar al-Assad said, "They [Israelis and Jews] try to kill all the principles of divine faiths with the same mentality of betraying Jesus Christ and torturing Him, and in the same way that they tried to commit treachery against Prophet Muhammad...."[128] Pope John Paul II listened to words lifted straight from the heart of Christianity. And he stood there--just stood there--heard them and remained silent. True, he could not well repudiate the words and story at the base of Christianity. Nevertheless, he was the same pope who in the Rome Synagogue in 1986 had emphasized, "Yes, once again, through myself, the church, in the words of the well-known declaration *Nostra Aetate*, 'deplores the hatred, persecutions, and displays of anti-Semitism directed against the Jews at any time and by anyone.' I repeat, 'By anyone.'"

Sixty years after the Holocaust John Paul II chose the same silence as Pius XII--the silence that had moved Camus to ask, "Who are we, anyway that we dare criticize the highest spiritual authority of the Century? Nothing, in fact, but the simple defenders of the spirit, who yet have a right to expect the most from those whose mission it is to represent the spirit."[129]

Not for nothing did Elie Wiesel call his first book *And the World was Silent.*

Ivan

The two of them were old friends, an odd pair, Christian and Jew, but friends for years. The story, at least as I remember hearing it, takes place in Russia during the time of the Tsar.

One day the Christian and his Jewish friend were having a friendly glass together at a roadside tavern. And, out of the blue, perhaps he was a little tipsy, the Jew came right out with it. The problem must have been on his mind for some time. "Ivan," he said, "do you love me?"

"What a question! Of course I love you."

A few minutes later the Jew asked again, "Ivan, do you love me?"

"I love you!" Ivan protested "I love you!"

A little later--for the third time--the Jew asked, "Ivan, do you love me?"

In exasperation Ivan protested, "Why do you ask me? How many times must I tell you? I love you, I love you. You are like an older brother to me!"

"Then why," asked the Jew, "--why don't you know what hurts me?"

ABRASHA'S STORIES

The Book

It came from Australia, unannounced, a slender volume sent to me by my cousin Fanya. The book was by Dr. Abraham Wajnryb. I had no idea who he was or what he would come to mean to me. I did discover soon enough that his story was a far from "ordinary" tale of the Holocaust. Both moving and difficult, his book revealed a fine intelligence. A total honesty stood behind its every word. I reviewed the book for a Jewish monthly in October, 1990:

> Six million stories have disappeared into the silence and darkness of the Holocaust. In a sense, each survivor who tells his story speaks not only for himself but for those whose stories must remain forever untold. It is, therefore a terrifying responsibility for a survivor to speak. It is perhaps an even more terrifying responsibility for him not to speak. To have survived and to remain silent is, in a way, to have joined those forever silenced and, at the same time, to have failed them, for if the victims of the Holocaust wished for anything, it was for their story to be told.
>
> Thus every survivor's story, well told or not, possesses intrinsic value, not only as testimony but as a precious document in the history of the Jewish people. Dr. Abraham Wajnryb's *They Marched Us Three Nights* is clearly the fulfillment of an obligation profoundly felt. It sheds light upon a time and experiences that continue to defy our understanding even as they continue to demand it.
>
> *They Marched Us Three Nights* is the only account, thus far, of the Dautmergen labor camp outside Schomberg in the Natzweiler region of southwest Germany. Of the 1,000 Jews transported there with Wajnryb from Stutthof in the autumn of 1944, fewer than 100 lived to see the last day of the camp in April, 1945. "Not one of the missing 900 was killed. They just died," the author comments matter-of-factly. He does not indicate how many of the 100 survived the "march into the unknown."
>
> Forty years after the events, Wajnryb recalls vividly the last day at the camp, the three "very long nights" of walking on "the road to death," and the days of freedom

that followed. But this book is far more than a record of his survival of the march.

Resorting to flashbacks, Wajnryb returns to the "vivid memories, painful feelings and strong fears" of the preceding four years of his captivity--to his daily confrontations with death in the Vilna ghetto and in the Kivioli (Estonia), Stutthof, and Dautmergen labor camps. While Wajnryb's rejection of a strictly chronological narrative form does not always make for easy reading, the flashbacks are essential to his exploration of the "soul searching" questions raised by those memories, feelings, and fears.

In 1938, one year before the Germans invaded Poland, Wajnryb, a 1936 graduate of the University of Warsaw, was one of the five young doctors to answer the call for volunteers to aid the thousands of Jews expelled by the Germans to Zbonszyn, a Polish town in the no-man's-land between Germany and Poland.

Trapped in the Vilna ghetto from its formation in 1941 to its liquidation in 1943, he served as the head of the division of infectious diseases in the ghetto hospital. Thus Wajnryb writes of his personal experiences in the Vilna ghetto and the labor camps not only from a personal point of view but from the special perspective of his profession.

Always acutely aware of the dangerous tricks time plays upon memory, Wajnryb recalls numerous episodes printed indelibly on his mind. But he is more concerned with the psychology of hunger, inertia, and fear underlying these events and unflinchingly analyzes their devastating influence on his own behavior and that of his comrades.

Though the prisoners at Dautmergen saw planes flying overhead, heard far-off bombardments, and knew that somewhere battles were being won and lost, Wajnryb writes, "Our war had another enemy, another front and another kind of fighting. The war that took place inside us--was against hunger."

He remembers a hunger that literally "took control of our lives," a hunger that like a disease, "penetrated all the cells of the brain and the body and seized control of our thoughts, words and actions so as to exclude all else." "The power of hunger," he writes, "is great indeed, perhaps the greatest and most corrupting of all."

Wajnryb finds the power of inertia at least as corrupting as the power of hunger and just as deadly. With scientific objectivity, he describes the psychology behind his own repeated failures to act, whether in the Vilna ghetto or on the death march.

Twice rejecting opportunities to escape the ghetto with his wife, Wajnryb admits that he lacked the will, the energy, and the courage to take charge of his destiny. "If my wife had not survived," he writes with chilling honesty, "her blood would have been on my hands." Similarly, he has only admiration for "Di Hunderte," the Jews of the Vilna underworld, who acted instinctively and were among the first to escape from the march and hide in the forest, while he and his comrades were almost completely paralyzed by their indecisiveness.

As if hunger and inertia were not enemies enough, Wajnryb also stresses the power of fear. "Under normal conditions," he acknowledges, fear enables "a person in danger to defend himself. But uninterrupted fear, days and years, undermines and destroys one's stamina, leaving him helpless and humiliated." It is fear, too, that powers the inertia "which took possession of us," so much so that "the greater the possibility of freedom seemed to be, the more intense was our fear."

On the third night of the march the moment of escape finally arrives. While still "oscillating between hope and despair," Wajnryb and his comrades spontaneously break their inertia and dash for the forest. "Suddenly all I knew was that I was running away. We all ran. What happened to me--the fog, the confusion and the escape--happened to the others as well. We all ran at once." The guards do not shoot, nor do they unleash the dogs. And the escape succeeds.

Wajnryb charts the psychology of freedom as accurately as he charts the psychology of captivity. The blue-striped ghosts emerge from the forest only when they hear a French motorcycle soldier announce their liberation with his shouts of "Liberte, egalite, fraternite." "We sat down on the edge of the road," Wajnryb writes, "and didn't know whether we were feeling the joy of freedom or a sadness for those who had been left behind, near the camp and the chimney, all those who would never hear the noise of the French motorcycle."

Freedom for Wajnryb is the French soldier's promise that "you will be able to start life again." Freedom for him is the overwhelming realization that "whatever we would do, it would be done of our own free will."

Freedom for Wajnryb also has meant the need through this book "to complete the mission of a survivor" to tell the story and "let the world know." *They Marched Us Three Nights* goes beyond the facts and evidence that constitute the testimony in the memoirs of many victims of the Holocaust. The book is the work of a man conscious of the ambiguities of life and concerned with the havoc wrought by doubt, confusion, fear, and tension upon lives that were caught in the grip of merciless Nazi power.

When the supplies of medicines ran low in the ghetto, Wajnryb found himself forced to confront the "complex moral dilemmas" involved in determining "who has the authority to decide who is to live and who is to die." But neither in these soul searching confrontations nor in the story of his escape does Wajnryb make any pretensions to heroism.

The escape, he writes, covered "only three days during an endless period of four very long and very cruel years of slavery. In retrospect I am often struck by the difference between the pomposity and unreality of the 'heroic' concept of escape when compared with those long years of utter deprivation. The preservation of the sense of dignity and human relations during those years required far more heroism."

Forty years after the events described in *They Marched Us Three Nights* Abrasha Wajnryb asks himself one final soul searching question: "Did I stand the test of this hard time?" He leaves the question unanswered.

His story speaks for itself.

I have spent my life with books. Books have saved my life. They have lost it too. But I am glad I first met Abrasha the way I did--in a book.

Without him there would have been no story.

The Reunion

I met Abrasha in person on January 2, 1991. These stories are based on notes I kept during the next two whirlwind weeks with him and Fanny.

*** *

We are at the bottom of the world, fourteen hours and seven thousand non-stop miles from Los Angeles. Within minutes we passed through customs and into the hands of Abrasha and Fanya. Since then life with Abrasha has been non-stop talk: medicine, psychiatry, Sydney, Vilna, Wilno, jargon, jokes, the Jewish connection.

In their seventh floor apartment on Bondi Street Fanya tries to tell me the "whole" story of her and Abrasha. They first met in spring, 1944, in the lager Kivioli in "Estland"--that is, in Estonia. The Germans sent Abrasha there after the liquidation of the Vilna Ghetto in September, 1943, only hours after they sent his wife Lusia, also a doctor, on a death transport to Majdanek. He did not know of her survival until after the war. Likewise, the Germans sent Fanya to Kivioli from the Kovno Ghetto, nor did she know what had happened to her husband Osya.

Abrasha worked in the hospital in the Kivioli camp but not as a doctor. He swept floors and performed other menial tasks. Fanya worked in a warehouse sorting clothes. The prisoners in the clothing warehouse sometimes received an extra piece of bread or a bit of meat, and she would bring what little extra she could to the hospital. There she met Abrasha, though he has no recollection of how they first met.

In July, 1944, only two or three months after their meeting, the Germans evacuated the camp and sent Abrasha, Fanya, and many other Lithuanian Jews to Stutthof. There they lost track of each other.

They did not see each other again for forty-five years.

A Stone

If humor is to be found in a situation, Abrasha will find it. If there is none, he is quick to create it. When an especially difficult situation arises--medical, social, or otherwise--Abrasha will face the challenge first off with his sense of humor. When he says, with a smile, "It is a problem and a half," you know that, never mind, he'll find a solution.

We were sitting at the kitchen table when the telephone rang. Abrasha dashed into the next room. A moment later I could hear him giving medical advice. From the sound of his voice he had to be speaking to a friend. The minutes dragged on. At last he returned.

"It was The Dentist, a friend of mine. He is seventy-three. Many years ago I helped him pass the medicine section of his dentistry exams. He has an eye problem. He went to see a specialist, but after a few visits, for some reason he stopped going to him. Now he needs to see the specialist again for an opinion, but he is too embarrassed to call for an appointment. It is a delicate situation, but I made the arrangement for him.

"He has no friends. He is a hypochondriac. You can see, with him a five minute phone call turns into a half hour discussion. He has to discuss his case from every possible angle. It is a pity, but for him talk is therapy. He has to rid himself of what is on his heart. And I have to listen. He is a problem and a half. We have an old Yiddish saying that when a man rids himself of what weighs on his heart, it is as though a stone falls from his heart," and he paused a moment, then added "*uhn es fahlt oyf yenems korn.*" And it falls on someone else's corn, says Abrasha, and laughs at himself, and we laugh with him because we know the pain he feels in his toe.

For Abrasha the only difference between a problem and a problem and a half is that the problem and a half takes a little longer to solve.

The Doctor

As I listen to Abrasha it is clear that his underlying philosophical approach to his profession is totally unlike what we hear from our doctor friends in America. "The difference," Abrasha explains, "is that in the U.S. the technical approach--tests--determines the diagnosis, while in the European style the technical matters are used to accept or reject the diagnosis."

Abrasha would be a rarity in America. He takes time to *talk* with his patient. Much like the psychologist, he probes for the real reason the patient has come to see him. Now that he is semi-retired, he has more time to talk to his patients, and they love him for the time he spends with them.

Abrasha's humor is infectious. When Perle raises the matter of migraine, for example, he explains, "Migraine is a double headache-- one for the patient, one for the doctor."

To explain an illness or a disease, he traces the medical term for it back to its Greek or Latin roots. He is always explaining, always turning to history, always joking. He also has a healthy skepticism toward his profession and its pretentions.

He recalls with relish the first words with which his professor of medicine at Warsaw University addressed his class: "Gentlemen, you are going to learn about so many problems of the diseases of life that

you will discover it would be much healthier not to have been born."
Then, with even greater relish, he reminds himself of the twist that
Sholom Aleichem's Yiddish wit gave to the same problem: *"ahz vi lahng
der toyt existirt iz keyner nit zikher mit dem lebn"*--that as long as death exists
no one is sure of his life.

Abrasha has apparently always been intent on finding out the *why*
of things. Ever since his childhood his family and others would say of
him, *"Er vil nor vissen fuhn vahnen di fis kumen."* That is, Abrasha was so
curious about things that he always wanted to know even where the
feet came from.

Abrasha's walk is firm, his voice confident. His air of self
assurance simply has to communicate itself to his patients, whether in
his office--that is, his "surgery"--or when he walks into a hospital
room. He understands his patients--and his friends--the way
Chekhov, also a doctor, understood his characters: with generosity
and life-saving humor.

Rounds

"On one of my visits to Israel Hilel took me along while he was
making rounds in his hospital." Abrasha was talking about his dear
friend Dr. Hilel Fryd, who had been with him at the Dautmergen
lager. Abrasha told the story of their being on the death march
together and of their escape from it in *They Marched Us Three Nights*.

"A stream of students followed us as we went from bed to bed.
Suddenly a woman patient jumped out of her bed. She ran over to
me, threw her arms around me, and she began to cry. I tried to calm
her. Then the words poured out of her. She began to thank me for
saving her life! It was in the hospital in the Vilna Ghetto--just before a
selektzieh was to take place. She told me how I threw a sheet over her,
how the German doctor making the *selektzieh* had stopped at her bed,

and how she had heard me tell him, 'This one doesn't need to be taken--she's already dead.'"

Abrasha paused. "But I didn't remember her." He said it as though even now he was trying to recall the original episode.

The problems of memory--memories of the Holocaust--trouble him deeply. He fears the tricks that memory can play. "Does one remember the event itself?" he asks himself. "Or does one remember the story that someone tells about an event--and then absorb it into his own reality and transform it into his own experience?" Abrasha is tormented by the possibility that he might unwittingly appropriate another's experience. He is scrupulously honest. And he says, "Many things happened there. One can't remember everything." That is why in his book he writes only of what he definitely remembered.

On a note of wonderment, he says, "I don't even remember how I first met Fanya."

"Praised be Jesus Christ"

"It was the only time I came through without *nissim*, without miracles." This is how Abrasha explains the only initiative he says he ever took to save his life during the Holocaust. Otherwise he declares himself to have been a victim of his own natural inertia, which he considers to be the unfortunate consequence of intellectualism.

It happened in September, 1939, just after the Polish defeat at the beginning of the war. Abrasha was an officer in the Medical Corps. He retreated with the rest of his unit to the town of Brody. The Red Army turned him back from the Rumanian border. But the Russians did give him permission to return to Vilna and allowed him and several of his fellow soldiers to board a train for Vilna. Well on their way, he and his companions noticed first one soldier, then another and another leave the compartment--and fail to return. They simply vanished from the train. Sensing something was wrong, Abrasha's companions chose him to make his way to the engineer to find out what was going on.

Abrasha reached the engineer and began with the customary "Praised be Jesus Christ." The engineer responded with "Forever and ever." And both said, "Amen." Because the Red Army men were within earshot the engineer could not talk freely. Nevertheless, he managed to tell Abrasha that the train was no longer in Poland but on Russian territory, heading toward Minsk, not toward Vilna. But what the train's final destination was he did not know--or could not say.

Then, perhaps taking pity on Abrasha, the engineer said, "You do not look like one of those who can jump off a train. You will kill yourself. Listen to me. Sit on the lowest step and let yourself fall off. Do not jump. Just before the tunnel comes I'll give three blasts of my whistle. Then go!" He did give three blasts, and Abrasha and four others fell away. They split up, then turned back in the direction from which the train had come.

Later, Abrasha learned that the train was bound for Kozelsk, a concentration camp for officers, not for ordinary POWs. The Polish officers who remained aboard the train eventually met their fate in the forest of Katyn, executed by the NKVD.

"Yes, I saved my own life," Abrasha said. "But it was not a heroic exploit."

The Execution

After escaping from the train that was carrying him to death at Katyn, where the Russians executed thousands of Polish officers, Abrasha walked two days and three nights toward Vilna. He managed to catch a train headed for Lida, where its passengers were told they would have a one hour delay before moving on to Vilna. While the train remained at the station, three or four seventeen-year-old Soviet "Revolutionary soldiers"--marked only by their armbands, their youth, and their rifles--picked out a dozen Polish civilians from among the waiting passengers. They also chose Abrasha.

The other passengers and other onlookers watched the entire frightening episode. "A squad of uniformed Russian soldiers came up to us," Abrasha said. "The Revolutionary soldiers put me and the others up against a wall. Then they blindfolded us. I heard the bolts click. I could feel the firing squad aiming its rifles. Then, suddenly, I heard the sound of the train pulling away! The show was over! The Revolutionary soldiers released all of us. They were Russian Jews. The Soviets chose them because they didn't trust the Poles."

The sham execution achieved exactly what the Soviets intended to achieve. "They wanted to create terror in the population. When I returned to Vilna, Professor Czarnocki told me how he had actually seen an execution at the train station at Lida! He had witnessed it with his very own eyes! I had to explain how I had been among those who were *not* executed because the execution had *not* taken place. Czarnocki just stared at me. Then he crossed himself in complete disbelief."

Lusia

When the Germans made the final selections at the liquidation of the Vilna Ghetto in September, 1943, they sent Abrasha to the Kivioli concentration camp in Estonia. They sent his wife Lusia on a death transport bound for Majdanek.

"I did not know what happened to her until after the war. She and three other young women saw a patch on the floor of their cattle car. They managed to pry it open and worked their way through. Two jumped and were killed instantly. But she and Clara Kowarska, a *shvester*, a nurse in Warsaw, survived. Clara was so beautiful that there was not a doctor who was not in love with her. They remembered the story of how I managed to escape from the train bound for Katyn, and they survived the fall from the train."

Lusia followed the train tracks in the opposite direction but far enough away from them so as not to be visible from any trains that might pass by. She finally came to a peasant farmhouse, knocked on the door, and called out the traditional greeting, "Praised be Jesus Christ." She crossed herself as the door opened and the traditional answer came back, "Forever and ever," and both said, "Amen."

Friendship established, to account for any possible slip-ups in her language she told them that she was a nurse who had been forced to work with the Germans. She ate with them. Then they told her to be careful on her way, just as they were careful, too, of escaped Jews. For they had heard that Jews frequently escaped from the trains. Why, only this very morning the bodies of two Jewish girls had been found near the railroad tracks.... Moreover, it might be a good thing to go to Bialystok. Why? Because the ghetto there had been liquidated, and "many cheap things" were now available to buy there.

Di Hunderte

Vilna, once known as the cradle of Jewish civilization in Europe, and still remembered as the Jerusalem of Europe, was also the home of *Di Hunderte*--"The Hundred"--a legendary gang of a hundred or more of the toughest Jewish hoodlums of the Vilna underworld. In *They Marched Us Three Nights* Abrasha remembers how they were the first to escape the march--on the very first of the three nights. Later, when he met some of them, he learned each already had his own apartment in the French occupied zone in Germany and was working with the Maquis.

Abrasha had more than a little admiration for them. "Only about fifteen in the barrack in Kivioli belonged to *Di Hunderte*. Sandkeh and his brother Shimkeh were among them. Shimkeh was the clever one. Today Shimkeh is in America. Sandkeh was the stronger one. He died of typhus. The Nazis singled out Sandkeh. They placed a fifty pound sack on his shoulders to torment him. It meant nothing to him. He stood with one arm akimbo. Then they put another sack of fifty pounds on him. The same. They added three more sacks. Sandkeh remained standing. When he walked off, even the SS admired him.

"*Di Hunderte* outsmarted the SS when they came to 'collect' the watches, rings, and other valuables from the barrack. The SS never got anything from them. They protected the doctors. At every bread distribution they took each doctor along to get him an extra loaf. They stole one loaf out of every ten. They were really masters. I don't know how they did it. But this was their way of life in Vilna. The camps were only one more obstacle for them to overcome in a life filled with obstacles.

"In 1936-37 the ONR, the *Obus Narodowy Radycalny*--the National Radical Camp--was a fierce anti-Semitic student organization that intimidated the Jewish students. But in Vilna the Jews fought back. *Di Hunderte* fought at their side. And the ONR couldn't do what it usually did.

"There was one called *Der Blinder Idiot*, the Blind Idiot. He was willing to do anything to become one of *Di Hunderte*. So they finally sent him out to prove himself--or maybe he did it on his own: he went to the Post Office and stole some parcels. He got caught and received five years. On getting out, however, *Di Hunderte* accepted him.

"Then there was *Leybkeh der Poyer*, Leybkeh the Peasant. He was the only one sent out to do *nahseh arbet*, 'wet work.' Murder, with a knife.

"*Di Hunderte* were *zjulikehs*, hooligans. But, all the same, they came to Velfkeh's, the most famous Jewish restaurant in all of Vilna. It was an extraordinary place. No comparison. But they went there just like the rich and famous."

While Abrasha admired *Di Hunderte* in many respects, he did not forget that there was a darker side to them. "They took money from some of the SS after the war to testify in their favor."

Runde

Unterscharfuhrer Runde was in charge of the hospital at the Kivioli camp. Abrasha hasn't forgotten him.

"Only Dr. Wolkowyski was allowed to practice as a doctor. Runde liked Dr. Wolkowyski. The rest of us who were doctors were delegated to do all the menial tasks around the lab.

"One day there was a selection. Twenty were selected, and Dr. Wolkowyski was one of them. They were taken out. We heard the shots. When Runde came back into the hospital he saw the anger and bitterness in our little group. He turned to face us. As if he could read our thoughts, he said, 'Yes, I killed him. And if I get an order to kill my daughter, I'll do it too!'

"After the war I received a letter from Germany requesting me to give testimony against Runde. But first they asked me to draw a picture of the camp--I suppose to prove I would be a trustworthy witness. I prepared to give testimony. Then I learned the case was moot. Runde had hanged himself.

Still thinking back into past time, Abrasha continued, "This same Runde was a guard on a transport to Dachau. My friend Tola Resnick was on it and Runde recognized him. He told Tola to jump off. Tola did--and saved himself.

"Ever since then I have wondered about Runde. By that time it was already obvious that Germany would lose the war. Did Runde save Tola to earn favor for himself after the fighting, for the time when he knew he would be put on trial? Or did he do it spontaneously, just because he recognized him? It is a question?

A Miracle Tale

Two days after their escape from the death march that began with the evacuation of the Dautmergen Camp, near Schomberg, in southwest Germany, Abrasha and his comrades--Dr. Szymon Gitelson, Dr. Mark Dworzecki, and Dr. Chaim Hilel Fryd--reached Saulgau, in the French Zone. The war would be over in a week. But for Abrasha it was already over. He collapsed on the steps of the Town Hall and was taken, more dead than alive, to the Saulgau District Hospital. He weighed 39 kilograms when he was admitted to the hospital. Through a fog he heard one of the nurses say, "This one is *kaput*." But he slowly recovered and, in time, joined his comrades on the staff of the hospital.

After leaving Saulgau Abrasha headed toward Munich with his friend Tola Resnick. They started from the French Zone, which had the fewest Jews, and set out for Munich, which at that time had about ten thousand Jewish D.P.s.

They went by way of Biberach. There two French soldiers told them about a Lithuanian woman who had a Jewish child in her charge and that both were about to be repatriated to Lithuania. She wanted the child to have a Jewish home. She did not know what to do. She told a story of having worked for a Jewish couple--and how, when the Gestapo came, and just before he was arrested, the father threw the three-year-old child into her arms.

Abrasha and Resnick went to see the woman and the child.

They went on to Munich and chanced to attend a lecture by a man urging the Jewish D.P.s to go on Aliyah Bet. Someone in the audience asked, "If you are so intent on Israel, why haven't *you* gone?" The lecturer, a vigorous, handsome man, answered, "I am looking for my child."

"We looked at each other and sensed something. Could this be the father? If so, we had a problem: how could we get him to Biberach? We knew both parts of the story--but how could we tell *him* anything? What if we were making a mistake? How terrible to raise his hopes for nothing.

"We went up to the speaker, a Lithuanian Jew. And without revealing our real reason for inviting him, we prevailed upon him to repeat his lecture in Biberach. He came. He saw the woman and the child, now about six. And it was in fact his child. The resemblance that we thought we had seen really existed. Father and son were reunited."

Abrasha paused, turned his head away for a moment. "I get emotional when I tell this story," he said.

"I Am Kusevitz!"

Abrasha remembered a story of another large meeting of D.P.s that he had attended. "Each of us had to stand up, give his name, and say a few words about himself. One man got up and gave his name. It sounded to me like 'Kusevitz.' At that very instant another man rose, and from the depths of the hall he roared back, '*I* am Kusevitz!' And suddenly two brothers were reunited."

Passing

Abrasha has a large circle of friends and acquaintances. The survivors among them, here as elsewhere, seem always "in touch" with one another, drawn together by a shared past beyond the grasp of outsiders. And it's so. They possess a knowledge no one else can have, and, often enough, they are possessed by it. Having more in common with each other than with a non-survivor, it is no accident, therefore, that one survivor marries another. It is no accident that they begin a "new" family together. About seven thousand survivors have made their home in Australia, mainly in Sydney and Melbourne. Most, I think, have come here to get as far away from Europe as they can. In a way, to know Abrasha's friends is to know something about Abrasha too.

The Kusmans, Sophia and Edik (Edward), for example. Survivors of Warsaw, both of them built new lives and a new home in Australia. They are gentle people. Edik is about eighty. He is a doctor too, recently retired. They live in a Federation home. Built around the turn of the century, the house is Victorian in feeling, comfortable if a trifle musty. Edik had his surgery in his home.

Sophia is proud of her gardening, Edik of his learning. Abrasha said, "Edik started to read when he was six--and he hasn't forgotten a thing he read since then." When Perle sat down at their piano and drew Yiddish songs from it, then Bach and Mozart too, Edik's face took on a look of pure joy. Edik lost himself in her music, as though he were listening to sounds of his Jewish youth.

Abrasha is not entirely sure how he and Sofia made it through to the other side of the Warsaw Ghetto wall before the 1943 Uprising. Either Edik got out on the tram after taking off his star or he went through the sewers. Sofia and her mother survived outside the Warsaw Ghetto. They "passed." She had papers and lived openly. She hid Edik. After the Warsaw Polish Uprising of 1944, the Germans deported both of them to Germany as forced labor. And still passing as Poles, they survived!

I look at them. Our talk is of flower gardens, Yiddish music, and life in Australia. Forty-seven years ago they were young and outwitting Germans and Poles and death.

Forty-seven years later we are sitting with them, having tea and cakes and a chocolate.

Nekomah

"Abrasha," I asked, "do you know any story of *nekomah*? Why does hardly anyone ever tell such a story? Weren't there ever any instances of it? There had to be."

He thought a moment, hesitated. "Well, I do have one such story. It was after the war. Szymon, Mark, Chaim Hilel, and I--we were all already active as doctors in the Saulgau hospital. Two or three times we discussed this very question of revenge without coming to any conclusion .

"Dr. Zoll, the head of the hospital, was a German. As a member of the defeated enemy he was very careful with us, very cautious. One day he brought in news that there was a sick German in need of the last available bed. Trying to keep on our good side, he asked us what he should do. As far as he was concerned, it was just as well to deny the German the bed. "We consulted each other. Instead of taking *nekomah* we decided to take the German into the hospital. We were doctors. Our duty--our first duty--was to heal the sick. How could we take *nekomah*? How could we take revenge?

The Surrogate

Abrasha took us to the home of Wanda Resler, on Sydney's "North Shore," where we met her and some of his other friends, survivors all.

This afternoon they told stories of their past, maybe for our benefit, strangers from America, yet privileged because we were connected to Abrasha and Fanny. They do not tell their stories in a straight line. Nor do they dwell on them. They tell them so quickly I come away thinking I have missed the essential innermost truth of the story they tell. Still, I am glad to hear their stories in their own still-living words.

Wanda is a Polish-Jewish beauty: elegant, stylish, charming, for all the world everything one might imagine a Polish countess to be. Her home reflects her personal beauty and good taste. It is as modern as anything on Chicago's North Shore, sunken living room, modern paintings, modern lamps and all. When I brought up the question of *nekomah*, she said she had just such a story.

Wanda went into hiding--was it in Warsaw?--with false papers. "With money you could buy a birth certificate," she said. "And once you had a certificate it could become the basis for other papers and documents. For money." Even with papers one faced the constant danger of betrayal by the Poles who could uncannily "smell a Jew" by his walk, by his carriage, by his way of carrying a shopping bag. "They could stop you and demand five hundred zlotys--or the Gestapo." These were the *smalczovnikes*, the blackmailers.

"One day, after the war, I passed a group of people standing around watching a Pole at work digging a hole. I asked who he was and what was going on. They told me that this man had a specialty. He used to take Jewish babies and kill them by smashing their heads against a wall.

"I was still carrying the bottle wrapped in a newspaper that I used to carry for protection. When I heard the story, I thought I would smash his head in with it. But I could not take *nekomah* in this way. It was not in me.

"Not long afterward, I met a Soviet officer, a Russian Jew, a communist. I told him the whole story. I gave him the name of the Pole. I told him where he lived. Perhaps he could do something. A week later he told me, quite simply, 'I have done what it was necessary to do.'"

Wanda's sister survived six years of hiding and suffering. She committed suicide after liberation.

The Hidden

Genya Gottlieb came late to Wanda's home. She is a woman full of fire. She told of being hidden by a Ukrainian peasant. "She was a witch. She demanded money and threatened to go to the Germans." Aware of the danger to Genya, a friend of her father--a "good" Ukrainian, she said--went to the peasant woman and warned her that soon the war would be over and that if she wanted to save herself from retribution by the Russians she had better continue to protect Genya.

"When the Germans retreated, I remained in hiding in the cellar. A week after they were gone, the good Ukrainian threw a stone into the cellar, with a note attached: it said I must remain there until it was safe to come out. I knew that there had been previous German retreats and advances in the area and that each time the Germans had managed to capture and kill a few more unwary Jews. So I remained hidden. But then the house was bombed! Luckily, I escaped injury. The Germans had retreated for good."

Genya also remembered two young Jews she had known. "One was very big, fat, and heavy. The other was normal. They also survived in hiding--under a stable floor. They had only watery potato soup to eat, just enough to keep them alive. All the waste of the animals above them fell through upon them. But they survived the ordeal of hiding. When the advancing Russians liberated them, the fat one was reduced to almost nothing in size. Yet a week later the Russians took him and the other one into the army. The fat one was killed. After all his suffering."

I had heard similar stories before. But whatever their similarities, the stories were never really alike. Genya spoke rapidly. The anguish of the fear of betrayal and the agonies of hunger, torments that had lasted weeks and months, if not years, took Genya only a few moments to tell. In one sense, those moments told everything--and in another they told almost nothing.

Homecoming

One day I asked Abrasha the inevitable question. "Abrasha," I said, "Where do you come from?"

"From Kielce."

"Kielce!"

"Yes."

"Abrasha, you have to tell me more. I want to know what happened there." I already knew, or thought I knew, what had happened there. But I wanted to hear what Abrasha had to say.

"I did not return to Kielce after the war," he said, "but I have a dear friend who did. We know each other for over seventy years. We are both from Kielce."

Abrasha has told me of the competition that has occurred among survivors almost since the very beginning of the liberation. Rivalries, he says, have developed concerning who has had the worst experiences: the concentration camp prisoner, the labor camp prisoner, the ghetto dweller, the partisan, and so on. A hierarchy, he says, has actually developed concerning the place and extent of suffering! He is appalled. I think it tells him something about human nature he would rather not know.

Abrasha took us to meet Ignatz Herman. Ignazty's experience doesn't fit into any of the "usual" categories: his story of the Holocaust took place after the Holocaust.

He is two or three years younger than Abrasha. He is quick in speech and movement as he tells the story.

————

After the war I made my way back toward Kielce to look for my family. As I approached town, walking along the river's edge, I heard the sound of trouble. I saw perhaps a dozen women--and they were wailing.

"What's wrong? What is going on?" I asked.

"Haven't you heard?"

"No."

"There--over there in that house--they found the heads of Christian children! The Jews did it! They needed blood for their matzos!"

I left them. I immediately got rid of most of my clothes. I turned up my collar to look like a peasant. I knew I must not be recognized as a Jew.

I entered the city and saw what was going on. Poles with hammers, sticks, iron chains, and metal bars were running through the streets like a wild river, looking for Jews to beat and kill. I turned off into a side street, away from the crowd, and reached the shoemaker's shop where I knew the owner, and I asked for shelter. He took me in. He quickly put me behind a machine and placed a newspaper in my hands. He told me to keep it in front of my face so that none of his customers would see me. When his daughter came into the shop and saw someone strange behind the machine, he told her that what she had noticed was none of her business--and he ordered her to leave the shop. She left.

And so it was.

For about a week. The shoemaker hid me by day and by night. After a week the Communists from Warsaw sent in the militia to "restore" the very order they had allowed to riot. Two militiamen took me into custody. They said it was for my own safety, and they brought

354

me to the police station, where they gave me shelter and food and protection. In the police station I learned that I was one of about forty to survive the pogrom.

When I came into the station, the others could not believe what they saw. "*Ignatz, dos bist du?* Ignatz, it is you?" they said. Some were badly injured, others less so. All the others had been killed. I saw them lying in the street. They had been beaten and beaten until they died.

_____

Ignatz's twists of language, the look in his eye as he spoke, the shrug of his shoulders, the sound of his voice multiplied his story beyond his words into a living footnote to the Holocaust.

The Kielce "pogrom" took place fourteen months *after* the end of the war--on July 4, 1946.

The Rainbow

An afternoon of thunder, lightning, rain. Then the sun appeared, highlighting Sydney's skyscrapers. And a rainbow. Which led Abrasha to tell the biblical story of how after the Flood God promised that should man disappoint him and disobey him again, He would send a rainbow before the next one--as a warning.

We sat around during the evening looking at photographs of Abrasha and Fanya, of his sister and friends. But most of all I was taken by some photos of olden times, of Abrasha's childhood in Kielce, in particular of Abrasha in a white suit, standing with one foot crossed over the other, and with one hand to his head in a thinker's pose. He could have been--what?--nine? ten? Another was of Abrasha as a little boy, together with his two sisters. He wears an overcoat and a high Russian fur hat. The photos capture a time, a place, a way of life only two decades before the Flood.

They evoke a cascade of reminiscences about Abrasha's life. The air is thick with talk about Yiddish words and Hebrew words, about poets, ideas, events, about matters Russian and Polish. "He loves the Polish language," Fanny interrupts. "When he hears it, it turns him into another person."

Abrasha knows Abraham Sutzkever and *Di Goldene Keyt*. He knew Janusz Korczak. He knew Abba Kovner in the Vilna Ghetto. Chaim Grade's first wife died there in his hands. We speak of Aron Vergelis, the Communist editor of *Sovietische Heimland*, who has changed his tone and tune somewhat, but much too late. We speak of Peretz Markish's son, who has left Israel somewhat unhappily; it is not known whether he expects to return. And H. Leivick. Chaim Herzog. The Palmach. The Haganah.

And back to the Vilna Ghetto. Unlike Chaim Lazar, Abba Kovner, and others, Abrasha was never a member of the underground. Yet they trusted him. Abrasha's hospital, where he headed the division of infectious diseases, was at the center of things. All the bits and pieces of information came his way there so that he had a better idea of the whole picture than most. He could put Lazar and Chwonik in the hospital, one with an arm deformed by tuberculosis, the other with a hand crippled by polio, and keep them safe and temporarily out of harm's way, to pursue their plans. He knew them all.

He knew the terrible dilemma that Kovner and his partisan group faced: to travel light and escape to the forest--or to take with them the women and children who sought their help. Knowing that one child could threaten the success of their entire venture, they made the hard choice--and doomed perhaps a hundred to death.

He knew Jacob Gens, the head of the *Judenrat*. "If at the end of the war it had been found that his strategy had succeeded in saving 20,000 Jews at the cost of 40,000, he would still have been considered a heroic figure. But because he lost most of the Vilna Ghetto population, despite the plans he had to save it, he is considered a villain. The failure, despite good intentions, is a negative." There can be much good in what turns out badly, he says, just as there can be much that is bad in what turns out well. Always Abrasha returns to the impossible choices facing the Jews in a world where morality no longer existed. What most people who talk about the Shoah simply don't understand, says Abrasha, is *"ahz es iz geven ah gantz andersh velt."* That it was a completely different world.

Abrasha touched on the story of Yitzhak ("Antek") Zukerman and his mental depression. "People wanted to know. How could a general leave his troops and save himself? Anielewicz died inside the Warsaw Ghetto, while Antek saved himself outside the Ghetto. The question was raised after the war--and it hung like a cloud over his head."

A mention of Gallipoli reminds Abrasha of Dunkirk. "You know, the English called Dunkirk a victory when it was really a great defeat. They saved 300,000 Englishmen at the expense of half a million French--and they called this retreat a victory! Only the English could get away with that. This is what you call *chutzpa!*"

Abrasha's mind is boundless and bountiful.

The Definition

To ask questions, which is the Jewish way, says Abrasha, is to oppose fanaticism. "But this is not the way of the Yeshiva students," he says. "They do not ask questions of the Bible. They study Talmud and refer to the Bible only for the legal problems, not for the stories. For them 'To place a fence around the Torah' means not to question it."

Nor can Abrasha understand how Joseph Caro--a master of the mysticism of the Kabbala--could have written the *Shulkhan Arukh.* Abrasha argues that the precision with which he set down the exact laws to be followed by a practicing Jew is completely antithetical to his

Kabbalism. "I have put the problem to others," he says, "but I have never received a satisfactory answer."

Another paradox that disturbs him concerns Halacha. "According to the Orthodox," he says, "Halacha is now frozen. But originally Halacha had just the opposite meaning. It meant continuation, on-goingness. Halacha went on with you in life, trying to teach you with respect to new developments in life. The Orthodox attitude toward Halacha is now in direct contradiction to what it is supposed to be."

If Abrasha has his problems with Orthodoxy, he has none when I ask him to define "a good Jew." Without hesitation he says, "I believe a good Jew is any kind of a Jew who is proud of being a Jew and expresses with love his belonging to the Jewish people."

Horace

Abrasha works in his "surgery"--in his office--two to two and a half hours a day. He is up-to-date in his profession. He loves his surgery. But his philosophical and psychological cast of mind makes him unlike any other doctor I have ever known. He is a doctor schooled in the humanities. His language is rich in allusion and illustrations. Not only is there a story above or below the surface of whatever he is saying, but the story always has a point, and the point always points inward. His mind is bursting with ideas. Though he is not a Litvak, he might as well be because he speaks with the *khokhmah* that is the mark of the Litvak--that is, with wit, intelligence, humor, and wisdom.

"I would rather treat ten Australians than one Jew," he says with a twinkle in his eye.

I am astonished and puzzled, so I fall into his ambush and ask, "Why?"

"The Australians," he tells me, "hardly ever ask a question. The Jew always does. And not only that, he tells you of his own diagnosis, a friend's diagnosis, how the medicine the doctor has prescribed failed to work for his aunt, etc., etc., and finally he winds up with 'Doctor, could you help me get a second opinion?'"

Of course I laugh. I could listen to his stories day and night. It occurs to me that he may be telling them because he knows he has a good listener in me. But no, it's more than that. He is simply full of life and humor and is just a great storyteller. And what with my notebook and all, maybe he thinks I am more than just a good listener. Anyhow, I dread the day we will have to leave Sydney and go on our way.

Last night I caught a glimpse of Abrasha typing away in his study, probably on a script of political commentary for the radio or on an article arguing for the need to preserve and protect the memory of the Holocaust. So this morning I got around to suggesting that he ought to write more--more than just for the Yiddish press and the Yiddish radio. I reminded him of doctors who were also writers... Chekhov... Maugham... Bulgakov....

I think he understood the direction I was taking, because without missing a beat, as if to corroborate my faith in words, and perhaps his own, he quoted in Latin a line from Horace: "I have built me a monument more lasting than bronze."

The Boomerang

Our two bags were packed. They stood in our room, ready for our departure. Abrasha bounded into our room. "*Nu, kinderlakh*," he said, "*s'iz sheyn tzayt.*" He and Fanya refer to us as *kinder* and *kinderlakh* in the family sense. At our age we are still *kinderlakh*, little ones, to them! "It's time," he says.

We carry our bags to the elevator, then down to the car that is waiting for us. We pile the bags into the trunk. It is an awkward moment. I feel the thump in my heart. My throat tightens. The motor is running. Fanny hugs us and kisses us and gives us a box of candy. It is time to part. There is a certain quick sadness at the core of these last moments.

Abrasha and I embrace. He plants a kiss first on one cheek, then on the other, the European way. Then he hands me a half-size boomerang. He has saved it for this moment. He has written a poem on it--in Yiddish! It urges us to return--like the boomerang.

Two weeks in Abrasha's presence: they will leave their mark. Forever. Perhaps we shall meet them next year when they will spend the Australian winter in Israel.

L'hitraot.

FANYA'S STORIES

Dani Birger

All Fanya's stories are extracts from recorded conversations we held in Highland Park, Illinois, in August, 1995.

***

October 28, 1941, was "the big *Di Groyse Aktzieh*."

All the Jews of Kovno were ordered to assemble at the Democratu Platz at six o'clock in the morning--all the labor brigades--each one with his family. Wives, children, grandparents, everyone. Anyone found at home, no matter for what reason, would be shot.

We were five in the family: myself, Di Mameh, Der Tateh, my brother Aharon, and Osya. My father's labor brigade was one of the smaller ones. We all went. It was winter cold. All of us stood grouped together in the last row of my father's brigade. Osya was sick with typhus. He had a fever of 39.8 degrees. Three weeks earlier, when the Germans heard of the typhus epidemic, they burned down the hospital with everyone inside. Our doctor said, "Do not let anyone know. Take him to the Platz. It is one death or another. Take the chance."

Osya was weak. We knew he could not stand on his feet. We took a stool for him. We thought we would hide him as long as possible inside our group.

At the Democratu Platz there was a *selektzieh*. To the right: good. To the left: bad. It grew later and later. We stood there from six in the morning until five at night. Dani Birger, one of the Jewish policemen, saw us standing grouped together. He knew the family. He came over to us and burst out, "Divide up! Divide up! Half and half! For God's sake, do not stand together!" Then he moved quickly away. With those words he saved us.

The Commandant--his name was Jordan--started to come in our direction. He was a young German and beautiful, a handsome man. He came toward us. He let everyone through. But when he came to us--we were three and two now--he stopped. Right in front of Osya. Osya stood up as though his life depended on it. And quickly he spoke up, "I work at the airport!" Osya spoke up for all of us. I don't know how he did it. As soon as Jordan left us we took hold of Osya--I on one side, Aharon on the other--to keep him from falling over. We held him like that for five more minutes. Dani saw it all. From a distance I saw him raise his hands to heaven.

The next day the ten thousand Jews who were chosen in the *selektzieh* were shot at *Der Nayenter Fort*. It was the largest single execution of Lithuanian Jews.

Vaivara

From the Kovno Ghetto we were all transported to a lager called Vaivara, a *Ka Zet*. In Estonia. Di Mameh and I remained there. The men were sent elsewhere. It was surrounded by a wasteland. No one lived in the area. The Germans used to count us early every morning, then send us out of the lager to do "black work." We had to dig the frozen earth from morning until late at night and carry it from one place to another with no purpose to what we were doing. Men and women did the same work. There was no difference.

I met a girlfriend who had gone to school with me. She was older and a year or two ahead of me. She worked in the clothing warehouse. She asked the Germans for me and got me a job there too.

People got sick with the spotted typhus, which comes from dirt and lice. And it spread. We had no place to wash or bathe. There was no water. It was an epidemic. There was no medicine and people died like flies. The Germans closed down the lager. It is a wonder they did not burn it down. Di Mameh and I fell sick.

364

I did not know anything about the others. Then my brother came from another lager. I brought him to Di Mameh. Di Mameh was sick. When she saw him, she said, "What are you doing here?"

A little while later the Germans began to send people out of the lager to other lagers because the Russians were approaching. Little by little they had to liquidate the lager. It was then that they took Di Mameh away from me. A large group had to be sent out, and Di Mameh and my brother were among them. A month later they sent the rest of us out too.

The Magicians

They drove us by foot on a road where all we saw was snow. The snow was up to our knees. We walked several days barely holding out. I ate snow. Friends of mine warned me not to do this--but too late.

At last, exhausted, we arrived at the lager called Kivioli. I do not remember the camp commander's name. Kivioli consisted of two lagers: the "little lager" and the "big lager." At first they brought us to the little lager. There I encountered *Di Hunderte.*

I did not want to eat. I was so sick from eating the snow that I couldn't even think of eating. I felt very bad. I felt as though I were dying. My friend Shura Visnitzky was with me. She brought me to *Di Hunderte*, a gang of thieves and hoodlums from the Vilna underworld. She wanted to force me to eat. One of them gave me a sandwich with butter and with *chazer*, with ham. "You will eat," he threatened me. I ate one sandwich--then I asked for more. He gave me another.

The sickness left me. I became well.

Where did they get this food? First of all, they had money. They had stolen it in Vilna. With money and with gold they could do anything. Abrasha told me that when bread was brought into the lager, in their hands one hundred loaves magically became two hundred. They were experts. I don't know how they did it, but they did. The Germans took away everyone's watch. But from them you could not take the money and the gold. They hid it somehow. You never know how a *gonif,* a thief, works. They were magicians. You don't know how they did it. The Germans were afraid of them.

There were only ten, maybe fifteen of them in this lager.

Aharon

I asked after everyone--who was where. Prisoners came to us from other lagers to pick up clothes from the warehouse. I learned where my brother Aharon was from them. But I do not remember the name of his lager. He did not need clothes. He needed food. I used to send him food through them so that he should get well. I sent butter. I sent bread. I sent *chazer.* I sent sugar. But they didn't give him what I sent. When he wrote me, "Rescue me. Send me as much as you can. Send whatever you can. I do not get anything from you," I knew he was not getting what I sent.

And when these people brought me his documents, I knew my brother was no longer here. I began to beat them. They let me beat them. And the German stood and watched as I beat them. He took pleasure in it even though he did not know why I was beating them.

I did not tell Di Mameh that he had died. I knew he was her *liebling* and that she still hoped. One day she went off to work with a group--to peel potatoes. Someone told her. Imagine what I had from her: the hysteria, the crying, the weeping.

This also passed.

The List

Then they sent us into the second lager, where we were divided up. We had a decent bed. We didn't lie on wooden boards, as before, but in bunks, one above the other. At least our group did. It was considered one of the better lagers. At least we had a bed.

One day Abrasha came and told me Di Mameh was in the lager. She had come on the latest transport to Kivioli, from the lager called Ezeda. Abrasha had a friend who worked in one of the offices and he had asked to have a look at the list of arrivals. Abrasha looked and he found the family name on the list. I didn't know she was there. I only knew that a new transport had been brought in. I thought *"efsher,"* maybe she might have been on it. Everyone always wanted to know if someone in his family was on any list of arrivals. Abrasha went and asked. And he came to tell me.

I went to see her. She was not ill. No one was ill.

They had put all the people from the transport into the hospital, separate from the rest of us. Di Mameh was among them. When the Germans brought such a group from another lager, it meant that they were going away to their death. I had no doubt at all that they were going to shoot these people.

I wondered what I could do. I had to get her out of the hospital. I discussed the matter with friends and decided to approach the Commandant of the camp. What more could they do than kill me?

The Appel

I went to the German living quarters, to the corridor where the Commandant lived and I hid behind a great stove. I thought that sooner or later he would have to come out to go to the toilet. It was so. When he did, I came out from behind the stove. He was startled, a little frightened. But he saw it was me. He knew it was me because he had seen me working in the clothing warehouse.

He took me into a second room and asked, "What is the problem?" He asked me to sit down. I did not. I told him my mother was among the new arrivals in the hospital. Then I played on his emotions. I said he must have a mother--that he must surely be homesick for her, that I had not seen my mother for years, and that I wanted her to remain in our lager, that he was a good lager fuhrer. "You are a good man," I said. "It is good in your lager. I want to take her out of the hospital. I want my mother to remain here."

He asked, "Is she healthy?"

"Yes, she is healthy."

"Are you sure?"

"Yes, I am sure."

He looked at me. Something was going on in his mind. "Tomorrow morning," he said, "when those people have been called out on the *appel*, remind me to take out your mother." My heart became lighter.

I went to my mother and said, "Mameh, if they call out for you at the roll call, you must come out. Do not just stand there and remain behind."

The next morning Shura, Abrasha, and all my *chaveyrim* who worked with me stood watching and waiting in a barrack a short distance from the *appel*. Everyone from the hospital was led out for roll call, Di Mameh too. As soon as I saw the lager fuhrer--he was walking with another German (I do not know who he was)--I went out for him to see me and remember. He motioned with his hand that everything was in order. That is what I understood.

368

He went over to where the group of prisoners was standing. He stopped. No one in the lager had a name. Only a number. But he called out, "Who is the mother of Fanya? Come out!" She did not move. Three times he called out. And she did not move. I ran out and said, "Mameh, come out! He is calling you!" Only then did she come out.

He called me over to him. "Is this your mother?"

I said, "Yes."

"You have a place for her?"

I said, "Yes."

"Take her."

She began to tremble--all over. "Mameh," I said, "calm yourself. Why didn't you come out when he called you?"

"I was afraid," she said.

Quickly I led her to our block, to the room where the rest of us lived. "Sit here," I said.

The *appel* ended. I did not see what was going on there. Later I learned that they gathered all the people, told them to get into a waiting truck, and took them away. They were a large group, fifty or sixty people. An hour later the truck returned with their clothes.

Di Mameh did not know what happened. And I did not tell her. I saw their clothes. I did not want to tell her. I kept many things from her.

She remained with me in the lager. After this we were never separated. She remained with me to the end--until the last day.

Ten Percent

A month later there was the Ten Percent *Aktzieh* in Kivioli. That is what we called it. What it meant was that from every lager the Germans "took away" ten percent of the people, not only from ours.

They ordered the prisoners out for roll call. They ordered us to stand in squares one meter apart. I placed Di Mameh on the left side. The Commandant and the head of the SS came toward us from the left side. The head of the SS went through all the rows and came to a stop right in front of Di Mameh.

I took a look at the lager fuhrer, and he took a look at me--and he recognized Di Mameh. He felt something. He went over to the head of the SS. "This woman I do not give up to you. She is my best washerwoman. I cannot give her away."

"Good," he answered. "Keep her," he said and walked on.

The Baker

We had another *Aktzieh*—when the lager fuhrer sent out those he had taken a dislike to.

One was a doctor, Abrasha's friend. They knew each other in Poland. I didn't know him. I don't know why the lager fuhrer hated him. I don't know the details.

Another was Kuske Probeh. He hung around with *Di Hunderte*. Whether he was one of the *chevreh* I do not know. He was not as common as they were. He said he was a baker and that he had a bakery in Vilna. He was taken and locked up with the others the lager fuhrer wanted to get rid of. All of them were taken to a different block in the middle of the night.

370

At four a.m. there was a sound at our door. Shura and I jumped up. I said, "Shura, what's happening?" She said, "I don't know. Someone is knocking." We got up to look. It was Kuske Probeh standing there. He had gotten out of the building where he had been locked up.

"Shura! Fanya! Come with me! I am getting out of the lager."

"You are crazy," I said. "What do you mean you are getting out of the lager! The first Est who will see you will kill you." The Estonians were terrible anti-Semites. Many Jews wanted to escape. The Estonians used to take their money, then betray them.

"I have nothing to lose," he said. "He is sending me to my death."

I said, "I can't go. I won't go. I have Di Mameh. I have just barely gotten her back." And Shura said, "I won't go either."

So he left. We watched him go. He limped on one foot. He went to the fence. We accompanied him with our eyes. We saw how he went. We saw him cut the barbed wire. And we saw him disappear into the forest.

Shortly afterward we were taken away--just before the Russian army came. The Germans took us by train from Kivioli to the lager Klooga, where they burned Jews. It is a port where they took us to the ship.

Later, we learned from those who met him that he remained alive. He did not stay in the forest long. He avoided everyone. He ate berries that he found. Kuske Probeh saw us from the forest the day the Germans were leading us away to the train.

Kuske Probeh knew Shura and me because we worked in the clothing warehouse. I don't know what happened to him. I heard he went to Poland. I have asked many people about him. But no one knows what happened to him afterward.

371

All the others were killed--Abrasha's friend too. I know because I saw their clothes, which were brought back to the warehouse where I worked. When the truck returned, the doctor's fourteen year old son forced his way into the warehouse and found his father's clothes.

Today the son is in Israel, a well-known pianist. The doctor's wife is also in Israel. I have seen her. Whenever Abrasha came to Israel he would go to visit her.

Klooga

From Kivioli they took us to Klooga. It was a *shrecklikher* lager. The Germans burned a great many people there. First they put down a row of tree trunks. Then they placed a layer of bodies on them, then another layer of wood, then another layer of bodies. And then they set them all on fire until they were burned up. Maybe some of the people were still alive. I don't know. For me it was *shrecklikh*, terrifying. Not for the Germans. The Germans took us to the ship. They even took people off the ship to kill them in Klooga.

Stutthof

From Klooga they took us to Stutthof. The whole lager was taken on board the ship. Stutthof--that was a terrible lager.

First they took us to a bath and told us to take off all our clothes. Then they poured cold water on us. Afterward they gave us other clothes. They would wake us in the middle of the night--at three in the morning--and drive us out of the block to freeze in the bitter cold. They gave us nothing to eat. They gave us *kropoveh* to eat. It has nettles. It is a kind of poison ivy. If you touch it with your hands, it burns and the skin erupts. They cooked it.

Abrasha was on the ship and went to Stutthof also. I saw him from far away. My father was there also. I saw Osya also. They came from other lagers--Der Tateh from Goldfields and Osya from Port Kunde. The Germans evacuated Estland because the Russian front was approaching. I talked with Der Tateh through the barbed wire. Also with Osya.

"If we remain alive," Der Tateh said, "we will meet each other again in Kovno." This, I think, is why Di Mameh went back to Kovno. This is why she dragged herself to the devil.

We were in Stutthof three weeks. Stutthof was torture. It had a crematorium, and Der Tateh was cremated there--from the gas chamber.

Candles

Before the cold water "bath" we were on the dirty side of Stutthof. After it we were on the "clean" side.

While I was on the dirty side I saw the woman who was the doctor in the gymnasium where I studied in Kovno. She was unmarried, an "old maid," a very good woman. But she was white-haired, an older woman. What I mean is that in my eyes she looked old. We all slept on the ground. She lay not far from me. They gave us nothing. All of us were dirty.

In the morning when we got up, I saw she does not get up. I said to one of my friends, "Take a look. Dr. Kambert is not getting up. Maybe we should wake her." My friend went over to her and came back.

"She is no longer here. Then she said, "Ah, now I understand."

"What do you understand?" I asked.

373

"Last night before we went to sleep she came over to me. She knew I had worked in a pharmacy, and she asked me if sixty of such and such tablets were enough to bring death. I said yes. It did not occur to me that she had them with her and was going to take them. She took them and she went to sleep. And did not get up again."

She knew already what she would have to go through if she went with us. So she went away.

Some people had candles with them. I don't know where they got them. They placed them around her and lit them. We left her there on the dirty side.

The Third Time

We were in Stutthof three weeks. It was a separate world. Shura was with me the whole time. Otherwise I met no one.

Then--at roll call--I met a Jewish girl I had known in Kovno. She had converted. She wore a cross around her neck and had dyed her hair blond. But she was in the lager like a Jew. She was a Kapo. And she made trouble around her. I recognized her because as a student she used to buy little hats from my father. We would see her in the street--a prostitute, not one of the finer people. A Jewish prostitute, yes.

As I was standing there with Di Mameh, she came over and took her from me, and sent her to one side. She left me with my group. Di Mameh called me to her from the other side and said, "Do not let me go alone. They will take me away."

I did not understand. I said, "What do you mean we won't go together? Of course we'll go together."

She said, "No, they are already sending me elsewhere. Go," she said, because she recognized the Kapo too, "go and ask her to let me go with you." Di Tante already understood. I did not.

I went over to the Kapo and I said, "Do you remember me?"

"Of course I remember you."

"Then you must remember my mother also--better than me."

"I remember her."

"Then why did you send her to the other side?"

"Who did I send away?"

"You sent *my* mother away."

"Listen to me. I am going to turn my back. I will not look. Take her back with you."

Maybe she did not recognize Di Mameh. All she saw was an older woman. I was nineteen, twenty. How old could Di Mameh have been? She was forty--an older woman. The Kapo turned her back and went off. I went to Di Mameh and dragged her with me to my group, dragged her into the middle of it so no one should see her anymore.

This was the third time I rescued Di Mameh.

The others were sent away to the crematorium.

Oxentzol

The Germans put us on a train and sent us from Stutthof to Oxentzol, between Hanover and Hamburg.

There we had to work in a munitions factory. I worked at a machine that made bullets. On the night shift. I still have the marks on my hand from the oil that flew from the machine and dropped into the scratches and cuts on my skin. Di Mameh worked there too, cleaning up with the broom, picking up things, and doing such work. Until the end of 1944. We were not bothered. We would go to work, then come back. There would be a roll call. They would count us.

We had a good lager fuhrer. He would let us sing songs. He would even *tell* us to sing songs. If he saw someone did not have good shoes, he saw to it that they got good shoes. Whoever needed a dentist was taken to the dentist. He was a very good Commandant.

But the SS girls saw he was too good to the Jews--so they informed against him. And he was ordered to the front.

He cried when he said goodbye to us. He said, "I *hope* you will remain alive, that you will not have to suffer much longer." And he left us.

Ten Days

A madman came to replace the good lager fuhrer at Oxentzol. He was there only a short time. Bombs from the English side began to fall around us more and more. The Germans decided to evacuate us-- to transport all of us to Bergen-Belsen by train. It was shortly before the end of the war, and the same SS girls who had betrayed the good lager fuhrer begged us not to betray them and reveal who they were.

Unfortunately we arrived at Bergen-Belsen. I'll never forget it. For ten days--we had no food to eat--no water--nothing. How did Di Tante get through those days? How did we all get through them? She was always heavy, yes? Well, she became as thin as my finger--very thin. People lay dead everywhere...piled high...thrown one on top of the other.... Sick ones. Skeletons wandered around. In Estonia-- where we were--we were only Jews. Others? I don't imagine, but I don't think so. We were Jews from Vilna and from Kovno. But this was an international lager. It held everyone, not just Jews: Germans, Poles, French, all nations, from the whole world, even Gypsies.

On the ninth day the Germans said we would all get not just a piece of bread but a whole loaf. Di Mameh and I said we would not eat the bread. How could the Germans become so good so suddenly? We knew the bread had to be poisoned. We did not *know*. But anyone who could still think a little about such matters *knew*. It couldn't be otherwise. They had given us nothing for nine days--no water, nothing--and now suddenly to get a loaf of bread? It had to be poisoned.

The next day--when they were to give us the bread--the Germans were in their barracks, drinking, carousing, singing songs that they were getting rid of the Jews. We were told this later.

Later we also learned that an English tank had lost its way in the area and had stumbled on the lager, then gone back to report what it had found. They returned with English soldiers who surrounded the lager and entered. They found the Germans who were drinking and singing and took all of them prisoner.

Those of us who still had our senses about us told the English that we were supposed to get bread that day. The English discovered where the bread was kept, locked it up, and let no one have any. They took one loaf, analyzed it, and found that one bite was enough to kill a person.

What did the English do? They should have given the Germans the bread to eat.... Kramer--the lager fuhrer--they hanged him later. The English forced the Germans to gather all the dead--they worked very hard. The others? Yes or no, I don't know if any were shot. It was not my concern.

The English distributed canned food, fat food. People fell upon the food. As a result, ten thousand people died--from dysentery. We remained alive by not overeating.

But on the last day before the liberation, someone gave Di Mameh a push, and she fell and broke her foot. The English took her to the hospital. She lay in bed. They made her a cast, but it wasn't done right. Later they took her to a better hospital, where she became better.

The English took us to a little town called Belsen, an SS town. They had cleaned out the SS. They gave us hot water to bathe in. They gave us a decent bed with white sheets. We began to feel human.

Belsen

We were in the city Belsen three months. I worked there in a cafeteria for the English military. I didn't have a bad life...I lived...I wasn't rich...I had no money...you weren't allowed to have money. But I lacked nothing...not food...nothing...I had my own room. I lived as though I were in a hotel. Di Tante was in the hospital with her broken foot for two or three months.

Meanwhile, I worked very hard in the cafeteria. There I met an English officer, a handsome fellow. He began to come every day to see me...to eat...to have coffee.... I was not a waitress. I stood behind the buffet. I would get whatever the soldiers asked for. He came only to me. He must have liked me. Probably. I don't know why.

One day he asked me to come to a party they were going to have in the English camp. I said, "I don't know. I cannot." I didn't want to. So he went to my superior and asked him to tell me to go.

My superior took me aside and said, "I guaranty you that all will be correct and proper. You can go." So I said, "If you come with me,

378

then I'll go." He said, "Good. You want that? I can come." I said, "Yes, I want it."

I don't know what I was afraid of. I can't say today what I was afraid of then. I was not interested in the officer. Just to go--? I didn't know any English. I had learned only a few words, those that were necessary for my work. I stood and worked with a dictionary.

So my superior came with me. I didn't let go of him. I said, "You must not leave me or go off anywhere. You must sit with me." I was twenty-four at the time. I was nineteen when the war began--plus five years. I went. There were so many beautiful tables filled with so many good things to eat. The officer never left me. He wanted to show me everything.

He came to see me every day. Until I told him I was leaving.

My superior became very angry with me when he heard I was going to Russland. He argued with me for days. "You will have a hard life...talk to your mother...you won't have a life."

Many people came from America, Germany, France to Bergen-Belsen--Jews, rabbis without beards. Each one agitated in favor of his country and for us to leave Russland behind. But it was no use. Di Mameh said she must find Der Fohter, that she must go back to Kovno to find my father. When I fought hard and begged her not to do this, she said, "If you do not go with me, I will go alone." This is how she went "home" for the second time in her life. I was a good daughter. I went with her.

Of Di Mameh's first failure I know only that she had the papers to go to America and was prepared to go--when the first World War broke out.

Bialystok

We were brought to the Russian sector. I soon saw our misfortune.

The Russians immediately sent us to clean the toilets. I said to Di Mameh, "This is what you wanted?" She did not reply. I did not go to clean the toilets. But we could not go back anymore.

Then we began to travel--to go and go and go. We went only a short way by train--through Berlin. I and a few other young ones sat on the roof of the train because there was no room inside. The rest of the way we went on trucks. Through Poland--Warsaw--on the trucks. We were two Yiddish women on a truck full of Litviner. No other Jews. If only there had been.

In Bialystok I jumped down to stretch my legs. And I came upon a red-headed Jew, the first I had ever seen. A Jew with red hair! He came over to me.

"You are Paylish? Little girl, you are a Yiddishkey?"

Mocking his dialect, I answered, "Yes, I am a Yiddishkey!"

"Where are you going?"

"Home."

"Where is your home?"

I said, "In Kovno."

"With whom are you traveling?"

"With Di Mameh. Why are you asking me these questions?"

"Do you know that people are running from there? People are coming *here* and you are going *there?*"

I said, "Mameh, do you hear what he says?"

She said, "I hear. We have traveled through all of Europe. We are almost home. We will go on to the end."

"But, Mameh, you hear? People are running from there." She did not want to hear anything.

"How would we live here if we remained here?" I asked him.

"There is a Committee--they help people. Jews gather together here. You won't get lost. *There* you will get lost!"

Nothing helped. Di Mameh was stubborn. She did not know what had happened to Der Papah. But I--I could imagine.... Der Papah had already had a stroke at home...and he was in a lager...in a lager like Stutthof...and if they had already decided to send Di Mameh to the ovens, then they must have sent him away for certain. And that is how it was.

He was a sick man and did not look good. They kept the young ones and sent the old ones away. I was certain Der Papah was no longer here. But I could not say to her, "What are you looking for? He is no longer here." I would not say it to her--not on my life. But when we came to Kovno and she saw he was not there, she understood he was not alive.

I knew my brother was no longer here. Did I tell her that? No, I did not tell her that either. I could not.

The Ring

The time came when the Jews of Kovno were to be confined to the ghetto. My mother and father gave most of our most valuable possessions, including my piano, to the wife of the man who worked for my father--to hold for us until better times. The woman took the ring off my finger.

Once in the ghetto, it became a matter of life and death for us to get food and other things we needed. So one day I walked beyond the ghetto limits, removed the Star of David from my arm, and went to the woman to ask her to return some of our possessions so that I could barter them for life itself. When I came to the woman's home, I saw an SS man sitting at the kitchen table! Even so, I called the woman to the door and asked for her help. The woman said, "You see who is at my table? Get out!" She refused to give up anything.

It was the same when we went back to Kovno in 1945. We looked for the family that held our things. They were ready to meet us with empty hands. They returned nothing to us. They told us they had sold everything for food. A lie. What things? Everything that is in a respectable home. The piano I played on. The name of the family was Boginsky.

We gave up Kovno and went to live in Vilna. One day I went from Vilna to Kovno with some of my colleagues. By chance I saw the woman in the street. She was coming toward us. I forced her to stop, and I confronted her. "What a beautiful ring you are wearing! Where did you get it?"

"Oh, I bought it."

I asked to see it--and I pulled it from her finger. And I told my companions what had happened. When the woman started to run away, one of them stopped her. I faced her again and said, "I do not want anything from you! You are a thief! A thief! You will die! You will die!" I shouted it again and again. I could not help myself.

Two years later she died of cancer. He did too. They paid for everything. Sometimes I think there is a God in heaven after all.

The Grand Inquisitor

Osya found cousins who, like us, had come to live in Vilna. In 1957 one of them was permitted to go to Poland. Before he left, I asked him, "You are a Taraseisky?"

He said, "What do you mean *a Taraseisky?*"

"Send us papers so we can get out too."

He said, "Not I."

I said, "Why not?"

"They will say you are not Polish."

"What does it matter to you? You are getting out. What does it bother you if we will also go?" He was a Communist. He was so holy you couldn't say a word to him. He didn't want to help. And so it was.

So in 1957 I went to a lawyer I knew and I said, "I want to make documents in Di Mameh's name. I want to go to Poland and from Poland I want to go to Israel."

He said, "Go to where the ghetto was in Vilna and look for the number of a house that is ruined. And I'll make documents that your mother lived in Vilna in such and such a place at such and such a time."

I went and I did everything he told me. He made the documents, and no one knew. I took them to the proper bureau.

A week later the police called me in. A man with a Jewish face stood outside the entrance to the police station. He said, "You are so and so--?"

I said, "Yes."

"Come with me."

He took me into the KGB--on the Prospekt Lenin. It is where the statue of Lenin faced the great building, the KGB. He took me to the second floor. He opened one door, took me in with him, then through another door into a huge room.

"Who made you these false documents?" he demanded. "You were born in Liteh. You are not a Polish citizen. Your mother is not a Polish citizen. Your mother did not live in Vilna. Who made you these documents?"

"No one made them. And my mother lived in Vilna." I stuck to my story. "I went to the Archive and I got the documents. I made a request to find out where she lived, and I got the documents, official documents, from the Archive."

It did not help. He kept me in that room for three hours, tormenting me with his questions. Finally, he saw he could pull nothing out of me. So he wrote out an exit pass to permit me to leave the KGB building. As he gave it to me he promised me, "In your whole life you will *never* get out of Liteh."

I don't know how I did it, where I got the nerve, but I answered him, "I hope that you will not sit in this place for *your* whole life!" And as I said it to him a shiver went through my body.

I flew down the stairs--two floors--I don't know how. I ran right into Osya's arms! He was standing outside there waiting for me. Three hours long. Can one imagine what he went through?

No Exit

Nothing happened to me at my work. Nor did they take Osya off his job. But they blocked his advancement. They told him so at his work. The KGB let it be known at his place of work and at mine.

My own director said to me, "You want to leave here? What are you missing here?"

I said, "You live among Litviner. You live in your land. This is not my land."

"It *is* your land. Your land is occupied."

"But you are living out your life with your own language. You are living out your life with everything that is yours. I want to live among my people also. *You* may do so and *I* must not?"

It was then that he told me that my firm had received a letter from the KGB. He said, "Nothing will happen to you. It doesn't matter to me if you do want to go or you don't want to go. But it seems to me something will happen to your husband."

Osya had close friends that worked with him. They told him that there too at work they had received such a letter. And it was so: they did not let him go higher. This troubled him very much. He was worth much more than he earned. And he knew it. And everyone respected him.

In 1971 we requested exit papers for the second time. The day after we presented our documents Osya was fired from his job. They told him to go--because he was not faithful enough for them.

No Equals

She went away quickly.

She sat with us in the evening watching television. It was nine p.m. She said she was tired and wanted to go to sleep. She was not sick. I took her to her bed. She undressed and lay down to sleep. Osya and I went on watching television. Around eleven we went to bed. The house was quiet, still, peaceful.

In the middle of the night I heard her calling me. I got up and went into her room. She was sitting on her bed, and she said, "It hurts me terribly here," and she pointed to her heart. Osya was up and I told him to get dressed and call for emergency help. We did not have a phone in the house. We were ten years in Israel and had no phone. He got dressed and left to call for help. I brought her a glass of water, and she threw the water over herself. She felt she was burning. I dried her off. A doctor came, but not with an ambulance. He came with an ordinary car and a driver. He listened to her heart and immediately called for an ambulance on his phone. It came quickly. They put her on a stretcher. She asked me, "Where are you taking me?" I said, "To the hospital. You are not well." Those were her last words.

They took her down the stairs and placed her in the ambulance. I sat in the ambulance with her. The ambulance didn't just go. It flew-- so fast that I took her in my arms so she should not fall. I understood it was not good. I told the driver to go still faster. Osya followed behind us in his car.

The doctor, meanwhile, had called ahead to the hospital, and they were already waiting for us when we arrived. They took her inside immediately. They did not let me go with her. I saw them bring one machine, then another machine. I don't know what they brought. A half hour later the doctor came out--I was standing with Osya--and he asked, "Whose mother is it?"

I said, "Mine."

He said, "Come in." We went into another room. He said, "Sit down." I already understood she was no longer here. He said, "We did everything." When we brought her she was already clinically dead. "We tried electric shock. We tried everything we could. I'm sorry."

When we came home, her pillow was still warm.

All along she had said, "I know I will not live forever. I know I shall die. I do not want a *langeh bet*--I do not want to lie in bed and suffer. I want to go quickly." And that is how she died. She was 82. She died July 31, 1978.

She had a large funeral. My co-workers came. A Rov said prayers. Osya said Kaddish. Our *chaveyrim* came--all of them knew her. But none of her equals--because she no longer had any.

Australia

Where was Abrasha during this time? I don't know. I saw him for the last time in Stutthof, when I also saw Osya and Der Papa. I knew nothing of him after that. I returned to Russland. A few years later, back in Vilna, I learned he was alive and in Australia.

A friend of mine, who was with me in the lager, had a sister in Vilna, a Communist. We met and she told me she had met Abrasha in France and that he had received papers to go to Australia.

Abrasha had wanted to go to Israel. But while he and his wife were in France waiting for papers to go to Israel, Abrasha's wife learned a friend of hers from Vilna was living in Australia, and she asked others who were going to Australia to find her friend and tell her that she and Abrasha were in France and to give their address. As soon as their friends in Australia learned where Abrasha and his wife were, they sent papers for them to come to Australia.

Abrasha wanted very much to go to Israel even after he was in Australia. His wife did not want to go. That is why they remained in Australia.

There it is, the whole story.

The Practice

Abrasha understood illness. Everyone believed in him. All his *chaveyrim*. Each had a different doctor, but they would come to him to see if they needed to take whatever each doctor had prescribed.

In his last years he gave up some of his practice. It was hard on him. He went to his surgery because he wanted to go. He loved it. Patients came specifically for him, just to talk to him. And he used to listen. But he gave up many of his patients to the other doctors.

Abrasha originally had his practice in his home--in his previous home. When I came, he said he wanted to give up the home, but not his practice. He still wanted to go out of the house to work. We looked for another house.

A friend of his son was always in Abrasha's home, as a child, as a student. He loved Abrasha. Abrasha was a friend of his father. His father died in Abrasha's arms. The young doctor--the friend to Abrasha's son--proposed that Abrasha join him in the surgery he shared with two other doctors and offered him the office his mother, also a doctor, had used until she retired. He loved Abrasha like his own father. When Abrasha would go off traveling, he would embrace him, kiss him. When Abrasha would return, he did the same. He didn't know what to do for Abrasha. He was more a son to Abrasha than Abrasha's son was to him.

The Writer

What drove Abrasha so much about the Shoah? I don't know. He used to tell about his nightmares after the Shoah...always dreaming about the lager...how he would jump up screaming from his sleep. I don't know whether he decided himself to write his experiences or his wife told him or his *chaveyrim* told him. But he began to write. After he began to write, he told me, he calmed down. He stopped screaming in his sleep. He stopped having nightmares. He became more and more calm. He wrote his book *They Marched Us Three Nights* in Hebrew and in English.

He spoke only of the Shoah. He had his circle. His *chaveyrim* gave him support. He had someone to talk to. I would go everywhere with him--to a dinner, a lunch--always there was one theme: the Shoah. One theme. And I would die listening to their talk.

He also wrote his memoirs, but it was not a book. He wrote about his whole life--his memories--and made three copies: one for his son, one for his daughter, one for his sister's children. All three have the same one--in English. Typewritten. His sister has something, also typed, about the ghetto. I saw it. I think it is in Hebrew, in *Ivrit*--for her only.

Polish was Abrasha's mother tongue. He loved Polish. His father taught him *Ivrit*. His mother, Yiddish. And he wrote articles in a beautiful Yiddish. He loved to write in Yiddish.

Abrasha's Death

A few days before his death Abrasha lay in the hospital. He wasn't supposed to get out of bed, but he awakened in the night, jumped up, ran to the nurse, and said, "My friend Dr. Fryd has fallen! He is dying! He needs help! Help him! The nurse put him back to

389

bed, calmed him, and said she would help Dr. Fryd. She called Abrasha's doctor and told him what had happened.

Abrasha was certain of what he had done. He told me. He told everyone. I didn't know till he told me. When I came to see him, he said, "Do you know what happened to me?" and he told me how he had jumped out of bed...how he wanted to help Fryd who lay on the floor dying...that the nurse had put him back to bed...and that she had informed the doctor.

Two days later the same thing happened! He jumped out of bed, ran to the nurse, and screamed, "My *chaver*--he is dying! Sensing Abrasha could die at any moment, his doctor tried to soothe him and said, "Calm yourself. We will help your friend. We are in the hospital."

Abrasha died a few days later.

When I told Professor Fryd the story, he said, "Abrasha was correct--but it was just the opposite! It was on the second day of the three day march--the day before we ran away. It was Abrasha who fell and was in danger of dying. He had no more strength, and I forced him to hold on. I helped him through."

The doctor understood that Abrasha was remembering something that had happened long ago and had remained in his mind. It was a kind of premonition of death. But to me it is a great question mark. I don't understand it.

Telling the Story

I lived with a man whose whole life was bound up with the Shoah. He talked of the Shoah. He worked on the Shoah. All his books were about the Shoah. I was not able to find a single book in his library that I was able to read all the way through. I couldn't.

While we were in Sydney a documentary film on the Germans was going to be shown on television. He wanted to see it. He knew I did not. Abrasha said, "Come, see it with me. Don't let me sit alone. What can happen?" I watched the film. And all night long I walked around. I did not sleep. I did not sleep all night--and he saw I did not. From that time on he did not trouble me about such matters.

I go to the library in Israel. I read a great deal. I can't go out when it is hot. So I sit at home and read. I don't always know the contents of a book beforehand. Sometimes I borrow a book and I find it deals with the whole story--the Shoah. I close the book. I don't read it. I can't. I take it back to the library, and I exchange it for another.

There are some people who live with it. Abrasha lived with it. There are people who can't exist without it.

And then there are people--Professor Fryd, for example--he did not once tell his children of what happened with him there. He did not write down a single note. He doesn't want to hear about it. When people speak of the Shoah, he goes out of the room. Until today. He is 81, 82 years old. He can't. I can't either.

I do not talk to Fima about the Shoah. Nothing. First of all, he does not ask. It can be that he spoke with Osya. He used to sit and talk with Osya often--I don't know about what. But not with me. He knows everything about Di Tante. I believe Osya told him many things. But he did not learn anything from me. I did not talk to him about it. And I won't.

AFTERPIECES

A Journey

When I was a child, the existence of grandparents always puzzled me. For some reason I had none. All my playmates had them. Or so it seemed. One grandparent was puzzlement enough, but some had two or three. I learned you could even have as many as four. For a long time the arithmetic of the matter escaped me. All I really knew was that I was born without any, had never had any, and was unlikely to acquire any in the future. And that was that.

Of course I held my parents responsible for depriving me of grandparents--and the privileges that came with them. Even though they invariably looked "old," grandparents, I saw, were useful to have. They were reliable sources of candy, good feelings, and answers to troublesome questions. Candy and good feelings I could do without. But I missed answers to big questions.

So it was that when we took off for the USSR in 1970, I was not in search of roots--because I had none. Genealogy was not the spur. I still had plenty of questions, though, better than those of childhood. But it was too late to put them to my mother and father and get the answers I craved. From the very outset they had deprived me of one generation, and in dying they had already deprived me of another.

Somewhere in the back of my mind I might have been hoping that maybe--just maybe--I'd still be able to find an answer or two on the other side of the ocean. My father's sister and his niece existed in old letters. I knew they had survived the concentration camps and could still be alive behind the Iron Curtain. Looking for them would be an adventure in itself. Finding them might fill in the blanks in my father's story.

I had no idea that the Tante's story would become part of my own.

Only afterward, belatedly, did I come to understand that connection was itself an answer. Only after reading and re-reading the letters, only after deciphering the postcards, did I come to realize the meaning behind Dora's hope in 1914 that "we shall be able to see each other." To her, *meshpokhe*--family--meant connection. "If we cannot see each other," she said, desperate for connection, "let us hear from each other." Requesting photos, she said, "I would like to see everyone, if only from a distance." For her, connection was all, as it could only be in one so bitterly cut off from husband and son. It was a passion that never left her. As we took off for the USSR I had no idea that I would be connected to her story, that hers would be connected to mine. Or that the connections would take me where I had never thought of going. And that I would become responsible for the future of the whole story.

I grew up during a time when "taking a trip" meant you took the train, and taking the train meant you would have an adventure. Airplanes were common enough, but they were for the well-to-do, businessmen and such. Or for special occasions. Nowadays hordes of tourists fly everywhere to visit the world. Not for them Thoreau's remark "I have traveled a good deal in Concord." They bring back trinkets, stories of hotels and restaurants, show pictures taken--but rarely tell what I would most like to hear: news of the world and themselves in it.

When our plane left for Europe I did not know that I had embarked not on a trip but on a journey. A journey of years. Of stories. Of stories within stories, of stories added to stories. A journey into more than one dimension, into both outer time and inner. I had no idea of the connections awaiting me in Vilnius or in the journey I had yet to take in postcards, letters, diaries, in visiting and re-visiting scenes, memories, feelings, and ideas.

I had no idea I was on a journey that would be a turning point in my life.

396

After Vilnius, no matter which way I turned, no matter where I looked for information and understanding, I found myself facing the Holocaust. After Vilnius, I was to learn as never before that the Holocaust was the point of reference by which I must measure what I see and hear in the world around me. That the point of reference would provide me with a point of view from which to have a point of view.

The journey that really began with my father, that eventually took me to Vilnius and back, reaches into each word I write today.

Tulu

Tulu, our guide, is twenty-four years old, a college graduate, modern and emancipated. Her father is an officer in the Turkish air force. She was pointing her finger at the wide open, windblown landscape before us, and saying, "There. You see? This is Cappadocia. It means 'the land of beautiful horses.'" She paused a moment to give us a chance to absorb the scene, long enough for one of our fellow tourists to complain, "But there are no horses." With a smile concealing the barest touch of pity, she turned to him, then startled us all. "Imagination," she said, "makes the world."

In the theater of my imagination the magic lantern is forever clicking in its slides to make my world. I can be alone or with others, no matter the hour or the place, when suddenly, unsummoned, the lantern turns itself on, clicks a slide into place, and instantaneously transports me into a present very different from the one I am still in. With each slide I lead a double life, actor and spectator in the world it makes for me. When the lantern turns itself off and I return from the scene, I know I have been there before and will journey there again to find my way into its story and beyond.

Abrasha's story of the Kusevitzes took him less than a minute to tell. It is his shortest story--and one of his longest. Only the imagination that makes the world can get you there.

I hear one Kusevitz identifying himself to the audience: "I am Kusevitz." And I sense the electric shock--then the joy of his brother's contradiction roaring back to him: "*I* am Kusevitz!" An incredible thrill shoots through the hall, through the heart--mine, everyone's. I can see this Kusevitz come running down the aisle to his brother. I can see them enveloping each other, kissing, weeping. It is a seldom scene.

Offstage, behind them in the silent darkness of the hall, a very different scene is unfolding, an invisible scene, in which each survivor in the audience shares this reunion of the Kusevitzes--yet suffers in silence, forever alone with the bitter knowledge of why he will never be able to share it. Like the Kusevitzes, each one has come to listen and wait, has come with a glimmer of hope to hear a familiar voice. But the tension between hope and fear has snapped, leaving behind palpable disappointment. Leaving behind jealousy. And guilt. And endless sorrow.

Each slide is a call to the imagination that makes my world. Each time the projector's cassette stops to insert another slide I rediscover yet another moment that will never let me go.

Lenin's statue. It stood in front of KGB headquarters in Vilnius. It has been removed by now, removed, surely, to some outdoor graveyard for the hundreds of such statues once scattered throughout the Former Soviet Union to proclaim "the radiant future." It has become a relic, an artifact. But in the slide Lenin still stands with his arm out flung, forever the orator, ruling over Vilnius's Red Square, still the icon of murder. The bench that stood opposite him across the street has vanished--to make certain no one can sit to watch who goes into the building and who comes out. Osya stands on the sidewalk at the door to the building, waiting for Fanny to hurl herself into his arms after her escape from the Grand Inquisitor. And so do I.

Again--and forever--the door opens and Di Tante stands there in her brown raincoat. She enters her neighbor's apartment to stand before two total strangers. From America. One speaks Yiddish to her, telling her that I am Henoch's son--and my brother's brother. Quickly she comprehends the incomprehensible. She is cool, self contained. No scream, no shout, no tears, no embrace. The crook of her index finger beckons us to follow her--and so to enter forever into memory.

The lager Kivioli. Another scene. A recurrent nightmare. Fifty-five or sixty arrivals from the latest transport have assembled for the *appel.* They do not know it, but just out of sight the lorries are already waiting to take them to their death in some forsaken forest. The motors are running. The Commandant of the lager is there for the roll call. He calls out for Di Tante once. She does not move. He calls out for her a second time. Again she does not move. Fanny, Abrasha, and their comrades are watching from their block. They are bursting with anxiety. The Commandant calls out a third time. Still Di Tante does not move. But Fanny does and runs into the scene, desperately begging her to come out, literally dragging her back into life. Years later Fanny tells me, "She had the psychology of the camps. She knew any little thing could grow into life--or death."

The English Zone of Germany. Liberation and freedom. Di Tante and Fanny--mother and daughter--confront each other. I see and hear the scene. Di Tante is determined to find her husband Chaim. Fanny knows he cannot be alive. But Di Tante is stubborn. She refuses to give up hope. She will not abandon him. She will go back to Kovno to look for him. Nothing can sway her. If need be she will go without her daughter. Again life hangs in the balance. This is no stage play.

The lantern focusses on a scene that never took place. Di Tante is having a fall coat made. Fanny has bought the material for it with the pocket money we have given Di Tante. "The coat is very beautiful," Di Tante says, "and when it is finished I want to dress up with a pretty pocketbook from Leningrad and have my photograph taken and send you the pictures." She was going to do it in the spring. She never took that photograph. But I have it anyway.

Vilnius. Di Tante's birthday. Fanny and Osya and their *chaveyrim*--comrades all--have gathered around the table to celebrate the occasion with their "Babushka." They all know her because she is someone to know. For years they have tasted the dishes she has made for them--and her wit, too. You can feel the love flowing toward her from all around the table--all of them survivors of the Holocaust, all of them long since caught behind the Iron Curtain. And she feels their love. And with a motion of her hand, determined to let no one see, she hides the tear in her eye.

December 26, 1971. Di Tante stands on a carton packed with clothes. She is writing her last letter to us from the USSR. Like Fanny, Osya, and the children, she is packed and ready to go. In a few days she and the whole family will be in Vienna, then Israel. The *schifskarte* for 1914 passage from Antwerp across the Atlantic have been transformed into airline tickets for a flight to Israel. She ends her letter, more meaningfully than ever, "With great love and kisses." Fifty-eight years late.

My father. He sits at the kitchen table. He is writing one of his letters to his sister Dora--in Yiddish, not Russian. He writes it on December 30, 1958. I will not read it until Vilnius, 1970, when I hold it in my hands. "Nevertheless," he writes to her, "it is good to be alive to hear from each other. At least we are among the living." Words for my imagination.

At home the magic lantern lights up my brother's *Ah Malakh Veynt*--lights up his imagination in my own.

These scenes--these and all the others--they say, "Imagination makes the world."

A Normal Life

At the festivities following the marriage ceremony for a young friend of ours his grandmother, a survivor of a ghetto in Poland, rose to the microphone to say a few words to her grandson and his new wife. As she reached the end of her little speech, she paused for a few moments, perhaps to think back on her own Jewish history. Then, quietly, offering words that came from a private region known only to survivors of the Holocaust, she said, "What can I wish you? What I wish for you is a normal life."

When I was five, for all I knew, "normal" meant you had a mother and a father, also an older brother who went to high school and played tennis with a red-haired girl in Franklin Park across the street.

Normal for us ended quickly and abruptly in 1930. The Depression hit. Hard times. And nowhere an end to them in sight. Hitler, Germany, and Japan were waiting in the wings. When World War Two hit, first in Europe, then in the Pacific, the whole concept of "normal" became obsolete. At home, in spite of the inescapable realities, we clung desperately to the concept of normal because we had started with it. But the truth is, Depression and War loomed over daily life like nothing else to tell us our world would never be normal again. The truth is: the abnormal was becoming the norm.

Times were bad, very bad, in America and for America. But bad as they were they were heavenly compared to what was to befall Europe. There, before I was born, the slaughter of the first World War and the pogroms afterward had already doomed normal life. Between the wars, during the period of Lithuania's independence, Di Tante had time to taste a normal life in her marriage, her two children, and the thriving business she helped create. But normal was only temporary, a reprieve. It lasted long enough to become a memory that, by contrast, would only magnify the horror to follow.

Normal ended when the German-Soviet Pact took effect in June, 1940, when the USSR took over Lithuania, exiled many Jews to Siberia, and effectively put an end to a viable Jewish community. A year later the Germans attacked the USSR, drove the Russians from Lithuania, and began the Holocaust. On December 1, 1941, Karl Jaeger, commander of *Einsatzkommando* 3, reported that with the exception of Jews remaining in the Kovno, Shavli, and Vilna ghettos, his unit had "achieved the goal of solving the Jewish problem in Lithuania." The Soviets ended "normal" in Lithuania. Within six months the Germans and their Lithuanian collaborators uprooted and destroyed it entirely. Forever.

"I lived through two wars. Twice I lost everything," said Di Tante. What could normal mean to her after all that she had lost? What normal life could there be for Shaynke Chaya, the Tunnelerkeh, who was so "much to be pitied?" "No one is left from her family," said Di Tante. "All killed...no child, nothing. Hitler murdered them all." And what of the quarter of a century lived out under communism? Di Tante and her family stubbornly refused to surrender. They did not give up Jewish life--the holidays, an anniversary celebration, a birthday, the birth of a child: all had a semblance of normal. But it was a normal under relentless communist siege. It was a normal surrounded by the poisonous futility, waste, and corruption of a police state that ruled by fear--a normal not free to be itself.

Maybe there is no such thing as normal at all.

Or maybe normal is normal after all, a necessary breathing time between periods of abnormal disaster and evil. Maybe normal is what enables us to tell the difference between the two. Maybe it's what's necessary to give us time to recuperate before the next onslaught, to withstand insanity and give us just enough of a taste of hope and possibility to go on with life.

"I wish for you a normal life," she said. Simple words speaking special love, but drawn from the whole story of her abnormal knowledge.

The Besht

Two generations after the Holocaust many Germans are increasingly suffering from "Holocaust fatigue."[130] They are tired "of seeing their history reduced to the 12 Nazi years."[131]

What German, young professional or pensioned grandfather, wouldn't want to be freed of the guilt and shame he feels the world has imposed upon him? What German wouldn't want to close the door on the Holocaust? The current term in Germany for what they would like is *Vergangenheitsbewältigung*--a "coming to terms with the past," a "mastering of the past," even an "overcoming, an overpowering of the past." What they really want, for lack of a better word, is "closure," an end to the dead past. They would like nothing better than to close the door on the past and lock it away forever. "We were born after," they say. "We are not responsible. You can't blame us for the Holocaust. The Holocaust is over and done with." For them it is "Case closed." But not completely. The reporter covering the opening of Berlin's Jewish Museum suggested otherwise: "Chic, modern, reunited and wealthy, a postwar German generation blessed by the accident of a later birth came to celebrate the 2,000 year history of a religious minority that Germany absorbed, honored and then incinerated, in a paroxysm of hatred that will never be fully understood or forgotten."[132]

If postwar Germany longs for closure, Christianity, in one respect at least, rejects closure entirely: it has never forgotten the killing of Christ or the crucifixion, which long ago set the stage for the Holocaust. There is no way the Church can afford to forget the crucifixion. The crucifixion is the very life's blood of Christianity. It can't deny the very reason for the existence of the Church. Why is there anti-Semitism in a Poland without Jews? In the Former Soviet Union, where the Russian Orthodox Church is still a powerful force? And elsewhere across Europe and the West? Because, in the end, when all is said, there is no closure with respect to the crucifixion. How can a United Nations pass a "Zionism is racism" resolution?

How can students at English universities and on American college campuses--institutions of higher learning and enlightened thought--vote their agreement to such a slogan? How is it that there and elsewhere--in an awful reversal of killer and victim--the Jew has become the Nazi? In whatever form it reveals itself there is no closure in most of the Christian world on the longest hatred.

True, there have been regrets, apologies, calls for dialogue, and declarations of reconciliation and well-meaning efforts toward it. There are new teachings, but in the everyday world far from the world of theologians and scholars the reality is otherwise. In his article "What's Taught, Learned About Who Killed Christ" Gustav Niebuhr points out that for many observers close to the scene "there remains a gap between the nuances of scholarship and the understanding of ordinary believers."[133] The chilling interview of the Polish townspeople in front of their church in Claude Lanzmann's *Shoah* is a vivid example of the wide gap between the new in Catholic thinking and the continuing power of the old. In June, 1998, Kazimierz Switon, a former member of the Polish parliament, planted the first cross outside the Auschwitz concentration camp. A year later three hundred crosses had sprouted there. Government authorities had them removed. Only one cross remains there, the cross John Paul II used in his celebration of the Mass at Auschwitz in 1979. The crosses at Auschwitz did what the cross has done throughout the long history of Christianity's relationship to the Jew. They reminded the Jew of the centrality of the cross to Christianity--and therefore of what Christianity remembers most powerfully. Christianity's essential rejection of closure with respect to the crucifixion is precisely what makes such closure equally impossible for the Jew.

Until 1960-61 native born Israelis--the Sabras--had their own problems with closure. Not for them the Holocaust. Not for them the experience of Europe's Jews. They looked with shame, sometimes with scorn, upon the Jews who went "like sheep to the slaughter." They were often less than understanding of the few survivors of the Holocaust who managed to reach Israel. The Sabras considered themselves the "new" Jews, worlds removed from the *shtetl* Jew and his "diaspora mentality." Woefully uninformed about the Holocaust, they saw it as better off forgotten. They saw it as a blot upon Jewish history, not as a part of their own history. It took the capture and trial of Adolf Eichmann to reveal what they had closed off from themselves. The Eichmann trial forced them to face what is essential to their history. The trial became a turning point in their consciousness. They learned there could be no closure regarding the Holocaust, that its repetition would be an ever-present threat.

They learned what Jews worldwide know: that there is no statute of limitations for murder--not for one murder, not for six million. They learned that while forgiveness is possible for some things, there can be no forgiveness for the Holocaust. At the turn of the twentieth century apologies for the Holocaust have been flying thick and fast. But how can you even ask forgiveness for what is unforgivable? How do you close the door on a past that is unforgettable? The door won't close. Where there can be no forgetting, closure is impossible. The Holocaust permits no closure on memory. At a memorial gathering at Auschwitz Elie Wiesel was moved to say, "God of forgiveness, do not forgive these murderers of Jewish children here." Wiesel was speaking for all the children that were the first target of the Nazis: one and a half million children. To reject forgiveness, to refuse it, is to prevent forgetfulness, to keep memory alive, to forestall closure. Memory is what makes closure essentially impossible.

Memory is what makes life possible. Where memory no longer exists--to be a victim of Alzheimer's or amnesia--is to be deprived of all that makes us human. To be alive but without memory is to experience a living death without even knowing that you are undergoing the experience of a living death. What does "forgetting" mean? It means you lose the capacity to differentiate--right from wrong, good from evil. It means what Archbishop Olivier de Berranger said in 1997 at Drancy in his apology to the Jewish people for the silence of the French Catholic Church during the Holocaust, that "Conscience is formed by memory and no society can live in peace with itself on the basis of a false or repressed past, anymore than an individual can."[134]   In rejecting closure with respect to the Holocaust the Jew asserts his humanity--and makes closure equally impossible for Christianity.

Is there, then, no hope at all for closure--for Christians and Jews, for Germans, Lithuanians, French, and others--who, one way or another, have been touched by the Holocaust?   Probably not--at least not for the foreseeable future. If there is any hope at all for closure, it lies perhaps in the words of Israel Baal Shem Tov (the Master of the Good Name).   The Besht, as he is called, founded the Hasidic movement in eighteenth century Eastern Europe. He was the first of the great Hasidic masters. "Forgetting," he warned, "lengthens the period of exile. In remembrance lies the secret of deliverance." He intended his words for his followers, but ever since then his words have articulated their special burden of truth for all Jews who have any sense at all of their place in Jewish history. I don't think he had Christians in mind when he said them. But they contain an offer that applies at least as powerfully to Christians--Christians who, since the Holocaust, have any sense at all of their place in Jewish history. In a way, incredibly enough, the Besht turns out to be a better Christian than the Christian!

Expiation? Atonement? Sincere as the Christian desire for them may be, they are next to impossible to attain. Sincerity is no substitute for knowledge--the knowledge of what the Holocaust actually was. But if they were at all attainable, why maybe then one could imagine the Besht saying, "OK, if that's what you truly want, you have to go back to where you came from. *All* the way back. Maybe then."

Fargest Unz Nit

What, then, of my father's *schifskarte*, letters, and packages sent so long ago?

Amalek was not part of my father's vocabulary. He knew him only as Nickolai, reason enough, though, to leave the Old World for the New. But my father was eighteen, too, and he had a touch of the wanderlust. Nor could he have been immune to the spirit and tensions of his time. Whatever his reasons, and there must have been others, he must have known crossing the ocean meant separation from his family forever, but it did not mean he could abandon his mother or his little sister. He worried for them, cared for them. The *schifskarte*, letters, and packages are "history" now, reminders of how geography is destiny in Jewish history. But they were also once an expression of love beyond duty. "Each month," Di Tante remembered of her brother Henoch, "he sent money to Di Mameh." Sent *schifskarte* for her and Di Mameh. Sent for his brother Max. Sent packages to his sister when he was able. Sent a touch of hope when he could. It was not in him to forget what he had left behind.

The Baal Shem Tov was not part of my father's vocabulary either. My father was a Litvak, after all, and far removed from the world of the Hasidim. He did not know the Besht's axiom that "Forgetting lengthens the period of exile. In remembrance lies the secret of deliverance." He did not need to know it. In his own way he simply lived it.

What, then, of the *schifskarte*, letters, and packages for Di Tante? Of that first turning point in her life, that first time she turned back? She explains that in 1914 "we had two tickets for ship's passage-- Mama and I--that my good brother sent to bring us to him in America. But it was not to be...." In her "biography" she recalls, "The First World War began in 1914. This was also terrifying. When the war began all the Jews were sent away. The reason given was that Kovno had a fortress and the Jews were considered the worst enemies and spies. So I, a little girl, and my sick mother were considered enemies. You can imagine the suffering and troubles I endured. This can in no way be written out. I was a little girl but faithful....Would you say otherwise?" Di Tante and her mother were expelled from Kovno in 1915. From then on Di Tante remained with her mother, eventually to return to Kovno. Maybe the truth is that she could not--would not--pursue America and leave her mother behind.

What, then, of that second turning point in her life, in 1945, when for the second time she turned back to Kovno? It, too, hinged on a refusal, this time her refusal to leave her husband Chaim behind if there was even the remotest chance that he had survived the concentration camps. Hers was a loyalty beyond all reason. It was not in her to forget him. Within the woman she had become there was still "a little girl but faithful....Would you say otherwise?"

"*Fargest unz nit!*" These were Osya's last words to us in 1970. They followed us as we turned away from him, Di Tante, and the family to board our plane. Back then they were plea, hope, warning, fear. Even as he called them out to us I knew they would remain with me forever. They always return me to him and lock me to that moment. But they reach far out beyond him and his urgency. *Fargest unz nit.* Do not forget us.

Fargest unz nit. This is the theme.

Mann Trakht

In the beginning were two postcards.

"*Mann trakht uhn Gott lakht,*" Di Tante wrote to my father. She knew her proverbs.

The problem is that the English translation--"Man thinks and God laughs"--does no justice to the Yiddish, the pointed rhyme, or the deeper meanings. My brother called one of his statues *Fartrakht.* It is a figure of an old Jew sculpted from a single log. His eyes almost closed, he holds his beard with his right hand, keeps his left behind him in the classic pose of an old Jew "lost in thought" in an old world of his own making. The "*trakht*" inside "*fartrakht*" suggests depths in the "*trakht*" of the proverb far beyond the English "thinks." Paired as they are, man and God, *trakht* with *lakht*--God's laughter--this proverb opens immense areas of history, theology, philosophy, and God knows what else. At the same time it is more ironic, more subversive than any other I know, more terrifying, too, for its implication of a cosmic joke.

In my grammar school and high school years I knew little enough about my aunt and her history. Dimly I knew she was to have come to America. What had happened? Why didn't she come? What about *schfskarte*? In the beginning I did not know, nor for decades later. And all the while the "answer" was lying there undisturbed in the orange lacquer box--but illegible even if I could have mastered the miniscule Yiddish handwriting on Di Tante's postcards. I had no idea how history begets history.

In June, 1959, she wrote, "In the year '14 we had two tickets for ship's passage--Mama and I--that my good brother sent to bring us to him in America. But it was not to be. The tickets were for passage from Antwerp. Just then the war broke out....And that, my dear ones, is how my life worked out."

Well, not exactly.

Nowhere in her writings or elsewhere does she explain why she did not use the *schifskarte* my father had sent her. Perhaps the chaos of the war upset her world and made leaving it impossible. Perhaps she lost the two tickets because of the war. Either way, though, afterward she could have written her brother to send tickets to her again. She did not. What happened? I suppose life happened. Did her mother decide to remain in Kovno? Did Di Tante refuse to abandon her mother? Did she give up her dream of America for other dreams? Marriage? A family? I have no way of knowing. All I know is that she went home--to Kovno.

In 1991 Fanny recalled that after Di Tante had recuperated from the foot broken in Bergen-Belsen, "Di Mameh began to complain that she must find Der Fohter, that she must go back to Kovno. When I

409

fought hard and begged her not to do this, she said that if I did not go, she would go alone. I was a good daughter--and I went. And this is how she went 'home' for the second time in her life."

Twice Di Tante "went back." Twice she chose. Once under Nikolai. Once under Stalin. The first time--though she could not have known it--her decision to remain in Europe meant she and her family would be trapped in the Kovno Ghetto. The second time, her decision to go back home to Kovno to search for her husband--a hopeless search--meant she doomed herself to be trapped in the Soviet Union. Worse, the first mistake laid the groundwork for the second.

Every life bound up with hers felt the consequences, the ultimately terrifying consequences of her decisions. I do not know how she lived with the knowledge of these consequences, these tragic, unintended consequences. I cannot bring myself to imagine the sorrow and the anguish that must have haunted her thoughts. What words can describe such suffering, such pain? No human being should have been expected to pay such a price--not Di Tante, she of such kindness, goodness, *khokhma*. She of the good intentions. No, not Di Tante.

No. There must be a way to blame the history of the twentieth century. There must be a way to blame History--the history that begets history that, in turn, begets history.

...uhn Gott lakht.

The Telephone

For decades now I have gone where historians, theologians, philosophers, and other scholars of the Holocaust have taken me, and I admit they have taken me far indeed. But for all that they may have discovered in pursuing the Holocaust in terms of their specialties, I have found that for the most part they have pursued the facts rather than reached into the heart of the matter. The Holocaust is more than a "subject" for study.

When I come away from them I often feel that they and their special vocabularies have missed the mark. Of necessity the very words they use tend to be cool, objective, analytic--far removed from the flames, far from the Ninth Fort. The unique world of testimony, memoir, and fiction--so called "Holocaust literature" at its most honest--is closer to the truth. When I open Chaim Kaplan's *Diary* and begin to read, I forget myself, lose all sense of present time and place, forget even that I am reading. Kaplan immerses me in the Warsaw Ghetto and I cannot get out. Avraham Tory's *Diary* takes me into the Kovno Ghetto and Ephraim Oshry's Yiddish holds me in his *Churbn Lite*, his "Chronicle of the Destruction of the Sacred Jewish Communities of Lithuania, 1941-1945." Ilya Ehrenburg and Vasily Grossman do the same with the testimonies they compiled in *The Black Book* to indict the "German-Fascist Invaders" who murdered Jews in the USSR and in the death camps in Poland.

When I begin to read "The People Who Walked On," in Tadeusz Borowski's *This Way for the Gas, Ladies and Gentlemen*, I know I have entered a place where the concept of a normal life no longer exists. It is "fiction" unlike any fiction ever written before. In this story the narrator is a worker prisoner in Auschwitz like Borowski himself. He has the Sunday off and he is the goalkeeper for his soccer team. Retrieving a ball that has rolled out of bounds behind the goal, he notes that a train has arrived on the ramp behind the field and begun to disgorge its cattle cars. He sees women "already wearing summer dresses" and men in their white shirts falling into a procession growing ever larger. He sees them look in the direction of the field. Returning to the game, he puts the ball back into play. It goes back and forth on the field, first one way, then another, again, and again. Once more it gets past the goal. When he goes to retrieve it he sees the ramp is empty, that the train has gone, and "not one person remained." His only comment: "Between two throw-ins in a soccer game, right behind my back, three thousand people had been put to death." But it is enough--enough for you to know that Borowski has taken you where you have never been before.

Elli, a memoir by Livia E. Bitton Jackson, is the experience of a thirteen year old girl flung into the inexorable pattern: expulsion, ghetto, deportation, cattle cars, Auschwitz. Elli survives, but she will long forever for her lost world and be forever inconsolable: "Our entire world rose up like smoke into nothingness, all those achingly dear to us. They are all gone, robbed of life."

The bystanders who watch the Jewish exodus to the ghetto, she understands, "are on the other side of the fence. A world separates us because they do not understand. But we all within the fence, we understand."

And, as ever, understanding is at the heart of the matter. "How can anyone understand the aching that is Auschwitz?" she asks. "The compulsion to fill the void that is Auschwitz? The search, the reaching out. The futility. The irrevocable statement that is Auschwitz. Who can understand the inconceivable futility that is Auschwitz. The loss of perspective. The loss. The total, irreconcilable loss."

"I belong to this void," she says. "Nothing can change that. Nothing. My search for a home, for human relationships, for knowledge. This is one unalterable allegiance. This is where I belong. To Auschwitz."

The scholars in the academy are not equipped to enter Elli's territory, nor Primo Levi's who, shortly after his return from Auschwitz in 1946 wrote a poem called "Shema," a title and a word which refers immediately and directly to "Hear, O Israel, the Lord is our God, the Lord is One," the key statement at the very heart of Jewish faith:

You who live secure
    In your warm houses,
      Who, returning at evening, find
Hot food and friendly faces:
    Consider whether this is a man,
    Who labours in the mud
    Who knows no peace
    Who fights for a crust of bread
    Who dies at a yes or no.
    Consider whether this is a woman,
    Without hair or name
    With no more strength to remember
    Eyes empty and womb cold
    As a frog in winter.
Consider that this has been:
I commend these words to you.
Engrave them on your hearts
When you are in your house, when you walk on your way
When you go to bed, when you rise:
Repeat them to your children.
    Or may your house crumble,
    Disease render you powerless,
        Your offspring avert their faces from you.[135]

This "Shema" could only have been dictated by Auschwitz.

"Immerse yourself" said Dr. Elkes in his Last Testament. But immersing yourself is an internal affair and therefore has its dangers. Sometimes it happens, though, that you do immerse yourself. You never know you are immersing yourself when you do it. You know that you have immersed yourself only after you have returned from immersing yourself. You know you have been there when you remember feeling "Zero at the bone." That's what Emily Dickinson called it. It is where Kaplan, Borowski, Levi, and Elkes himself take you. The danger is that you may not find your way back--that you will

413

forever after be somewhere else, never knowing that you didn't get back in time.

My phone rings and rings again, and again. It breaks the silence surrounding me. I am grateful for the aftershock. It tells me I am back home again.

Der Nayenter Fort

You always come back to it. There were other forts encircling Kovno where the killing took place--the Seventh Fort, the Fourth Fort. But the Ninth Fort—*Der Nayenter Fort*--the worst of them, is still the least known major killing center of the Holocaust. The Ninth Fort was the Lithuanian Auschwitz.

The Germans followed a pattern in their larger-scale operations during the Holocaust. They took Jews from their homes by deception, threat, or force, brought them to a central location, sent them to a ghetto, then to a concentration camp or straight to a death camp. The efficient train system inexorably transported the Jews to their destination. Trains transported "foreign" Jews to Kovno. They were then generally marched directly to the Ninth Fort. The Kovno Ghetto, however, was unusual in at least one respect. The Kovno Jews did not have to be rounded up to be transported anywhere. They were simply forced into Slobotkeh. Thereafter, the Ninth Fort was always ready for them.

In the title story of *This Way for the Gas, Ladies and Gentlemen*, Henri counsels the narrator--both of them working prisoners at Auschwitz-- "Patience, patience. When the new transports come, I'll bring you all you want." What he promises him is the best he can find from the food and clothing the doomed Jews leave behind them on the ramp where they are debarked from the trains. But the narrator has deep and not unreasonable concerns. What will happen, he demands to know, when the transports stop coming. "One hears all kind of talk, and, dammit," he worries, "they'll run out of people."

414

The Germans and their Lithuanian collaborators did run out of Lithuanian Jews. A surviving remnant--the Association of Lithuanian Jews in the American Zone in Germany--knew the awful truth. As "living witnesses" to the destruction of Lithuaniana Jewry they held a conference in Munich in mid-April, 1947, to declare to the Jewish and non-Jewish world the "Guilt of the Lithuanian People in the Extermination of Lithuanian Jewry." "To our great sorrow we must assert that the smaller Jewish communities in the Lithuanian provinces were destroyed exclusively by Lithuanians and the larger communities with their full participation." They charged every level of Lithuanian society--the intelligentsia, government officials, farmers, craftsmen, workers, etc.--with active cooperation with the Germans.[136]

A half century later, the Lithuanian poet Sigitas Geda was uncommonly well aware of the Lithuanian role in the destruction of Lithuanian Jewry. Deeply moved by the Last Testament of Elkhanan Elkes, he republished it in his *Athens of the North* and wrote of it, "We have not paid our debt. It does not matter that we didn't know we had a debt. It does not matter that we, or our parents, or our grandparents, did not kill anyone. We belong to a nation that raised murderers. I am afraid that any decent person reading this text will stop smiling. I feel it in myself and through myself" (13 May 1995).[137]

"The Germans will never forgive the Jews for Auschwitz," says Bonn journalist Wolfgang Storz. "They know their guilt, but don't want to be reminded of it."[138] Lithuanians will never forgive the Lithuanian Jews for their Auschwitz either.

Debts

The call came on a Sunday afternoon in mid-November, 1993. It was from my cousin Fanya in Sydney. The moment I heard her voice, I saw myself again looking out the window of their seventh floor apartment on Bondi Road, looking out at the Opera House gleaming full sail in the distance. Surprised and delighted to hear her voice, I shouted my joy and laughter thousands of miles down to the edge of the world.

"Do not laugh," she cut me off. "Abrasha has died."

For years hardly a week goes by that I do not somewhere come upon the death notice of yet another survivor of the Holocaust. Sometimes the obituary will carry a few lines about a miraculous escape. But there is no escaping the nameless ache that takes hold as I read it. There is no escaping the toll that death is taking among the ever-thinning ranks of the survivors at the very moment that the old enemies are re-emerging in the shape of new Nazis to spread the poison of anti-Semitism once again.

I cannot measure my debt to Abrasha. I owe him for memories of two of the happiest weeks in my life--for two weeks of non-stop conversation with him in January, 1991.

How many times since that call have I taken *They Marched Us Three Nights* from its shelf in my library to listen to Abrasha's voice again.

To hear again the story he tells of Lubocki the teacher, who made a statement by invariably introducing himself as "Lubocki the teacher," no first name necessary. Lubocki was a Yiddishist and saw the teaching of Yiddish as "the solution for all Jewish problems." Abrasha tells how Lubocki would often come to visit a student or a fellow teacher in the Vilna Ghetto hospital, how he would remain afterward to talk philosophy with Abrasha, and how they became fast friends even though Abrasha's Warsaw accented Yiddish could only have grated on Lubocki's Lithuanian ear.

Lubocki and Abrasha were both deported to Kivioli. And both became patients in the camp hospital. Often they heard shots outside the hospital walls, marking the executions of those too slow in recovering. One day, much weakened by illness, Lubocki, an agnostic, turned to Abrasha and said, "You are young and you may leave this room, join the other prisoners and be transported somewhere to

416

another camp. One day you may return to a free world. If you ever meet Wilnoites who have heard of Lubocki the teacher, tell them you were with him in the last hours of his life and you heard his last warning: Don't deprive children of the word of God unless you are sure you have a better substitute...there is no better substitute."

Abrasha kept his promise to Lubocki. "For many years afterwards," he said, "I would retell the story to anyone willing to listen. The Wilnoites listened eagerly. To others, whether they liked it or not, I also told the story."

I open Abrasha's book to see again the scene of the blessing in the Bavarian forest. Five of them had just made their escape from the death march: Abrasha, Szymon Gitelson, Mark Dworzecki, Chaim Hilel Fryd--doctors all--and one remembered only as Badanes. After years of ceaseless hunger they had managed to find real food. Yet, there in the forest, they all stood and waited quietly for Fryd to say the blessing before they fell upon it. Abrasha recounts how thirty-five years later, overcome by memory, he had the privilege of saying the same blessing, the *Shehekheyanu*, at the Passover Seder in Chaim Hilel's home in Tel Aviv. I cannot go to a Seder now without hearing him say, "Blessed art Thou, O Lord, King of the Universe, Who has kept us alive, and preserved us, and enabled us to reach this season."

Abrasha loved his patients, even those who drove him to distraction. Surely he could only have loved the patient who came in one day complaining of exhaustion. Abrasha asked if it was the heat that was troubling him. "No, Dr. Wajnryb," he answered, "it's not the heat. It's the humanity."

I still have fixed in my mind the image of Abrasha hunched over the typewriter in his study, his fingers leaping over the keys. His last article appeared in *The Melbourne Yiddish News* less than a month before his death. He called it "We Must Not Be Silent." Drawing upon Deborah Lipstadt's *Denying the Holocaust*, he took direct aim at Robert Faurisson, Jean-Marie Le Pen, Leon Degrelle, and other Holocaust deniers, but especially at David Irving who was then seeking

417

government permission to enter Australia to sell his own brand of Holocaust denial.

Abrasha's final paragraph was a warning to those in the Australian Jewish community who counseled silence and a low profile in the Irving affair. It was also a protest against all deniers of the Holocaust. "We, the still miraculously living survivors of the remnant," he wrote, "have the full right to protest! We promised the murdered and the burned, those tortured to death, that we will tell and transmit to future generations what took place there. We tell and we shall continue to tell. Now there lies an even more holy debt upon us: to discredit the lies and disqualify their authors. This is the debt we pay. The moral power of the debt is a lot stronger and more significant than...[the] call to silence! This is not the road to take!"

Abrasha knew the moral power of the debt. He knew no one could ever tell the whole story. He also knew it had to be told and that the telling must continue. Abrasha never ceased paying his debt.

And I shall never be able to pay my debt to him.

The Impossible

Whenever I heard Di Tante or some other survivor say *uhn azoy iz geven*--"and so it was"--I knew the words did not simply signal the end of a story: they asserted the story was testimony beyond question. When Fanny or some other survivor would say, "There it is, the whole story," I knew the same stamp of finality and truth had been affixed to it.

Still, whenever I hear a survivor speak--or keep his silence--I know the one question I fear to ask, have no right to ask, and do not ask is the question I want most to ask: "How did you survive?" Survivors know something I do not know. They have a special knowledge that they do not offer to share. I know my question is off-limits. And yet I am desperate to know the answer--as though my life depended on it.

Di Tante and Fanya were not strangers. They were *familye*, after all: they, if anyone, would surely reveal the secret to me. If anyone knew it firsthand, they did. They were not only eyewitnesses: they had lived the secret. If only they told me the secret, I might live off it forever.

And so, instead of asking the main question directly, from time to time I would go roundabout and ask them for their memories--of people, places, events in times past. Of my father. Of Kovno. The War. Perhaps, by some chance, they'd tell me.

Or I'd search the letters. I do not possess every letter Di Tante wrote my father, my brother, or me, but beginning with the first one I do have, written in 1958, reading them invariably puts me in suspense. And invariably I think I will discover something I have somehow overlooked--some clue to the answer.

Di Tante is not one who fears putting pen to paper. But when she comes to write of the Shoah, she has to admit "it doesn't come out in the writing as it did in life." When the war came to Kovno in 1941, she says, "Everything was taken from us, and we were sent into the ghetto....It was a sorrowful time. We were fenced in with barbed wire and guarded by many soldiers. They used to force us to work." But then she stops short and says, "You can imagine for yourself how they tormented us." When she writes of her son's death, she says again, "You can imagine the effect of all this on me. I write in brief: one can't put everything down on paper."

She tells my brother how "through great wonders and miracles my daughter and I remained alive," how her husband and son did not, and adds "when we turned back home--what home? when home?--we didn't even have anything to eat or anything to begin life with." Again she stops short: "You can imagine how tragic it was." As for "that beautiful lager Bergen-Belsen," she says, "Can any books describe these matters? Impossible."

To me she explains, "To write all that you ask is impossible. This can only be done verbally." Moreover, "If I were to write you everything about the war...what will all this be for you except grief? I do not want to tell you what Fanya and I suffered. I cannot forget this. But why do you too need this grief?"

The Impossible, she maintains, is too much for her to convey, too much for another to absorb. Her own words fail in the face of the Impossible. She counsels me to use my imagination. But how can one imagine the Impossible? Imagination cannot go beyond itself. How is one to imagine what is beyond the imagination of mankind?

Still, I did not give up. When I wrote to her in Israel, I offered a business arrangement: a dollar a page for all she would write about her past. She shot back in February, 1972, only days after her arrival there, "I understand your joking about paying me for my writing....In the next few days I will send you all that I remember of the old days. As for the cost, we will no doubt come to terms. Or will we both have to bargain?" In March she rewarded me with "My Biography."

"Only ten pages for a whole life? Impossible!" I complained. "Tante," I said, "for a thousand pages you can earn a thousand dollars!" The ten pages were all that there were to be.

But Di Tante understood the problem. "It seems to me I have written much," she said, "and if it is too little, you can add as much as you like. Whatever you add will still not be enough. But now you will have work to do, with so much to read and add." And she left me with the problem.

I have worked and read and discovered stories to add. Whatever I have added is still not enough.

The whole story? There is no whole story.

Ah Malakh Veynt

Several of my brother's sculptures have been living with me since he died. And I with them. I have grown older with them. I love them, not least of all for the story each one tells.

Ah Malakh Veynt is a sculpture unlike any other my brother created. It is different from all the others in its composition and execution. It is stark in mood and abstract in form. No whimsy or humor here. It blocks out its space darkly.

You can always identify my brother's work by the hands that appear in them. They appear in sculpture after sculpture, never twice the same. They are his signature. In this sculpture what you see first of all are the hands. Hands everywhere. The central figure seems enveloped by hands. You can't help but focus on these hands because they are larger than the face of the central figure itself.

When someone asks me about this piece I tell him to count the hands. Almost every time people will come up with the wrong number. You have to count all the hands before you can begin to understand the sculpture. Eventually you can single out six large hands, all of them related but each different from the others. One hand thrusts upward in defiance. Each of the other five expresses a different idea, a different emotion. The two hands of the central figure cover its face up to its eyes. You can easily miss the final two hands, one on each shoulder. They appear unaccountably from somewhere behind the figure. Ten in all.

My brother called his sculpture *Ah Malakh Veynt*--An Angel Weeps. He took the name from a Yiddish poem. The six hands? The six million. The hand on each shoulder? The hands of God.

My brother was not a believer, and *Ah Malakh Veynt* is not a "religious" statue. Not in any ordinary sense. You do not see the tears behind the angel's hands. But if you see them you realize my brother's sculpture is a poem.

EPILOGUE

In his story "A Visit" Tadeusz Borowski writes how those who were doomed to die in Auschwitz "begged the orderlies loading them into the crematorium trucks to remember what they saw. And to tell the truth about mankind to those who do not know it." *This Way for the Gas, Ladies and Gentlemen* does for them exactly what they wanted. Its stories are not in the realm of "ordinary" literature. They come from the realm of the Holocaust universe, from a region beyond the imagination of mankind. They carry messages from the other side, from the anti-world. Messages of indisputable truth.

Like Borowski--like any serious poet--my brother was a "maker." He sketched on paper the figures he saw in his imagination; he envisioned them embodied in a block of wood or a log. Then, as the chips flew, his mallet and chisel materialized them, breathed the breath of life and freedom into them. For all the humor with which he sometimes endowed them, they have stories to tell of truths from this side of the divide to those who do not know them.

How often did Di Tante exclaim "What can happen in a lifetime!" and "What can happen in five short days!" She wrote fragments of her story and lamented the impossibility of telling the rest. She lived her stories on both sides of the divide. Fanny and Abrasha told me stories that they, too, had lived on both sides of the divide. But it was Di Tante, overwhelmed by the wonder of our appearance in her life--coming from one side of the curtain to her on the other--who in one breath declared, "This is only to be read in stories," and in the next proclaimed, as proof to herself and to all, "But, after all, this is true!"

I often hear my stories on the Green Bay Trail, especially when I have the path all to myself. When I catch a glimpse of the rails heading north to Kenosha or south to Chicago, I am as fascinated as ever to see their parallel lines merge and magically disappear in the far distance. I know that sooner or later, but on time, I will hear the blast of the horn and the roar and rumble of the outbound or the inbound as it passes me by. Though the sounds will break the silence around me, I take a certain comfort in them. I know they belong to a train that if it takes me anywhere, it is to Chicago and back.

It is 2004. I see wild flowers bordering both sides of the path, hear the hum of September bees as I walk north toward town. The intermittent sun shines through the overarching trees.   Where the path ends at a parking lot about a block before the central train station, I leave it and cross the street to continue on the sidewalk.

I walk in freedom past the Town Hall where the flag snaps red, white, and blue against a blue sky. A cool northeast wind blows toward me from Lake Michigan, and I push against it to pass the town library. The civic sculpture on its lawn holds no meaning for me, and I do my best to ignore it. The center of town goes about its business as though there were peace in the world. I mail my letter in the mailbox in front of the bank, turn back on the sidewalk, pass the library again and the Town Hall. Across the street the clock in the tower of the central train station tells me what time it is. Time to retrace my steps.

There is no whole story. But there are stories. Stories to wonder over. Stories that insist on living, like all stories that have truth to tell about mankind in the twentieth century to those who do not know it. Abrasha told and retold the story of his friend Lubocki to those who were willing to listen, and "To others, whether they liked it or not," he said, "I also told the story." In the last paragraph he wrote before his death he said again about the Shoah, "We tell and we shall continue to tell."

There is no whole story--only a story made out of stories and fragments of stories, a story carved out of memories and into existence. And, yes, *ahzoy iz geven*--and so it was. And so it is. And the telling will continue. Because in memories begin responsibilities. Because in stories begin responsibilities.   And because I am mindful that my familiar path could well have been another, that it could have led as easily to the Ninth Fort as to my home.

Bibliographical

Anissimov, Myriam. *Primo Levi: Tragedy of an Optimist.* Woodstock, N.Y.: Overlook Press, 1999.

Appelfeld, Aharon. *Beyond Despair.* Translated by Jeffrey M. Green. New York: Fromm International Publishing Corporation, 1994.

Bergelson, David. *Naye Dertseylungen.* Volume 1 of Selected Works. Buenos Aires: ICUF Publishers, 1949.

Borowski, Tadeusz. *This Way for the Gas, Ladies and Gentlemen.* Translated by Barbara Vedder. New York: Penguin Books, 1976.

Camus, Albert. *Resistance, Rebellion, and Death.* Translated by Justin O'Brien. New York: Alfred A. Knopf, 1961.

Documents on the Holocaust. Edited by Yitzhak Arad, Israel Gutman, and Abraham Margaliot. Jerusalem: Yad Vashem, 1981.

Encyclopedia of the Holocaust. Israel Gutman, editor-in-chief. New York: Macmillan Publishing Company, 1990.

Faitelson, Alex. *Heroism & Bravery in Lithuania, 1941-1945.* Jerusalem: Gefen Publishing House, 1996.

Frank, Niklas. *In the Shadow of the Reich.* Translated by Arthur S. Wensinger. New York: Alfred A. Knopf, 1991.

Gar, Josef. *Umkum fun der Yidisher Kovne.* Munich: Central Committee of the Liberated Jews of the U.S. Zone, 1948.

Greenbaum, Masha. *The Jews of Lithuania: A History of a Remarkable Community: 1316-1945.* Jerusalem: Gefen Publishing House, Ltd., 1995.

Hartman, Geoffrey, ed. *Bitburg in Moral and Political Perspective.* Bloomington: Indiana University Press, 1986.

Hidden History of the Kovno Ghetto. Boston: Bullfinch Press, 1972. A project of the U.S. Holocaust Memorial Museum.

Hilberg, Raul. *The Destruction of the European Jews.* New York: Harper Colophon Books, 1961.

Kaplan, Chaim. *The Warsaw Diary of Chaim A. Kaplan.* Revised and translated by Abraham I. Katsh. New York: Collier Books, 1973.

Mishell, William W. *Kaddish for Kovno: Life and Death in a Lithuanian Ghetto 1941-1945.* Chicago: Chicago Review Press, 1988.

Morse, Arthur D. *While Six Million Died: A Chronicle of American Apathy*. New York: Hart Publishing Company, Inc., 1967.

Oshry, Ephraim. *Churbn Lite: The Ruins of Lithuania: A Chronicle of the Destruction of the Sacred Communities of Lithuania 1941-1945*. New York and Montreal: Oshry Book Committee, 1951.

_____. *Responsa from the Holocaust*. Translated from the Hebrew by Y. Leiman. New York: Judaica Press, 1983.

Ringelblum, Emmanuel. *Notes from the Warsaw Ghetto: The Journal of Emmanuel Ringelblum*. Edited and translated by Jacob Sloan. New York: McGraw-Hill Book Company, 1958.

Talmage, Frank E., ed. *Disputation and Dialogue*. New York: Ktav Publishing House, 1975.

Tory, Avraham. *Surviving the Holocaust: The Kovno Ghetto Diary*. Edited by Martin Gilbert and translated by Jerzy Michalowicz. Cambridge, Massachusetts and London, England: Harvard University Press, 1990.

End Notes

1 All figures for Jewish emigration from USSR are from Robert O. Freedman, ed., *Soviet Jewry in the Decisive Decade, 1971-80* (Durham, North Carolina: Duke University Press, 1984), p. 22.

2 Joseph Gar, "Concentration Camp Bergen-Belsen," in *Holocaust and Rebirth: Bergen-Belsen, 1945-1965* (New York: Bergen-Belsen Memorial Press, 1965), p. LXXXI.

3 Ephraim Oshry, *Churbn Lite: The Ruins of Lithuania: A Chronicle of the Destruction of the Sacred Communities of Lithuania, 1941-1945* (New York and Montreal: Oshry Book Committee, 1951), p. 84.

4 Avraham Tory, *Surviving the Holocaust: The Kovno Ghetto Diary*, ed. by Martin Gilbert and trans. by Jerzy Michalowicz (Cambridge, Massachusetts, and London, England: Harvard University Press, 1940), pp. 503-07.

5 William Mishell, *Kaddish for Kovno: Life and Death in a Lithuanian Ghetto 1941-1945* (Chicago: Chicago Review Press, 1988), pp. 170-71.

6 Alex Faitelson, *Heroism & Bravery in Lithuania, 1941-1945* (Jerusalem: Gefen Publishing House, 1996), p. 177.

7 *Kovno Ghetto: A Buried History* (1997). Written and narrated by Martin Gilbert. Directed and produced by Herbert Krosney for A & E Network and the History Channel.

8 All remarks in this paragraph are from Kadushin's remarks made at the Washington, D.C. exhibit. All other remarks are from the documentary.

9 Josef Gar, *Umkum fun der Yidisher Kovne* (Munich: Central Committee of the Liberated Jews of the U. S. Zone, 1948), p. 74.

10 Masha Greenbaum, *The Jews of Lithuania: A History of a Remarkable Community: 1316-1943* (Jerusalem: Gefen Publishing House Ltd., 1995), p. 325.

11 *Umkum*, p. 78.

12 *Documents on the Holocaust*, ed. by Yitzhak Arad, Yisrael Gutman, and Abraham Margaliot (Jerusalem: Yad Vashem, 1981), pp. 405-06.

[13] Dov Levin, "Ruins and Remembrance" in *Hidden History of the Kovno Ghetto* (Boston: Bullfinch Press, 1972), p. 224.

[14] Dov Levin, *Lietuviu Aktyvistu Frontas* in *Encyclopedia of the Holocaust* (New York: Macmillan Company, 1990), p. 876.

[15] Faitelson, p. 21.

[16] *Documents on the Holocaust*, pp. 389-90.

[17] Mishell, p. 28.

[18] Tory, p. 61.

[19] Jaeger Report in Appendix A, *Kaddish for Kovno*, p. 388.

[20] *Ibid.* The "shooting paradise" term is Martin Gilbert's emendation for the obscure "parade shooting" in the Jaeger Report. See his *The Holocaust: A History of the Jews of Europe during the Second World War.*

[21] Tory, p. 61.

[22] Ephraim Oshry, *Responsa from the Holocaust*, trans. from the Hebrew by Y. Leiman (New York: Judaica Press, 1983), p. 161.

[23] Faitelson, p. 91.

[24] Jaeger Report, in Appendix A of *Kaddish for Kovno*, p. 386.

[25] *Churbn Lite*, p. 83.

[26] *Ibid.*, p. 81.

[27] Arthur D. Morse, *While Six Million Died* (New York: Hart Publishing Co., Inc., 1967), p. 210.

[28] Claude B. Foster, "Historical Antecedents: Why the Holocaust?" in *The Annals of The American Academy of Political and Social Science* (July, 1980), p. 15.

[29] (http://www.pbs.org/wgbh/amex/holocaust/filmmore/reference/primary/barmemo.html)

[30] Morse, p. 91.

[31] Tory, p. 238.

[32] *Responsa*, p. xviii.

[33] *Ibid.*, p. xx.

[34] *Churbn Lite*, p. 85.

[35] *Responsa*, p. 190.

[36] *Churbn Lite*, p. 309.

[37] *Hidden History of the Kovno Ghetto*, p. 215.

[38] *Responsa*, p. 210.

[39] *Churbn Lite*, p. 137.

[40] *Ibid.*, p. 310.

[41] *Responsa*, p. 148.

[42] Chaim A. Kaplan, *The Warsaw Diary of Chaim A. Kaplan*, rev. and ed. by Abraham I. Katsh (New York: Collier Books, 1973), p. 139.

[43] Yair Sheleq, "Digging for the ghetto's terrible history," (Http://www.haaretz.com/digging-for-the-ghetto-s-terrible-history-1.13908), July 24, 2004.

[44] Emmanuel Ringelblum, *Notes from the Warsaw Ghetto: The Journal of Emmanuel Ringeblum*, ed. and trans. by Jacob Sloan (New York: McGraw-Hill Book Company, 1958), p. 301.

[45] Tadeusz Borowski, *This Way for the Gas, Ladies and Gentlemen* (Penguin Books, 1976), p. 11.

[46] *Ibid.*, p. 17.

[47] *Documents on the Holocaust*, p. 398.

[48] Roger Cohen, review of Frederick Kempe's *Father/Land* in *The New York Times Book Review*, July 11, 1999.

[49] George Will, " Holocaust Museum: Antidote for Innocence," *The Washington Post*, March 10, 1983.

[50] George Will, "The Stones of Treblinka Cry Out," *The Washington Post*, September 10, 1989.

[51] Johnny Heller, "NU prof pursues war-crimes case vs. Nazi suspect," North/Northwest Supplement *Suburban Sun-Times*, April 11, 1980.

[52] Tory, p. 411.

[53] Ringelblum, p. 65.

5

54 Speech in Munich, December 17, 1922. See Robert Wistrich, *Hitler and the Holocaust* (New York: Modern Library, 2001), pp. 122-23.

55 Speech to American Jewish Committee Interreligious Affairs Commission, *Jewish Press*, June 2, 1978.

56 Eliezer Berkovits, "Judaism in the post-Christian Era," *Judaism*, Vol. 15, 1966, collected in *Disputation and Dialogue,* ed. by Frank E Talmage (New York: Ktav Publishing House, 1975), p. 288.

57 *Umkum,* p. 42.

58 *Ibid.*

59 *Ibid.,* p. 279.

60 *Responsa,* p. xxiv.

61 *Ibid.,* p. xxv.

62 *Umkum,* pp. 50-51.

63 Tory, p. 209.

64 *Responsa,* p. 35.

65 *Ibid.,* p. 99.

66 Tory, p. 383.

67 Lucy Dawidowicz, "The Rise and Fall of Yiddish, *Commentary*, LXX, No. 5 (November, 1980), p. 43.

68 Myriam Anissimov, *Primo Levi: Tragedy of an Optimist* (Woodstock, N.Y.: Overlook Press, 1999), pp. 339-40.

69 *Ibid.,* p. 393.

70 In "A Conversation with Philip Roth," in Aharon Appelfeld, *Beyond Despair,* trans. by Jeffrey M. Green (New York: Fromm International Publishing Corporation, 1994), p. 63.

71 Quoted in Haim Chertok, "The 'Jewishness' of the Israeli," *Israel Scene* (Aug./Sept., 1990), p. 9.

72 *Ibid.*

73 Appelfeld, *Beyond Despair,* Lecture Two, p. 39.

[74] David Bergelson, *Naye Dertseylungen* (Buenos Aires: ICUF Publishers, 1949), pp. 49-65. Concluding quoted passage is my own translation from the Yiddish.

[75] Raul Hilberg, *The Destruction of the European Jews* (New York: Harper Colophon Books, 1961), p. 3.

[76] *Ibid.*, p. 4.

[77] *Ibid.*, p. 3.

[78] James Carroll, "The Silence," *The New Yorker*, April 7, 1997.

[79] Giuseppe Grassano, "A Conversation with Primo Levi (1979)," collected in *The Voice of Memory: Interviews 1961-1987*, ed. by Marco Belpoliti and trans. by Robert Gordon (New York: New Press, 2001), p. 122.

[80] Niklas Frank, *In the Shadow of the Reich*, trans. by Arthur S. Wensinger (New York: Alfred A. Knopf, 1991), p. 380.

[81] *Ibid.*, pp. 370-71.

[82] Tory, p. 222.

[83] Ringelblum, p. 129.

[84] A. Roy Eckardt, "Toward a Critical Assessment of Christian Theology in the Aftermath of the Holocaust: A Few Marginal Notes upon the Singularity of the *Shoah* and the End of the Christian Era," a paper prepared for "Thinking About the Holocaust: A Scholars' Conference Devoted to Historiographical and Theological Questions," Indiana University, November 3-5, 1980, p. 18.

[85] Remarks of President Reagan to Regional Editors, White House, April 18, 1985. Geoffrey H. Hartman, ed., *Bitburg in Moral and Political Perspective* (Bloomington: Indiana University Press, 1986), p. 240.

[86] William L. Shirer, *The Rise and Fall of the Third Reich* (New York: Simon and Schuster, 1960), p. 968.

[87] Mark Harris, *Wake Up, Stupid* (New York: Alfred A. Knopf, 1959), pp. 237-38.

[88] Sergio Minerbi, "The Visit of the Pope to the Holy Land," Israel Ministry of Foreign Affairs, July l, 2000. (http://www.mfa.gov.il/MFA/MFAArchive/2000 2009/2000/7/The

%20Visit%20of%20the%20Pope%20to%20the%20Holy%20Land%20-%20Sergio%20It)

89 Eliezer Berkovits, "Facing the Truth," *Judaism*, Vol. 27 (Summer, 1978), p. 326.

90 Eliezer Berkovits, "Judaism in the post-Christian Era." See Note 56, *Disputation and Dialogue*, p. 289.

91 Quoted in Sergio Minerbi, "John Paul II and the Jews," Israel Ministry of Foreign Affairs, March 1, 2000.
(http://www.mfa.gov.il/MFA/MFAArchive/2000_2009/2000/3/John%20Paul%20II%20and%20the%20Jews%20-%20Sergio%20Itzhak%20Minerbi)

92 *Ibid.*

93 *Ibid.*

94 Henryk Grynberg, "Appropriating the Holocaust," *Commentary* (November, 1982), p. 56.

95 Interview by Manfred Gerstenfeld, "Two Steps Forward, One Step Backward," *Israel Scene*, week ending January 1, 1992.

96 Berkovits, "Judaism in the post-Christian Era," in *Disputation and Dialogue*, p. 287.

97 Victor L. Simpson, Timesunion.com, October 3, 1997.
(http://alb.merlinone.net/mweb/wmsql.wm.request?oneimage&imageid=5832328)

98 Quoted in Chicago *Sentinel*, February 23, 1978.

99 *Ibid.*

100 B. A. Robinson, "A Roman Catholic apology for the past sins of its members." (See under: Release of the apology document.) Ontario Consultants on Religious Tolerance, March 8, 2000.
(http://www.religioustolerance.org/popeapo1.htm)

101 Tom Bethell, "Is the Pope Overdoing the Apologies?" Beliefnet, 2000. (http://www.beliefnet.com/Faiths/Catholic/2000/03/Is-The-Pope-overdoing-The-Apologies.aspx)

[102] John Paul II, General Audience, March 1, 2000
(http://www.vatican.va/holy father/john paul ii/audiences/2000/doc
uments/hf jp-ii aud 20000301 en.html)

[103] Victor L. Simpson, *The Standard-Times*, June 21, 1998.

[104] Quoted in Sergio Minerbi, "The Visit of the Pope to the Holy
Land," Israel Ministry of Foreign Affairs, July 1, 2000.
(http://www.vatican.va/roman curia/secretariat state/2003/document
s/rc seg-st 20031018 sodano-xxv-pontificate en.html)

[105] Quoted in Marc Perelman, "Catholic-Jewish Parley Is Called
'Last Chance' For a Historic Dialogue," *Forward*, April 27, 2001.
Cassidy spoke in Baltimore, February, 1999.

[106] Harold Schulweis, "Sleeping Through a Revolution," *Forward*,
October 22, 1999.

[107] John Leo, "Catholic Apology for Jews' oppression still not
enough," *The Gainesville Sun*, March 21, 2000.
(http://news.google.com/newspapers?nid=1320&dat=20000321&id=M
4ZRAAAAIBAJ&sjid=ygYEAAAAIBAJ&pg=6264,5382941)

[108] "The Vatican and the Holocaust: A Preliminary Report,"
October 26, 2000.

[109] Quoted in Ronald Rychlak, "Pope Pius XII Study Group: A
Wasted Opportunity."
(www.catholicleague.org/research/piusXIIstudygroup.htm)

[110] Walter Kasper, "The Jewish-Christian Dialogue: Foundations,
Progress, Difficulties and Perspectives," Jerusalem, November 19-23,
2001.

[111] Haim Shapiro, "Vatican Still Refuses To Open Holocaust
Records To Jewish Scholars," *The Jerusalem Post*, November 2, 2001.
(www.jpost.com/editions/2001/11/02/News/News.37419.html)

[112] *Ibid.*

[113] *The New York Times*, March 17, 1998.

[114] *The Jerusalem Post*, International Edition, January 15, 1994.

[115] Sergio Minerbi, "Pius XII," *Encyclopedia of the Holocaust*, Vol. 3,
p. 1139.

116 Papal message of May 16, 1995.
(http://www.ewtn.com/library/papaldoc/jp2wwii.htm)

117 Chaim Herzog, "A Historic Victory for the Jews," *The Jerusalem Post*, January 15, 1994.

118 David Kertzer, *The Popes Against the Jews* (New York: Alfred A. Knopf, 2001), p. 225.

119 *Ibid.*

120 A Catholic Timeline,
(http://www.shc.edu/theolibrary/resources/Timeline.htm)

121 Frank Talmage, *Disputation and Dialogue*, pp. 256-57. See Note 56.

122 Eliezer and Dov Berkovits, "Morally bankrupt still," *The Jerusalem Post*, International Edition, week ending May 9, 1992.

123 Ernie Meyer, "Remembering for the Future: The impact of the Holocaust and genocide on Jews and Christians," *The Jerusalem Post*, International Edition, week ending August 13, 1988.

124 Schneir Levin, Letter to Eugene Fisher, National Council of Catholic Bishops, *Midstream*, Nov./Dec., 1998.

125 Anne O'Hare McCormick, *The New York Times*, March 3, 1943. Also quoted by Max Frankel in his mea culpa, "Turning Away From The Holocaust," *The New York Times*, November 14, 2001.

126 Albert Camus, "The Unbeliever and Christians" in *Resistance, Rebellion, and Death*, p. 71.

127 *Forward*, October 26, 2001.

128 Anti-Defamation League "Open Letter," *The New York Times*, May 13, 2001.

129 Quoted by Jacob Baal-Teshuva, "Awaiting 'The Deputy,'" *New Leader*, February 17, 1964.

130 Roger Cohen, *The New York Times*, August 15, 2000.

131 Roger Cohen, *The New York Times*, March 20, 2001.

132 Steven Erlanger, *The New York Times*, September 10, 2001.

133 *The New York Times*, April 29, 2001.

[134] Roger Cohen, "French Catholic Church Apologizes for Silence on Holocaust," *The New York Times*, October 1, 1997.

[135] Primo Levi, *Shema: Collected Poems of Primo Levi*, trans. from the Italian by Ruth Feldman and Brian Swann (London: Menard Press, 1976).

[136] *Umkum*, pp. 268-69.

[137] Solomonas Atamukas, "The Hard Long Road Toward The Truth: On The Sixtieth Anniversary Of The Holocaust In Lithuania," *Lituanus*, Lithuanian Quarterly Journal of Arts and Sciences, Vol. 47, No. 4, Winter 2001. (www.Lituanus.org/2001/01_4_03.htm)

[138] Ernie Meyer, "Transforming guilt into understanding," *The Jerusalem Post*, January 23, 1993.

ABOUT THE AUTHOR

Irving Abrahamson grew up on the West Side of Chicago, graduated from Marshall High School in 1943, served in the U.S. Navy (1944-46). He returned home from duty in the Pacific and China to become part of the storied post-War G.I. Bill Generation that changed America. He graduated with a B.A. from Roosevelt University, then with an M.A. from the University of Chicago. He won his doctorate from the University in 1956. He taught English at Roosevelt University, briefly at the University of Illinois (at Navy Pier), then joined the faculty of the Chicago City Colleges (Wilson and Kennedy-King) in 1956, retiring as a professor in 1988.

Outside the formal academic world, from 1970 to 1989 he was a frequent book reviewer for the Chicago *Tribune*, the Chicago *Sun-Times*, and other publications. He compiled the uncollected and unpublished works of Elie Wiesel and edited them into the definitive three volume *Against Silence: The Voice and Vision of Elie Wiesel*, published in 1985, shortly before Wiesel won the Nobel Prize for Peace. He was a Special Advisor for the U.S. Holocaust Memorial Council, the forerunner of the Museum.

His work at various times as script editor and/or story consultant for Carlo Ponti (Champion Films) and Zev Braun Productions took him to Rome and Hollywood for work on a number of feature films, among them: *The Pedestrian* (directed by Maximilian Schell and starring him); *The Babysitter* (directed by Rene Clement, starring Maria Schneider and Robert Vaughn); *The Flower in His Mouth* (directed by Luigi Zampa, starring Jennifer O"Neill, James Mason, Franco Nero); *Angela* (directed by Boris Sagal, starring Sophia Loren). He was story consultant for Howard Fast's *Freedom Road*, a TV mini-series directed by Jan Kadar and starring Muhammad Ali.

He has traveled widely with his wife Perle. One of their trips has become *The Whole Story.*